Lecture Notes in Computer Science

Edited by G. Goos and J. Hartmanis

145

Theoretical Computer Science

6th GI-Conference
Dortmund, January 5 – 7, 1983

Edited by A.B. Cremers and H.P. Kriegel

Springer-Verlag
Berlin Heidelberg New York 1982

Editorial Board

D. Barstow W. Brauer P. Brinch Hansen D. Gries D. Luckham
C. Moler A. Pnueli G. Seegmüller J. Stoer N. Wirth

Editors

Armin B. Cremers
Hans-Peter Kriegel
Lehrstuhl Informatik VI
Universität Dortmund
Postfach 50 05 00
4600 Dortmund 50
West Germany

69504167

MATH-1

CR Subject Classifications (1982): D.3.1, D.4.1, E.1, F.1.1, F.1.2, F.2.2, F.3.1, F.3.2, F.3.3, F.4.1, F.4.2, F.4.3

ISBN 3-540-11973-6 Springer-Verlag Berlin Heidelberg New York
ISBN 0-387-11973-6 Springer-Verlag New York Heidelberg Berlin

Printed in Germany

Printing and binding: Beltz Offsetdruck, Hemsbach/Bergstr.
2145/3140-543210

FOREWORD

The 28 papers in this volume were contributed for presentation at the 6th Biannual GI Symposium on Theoretical Computer Science, held in Dortmund, Germany, January 5-7, 1983, sponsored by the Special Interest Group for Automata and Formal Language Theory of the Gesellschaft für Informatik. In addition to the 28 contributed papers there are three invited papers.

The papers were selected on September 23, 1982, at a meeting of the Program Committee from 82 extended abstracts submitted in response to the Call for Papers. The papers generally represent preliminary reports of continuing research. It is anticipated that most of these papers will appear in more polished form in scientific journals.

The conference organizers wish to thank all those who submitted abstracts for consideration, those colleagues who helped in the evaluation of the many abstracts (see next page), the sponsoring organisations for their assistance and financial support (see next page), and the many individuals who contributed to the success of the conference.

Local Arrangements

V. Claus (chairman)
K. Ambos-Spies
A.B. Cremers
J. Grollmann
H.P. Kriegel
M. Staegemeier
F. Wankmüller

Program Committee

K.R. Apt
L. Boasson
A.B. Cremers
J. Eickel
P.v. Emde Boas
K. Indermark
R. Loos
K. Mehlhorn, Chairman
M. Paterson
W. Paul
G. Plotkin
B. Reusch
G. Roucairol
H. Walter

Referees

H.-J. Appelrath
J. Bergstra
E. Börger
U. Brandt
G. Brebner
E.O. de Brock
R.M. Burstall
V. Claus
G. Costa
Ch. Crasemann
A.B. Cremers
W. Damm
F.M. Dekking
H.D. Ehrich
A.J. van Es
E. Fehr
D. Friede
H. Ganzinger
M. Gordon
I. Guessarian
E. Hangel
H. Heller
M. Hennessy
R. Höllerer
W. Hoffmann
K. Indermark
M.R. Jerrum
G. Jochum
R. Kemp
D. Killar
H.A. Klaeren
H.C.M. Kleijn
H. Langmaack
J. van Leeuwen
H.W. Lenstra Jr.
J.K. Lenstra
C.W. Lermen
W. Menzel
J. Merkwitz
W. Merzenich
A. Mycroft
F. Nielson
H.R. Nielson
A. Pettorossi
J.M. Pflüger
A. Poigné
L. Priese
J. Reichardt
W. Reisig
D.E. Rydeheard
B. Schinzel
D.A. Schmidt
O. Schoett
M.W. Shields
F. Simon
M. Smyth
C. Sturtivant
W. Thomas
A. Ultsch
K. Unterauer
P.M.B. Vitänyi
H. Waldschmidt
K. Weihrauch
R. Wilhelm

Sponsoring Organizations

Universität Dortmund
Stadt Dortmund
IBM Deutschland AG, Stuttgart
mbp Dortmund
Nixdorf Computer GmbH, Paderborn
Stadtsparkasse Dortmund
Uhde GmbH, Dortmund
Union Brauerei, Dortmund

CONTENTS

INVITED LECTURES

CONTRIBUTED PAPERS

PARTIAL FUNCTIONS IN CONSTRUCTIVE FORMAL THEORIES*

Robert L. Constable
Cornell University

ABSTRACT

Partial functions abound in modern computing theory, and so any system which purports to naturally formalize it must treat them. Surprisingly the most common treatments do not work well for constructive formal systems, i.e., for those with computational content. Since constructive formal systems are significant in computer science, it is important to give an account of partial functions in them. This paper does that by construing a partial function $\phi:N\to N$ as a total function $f:D_f\to N$ for D_f an inductively defined set generated simultaneously with f. This idea has appeared in other guises, at least in the author's previous work, but here it is presented in a pure form. It is compared to Scott's method of using total functions on domains. A formal system of arithmetic is defined to illustrate the ideas. The system is shown consistent relative to constructive type theory; from this result important corollaries are drawn about using the theory as a programming language.

KEY WORDS AND PHRASES

automated logic, Heyting arithmetic, constructivity, intuitionistic predicate calculus. partial functions, recursive functions, programming logics, program verification, type theory, type checking

I. INTRODUCTION

1.1 Primitive and General Recursion

In 1888 or so Dedekind considered a class of recursive function definitions over the natural numbers N = {0,1,2,...} which we now call <u>primitive recursive</u>. Essentially they have the form

$$f(n,x) = \underline{if}\ n=0\ \underline{then}\ g(x)\ \underline{else}\ h(n,f(n-1,x),x)\ \underline{fi}.$$

In the early 1930's Herbrand considered a more general class of recursive definition, say of the form

*This work was supported in part by NSF grant MCS-81-04018 at Cornell University and in part by SERC Grant GRB 59471 from Great Britain at the University of Edinburgh, Scotland.

$$f(n,x) = exp$$

where exp can contain arbitrary occurrences of $f(t_1,t_2)$ for expressions t_1, t_2. These are now called general recursive definitions and we recognize in them the style of recursive definition allowed in programming languages such as Lisp or Algol.

The meaning of primitive recursive definitions is immediately clear. They define functions from numbers or n-tuples of numbers to numbers. But because it is possible to write general recursive definitions of the form $f(n) = f(n+1)$, it is clear that these definitions do not denote such functions. One approach to their meaning which has been extensively studied considers them to be partial functions, that is functions which may be undefined at some (or all) of their arguments. The subject of Basic Recursive Function Theory (BRFT) as founded by Kleene takes the concept of partial recursive function as fundamental. One of the formative results of the theory states that there is no recursive enumeration of those partial recursive functions which are defined on all inputs, i.e., the total recursive functions.

1.2 Formalizing General Recursion - Difficulties

Although the theory of partial recursive functions is very elegant, there are certain difficulties with formalizing it that stem from the fact that the total functions are not recursively enumerable. Essentially the difficulty is how to treat a term such as f(t) if f is not defined at t. This is a special case of the linguistic issue of "terms that do not denote" such as "the king of France in 1982."

1.3 Avoiding the Problem

There are formal theories of partial recursive functions so the difficulties are not absolute. For instance any formalization of set theory will solve the problem, but it usually does so by treating f(t) as an "abuse of notation." A function is defined to be a special kind of relation, so the basic notation is that a certain pair $\langle x,y\rangle$ belongs to the relation f. If t is not in the domain of f, i.e., if f is not defined at t, then $\langle t,y\rangle$ does not belong to f for any y.

Kleene showed how to formalize BRFT in elementary number theory in terms of the relation $f(x) \simeq g(x)$ which means "if either f(x) or g(x) is defined then so is the other and their values are the same." But again the term f(x) is a fiction in the theory and does not have meaning itself.

1.4 Extensions to Total Functions

One way to treat f(t) when f is undefined at t might be to regard it as some arbitray number, about which we know nothing. In this view the definition $f(x)=exp$

denotes any of a class of total functions consistent with f(x)=exp when f(x) is defined. Classically this interpretation is acceptable (see [2]), and it obviates complex type checking. But constructively the interpretation is flawed since from the equality f(x)=f(x) for any x in N, we can deduce $\exists y.(f(x)=y)$. From this we expect to be able to calculate the number y, giving the value of f(x) which is not possible for $x \notin D_f$.

Another classical approach to this problem is to extend the partial function to a unique total function. These extensions are not always very useful, e.g., as in the case of 1/x, but they solve the problem of type checking. However constructively not even this option is possible because there are partial recursive functions which cannot be extended to any total recursive function.

1.5 Extended Domains

John McCarthy who in the early 1960's was laying the foundations for a theory of general computer programs recognized the difficulties caused by partial functions, [12]. In the early 1970's Dana Scott forcefully advocated a theory of partial functions obtained by extending the domain of numbers, for instance, to include a special element, called bottom, written ⊥. One says that f(t) is undefined by writing f(t) = ⊥. Now the term t(n) has precise meaning for all numbers n. This approach as been extensively pursued [4,5,10,13,17] and has been rigorously formalized in the LCF system of Robin Milner and his colleagues [7].

One difficulty with the McCarthy, Scott, Milner, etc. approach is that the new element ⊥ complicates the basic theory, say in this case that of the extended natural numbers $N^+ = \{\bot, 0, 1, 2, \ldots\}$. Another difficulty is that unlike the Kleene approach, this theory is not constructive as written, i.e., where ⊥ is considered a canonical element of N^+. That is, given a partial recursive function $\phi: N \to N$, its natural extension to $\phi^+: N^+ \to N^+$ obtained by putting $\phi^+(n)=\bot$ if $\phi(n)$ is undefined is not effectively computable. It is possible to interpret such a theory constructively as Scott advocated [15] or as done by Herbert Egli and R. Constable [5]. Indeed LCF stands for "Logic of Computable Functions." But the conceptual cost of the constructive theory of N^+ is high, e.g., the basic objects are not numbers but computations of numbers and the basic equality is no longer decidable, so N^+ is not discrete, and the notion of a computation returning a value involves fundamentally the idea of approximations, even in the natural number case.

1.6 Inductively Defined Domains

A common _informal_ way of dealing with partial function such as 1/x in algebra and analysis is to regard them as total functons on a subset of their apparent domain, e.g., 1/x maps from the subset of nonzero reals to reals. In the case of a general recursive definition f(x)=exp we can find uniformly an inductively defined subset of N, D_f, whose members are precisely those numbers on which f is defined, D_f may be empty. The definition f(x)=exp determines a unique function $f:D_f \to N$. This function we can take to be the meaning of the definition, and we call D_f the domain of the function.

Although we know what f(x)=exp denotes and we have granted f(t) real status for $t \in D_f$, there remains the question about the meaning of f(t) when $t \notin D_f$. We might say that f(t) is not a well-defined term and has no semantic content. Thus the formula $\forall x.(P(x) \Rightarrow f(x)=f(x))$ might be meaningless unless $P(x) \Rightarrow D_f(x)$. However such an approach would mean that knowing whether a term or formula is well-defined may be an extremely difficult mathematical problem in some cases, because one would have to know in general whether $P(x) \Rightarrow D_f(x)$ for arbitrary predicates P. This is not the customary way of treating syntactic issues in formal systems, expecially those for programming languages. On the contrary, custom dictates that such issues are efficiently decidable. Are we to view this custom as mere happenstance or as well learned principle?

1.7 Outline of the Paper

In section II we define a theory called General Recursive Arithmetic, GRA, which treats partial functions f as mappings from $D_f \to N$. The theory is presented in such a manner that it can easily be generalized to a type theory which we consider to be the type theory generated by GRA.

In section III we show that all partial recursive functions are definable in GRA. In section IV we interpret GRA in the Intuitionistic Type Theory (ITT) of Per Martin-Löf thereby revealing GRA's constructive content. This involves giving a type theoretic treatment of least fixed points.

II. GENERAL RECURSIVE ARITHMETIC

2.1 Syntax Conventions

The syntax is presented using BNF with the following conventions. A term such as "proof" will denote a particular element of the syntactic category "Proof." After each definition we list the metavariables used to denote arbitrary members of the class when we want compact notation, e.g., t, t_1, t_2,... for terms. A vertical bar, |, is used to separate clauses.

The disjoint union of syntax classes A and B is A+B, and the ordinary union is $A \cup B$.

We assume that identifiers (id and Id) comprise at least finite sequences of upper and lower case letters and numbers. But we may also allow other alphabets and special symbols. We also assume that the concept of a list of elements from a set A, witten A list, is understood. Lists are written $(a_1, a_2, \ldots, a_n)$ with a_n the head and $(a_1, \ldots, a_{n-1})$ the tail; concatenation is denoted by juxtaposition, i.e., $(a_1, a_2, a_3, a_4) = (a_1, a_2, a_3)a_4$.

2.2 Syntax Equations

1. Let Nexp abbreviate "numerical expression."
   Nexp ::= id | id(Nexp list) | (nexp → nexp, nexp) | (nexp id nexp)
   $t, t_1, t_2, \ldots$ denote numerical expressions. The expression $(t \to t_1, t_2)$ is a form of conditional, if t=0 then t_1 else t_2.

2. Constants ::= a certain list of reserved identifers such as +, *, -, /, 0, 1, N, false, etc.

3. For now we put Term ::= Nexp.

4. Atomic formula ::= id | $t_1=t_2$ | id(Term list) | D_{id}(Term list)
   We call id and D_{id} as they occur here predicate names.
   $P, P_1, P_2, \ldots$ are used to denote predicate names.

5. Formula ::= atomic formula | formula & formula | formula ∨ formula
   formula⇒formula | ∀ Id list.formula | ∃Id list.formula | (formula)
   $F, F_1, F_2, \ldots$ denote formulas.
   The operators have their usual precedence: {∀, ∃}, &, ∨, ⇒
   (⇒ is right associative), so ∀x.x=0 ∨ P(x) ⇒ Q & R ⇒ S is
   (∀x.(x=0) ∨ P(x)) ⇒ ((Q & R) ⇒ S).

6. We say that a formula F is positive in predicate names $P_1, \ldots, P_n$, written $Pos(P_1, \ldots, P_n)$, iff none of the P_i occur in it or if it has the form P_i(Term list) or if A and B are $Pos(P_1, \ldots, P_n)$ and F is A & B, A ∨ B, ∀ Id list.A or ∃ Id list.B or if A is $Neg(P_1, \ldots, P_n)$ and B is $Pos(P_1, \ldots, P_n)$ and F is A ⇒ B.

   We say that F is negative in predicate names $P_1, \ldots, P_n$, written $Neg(P_1, \ldots, P_n)$ iff none of the P_i occur in it (in which as it is positive also) or if A and B are $Neg(P_1, \ldots, P_n)$ and F is A & B, A ∨ B, ∀ Id list.A, ∃ Id list.B or if A is $Pos(P_1, \ldots, P_n)$ and B is $Neg(P_1, \ldots, P_n)$ and F is A ⇒ B.

   Note, some formulas such as $P_1(x) \Rightarrow P_1(x)$ are neither $Pos(P_1)$ nor $Neg(P_1)$.

7. Let Idt denote _typed identifiers_ defined as
   Idt ::= id:formula

8. Proof ::= id | id(Proof list) | λ Idt list.proof
   The necessary reserved identifiers and the type constraints on proofs will be defined later. We will also discuss the use of lambda terms.

9. Let "Fd line" abbreviate "function definition line."
   Fd line = _id_(Id list) = term | id _id_ id = term
   We call id(Id list) the _left side_ or the definiendum and "term" the _right side_ or definiens. We call the underlined id the _defined function_ (_symbol_), it can occur as an infix binary operator.

10. Function definition ::= _def_ (Fd line) list _fed_
    def id _from_ ∀ Id list.∃ id.formula _fed_
    In the first clause each defined function can occur only once in a left hand side.

11. Let Pd line abbreviate "predicate definition line."
    Pd line ::= _id_(Id list) = formula | id _id_ id = formula
    We call underlined id the _defined predicate_

12. Predicate definition ::= _def_ (Pd line) list _fed_ where each defined predicate occurs exactly once on the left side and each formula on the right is _positive in the defined predicates_.

13. Definitions ::= Predicate definition + Function definition

14. Claim ::= formula _by_ proof
    We discuss later _valid claims_.

15. Book ::= (Definition ∪ Claim) list
    We discuss below a _correct book_ which is one for which all definitions are well-formed and all claims are valid.

In the type theory section we will allow Term = Nexp + Proof. We will also replace Id list in 5, 6, 9 and 11 to be a typed id list. With these changes we will be able to define constructive type theory.

2.3 Constants

The only constants that we really need for arithmetic are _zero_, 0, and _successor_ s and the constants for proofs of 2.6. But the theory has a pleasing form if we also allow the formula _false_ and the formula N used to denote "truth."

We also reserve certain symbols for infix operatons to be defined later, namely +, *, /.

2.4 Well-Formed Terms and Well-Formed Definitions

Every term such as f(t) occurs in a specific context which includes definitions, theorems and variables. Indeed each term has a unique address consisting of the line number of the book in which it occurs plus the "decimal address" in the tree representation of the formula or proof in which it occurs.

Given a particular occurrence of a term (at an address), we can list all of the theorems that are written up to that point and all of the assumptions which "govern" that occurrence. For example in these lines

$$f(2) > 0$$
$$\forall x.(x>0 \Rightarrow x^3>0)$$
$$\forall x.(x>0 \Rightarrow f(2)/x>0)$$

if we examine the occurrence of f(2)/x, it is governed by the theorem f(2)>0 and the assumption x>0.

In order to state the conditions under which an occurrence of a term is well-formed, we must be able to say precisely what its context is. For each occurrence of a term in a book, say specified by address p, we define its context which consists of all theorems previous to the line in which p occurs plus all assumptions which govern p in its line and all variable bindings in whose scope p lies. To define those formulas which govern a position, denoted Gov(p,A), let A_p denote a formula A which contains the occurrence at address p. Let new(x) denote a variable name which has not been used previously in any formula up to the line we are examining.

$\mathrm{Gov}(p, A_p \& B) = \mathrm{Gov}(p, A_p)$, $\mathrm{Gov}(p, B \& A_p) = \Gamma(B) \cup \mathrm{Gov}(p, A_p)$

(so & is similar to <u>cand</u>)

$\mathrm{Gov}(p, A_p \vee B) = \mathrm{Gov}(p, A_p) = \mathrm{Gov}(p, B \vee A_p)$*

$\mathrm{Gov}(p, A \Rightarrow B_p) = \Gamma(A) \cup \mathrm{Gov}(p, B_p)$, $\mathrm{Gov}(p, A_p \Rightarrow B) = \emptyset$

$\mathrm{Gov}(p, \forall x.A_p) = \{\mathrm{new}(x)\} \cup \mathrm{Gov}(p, A(\mathrm{new}(x)/(x))$

$\mathrm{Gov}(p, \exists x.A_p) = \{\mathrm{new}(x)\} \cup \mathrm{Gov}(p, A(\mathrm{new}(x)/(x))$

$\Gamma(A\&B) = \Gamma(A)\cup\Gamma(B) = \Gamma(A\vee B)$ $\quad$ $\Gamma(A\Rightarrow B) = \{A\Rightarrow B\} \cup \Gamma(t)$ for all terms of $A\Rightarrow B$

$\Gamma(P(t)) = P(t)\cup\Gamma(t)$

$\Gamma(f(t)) = D_f(t)\cup\Gamma(t)$

Let A be $\forall x.B$ or $\exists x.B$ and let t be any term of A which contains no bound variable, then $\Gamma(A) = A \cup \Gamma(t)$.

Given any set of formulas and variable bindings $\mathbf{F}$, we define its immediate closure $\overline{\mathbf{F}}$ inductively as follows (writing $d \in \overline{\mathbf{F}}$ if d is any free term appearing in a formula or binding of $\overline{\mathbf{F}}$):

(i) $\mathbf{F} \subseteq \overline{\mathbf{F}}$

(ii) if $A \in \overline{\mathbf{F}}$, $A \Rightarrow B \in \overline{\mathbf{F}}$ then $B \in \overline{\mathbf{F}}$

(iii) if $A \& B \in \overline{\mathbf{F}}$ then $A \in \overline{\mathbf{F}}$, $B \in \overline{\mathbf{F}}$

(iv) if $d \in \overline{\mathbf{F}}$ and $\forall x.A(x) \in \overline{\mathbf{F}}$, then $A(d) \in \overline{\mathbf{F}}$

(v) if $t=t' \in \overline{\mathbf{F}}$, $A(t) \in \overline{\mathbf{F}}$, then $A(t') \in \overline{\mathbf{F}}$

(vi) and if $t=t' \in \overline{\mathbf{F}}$ and $t'=t'' \in \overline{\mathbf{F}}$, then $t''=t \in \overline{\mathbf{F}}$

Fact: If $\mathbf{F}$ is finite, say n elements (largest of depth m) then $\overline{\mathbf{F}}$ is finite with at most $O(n.\max(n,m))$ elements.

We say that a function term f(t) is well-formed at occurrence p in A iff $\overline{\mathrm{Gov}(p,A)}$ contains $D_f(t)$.

well-formed definitions

A definition is well-formed at a line in a book if and only if any functions or predicates which occur on the right but not on the left are previously defined in the book and each occurrence of them in the definition is well-formed and moreover no variable occurs on the left that does not occur on the right of the same equation. (All occurrences of the defined function on the right are considered well-defined.)

2.5 Domains

---

*We might also take $\mathrm{Gov}(p, B\vee A_p) = \Gamma(\neg B) \cup \mathrm{Gov}(p,A_p)$.

The key to treating partial functions in this system is the simultaneous definition of functions f and their domains D_f. The domain definition can be generated automatically from the function definition. The rules for doing this are given here inductively. They are stated for one argument functions but generalize to $f(x_1,\ldots,x_n)$ trivially. Also for simplicity we assume that f is defined in terms of g_i which are defined or base functions. (Sometimes for typographical simplicity we write g_i as gi.)

Let N(x) be the predicate meaning "x is a nonnegative integer," i.e., x=x since there is only one type.

1. $D_s(x) = N(x)$
   $D_c(x,y) = N(x)\&N(y)$ for c = *, +, -
   $D_/(x,y) = N(x)\ \&\ y \neq 0$

2. If $f(x) = h(g_1(x),\ldots,g_n(x))$ then
   $D_f(x) = D_h(g_1(x))\ \&\ldots\&\ D_h(g_n(x))\&D_{g1}(x)\&\ldots\&D_{gn}(x)$

3. If $f(x) = (b(x) \rightarrow g_1(x),\ g_2(x))$ then
   $D_f(x) = D_b(x)\&(b(x)=0\&D_{g1}(x)\ \vee\ b(x)\neq 0\&D_{g2}(x))$

These three clauses will be used in giving axioms for the system. Notice that all the formulas on the right side are positive in D_f.

2.6 Axioms and Rules

We present a Hilbert style proof system based on three rules of inference (two of which express essentially one idea, <u>application</u>) and several axiom schemes listed below. For each axiom we also provide a function which is its constructive realization. Proofs are terms built from these realizing primatives. Each proof has a type which is the formula that it proves.

To state some of these rules we need the usual concepts of <u>free</u> and <u>bound variables</u>, scope of quantifiers and definitions and the idea of a term being <u>free for a variable in a formula</u>. We assume all of these definitions as presented in Kleene [9].

Inference Rules

application

$$\frac{A,\ A \Rightarrow B}{B} \qquad \frac{\forall x.A(x) \quad t \text{ a well-formed term}}{A(t)}$$

existential

$$E_A \qquad \frac{A(t) \quad t \text{ a well-formed term}}{\exists x.A(x)}$$

Axioms - propositional

realizing term	name	axiom
K_{AB}	constants	$A \Rightarrow (B \Rightarrow A)$
S_{ABC}	composition	$(A \Rightarrow (B \Rightarrow C)) \Rightarrow (A \Rightarrow B) \Rightarrow (A \Rightarrow C)$
P_{AB}	pairing	$A \Rightarrow B \Rightarrow A \& B$
1_{AB}	1st projection	$A \& B \Rightarrow A$
2_{AB}	2nd projection	$A \& B \Rightarrow B$
L_{AB}	left injection	$A \Rightarrow A \vee B$
R_{AB}	right injection	$B \Rightarrow A \vee B$
N_A	nil	$(0=1) \Rightarrow A$
C_{ABC}	cases	$(A \Rightarrow C) \Rightarrow (B \Rightarrow C) \Rightarrow (A \vee B \Rightarrow C)$

axioms - predicate

$\lambda f.\lambda z.(\lambda x.f(z))$	generalization	$(C \Rightarrow A(x)) \Rightarrow (C \Rightarrow \forall x.A)$ C has no free x
W_{AC}	witness	$\exists x.A(x) \Rightarrow (\forall z.(A(z) \Rightarrow C) \Rightarrow C$*

axioms - equality

ref	reflexivity	$\forall x.(x=x)$
tran	transitivity	$\forall x,y,z.(x=y \Rightarrow y=z \Rightarrow x=z)$
com	commutativity	$\forall x,y.(x=y \Rightarrow y=x)$

axioms - functions for f a defined function

def	definition	$\forall x.(D_f(x) \Rightarrow f(x) = exp(x))$
fun_f	functionality	$\forall x,y(x=y \wedge D_f(x) \Rightarrow f(x)=f(y))$

We need also the schemes 2. and 3. for D_f from section 2.4 as axioms about functions.

*In place of this witnessing axiom we could use a constructive version of Hilbert's epsilon symbol to provide a witness. The axiom would be $\exists x.A(x) \Rightarrow A(\epsilon_{x(n)}A)$ where the parameter n will allow us to use different witnesses for each application of the axiom.

For D an inductively defined predicate defined by $D(x) = F(D,x)$

D-def	D-definition	$\forall x.(D(x) \Leftrightarrow F(D,x))$
D-ind	D-induction	$\forall x.(F(P, x) \Rightarrow P(x)) \Rightarrow \forall x.(D(x) \Rightarrow P(x))$

There are axioms for functions of n arguments as well.

axioms - arithmetic

dom_s	domain-s	$\forall x.(D_s(x) \Leftrightarrow x=x)$
fun_s	functionality-s	$\forall x,y.(x=y \Rightarrow s(x)=s(y))$
inj_s	injectivity-s	$\forall x,y.(s(x)=s(y) \Rightarrow x=y)$
N-ind	N-induction	$A(0)$ & $\forall x.(A(x) \Rightarrow A(s(x))) \Rightarrow \forall x.A(x)$

For brevity we omit the axioms for +, -, * and / since these functions can all be defined from successor.

III. REPRESENTATION OF THE PARTIAL RECURSIVE FUNCTIONS

3.1 Syntactic Representation

Suppose we have defined the partial recursive functions from recursion equations as in [9]. These definitions have precisely the same form as those allowed in the theory. So there is an isomophism from a recursion equation, say E_F, defining a partial recursive function F( ) and a function definition say <u>def</u> f. We will use this notation generally, allowing F to denote the principle function letter defined by the equation E_F and letting f be the corresponding identifier of the formal system.

We claim that the computation rules of the system permit the deduction $f(n)=m$ precisely when $F(n)=m$. To prove this we must show that we can deduce $D_f(n)$ if and only if n is in the domain of F( ). We term to this next

3.2 Semantic Equivalence

We let $\vdash A$ mean that A is provable in the system. We use the same notation for numbers and their numerical representation in the system. We can prove:

Theorem: (a) For all n and recursively defined F,
F is defined at n iff $\vdash D_f(n)$

(b) $F(n)=m$ iff $\vdash f(n)=m$.

IV. INTERPRETATION IN TYPE THEORY

4.1 Constructive Soundness

To know that a theory is constructively sound we might provide a computational semantics for it. We might do this informally or by interpreting it in a known constructive theory. If the known theory is implemented, then the interpretation can provide an implementation of the given theory. We say that a constructive theory is implemented when there is a computer program which will execute all of the functions definable in the theory and all of the functions which are proofs.

In this section we will interpret GRA in Per Martin-Löf's Intuitionistic Theory of Types, ITT-79 [11], a theory which is being implemented. We will also consider interpreting GRA in the closely related type theory V3 [3] which takes an intensional view of functions and this permits an especially simple treatment of partial functions.

4.2 General Recursive Arithmetic Type Theory

There is a surprisingly simple way to interpret GRA in type theory. The first step, which we consider in this section, is to define a type theory which we characterize as the type theory generated from GRA by the propositions as types principle. The second step is to map this "arithmetic type theory", denoted GRATE, into Martin-Löf's ITT-79. The interesting step is the treatment of recursive functions and inductive definitions. In this paper we have room to treat only the first notion.

The syntactic changes needed to define a type theory from GRA are very simple.

1. Let Term = Nexp + Proof

2. In lines 5, 6, 9 and 11 replace Id list by typed Id list, that is sequences of id:formula.

With these changes we must consider type-correctness as well as well-formedness of formulas. Indeed we must worry about whether a type expression is well-formed, which is not a common concern in logical systems.

A formula F, whether it occurs in type position, $\forall x$:F, or an assertion position, $\forall x$:T.F, will be well-formed under the same conditions as in GRA except that when assuming a formula such as $\forall x$:T(y).A(x) or $\exists x$:T(y).A(x) we assume T(y) is well-formed. This means we define an operation Γ_t similar to Γ except that in forming $\Gamma(\forall x$:T(y).A) or $\Gamma(\exists x$:T(y).A) we take Γ_t(T(y)) $\cup$ {new(x):T(y)} $\cup$ Γ(A(new(x)/(x)).

For the purposes of type checking the formula N is considered to be the type of nonnegative integers and _false_ is the empty type. So the numerical constants have their obvious types: 0:N, s(t):N for t:N. We also agree that the proof constants have as type the formulas which they prove according to the table of section 2.6. Moreover we interpret A⇒B as the function A→B, and A&B as the cartesian product AxB; so s has type N⇒N and defined recursive functions $f(n_1 x_1, \ldots, x_p)$ have type N&N&.p.&N⇒N where N&.p.&N means N&...&N for N repeated p times.

The universal quantifier ∀x:T is interpreted as the ΠxεT operator of type theory, so we have also the type checking rule that if f:(∀x:T.A(x)) and t:T, then f(t):A(t). ∃x:T is interpreted as ΣxεT.

Here are some examples of formulas in this type theory which we call GRATE for General Recursive Arithmetic TypE.

1. ∃f:N→N.∀x:N.∀y:N.(f(x)=f(y)).

2. ∃g:(∃x:N.A(x)⇒N).∀z:(∃x:N.A(x)).A(g(z)).

Number 2 says that there is among the functions from ∃x:N.A(x) into N one which is the witness function for the quantifier.

Notice that this is a formula scheme because we have not specified A, but A must be a formula which is well-formed as a function of x, so it cannot for example be (1/x = 1/x).

It is especially interesting that the axioms of GRATE are essentially those of GRA with type restrictions plus axioms giving the computational meaning of the proof term, e.g., 1(P(x,y))=x, 2(P(x,y))=y, Kxy=x, Sfgx=f(x)(g(x)), etc.

4.3 Partial Functions and Their Domains in Intuitionistic Type Theory

From the discussion in 4.2 it is clear how we are going to translate into ITT-79. We will take _false_ to be the empty type, ∅, N to be the type of natural numbers, & as cartesian product, ∨ as disjoint union, ∃ as Σ the infinite union and ∀ as Π the infinite product. But how will we translate partial functions f and their domains? How will we translate inductive definitions?

In this section we treat partial functions and their domains assuming the translator of proofs mentioned above. Given a function definition such as f(x)=exp we want to treat the right side as a functional, say λf.λx.exp. But if we do this without care λfλx.exp will not be type correct. To insure that such a functional makes sense we must be able to determine the domain of numbers x for which λx.exp is defined as a function of the domain of f. In order to do this, we must supply the functional domain information about f. This we do by providing a predicate F of type $N \to V_1$. The domain of f will be $\{x:N|F(x)\}$. So we will build a mapping denoted $\mathcal{E}$ from F and f to a new predicate, denoted D(F,f) and a new function denoted E(F,f). We write $\mathcal{E}(F,f) = <D(F,f), E(F,f)>$.

The basic idea is that we define a function $\mathcal{E}$ from predicates and functions F,f such that $f:\{x:N|F(x)\} \to N$ whose value is a pair $<D(F,f), E(F,f)>$ such that $E(F,f)\epsilon\{x:N|D(F,f)(x)\} \to N$. We use $\mathcal{E}$ to define a sequence of predicates and functions starting with F_o = <u>false</u>, $D_o = \{x:N|F_o(x)\}$, $F_o \epsilon D_o \to N$. We take $F_{i+1} = D(F_i, f_i)$, $D_i = \{x:N|F_{i+1}(x)\}$, $f_{i+1} = E(F_i, f_i)$. The fixed point is defined by taking a limit of the f_i which is essentially but not exactly

$$F_\omega(x) = \exists n:N.F_n(x)$$
$$f_\omega(x) = f_n(x) \text{ where } F_n(x).$$

The details of how this is done in type theory are somewhat tedious. In the first place, if we are to take a general approach to this, then we allow arbitrary predicates $F:N\to V_1$. But this means that $\mathcal{E}$ and consequently F_ω and f_ω will not be of small type (of level V_1) but will be of level V_2. If we use functions of level 2 in recursive definitions, then the fixed points are of level 3, etc. Thus in a general theory we must associate with each recursive definition a level number **l**. A complete account of partial functions on N will involve all levels of the type hierarchy.

Another complication is that each f_i maps from $\{x:N|F_i(x)\}$ which in type theory is $\Sigma x\epsilon N.F_i(x)$, i.e., a type of pairs. So we must keep track of the proof component of x. Our convention will be that x_1 is the numerical component and x_2 is the proof; so $x = <x_1, x_2>$. We will have to iterate to form $x_{1,2}$ etc.

Here are the details of the translation. Assign to each defined function f of GRA a <u>level</u> as follows. The level of each expression containing only base functions is 0. The level of a recursive definition f(x)=exp is one greater than the level of exp.

Let $S = \Sigma F\epsilon(N\to V_1)((\Sigma x\epsilon N.F(x))\to N)$. Given a well-formed expression exp of GRA with free f, that is with f a function symbol not previously defined, we want to associate with exp a mapping $\mathcal{E}\epsilon S\to S$. Given F we will treat each occurrence of f in exp as a mapping from $\Sigma n\epsilon N.F(n)$ to N. To do this we must regard each occurrence of f(t) in exp as an occurrence of $f(<t,p>)$ where p proves that t satisfies F, i.e., $<t,p>\epsilon\ \Sigma n\epsilon N.F(n)$. We know that such p must exist because we build the domain of E(F,f) to guarantee this. We show inductively how to build the appropriate functional expression E(F,f) once we have built its domain D(F,f).

The key point in making this work is that we regard $\mathcal{E}$ as a function which computes from exp the domain on which E(F,f) is defined. Thus if we consider an expression such as

$$b(x) \rightarrow g(x),\ h(f(j(x)))$$

then if b(x) is false but f is not defined at j(x), i.e., if b(x) is false, yet F(j(x)) is not provable, then x is not in the domain of $\mathcal{E}$(F,f). Whenever x is in the domain D(F,f), we will be able to extract from the proof of D(F,f) the necessary proof that F(j(x)). Define from well-formed exp with free f a mapping $\mathcal{E}$ from S to S as follows for $F \in (N \rightarrow V_1)$ and $f \in (\Sigma x \in N.F(x)) \rightarrow N$. $\mathcal{E}$(F,f) will be <D(F,f), E(F,f)> for E and D as below:

if exp is g(n) for g:N → N
then put $D(F,f)(n) = D_g(n)$. Note E(F,f) is $\lambda x.g(x_1)$.
if exp is h(t) for $h \in \Sigma x \in N.H(x)$ and t an expression such that H(t), then assume t has been translated by the procedure to have the form $T(F,f)(x)_1$ for $\mathcal{E}(F,f) = \langle D_T(F,f),T(F,f)\rangle$
then $D(F,f)(x) = D(F,f)(n) = \Sigma q \in D_T(F,f)(n).\ H(T(F,f)\langle n,q\rangle)$ and $E(F,f) = h(\langle t,p\rangle)$ where p is the translator of the proof of H(t).
if exp is f(t), then assume t has been translated say $\mathcal{T}(F,f)(x) = \langle D_T(F,f), T(F,f)\rangle$ so that $t = T(F,f)(x)_1$, then put $D(F,f)(n) = \Sigma q \in D_T(F,f)(n).\ F(T(F,f)\langle n,q\rangle)$ and $E(F,f)(x)=f(\langle t(x_1),p(x)\rangle)$ where p extracts from $x \in \{y:N \mid D(F,f)(y)\}$ the proof of F(t), i.e., p(x) is the second component of x_2. (We use $t(x_1)$ to denote t with x_1 for x.) Notice that $E(F,f) \in \{y:N \mid D(F,f)(y)\} \rightarrow N$.
if exp is $b \rightarrow t_1,\ t_2$ and b, t_1, t_2 have been translated so that

$$b = B(F,f)(x) \quad \text{with domain} \quad D_B(F,f)$$
$$t_1 = T_1(F,f)(x) \quad \text{with domain} \quad D_{T_1}(F,f)$$
$$t_2 = T_2(F,f)(x) \quad \text{with domain} \quad D_{T_2}(F,f)$$

then $D(F,f)(n) = D_B(F)(n)\ \&\ (b=0\ \&\ D_{T_1}(F,f)(n) \vee b=1\ \&\ D_{T_2}(F,f)(n))$ and $E(F,f)(x) = B(F,f)(x) \rightarrow T_1(F,f)(x),\ T_2(F,f)(x)$.

We now define the fixed point apparatus.

<u>Definition</u>: Given $\mathcal{E} \in S \rightarrow S$ define

$$F_0(n) = \underline{false},\ D_i = \Sigma n\in N.F_i(n),\ f_o \in D_o \to N,$$
$$F_{i+1}(n) = D(F_i,f_i)(n),\ f_{i+1} = E(F_i,f_i)$$
$$F_\omega(n) = \Sigma m\in N.F_m(n)$$

We define $f_\omega(x) = f_{x_{2,1}}(<x_1, x_{2,2}>)$. In order to show that f_ω is a well-defined function on N we need to prove:

Lemmas:

(1) For all n, $F_i(n) \Rightarrow F_{i+1}(n)$.

Definition: If $F(n) \Rightarrow G(n)$ for all n, and if $f\in\Sigma n\in N.F(n)$, $g\in\Sigma n\in N.G(n)$ and if $f(<n,p>) = g(<n,p'>)$ for all n such that $<n,p> \in \Sigma i\in N.F(i)$, $<n,p'> \in \Sigma i\in N.G(i)$ then we write $f \subseteq g$ and $<F,f> \subseteq <G,g>$. If $<F,f> \subseteq <G,g>$ and $<G,g> \subseteq <F,f>$ then we write $<F,f> \equiv <G,g>$.

(2) If $<F,f> \subseteq <G,g>$, then $\mathcal{E}(F,f) \subseteq \mathcal{E}(G,g)$.

(3) If $F_i(n)$ then $f_{i+1}(<n,p'>) = f_i(<n,p>)$
where p' is the proof of $F_{i+1}(n)$ known from (1) and $F_i(n) \Rightarrow F_{i+1}(n)$.

(4) Given any sequence of predicates F_i and functions f_i such that $F_i(n) \Rightarrow F_{i+1}(n)$ for all n, i, and $f_i \subseteq f_{i+1}$, then $D(\Sigma n\in N.F_n, f_\omega)(m) \Rightarrow \Sigma n\in N.D(F_n,f_n)(n)$ for all m.

Let $\mu n.P(n)$ denote the least natural number n such that P(n).

Definition: For $x\in D_\omega$ define
$f_\omega(x) = f_{x_{2,1}}(<x_1,x_{2,2}>)$.

We can now prove a compactness lemma.

(5) Compactness

If $\mathcal{E}(F_\omega,f_\omega)(x) = y$, then $\exists n\ \mathcal{E}(F_n,f_n)(x) = y$.

From these lemmas we can prove

Least Fixed Point Theorem:

(a) $F_\omega(n) \Leftrightarrow D(F_\omega,f_\omega)(n)$ for all n

(b) for all $x\in D_\omega$, $f_\omega(x) = E(F_\omega,f_\omega)(x)$.

"Combining (a) and (b) we conclude"

(c) $<F_\omega, f_\omega> \equiv \mathcal{E}(F_\omega, f_\omega)$

(d) If $<G,g> \equiv \mathcal{E}(G,g)$,
then $<F_\omega, f_\omega> \subseteq <G,g>$.

To show that f_ω defines a function $D_f \to N$ in GRA we must know that the value of $f_\omega(x)$ does not depend on the proof component. That is:

Independence of Proofs Theorem:

If x,y belong to D_ω and $x_1 = y_1$
then $f_\omega(x) = f_\omega(y)$.

4.4 Remarks on the Interpretation

A method similar to that described above can be used to interpret inductive definitions of predicates. In this paper there is no room to present the method. It is worth noting however that the interpretation into type theory provides an implementation of GRA as a programming language. Not only can any partial recursive function f be executed, but any function implicitly defined by the proof of a claim such as $\forall x.(P(x) \Rightarrow \exists y Q(x,y))$ can be executed. In this sense GRA can serve as a theory for program development as in the current PRL system at Cornell whose implementation has been led by my colleague Joseph L. Bates

ACKNOWLEDGEMENTS

I would like to express my appreciation to Stuart Allen who has constructively criticized much of what I have to say on this topic. I also thank Donette Isenbarger for so efficiently and carefully preparing the manuscript.

REFERENCES

[1]: Aczel, Peter, "A Introduction to Inductive Definitions", Handbook of Mathematical Logic, (ed., J. Barwise), North-Holland, NY, 1977, pp. 739-782.

[2]: Constable, Robert L. and M.J. O'Donnell, A Programming Logic, Winthrop, Cambridge, 1978.

[3]: Constable, Robert L. and D.R. Zlatin, "The Type Theory of PL/CV3", IBM Logic of Programs Conference, Lecture Notes in Computer Science, Vol. 131, Springer-Verlag, NY, 1982, 72-93.

[4]: de Bakker, Jaco, Mathematical Theory of Program Correctness, Prentice-Hall, 1980.

[5]: Egli, H. and R.L. Constable, "Computability Concepts for Programming Language Semantics", Theoretical Computer Science, 2, 1976, pp. 133-145.

[6]: Feferman, Solomon, "Constructive Theories of Functions and Classes", Logic Colloquium '78 (eds., M. Boffa, D. van Dalen and K. McAloon), North-Holland, Amsterdam, 1979, pp. 159-224.

[7]: Gordon, M., R. Milner and C. Wadsworth, Edinburgh LCF: A Mechanized Logic of Computation, Lecture Notes in Computer Science, Vol. 78, Springer-Verlag, 1979.

[8]: Howard, W.A., "The Formulas-As-Types Notion of Construction" in Essays on Combinatory Logic, Lambda Calculus and Formalism, (eds., J.P. Seldin and J.R. Hindley), Academic Press, NY, 1980.

[9]: Kleene, S.C., Introduction to Metamathematics, D. Van Nostrand, Princeton, 1952, 550 pp.

[10]: Manna, Zohar, Mathematical Theory of Computation, McGraw-Hill, NY, 1974, 448p.

[11]: Martin-Löf, Per, "Constructive Mathematics and Computer Programming", 6th International Congress for Logic, Method and Phil. of Science, Hannover, August, 1979.

[12]: McCarthy, John, "A Basis for a Mathematical Theory of Computation", Computer Programming and Formal Systems (eds., P. Braffort and D. Hirschberg), North-Holland, Amsterdam, 1963, pp. 33-70.

[13]: Scott, Dana, "Outline of a Mathematical Theory of Computation", Proc. 4th Annual Princeton Conf. on Information Sciences & Systems, Princeton, 1970, pp. 169-176.

[14]: Scott, Dana, "Constructive Validity", Symposium on Automatic Demonstration, Lecture Notes in Mathematics, 125, Springer-Verlag, 1970, 237-275.

[15]: Scott, Dana, "Data Types as Lattices", SIAM Journal on Computing, 5:3, September 1976.

[16]: Stenlund, S., Combinators, Lambda-terms, and Proof-Theory, D. Reidel, Dordrecht, 1972, 183 pp.

A Monte Carlo factoring algorithm with finite storage

(extended abstract)

C.P. Schnorr *
Fachbereich Mathematik
Universität Frankfurt
(joint work with H.W. Lenstra, Jr., Amsterdam)

September 1982

Abstract We present an algorithm which will factor an integer n quite efficiently if the class number h(-n) is free of large prime divisors. The running time T(n) (number of compositions in the class group) satisfies prob $[T(m) \leq n^{1/2r}] \gtrsim (r-2)^{-(r-2)}$ for random $m \in [n/2, n]$ and $r \geq 2$. So far it is unpredictable which numbers will be factored fast. Running the algorithm on all integers n·s with $s \leq r^r$ and $r = \sqrt{\ln n / \ln \ln n}$, every composite integer n will be factored in $o(\exp\sqrt{\ln n \ln \ln n})$ bit operations and fixed amount of storage space. In our analysis we assume a lower bound on the frequency of class numbers h(-m), $m \leq n$, which are free of large prime divisors.

1. Introduction

The problem of factoring an integer n into its prime power divisors is computationally equivalent to determining all ambiguous, reduced positive forms $ax^2+bxy+cy^2$ (notation: (a,b,c)), $a,b,c \in \mathbb{Z}$, with discriminant $b^2-4ac = -n$ ($b^2-4ac = +n$, resp.). In fact these ambiguous forms correspond to the relatively prime factorizations of n, i.e. to the pairs $\{n_1, n_2\}$ with $n = n_1 n_2$ and $\gcd(n_1, n_2) = 1$.
According to GAUSS (1801) the equivalence classes of forms with fixed discriminant Δ form a group under compositions the class group $G(\Delta)$. The order $h(\Delta)$ of this group is the class number. Multiplication in $G(\Delta)$ can be done efficiently working with representatives of classes. The ambiguous classes are the classes H with $H^2 = 1$.

* Research supported by BMFT grant 08 30108

In case of negative discriminant $\Delta<0$ there is a unique reduced form in each class, and this form can be efficiently calculated from any other class representative. Therefore, factoring n is computationally equivalent to determining representatives of all ambiguous classes in G(-n). The reduced forms of these classes correspond to the relatively prime factorizations $n_1 n_2 = n$ of n.

The new algorithm, given the first t primes $p_1=2, p_2=3, \ldots, p_t=n^{1/2r}$, will work with finite storage. Let $e_i = \max\{\nu: p_i^{\nu} \leq p_t^2\}$, then stage 1 of the new algorithm computes

$$H = H_0^{\Pi_{i=2} p_i^{e_i}}$$

for an arbitrarily chosen $H_0 \in G(-n)$. Then compute H^{2^k} for the smallest $k \leq \log_2 \sqrt{n}$ such that $H^{2k} = 1$. Clearly H^{2k-1} is ambiguous. n will be factored in this way if h(-n) divides $2^k \Pi_{i=2}^t p_i^{e_i}$ for some k. If stage 1 fails then stage 2 does a random walk through the group generated by H. Stage 2 will factor n if $\mathrm{ord}(H^{2^k}) \leq p_t^2$ for some k, i.e. if h(-n) divides $2^k \Pi_{i=1}^t p_i^{e_i} q$ with $q \leq p_t^2$.

With $p_t = n^{1/2r}$ stage 1 of the algorithm takes $O(p_t)$ compositions and for random composite $m \in [0,n]$ with probability $\gtrsim r^{-r}$ detects a proper divisor of m. Stage 2 also takes $O(p_t) = O(n^{1/2r})$ compositions and with probability $\gtrsim (r-2)^{-(r-2)}$, $r \geq 2$ detects a proper divisor of m. Running stage 1 on the integers $n \cdot s$ for $s = \lesssim r^r$, $r = \sqrt{\ln n / \ln \ln n}$, every composite integer n will be factored within $\dot{o}(\exp \sqrt{\ln n \ln \ln n})$ operations. The latter bound already takes into account the cost of the arithmetic. The cost for a composition in G(-n) is proportional to the cost of computing gcd(u,v) for numbers $u, v \leq n$. By standard algorithms, see KNUTH 4.5.2 exercise 30, this takes $O(\ln n)^2$ bit operations, i.e. binary Boolean operations.

The particular features of the new factoring algorithm are:

(1) it can easily be operated with fixed storage,

(2) it is Monte Carlo in the sense that every 1000-th integer will be factored about 1000 times faster than average time,

(3) the integers which will be factored very fast are randomly distributed, there is no way to predict whether a given m will be factored fast,

(4) the algorithm is of the parallel type, i.e. 1000 processors will factor 1000 times faster.

Properties (2),(3) seem to endanger the RSA-cryptoscheme, see RIVEST et alii (1978). In particular no methods are known that generate class numbers with large prime divisors.

2. Stage 1 of the algorithm

Let n be the integer to be factored. -n is the discriminant of some quadratic form iff $-n \equiv 0,1 \bmod 4$. The purpose of stages 1,2 is to find a nontrivial divisor of n, provided -n is a discriminant and h(-n) is a product of small primes. In order to factor general integers n, the main algorithm in section 4 applies stages 1,2 to multiples $n \cdot s$ with $-n \cdot s \equiv 0,1 \bmod 4$. If -n is a discriminant we can easily construct forms (a,b,c) with discriminant -n: choose a small odd prime p with $(\frac{-n}{p}) = 1$ and solve $b^2 \equiv -n \bmod 4p$ which yields $b^2 = -n+4pc$ for some $c \in \mathbb{Z}$. Hence (a,b,c) has discriminant -n.

Throughout sections 2,3 we restrict to the case $-n \equiv 1 \bmod 4$, consult the complete paper for the case $-n \equiv 0 \bmod 4$. Then the unit $1 \in G(-n)$ is represented by the form (1,1,(1+n)/4). This ambiguous class yields the improper factorization $1 \cdot n = n$. The other ambiguous classes correspond in 1-1 way to the relatively prime factorizations of n with nontrivial divisors.

Stage 1 Let $n \in \mathbb{N}$, $-n \equiv 1 \bmod 4$, be given.

1. for some $t \in \mathbb{N}$ compute the t first primes $p_1=2, p_2=3, .., p_t$.
2. choose $H_0 \in G(-n)$ arbitrarily.
3. $H := H_0^{\prod_{i=2}^{t} p_i^{e_i}}$ with $e_i := \max \{\nu \mid p_i^\nu \leq p_t^2\}$
4. $\bar{H} := H$, $e_* := \lfloor \log_2 \sqrt{n} \rfloor$
5. for $\nu = 1,2,..,e_*$ do
   [$S := H$, $H := H^2$, if $H=1$ go to 7]
6. go to the stage 2
7. (at this point S is ambiguous and yields some divisor of n)

Stage 1 by itself is the core of the new factoring algorithm. The improvements resulting from stage 2 are important for practical applications, but they scarcely influence the asymptotical time bound of the algorithm.

Fact 1 Suppose $h(-n) | \Pi_{i=1}^{t} p_i^{e_i}$ and $\mathrm{ord}(H_0)$ even, then stage 1 generates an ambiguous class $S \neq 1$.

In case $-n \equiv 1 \bmod 4$ every ambiguous class $S \neq 1$ yields a proper divisor of n. In particular, when n has d odd prime divisors, then $2^{d-1} | h(-n)$, and there are exactly 2^{d-1} ambiguous classes corresponding to the 2^{d-1} pairs $\{n_1, n_2\}$ with $n_1 n_2 = n$, $n_1 < n_2$, $\gcd(n_1, n_2) = 1$. Moreover, when n is composite and $H_0 \in G(-n)$ is chosen at random, then prob $[\mathrm{ord}(H_0)\,\mathrm{even}] \geq 1/2$. Hence stage 1 has a chance $\geq 1/2$ to find a proper divisor of n, provided $h(-n) | \Pi_{i=1}^{t} p_i^{e_i}$. A few repetitions of stage 1 almost surely generate a proper divisor of n, provided $h(-n) | \Pi_{i=1}^{t} p_i^{e_i}$ and n is composite:

Fact 2 Suppose $h(-n) | \Pi_{i=1}^{t} p_i^{e_i}$ and n is composite. If stage 1 is passed with H_0 chosen independently k times, then with probability $\geq 1 - 2^{-k}$ a proper divisor of n has been found.

Next consider the chance that for random $m \leq n$:

$$h(-m) | \Pi_{i=1}^{t} p_i^{e_i} \quad , \; e_i = \max\{\nu : p_i^{\nu} \leq p_t^2\} \; , \; p_t = n^{1/2r} \quad .$$

SIEGEL (1936) proved:

$$\forall \varepsilon : \exists n_\varepsilon : \forall m \geq n_\varepsilon : h(-n) \quad [m^{1/2+\varepsilon}, m^{1/2-\varepsilon}].$$

We will base the analysis of stage 1 on the following hypothesis

$$(2.1) \quad \left\| \begin{array}{l} \text{For all } n \text{ and } t: \\ \#\{m \leq n : h(-m) | \Pi_{i=1}^{t} p_i^{e_i}\} / (0.5n) \quad \geq \\ \#\{\bar{m} \leq \sqrt{n} : \bar{m} | \Pi_{i=1}^{t} p_i^{e_i}\} \quad / \sqrt{n}. \end{array} \right.$$

Recently CANFIELD, ERDÖS and POMERANCE improved the theoretical lower bound on the second term in (2.1) . We refer in particular to the proof in POMERANCE (1981):

Theorem 3 Let $\Psi(n,v) := \#\{x \leq n : x \text{ free of primes} > v\}$.

For every $\varepsilon > 0$ there exists c_ε such that for all $n \geq 10$ and all r with $n^{1/2r} \geq (\ln n)^{1+\varepsilon}$: $\Psi(n, n^{1/r})/n \geq (c_\varepsilon r \ln r)^{-r}$.

In practice however $\Psi(n,n^{1/r})/n$ is larger than the bound stated in theorem 3. From experimental data we conclude

(2.2) for all n and $r \leq \sqrt{\ln n / \ln \ln n}$: $\Psi(n,n^{1/r}) \geq r^{-r}$

and this yields stronger results.

Corollary 4 Assume (2.2) and (2.1). Then for all $n \geq 10^{20}$ and all $p_t = n^{1/2r}$ with $r \leq \sqrt{\ln n/\ln \ln n}$:

$$\#\{m \leq n : h(-m) \mid \Pi_{i=1}^{t} p_i^{e_i}\} / (0.5n) \geq 0.83\, r^{-r}$$

Proof $\#\{m \leq n : h(-m) \mid \Pi_{i=1}^{t} p_i^{e_i}\} / (0.5n)$

$$\overset{(2.1)}{\geq} \Psi(\sqrt{n},n^{1/2r})/\sqrt{n} - \Sigma_{i=1}^{t} p_i^{-e_i-1}$$

$$\overset{(2.2)}{\geq} r^{-r} - n^{-1/r}\, t$$

$$\geq r^{-r} - 1.1 n^{-1/r} n^{1/2r} / \ln n^{1/2r} \quad (\text{since } t = \pi(n^{1/2r}) \leq 1.1 n^{1/2r}/\ln n^{1/2r})$$

$$\geq r^{-r} - 2.2 n^{-1/2r} r / \ln n$$

$$\geq r^{-r}\,(1 - 2.2 r/\ln n)$$

(in fact $r \leq \sqrt{\ln n/\ln \ln n}$ implies $r^{-r} \geq n^{-1/2r}$)

$$\geq 0.83 r^{-r} \qquad \text{for } n \geq 10^{20},\ r \leq \sqrt{\ln n/\ln \ln n}\ . \ \square$$

Runtime of stage 1 If $H^{p_i^{e_i}}$ is computed by the binary method (see KNUTH 4.6.3) this takes

$$2 \log_2 p_i^{e_i} \leq 2 \log_2 p_t^2 \leq 4 \log_2 p_t$$

compositions in $G(-n)$. Since there are about

$$t \lesssim p_t / \ln p_t$$

primes $\leq p_t$, this yields a worst case bound of

$$\frac{4}{\ln 2}\, p_t \approx 5.8\, p_t \quad \text{compositions in total.}$$

On the average the binary method is somewhat more efficient.

It takes about $1.5 \log_2 p_i^{e_i}$ compositions to compute $H^{p_i^{e_i}}$ and therefore stage 1 will only take about $4.3\, p_t$ compositions in total. All together we have proved the following

Theorem 5 Assume (2.1), (2.2), and that for every discriminant $m \leq n$ (a single) $H_0 \in G(-m)$ in stage 1 is chosen at random. Then for all $n \geq 10^{20}$ and all $p_t = n^{1/2r}$ with $r \leq \sqrt{\ln n / \ln \ln n}$: stage 1 factors at least $0.2\, nr^{-r}$ discriminants $\leq n$ and takes about $4.4\, p_t$ compositions in $G(-n)$.

For practical applications we advise to choose somewhat smaller exponents e_i' instead of the e_i:

$$e_i' := \max\{\nu : p_i^\nu \leq p_t\} \text{ with } p_t = n^{1/2r} .$$

We used the larger e_i for proving corollary 4 by a crude argument. Asssuming $\Psi(n, n^{1/r})/n \overset{*}{=} O(r^{-r})$ one obtains corollary 4 for the e_i' :

$$\#\{m \leq n : h(-m) \mid \Pi_{i=1}^t p_i^{e_i'}\} \;/\; (0.5n)$$

(assuming that (2.1) holds for the e_i')

$$\geq \quad r^{-r} - \Sigma_{i=1}^t p_i^{-e_i'-1} \frac{\Psi(n^{1/2-1/2r}, n^{1/2r})}{n^{1/2-1/2r}}$$

$$\overset{*}{\geq} \quad r^{-r} - O(n^{-1/2r} \frac{n^{1/2r}}{\ln(n^{1/2r})} (r-1)^{-(r-1)})$$

$$\geq \quad r^{-r} - O(\frac{2r}{\ln n} (r-1)^{-(r-1)})$$

$$\geq \quad r^{-r} - O((r-1)^{-(r-1)}/(r \ln \ln n)) = r^{-r}(1 - O(1/\ln \ln n)).$$

(since $r \leq \sqrt{\ln n / \ln \ln n}$).

In fact experimental data by ODLYZKO show that for $r \leq \sqrt{\ln n / \ln \ln n}$:

$$\#\{m \leq n : m \mid \operatorname{lcm}(2,3,\ldots,p_t)\}/n > r^{-r} .$$

By (2.1) this means that the constant 0.83 in corollary 4 can be replaced by a constant> 1 even if the e_i' are taken for the e_i.

3. Using a Pollard-Brent recursion in stage 2

If $h(-n) \nmid 2^{e_*} \Pi_{i=2}^t p_i^{e_i}$ with $e_i = \lfloor \log_2 n / \log_2 p_i^2 \rfloor$, $e_* = \lfloor \log_2 \sqrt{n} \rfloor$ then stage 1 fails to factor n and computes

$$\bar{H} := H_0^{\Pi_{i=2}^t p_i^{e_i}} , \quad H := \bar{H}^{2^{e_*}} .$$

Stage 2 uses $H,\overline{H}$ and will most likely find a proper divisor of n within $O(p_t)$ steps, provided $\mathrm{ord}(H) \leq p_t^2$.

Stage 2 generates a random walk through the cyclic group $\langle\overline{H}\rangle$ with generator $\overline{H}$. With some function $f:\langle\overline{H}\rangle\to\langle\overline{H}\rangle$ let

$$\overline{H}_1 := \overline{H} \ , \quad \overline{H}_{i+1} := f(\overline{H}_i) \quad .$$

The function f must be chosen such that

(3.1) f is easy to compute

(3.2) f is sufficiently random

(3.3) every relation $\overline{H}_j = \overline{H}_k$ with $j\neq k$ yields an ambiguous class S, depending on $\overline{H}$, f,j,k .

It is known (see KNUTH (1981), exercise 3.1.12) that some $k<j\lesssim\sqrt{\pi/2}\ p_t$ with $\overline{H}_j = \overline{H}_k$ can be expected if f is sufficiently random and $\mathrm{ord}(\overline{H}) \leq p_t^2$.

We have two methods to design f and to associate the ambiguous class S to f, $\overline{H}$, j, k. Both methods will produce ambiguous classes S with $S\neq 1$ whenever $\mathrm{ord}(\overline{H})$ is even. Experience must decide which of the methods is more efficient.

<u>Method 1</u> For some $q\in\mathbb{N}$ choose random integers $a_i\in[p_t^2, 2p_t^2]$ for $i=1,\dots,q$. Precompute $\overline{H}^{a_i}$, $i=1,\dots,k$. For some random function $g:\langle\overline{H}\rangle \to\{a_1,\dots,a_q\}$ let

$$\overline{H}_1 = \overline{H} \ , \ \overline{H}_{i+1} = \overline{H}_i\overline{H}^{g(\overline{H}_i)} \qquad .$$

Use the procedure <u>search</u> below in order to find some $k<j$ with $\overline{H}_k = \overline{H}_j$. Then

$$\overline{H}_j\overline{H}_k^{-1} = \overline{H}^T \quad \text{with } T = \sum_{i=k}^{j-1} g(\overline{H}_i) \quad .$$

Most likely we will have $j\leq 2p_t$ which implies $T\leq 4p_t^3$.

Now suppose that

$$\mathrm{ord}(\overline{H}) \equiv 2^e \mod 2^{e+1} \ .$$

Then $2^e | T$, and we can easily compute $\bar{e} \geq e$ with

$$T \equiv 2^{\bar{e}} \mod 2^{\bar{e}+1} \quad .$$

Then $\bar{H}^{T\,2^{-\bar{e}}}$ has order 2^e and yields an ambiguous class

$$S := \bar{H}^{T\,2^{e-\bar{e}-1}} \quad \text{with } S \neq 1 \text{ provided } e \geq 1 \;.$$

Comment We have tested this method for cyclic groups of order $m \approx 10^6$ and $a_i = c^{\bar{c}+i}$, $c, \bar{c}$ fixed, $q=200$. We obtained average period lengths of about $3\sqrt{\pi m/8}$. Also q must slightly increase with m. This weakness relies on the commutativity of the recursion steps. Method 1 takes one composition per recursion step and computes a multiple T of ord(H).

Method 2 Choose a random function $g: \langle H \rangle \to \{0,1,\ldots,7\}$, choose $a_0, \ldots, a_7 \in [p_t^2 \,,\, 2\, p_t^2]$ at random and precompute $F_i := H^{a_i}$, $i=0,\ldots,7$.

Recursion on H (We compute $H_i = H^{c_i}$ and d_i with $d_i \equiv c_i \mod 2^{32}$).

$$H_1 := H \;, \quad d_1 := 1$$

for i=1,2,..., do

$$\left[\begin{array}{llll} F := H_i \;, & f := d_i & & \\ \text{if } g(H_i) < 4 & \text{then}\,[F := F^3 & , & f = 3f\,] \\ \text{if } g(H_i) \text{ even} & \text{then}\,[F := F^2 H & , & f = 2f+1] \\ H_{i+1} := F\, F_{g(H_i)} & , \quad d_{i+1} :\equiv & f + a_{g(H_i)} & \mod 2^{32} \end{array}\right]$$

Use the procedure search below in order to find some $k<j$ with $H_k = H_j$. Since $H_i = H^{c_i}$ and $H = \bar{H}^{2^e *}$, it follows $\bar{H}^{2^e * (c_k - c_j)} = 1$. We compute t such that $d_k - d_j \equiv 2^t \mod 2^{t+1}$. Almost surely t will be less than 32, and this implies $c_k - c_j = 2^t m$ for some odd m . It remains to compute $\bar{H}^m$ since $\bar{H}^{m 2^\nu}$ is ambiguous for some $\nu \leq t$. We do not compute m explicitely but we retrace the above recursion on $\bar{H}$. In the following assume $t \geq 1$. We leave it to the reader to compute $\bar{H}^m$ in case t=0.

Recursion on $\bar{H}$ (We compute $\bar{H}_i = H^{c_i/2^t}$ and $r_i = c_i - 2^t \lfloor c_i/2^t \rfloor$ for $t \geq 1$)

$\overline{H}_1 := 1$ (the unit class) , $r_1 := 1$

for i=1,2,..., do

$$\left[\begin{array}{llll} \overline{F} := \overline{H}_i & , & r := r_i & \\ \text{if } g(H_i) < 4 & \text{then}[\overline{F} := \overline{F}^3 & , & r := 3r \;] \\ \text{if } g(H_i) \text{ even} & \text{then}[\overline{F} := \overline{F}^2 & , & r := 2r+1] \\ r := r + a_{g(H_i)} & , & s := \lfloor r/2^t \rfloor & \\ \overline{H}_{i+1} := \overline{F}\,\overline{H}^s & , & r_{i+1} := r - s\,2^t & \end{array}\right]$$

It can easily be verified that $\overline{H}_i = \overline{H}^{\lfloor c_i/2^t \rfloor}$.

Hence $\overline{H}_k \overline{H}_j^{-1} = \overline{H}^{(c_k - c_j)/2^t} = \overline{H}^m$ with m odd. This yields

<u>Fact 6</u> Let $\mathrm{ord}(\overline{H}) \equiv 2^e \bmod 2^{e+1}$, $e<32$ and $H_k H_j^{-1} = 1$, then $\mathrm{ord}(\overline{H}_k \overline{H}_j^{-1}) = 2^e$.

Therefore $S = (\overline{H}_k \overline{H}_j^{-1})^{2^{e-1}}$ is an ambiguous class with $S \neq 1$ whenever $e \neq 1$.

<u>Comment</u> We have tested this method for cyclic groups of order $m \approx 10^6$ and $a_i = c^{(\overline{c}+i)}$ with $c, \overline{c}$ fixed, $2 \leq c, \overline{c} \leq 6$. We obtained average period lenghts $\ll \sqrt{\pi m/8}$. The tests "$g(H_i) < 4$?" and "$g(H_i)$ even?" are chosen as to be independent. The storage requirement of method 2 is strictly finite. The recursion on H takes about 3 compositions per recursion step. The recursion on $\overline{H}$ takes about 6 compositions per recursion step, since the recursion on H must be retraced in order to provide the $g(H_i)$. In the rare cases that the recursion on H finds some $k<j$ with $H_k = H_j$ we can well afford this complication in computing $\overline{H}_k \overline{H}_j^{-1}$.

<u>The search for $H_j = H_k$ with $k<j$</u> Let $H_1 = H$, $H_{i+1} = f(H_i)$. We follow an idea of BRENT (1980) and do not store all the H_i but only a fixed number of them.

When computing H_i the stored classes

$$H_{\sigma(\nu)} \;,\quad \nu = 1,2,\ldots,7 \;,$$

for sufficiently large i, will be such that

$$\sigma(\nu) \approx \sigma(1)\; 1.1^{\nu} \;,\quad \nu = 1,\ldots,7$$

$$1.1^7 \sigma(1) < i < 1.1^8 \sigma(1) \approx 2.14\sigma(1).$$

The recursion for H_i is continued until some $H_j = H_{\sigma(\nu)}$ has been found. The corresponding program looks like

Search $H_1 := H$, $\sigma(\nu) := 1$ for $\nu = 1,\dots,7$

for $i=2,\dots$ do

$$\left[\begin{array}{l} \text{compute } H_i \text{ from } H_{i-1} \\ \text{if } \exists\, \nu:\ H_{\sigma(\nu)} = H_i \text{ then } [k := \sigma(\nu)\ ,\ j := i \quad \text{stop}] \\ \text{if } 1.1^8\sigma(1) < i+1 \text{ then} \\ \left[\begin{array}{l} \text{store } H_i \text{ instead of } H_{\sigma(1)} \\ \sigma(\nu) := \begin{cases} \sigma(\nu+1) & \text{for } \nu \neq 7 \\ i & \text{for } \nu = 7 \end{cases} \end{array}\right] \end{array}\right]$$

Let λ be the period and μ the length of the non-periodic segment of the sequence H_i, e.g.

$$H_\mu = H_{\mu+\lambda} \quad , \; H_i \neq H_j \quad \text{for } i<j<\mu+\lambda \; .$$

Fact 7 The procedure search finds some $k<j$ with $H_j = H_k$ within $\leq 1.1\, m+\lambda$ recursion steps, $m := \max(\lambda,\mu)$.

Proof Since σ increases by the factor 1.1, σ will take some value $\sigma(\nu)$ with $m \leq \sigma(\nu) \leq 1.1m$. Hence the for-loop stops at the latest with

$$j = \sigma(\nu) + \lambda \leq 1.1m + \lambda$$

and finds the equality $H_j = H_k$ with $k = \sigma(\nu)$.

Under the assumptions that each of the $\mathrm{ord}(H)^{\mathrm{ord}(H)}$ functions $f: \langle H\rangle \to \langle H\rangle$ has probability $\mathrm{ord}(H)^{-\mathrm{ord}(H)}$, the stochastic behaviour of μ,λ have been well analysed (see KNUTH (1981), exercise 3.1.12) .

The expected values of μ and λ are

$$1+E(\mu) \;=\; E(\lambda) \approx \sqrt{\frac{\pi\ \mathrm{ord}(H)}{8}} \;+ 1/3$$
$$E(\mu+\lambda) \approx 1.25\sqrt{\mathrm{ord}(H)} \;- 1/3$$
$$\mathrm{Prob}\left[\mu+\lambda \leq \frac{\pi}{2}\,\mathrm{ord}(H)\right] \approx e^{-\pi/4} \approx 0.46 \; .$$

We conclude from fact 7 that the number of recursion steps in search is bounded as

$$\leq 2.1\sqrt{\frac{\pi\,\mathrm{ord}(H)}{8}} \;\leq\; 1.32\sqrt{\mathrm{ord}(H)} \quad .$$

If in stage 2 we compute the H_i for $i \leq 1.32\, p_t$ then most likely some relation $H_k = H_j$, $k<j$ will be found, provided $\mathrm{ord}(H) \leq p_t^2$. It remains to analyse the chance that $\mathrm{ord}(H) \leq p_t^2$. For each prime p, $p_t < p < p_t^2$ we assume that the frequency of class numbers $h(-m)$, $m \leq n$ which are divisible by p is $\geq p^{-1}$, and we assume that $h(-m)/p$ factors like random integers of size $\sqrt{n}/p$. By retracing the proof of corollary 4 we conclude from the assumptions (2.1), (2.2) :

(3.4) | For all r,n,t with $n \geq n_0$, $p_t = n^{1/2r}$, $r \leq \sqrt{\ln n / \ln \ln n}$:

$\#\{m \leq n : h(-m) \mid p\Pi_{i=1}^{t} p_i^{e_i}\}/(0.5n)$

$\geq 0.83\ p^{-1}\ (r-r/s)^{-(r-r/s)}$

for all primes $p = n^{1/2s} < p_t^2$

Summing over all p, $n^{r^{-1}/(1+\varepsilon)} < p < n^{1/r}$ this yields

$$\#\{m \leq n : h(-m) \mid p\Pi_{i=1}^{t} p_i^{e_i} \text{ with } p < p_t^2\}\ /(0.5n)$$

$$\geq 0.83 \sum_{n^{r^{-1}/(1+\varepsilon)} < p < n^{1/r}} p^{-1} (r-2/(1+\varepsilon))^{-(r-2/1+\varepsilon))}$$

(using theorem 4.27 in Hardy Wright it follows)

$$\gtrsim 0.83\ \ln(1+\varepsilon)(r-2/(1+\varepsilon))^{-(r-2/(1+\varepsilon))} \quad .$$

<u>Conclusion</u> Assume (2.1), (2.2) and that for every discriminant $m \leq n$ H_0 in G(-m) is chosen at random. Then $\forall\ \varepsilon > 0 : \exists\ c_\varepsilon > 0 : \forall n$ and all $p_t = n^{1/2r}$, $r \leq \sqrt{\ln n / \ln \ln n}$: stage 2 with $O(p_t)$ compositions factors at least $c_\varepsilon (r-2+\varepsilon)^{-(r-2+\varepsilon)} n$ discriminants $\leq n$.

The following table compares the success frequencies r^{-r} and $F(n,r,\varepsilon) = \ln(1+\varepsilon)\ (r-2/(1+\varepsilon))^{-(r-2/(1+\varepsilon))}$ of stages 1 and 2. $F(n,r,\varepsilon)$ is only a lower bound on the success frequency of stage 2. The number of compositions for both stages is proportional to $n^{1/2r}$.

n	r	ε	$n^{1/2r}$	r^{-r}	$F(n,r,\varepsilon)$
2^{100}	4	0.5	$5.8 \cdot 10^4$	$4 \cdot 10^{-3}$	$3.0 \cdot 10^{-2}$
2^{200}	5	0.5	$1 \cdot 10^6$	$3.2 \cdot 10^{-4}$	$3.5 \cdot 10^{-3}$
2^{300}	6	0.5	$3.3 \cdot 10^7$	$2 \cdot 10^{-5}$	$3.1 \cdot 10^{-4}$
2^{400}	7	0.4	$4 \cdot 10^8$	$1.2 \cdot 10^{-6}$	$2.3 \cdot 10^{-5}$
2^{500}	7.6	0.4	$8 \cdot 10^9$	$2 \cdot 10^{-7}$	$4.5 \cdot 10^{-6}$

4. The main algorithm

The new algorithm can be used for factoring any composite integer n. We apply stage 1 to multiples n•s of n such that -ns is a discriminant. Here we can either restrict to discriminants $-ns \equiv 1 \bmod 4$, or we can extend stage 1 to discriminants $-ns \equiv 0 \bmod 4$ (see the complete paper). The non fundamental discriminants -ns will be useless and should be discarded as far as possible. The discriminant Δ is <u>fundamental</u> if

$$\neg \exists\, w \in \mathbb{N},\ w \neq 1 : \Delta/w^2 \text{ is a discriminant.}$$

In fact, the class formula (see DIRICHLET (1893,1968)),

$$h(-m) = \frac{\sqrt{m}}{\pi} \prod_{p \text{ prime}} \left(1 - \frac{1}{p}\left(\frac{-m}{p}\right)\right)^{-1} \qquad \text{for } m < -4 ,$$

implies for gcd(w,m) = 1 and w square free :

$$h(-mw^2)/h(-m) = w \prod_{p|w} \left(1 - \frac{1}{p}\left(\frac{-m}{p}\right)\right) = \prod_{p|w} \left(p - \left(\frac{-m}{p}\right)\right) .$$

Hence for small w h(-m) and $h(-mw^2)$ have the same large prime divisors.

<u>Main algorithm</u> Let n be the number to be factored and $p_1=2$, $p_2=3,\dots,p_t$ the first t primes, $p_t = n^{1/2r}$ (the appropriate choice of t,r will be determined by the subsequent analysis).

1. s := 1
2. take the next s with gcd(n,s)=1 , $-ns \equiv 0,1 \bmod 4$ and $\neg \exists\, w \in \mathbb{N} : w^2 | s,\ w \neq 1,\ -ns/w^2 \equiv 0,1 \bmod 4$
3. run stage 1 on ns this takes $O(p_t)$ compositions. If stage 1 yields an ambiguous class S then go to 4, otherwise return to 2 and take the next s
4. if S yields a factorization of n then stop, otherwise go to 5
5. return to 3 and repeat stage 1 on ns with independently chosen classes H_0 until some factorization of n has been found. In order to prevent that merely useless ambiguous classes are generated, continue to build up the 2- Sylow group $S_2(-ns)$ of G(-ns).

The method to build up the 2 - Sylow group $S_2(-ns)$ will be described in the complete paper.

Run time analysis of the main algorithm   We separately consider

1. the number $T(n)$ of bit operations to be done till some s has been reached with

$$h(-ns) \mid \Pi_{i=1}^{t} p_i^{e_i} \quad , \; e_i = \max\{ \nu : p_i^{\nu} \le p_t^2 \} \quad .$$

2. the number of bit operations for building up the 2- Sylow group $S_2(-ns)$ of $G(-ns)$ which is negligible.

T(n) We will assume that corollary 4 extends to multiples of n:

$$(4.1) \quad \left\| \begin{array}{l} \exists\, c, n_0 \ge 0 : \forall\, n \ge n_0 : \forall\, m : \forall\, p_t = (nm)^{1/2r} \text{ with } r \le \sqrt{\ln n/\ln \ln n} : \\ \#\, \{ns : s \le m \wedge h(-ns) \mid \Pi_{i=1}^{t} p_i^{e_i} \} / (0.5m) \ge c\, r^{-r} \end{array} \right.$$

Our experimental datas in fact confirm the lower bound r^{-r} .
The assumption (4.1) implies

$$\forall\, n \ge n_0 : \forall\, p_t = (n\, 3r^r/c)^{1/2r} \quad , \; r \le \sqrt{\ln n/\ln \ln n}$$

$$\exists\, s \le 3r^r/c : h(-ns) \mid 2^{e_*} \, \Pi_{i=1}^{t} \, p_i^{e_i} \quad .$$

Since stage 1 takes $O(p_t)$ compositions, we have

$$T(n) = O(p_t \, r^r \, (\ln n)^2) = O(n^{1/2r} \, r^{r+1/2} \, (\ln n)^2) \quad .$$

Here $O(\ln n)^2$ takes into account the costs for the arithmetic. We choose $r = \sqrt{\ln n/\ln \ln n}$, $p_t \approx (n\, 3r^r/c)^{1/2r} = O(n^{1/2r} \sqrt{r}\,)$, then all together (4.1) implies

$$T(n) = o(\exp \sqrt{\ln n \ln \ln n}) \quad .$$

Conclusion   If (4.1) holds then the main algorithm, using only stage 1, takes $o(\exp \sqrt{\ln n \ln \ln n})$ bit operations to factor arbitrary, composite integers n .

If we also apply stage 2 then s will be bounded as $O(r-2)^{(r-2)}$, and this will save a factor of about $r^2 = \ln n/\ln \ln n$.

References

Brent, R.P. : An improved Monte Carlo factorization algorithm. BIT 20 (1980) 176-184.

Dixon, J.D. : Asymptotically fast factorization of integers. Mathematics of Computation 36 (1981) 255-260.

Gauss, C.F. : Disquisitiones Arithmetiquae. Leipzig 1801. German translation : Untersuchungen über höhere Mathematik. Springer, Berlin (1889).

Hardy, G.H. and Wright, E.M. : An Introduction to the Theory of Numbers. Oxford University Press, fifth edition (1979).

Knuth, D.E. : The Art Computer Programming, Volume 2, Seminumerical Algorithms. Second edition. Addison - Wesley (1981) .

Lejeune Dirichlet, P.G. and Dedekind, R. : Vorlesungen über Zahlentheorie. Braunschweig 1893. Reprint: New York (1968).

Lenstra jr., H.W. : On the calculation of regulators and class numbers of quadratic fields. Journées Arithmétiques 1980,J.V.Armitage (Ed.) Cambridge University Press (1982) 123-150 .

Mathews, G.B. : Theory of numbers. 1892. Reprint: Chelsea, New York (1962).

Monier, L. : Algorithmes de factorisation d'entiers. Thèse d'informatique. Université Paris Sud (1980).

Morrison, M.A. and Brillhart, J. : A method of factorization and the factorization of F_7. Math. Computation 29(1975) 183-205 .

Pollard, J.M. : A Monte Carlo method for factorization. BIT 15 (1975) 331-334 .

Pomerance, C. : Analysis and comparison of some integer factoring algorithms. Computational Methods in Number Theory, R.Tijdemen, H.Lenstra (Eds.)Mathem.Centrum,Amsterdam (1981?) .

Rivest, R.L., Shamir, A., and Adleman, L. : A method for obtaining digital signatures and public key cryptosystems. Comm. ACM 21 (1978) 120-126 .

Sattler, J. and Schnorr, C.P. : Ein Effizienzvergleich der Faktorisierungsverfahren von Morrison-Brillhart und Schroeppel. Preprint Universität Frankfurt 1981. to appear in Computing.

Shanks, D. : Class number, a theory of factorization and genera. Proc. Symp. Pure Math.Amer.Math.Soc. 20(1971) 415-440.

Schnorr, C.P. : Refined analysis and improvements on some factoring algorithms. Journal of Algorithms 3(1982) 101-127 .

Siegel, C.L. : Über die Klassenzahl quadratischer Zahlkörper. Acta Arith. 1 (1936) 83-86.

Wagstaff, S.S. and Wunderlich, M.C. : A comparison of two factorization methods.
Unpublished manuscript.

Zimmer, H.G. : Computational Problems, Methods, and Results in Algebraic Number Theory.
Lecture Notes in Mathematics 262.
Springer, Berlin-New York (1972).

THEORY OF CONCURRENCY CONTROL

Christos H. Papadimitriou
National Technical Univ. of Athens
9, Heroes of the Polytechnic Str.
Athens 624, Greece

ABSTRACT

This paper is a review of recent theoretical work on the problems which arise when many users access the same database. For a detailed exposition of this material, the interested reader is referred to a forthcoming monograph [Pa4].

1. Introduction

Database concurrency control studies the problems that arise when many programs access and update the same data simultaneously. There is now a vast applied literature on database concurrency control (see [BG] for a review and references). More recently, a *theory* of concurrency control has started to emerge. The goals of this theoretical work have been compatible with the goals of the theory of computation in general:

(a) To study the *whole spectrum* of possible approaches to the computational problem in hand, and (b) To show rigorously the *limitations* of these approaches.

The concept of programs with shared data is certainly not new in computer science. Concurrent programs and communicating processes are already well-studied. That theory, however, concerns itself with a set of programs that are *meant* to run together, and shared data are in part means of communication and synchronization. Correctness is a *collective* property of the programs. In contrast, in database concurrency control we have programs that were meant to run *in isolation*, and were designed to be *individually* correct. As a consequence, an interleaved execution of such programs may fail to be correct. The canonical example is the pair of two-step programs updating the shared integer variables x and y.

```
begin  x:=x+1;
       y:=y-1
end
```

and

```
begin  x:=2*x;
       y:=2*y

end.
```

Each of these programs preserves the invariant "x+y=o". However, certain *interleaved* executions of their steps fail to doso. (For example, try the execution in which the two steps of the first program occur between the two steps of the second). The problem in concurrency control is to avoid such "incorrect" executions, while allowing the correct ones. This is not achieved by rewriting the programs to include synchronization, but by designing algoritms which monitor the execution and intervene to change the order of execution whenever necessary, so that the resulting concurrent execution is correct.

The algorithm which achieves this is called the *scheduler.* The scheduler operates on-line on a shuffled excution sequence from the individual programs. Such sequences are called *schedules*. The output of the scheduler is another schedule, which is guaranteed to preserve the invariants. (See Figure 1)

On the surface the problem may be reminiscent of *program verification* After all, the scheduler must verify that a certain interleaved execution of some programs preserves an invariant. There are very strong reasons, however, which make the program verification approach inappropriate:

1. First, the scheduler must arrive at decisions at a speed comparable to the execution of the programs. This rules out realistically any automatic verification.

2. The precise semantics of the programs are not available to the scheduler. What is submitted to the scheduler is a sequence of accesses to the shared variables. Local variable computations are hidden from the scheduler. Even the invariants are usually not known.

These arguments point towards the more *syntactic* approach, which has been the framework of concurrency control theory. We introduce the basic concepts in the next section. Section 3 gives a closer look, to schedulers and their properties. Section 4 examines a class of concurrency control algoritms based on locking. Finally, in Section 5 we examine some recent theoretical results on the subject of distributed concurrency control. These results constitute one more instance of the principle, that computational problems become much harder in a distributed environment.

2. The Model

Let $P_1,\ldots,P_n$ be programs accessing and updating both local and shared variables. The shared variables are called entities. Let $T_1,\ldots, T_n$ be execution sequences of the respective programs with steps involving only local variables omitted. The remaining steps are either read steps of the form "temp:=x", where x is an entity and temp a local variable (denoted as R(x)), or write steps of the form "x:=f (temp1,...,tempk)" where x is an entity, f an uninterpreted function symbol, and temp1,...,tempk the local variables involved in all previous read steps of the same execution sequence (notation:W(x)). Concurrency control studies such syntactic abstractions of programs (i.e., sequences of read and write steps), called transactions. A schedule is an element of the shuffle of the transactions.

We must now define, what we mean by "correct schedule". The constraints are those exposed in the previous Section: The precise semantics of the programs (the interpretations of the functions f above) are not known, neither is known the invariant to be preserved. These constraints point towards our definition of correctness:
A schedule is correct if it is equivalent to a serial schedule, that is, a schedule in which the transactions execute one strictly after the other, without interleaving. We have, of course, to define schedule equivalence. Two schedules are equivalent if they are final-state equivalent as uninterpreted program schemata. Since schedules are straight-line schemata, this is a particular easy instance of this notion. The resulting notion of correctness is called serializability, a very widely accepted criterion.
In some sense, serializability is the most liberal notion of correctness possible, given the constraints mentioned above. For a formulation and proof of this informal statement, see [KP].

There is an interesting combinatorial characterization of serializability. Let s be a schedule, and let V be its set of transactions. We can assume that s is a full schedule, that is, it starts with a transaction which writes all entities, and ends with

a transaction which reads all entities. From s, we can construct a combinatorial object called a <u>polygraph</u> P(s)=(V,E,C).
E is a set of directed edges defined as follows: If transaction v reads an entity X in s, and the last write step in s before the R(X) step of v belongs to transaction u, then (u,v) $\in$ E. Now C is a set of <u>choices</u>, that is, paths of lengh two. If (u,v) $\in$ E, and transaction w$\neq$u contains another W(X) step writing the same variable, then we add to C the choise (v,w,u). Intuitively, this triple means that, in any serial schedule equivalent to s, transaction w must come either before u, or after v.

A digraph (V,A) is said to be <u>compatible</u> with the polygraph (V,E,C) if E $\subseteq$A, and for each choice (u,v,w) in C either (u,v) or (v,w) is in A. A polygraph is <u>acyclic</u> if there is an acyclic digraph compatible with it.

<u>Theorem</u> 1 [Pa1] Schedule s is serializable iff P(s) is acyclic.

Unfortunately, this criterion is of no algorithmic help:

<u>Theorem 2</u> [Pa1] Testing whether schedule s is serializable is NP-complete.

There are certain interesting versions of the notion of serializability. An important one is <u>view-serializability</u> A <u>view</u> of a transaction T in a schedule s is the set of values read by read-steps of T. Two schedules are <u>view-equivalent</u> if, for all interpretations, the views of each transaction in the two schedules are the same. A schedule is <u>view- serializable</u> if it is view-equivalent to a serial schedule.

View-serializability is a stricter notion of correctness than serializability. It has been argued [RSL] that adopting serializability leads to errors of concurrency. In [Pa4] it is shown that view-serializability is indeed the right notion of correctness, when the programs which originate the transactions have nontrivial control structure. Versions of Theorems 1 and 2 are true of view-serializability as well.

An even more restricted notion of correctness is the so-called <u>conflict - serializability</u>. We say that two steps of a schedule <u>conflict</u> if they involve the same variable, and they are not both read steps. Two schedules are <u>conflict - equivalent</u> if any two conflicting steps have the same order in both. A schedule is <u>conflict-serializable</u> if it is conflict - equivalent to a serial schedule. Given now a schedule s, constrct a directed graph D(s)=(V,E) an follows: V is the set of transactions of s. The pair (u,v) of transactions is in E if there is a step in u which conflicts with a <u>subsequent</u> (in s) step of v. We have:

<u>Theorem 3</u> [EGLT] Let s be a schedule. s is serializable iff D(s) is acyclic.

Therefore, conflict serializability is a less liberal notion of correctness, which however leads to a criterion which is much more manageable, both conceptually and algorithmically.

Finally, there is in the literature a modified <u>model</u> of transactions, the <u>action model</u>. In this model, steps are not distinguished between read and write ones. Each step, called an <u>action</u> , consists of reading <u>and</u> writing an entity. Thus a transaction can be considered as a sequence of steps, in which each write step is <u>immediately</u> preceeded by a read step on the same entity. Furthermore, this pair of steps cannot be separated in a schedule. Another point of view of this <u>action model</u>, is that we have now even less semantics: We cannot even tell the read steps from the write steps.

<u>Theorem 4</u> [Pa4] the action model, serializability, view - serializability and conflict-serializability coincide.

<u>3. Schedulers</u>

The scheduler is an algorithm which maps schedules to schedules. It operates <u>on - line</u>. This means that it examines its input schedule one step at a time, in order of arrival. For each step, it decides whether to <u>grant</u> it or to <u>delay</u> it. If a step is granted, then the scheduler possibly grants steps that had previously been delayed :

```
algorithm scheduler ;

var  a:step; p:state;
     Q:set of steps;

     procedure  schedule (b:step);

     begin  modifystate ;
         if test  (p,b) then
```

```
            begin
            output (b);
            modifystate;
            for each  c ∈ Ω do schedule(c)
            end
        else Ω:=ΩU{b}
    end;
    begin  (comment:scheduler);
    p:=initialstate; Ω:=Ø ;
    repeat  on  steparrival(a) do
            schedule(a)
    forever
    end;
```

The parameters that distinguish different schedulers are: the predicate test; the discipline for maintaining the state p of the scheduler; and the queuing discipline implicit in the for all loop.

It is quite realistic to assume that the schedule has another property, called optimism. This is defined and defended an follows: Let A be a scheduler, and let H be the set of all possible schedules of a fixed set of transactions. (The set of transactions is fixed for concreteness and comparison. Criticisms that this assumption is unrealistic are therefore not founded.) Then A(H) is the set of schedules output by A.

Intuitively, A(H) can be regarded as the set of schedules which the scheduler, in its limited sophistication, can recognize as correct.

It is therefore natural to assume that, if A is fed with a schedule in A(H), it never delays a step. Thus "optimism" is a kind of idempotency property. From another important point of view, A(H) can be regarded as a measure of the performance of the scheduler, as it captures the amount of parallelism allowed by A.

The more schedules there are in A(H), for fixed H, the "better" the scheduler.

The set A(H) presumably contains only correct schedules. We say that scheduler A implements the concurrency control principle $C \subseteq H$ if $A(H) = C$. A natural question arises: Given C, under what conditions can we design an efficient (i.e., polynomial-time) scheduler A such that $A(H)=C$? Our first reaction, namely "if and only if C is polynomial-time recognizable", turns out to be false. For example, suppose that C contains schedules, each of which consists of two halves. The first half is serializable schedule, whereas the second half is a serial schedule, equivalent to the first. A scheduler A with A(H)=C must decide, after seeing the first half, whether or not it is serializable. This is impossible to do in polynomial-time, by theorem 2, unless P=NP. This is despite the fact C is polynomial-time recognizable. The correct characterization is the following.

Theorem 5 [Pa1] Let C ⊆ H. There is an efficient, optimistic scheduler A such that A(H)=C iff the set of prefixes of C is in P.

Theorem 5 demonstrates the importance of complexity results, such as theorem 2 and 3.

An important factor in the study of schedulers in the information that the scheduler has about the transactions and individual arriving steps. This information is hidden in the parameters initialstate and modifystate of our stylized scheduler. Intuitively, the more information A has, the better its "performance" A(H). This can be proved rigorously [KP], based on a formalism which we omit. It folows from the results in [KP], for example, that serializability is the best performance achievable, when only syntactic information on the transactions is available.

4. LOcking

Locking is a very widely accepted technique for implementing concurrency control algorithms. In some sense, it is a methodology inspiredby operating systems and other classical synchronization problems. The idea is the following: We modify the transactions (in fact, the programs) by inserting P and V operations on binary semaphores. In a transaction, there is a V operation before a P operationon the same semaphore, and there are no nested V-P pairs on the same semaphore. Initially, all semaphores are 1. These insertions are presumably such that the semaphores by themselves guarantee correctness.

As before, let us fix a set of transactions, the set H of all schedules, and let L be a mapping which inserts lock-unlock steps (that is, V and P operations) as above. Let L(H) be the set of all schedules (after the removal of lock-unlock steps). L(H) is the measure of parallelism allowed by L, as in the case more general shedulers.

There is a difference, though. If we are given a clans C ⊆ H, in principle we can always design a scheduler A such that A(H)=C - complexity considerations aside. In contrast, it is quite intuitive that, with locking, we can only implement certain C's. A fundamental question arises: When can we implement by locking a given subset of H?

To solve this and other problems in locking, it is helpful to employ a <u>geometric methodology</u> [Pa2,Pa3]. First, let us just consider two transactions. In the coordinated plane, think of the two positive axes as representing progress towards the completion of the transactions. Integer points on the axes are steps of the original transactions (not lock-unlock steps). A point in the orthant is therefore a particular snapshot of their concurrent execution. A semaphore locked by both transactions is represented by a <u>forbidden rectangle</u>, delimited by the positionof the respective lock-unlock steps on the axes (see Figure 2) A schedule is thus an increasing curve from O to F, avoiding all rectanngles — and all grid points except O and F. Naturally, small perturbations of the curve may represent the same schedule. We can read the schedule out of any such curve, by simply enumerating the grid lines as they are crossed by the curve. In the light of the geometric intepretation, the question we asked in the previous paragraph can be rephrased as follows: Given a class C of curves, can we place restangles on the orthant so that C is the class of all increasing curves from O to F not crossing the rectangles?

There are two very intuitive necessary conditions that a set C of schedules of two transactions A and B must satisfy, in order to be implementable by locking:

(1) The serial schedules AB and BA must be in C as there is no way to "block"these schedules by locking.

(2) If two schedules S and S' <u>cross</u> when considered as curves (this means that in the beginning S is "ahead " of S' in the execution of, say, A, and later it falls "behind" —we omit the formal definition, see Figure 2) then the "hybrids " S_1S_2' and $S_1'S_2$ are also in C. This property in some sense captures the memorylessness of binary semaphores.

<u>Theorem 6 [Pa3]</u> Let C be a set of schedules of two transactions. Then C is realizable by locking iff properties (1) and (2) hold.

Theorem 6 also gives a characterization of locking for more than two transactions. If S is a schedule and i,j transactions, let S_{ij} be the schedule with all steps of transactions other than i,j omitted.

<u>Corollary</u> Let C be a set of schedules. Then C is realizable by locking iff for each <u>pair</u> of transactions i,j these is a set S_{ij} of schedules realizable by locking such that

$$C = \{s: \text{for all } i,j,\ s_{ij} \in S_{ij}\}.$$

Theorem 6 and its corollary delimit the expresive power of locking as a concurrency control primitive. They can be considered as <u>positive</u> results, in that the nontrivial direction is the sufficiency part.

In the practice of concurrency control, the semaphores involved are not uninterpreted, as we have considered them so far, but are closely related with the <u>entities</u> of the transaction. Each entity has its <u>lock bit</u>, and the P and V operations restrict access to the entities. Each entity is locked before its first access by a transaction, and unlocked after the last. It is this connection that brings out some of the most interesting work on locking.

Geometry is very helpful here. Schedule equivalence has as a geometric analog <u>curve homotopy</u> on the orthant, with the grid points that correspond to conflicts removed. <u>Safety</u> (i.e., avoidance by locking of all non-serializable schedules) has also a nice geometric characterization [Pa2], leading to efficient algorithms [LP,SW]. For more than two transactions, the problem of safety becomes NP-complete [Pa2]. The problem of <u>deadlocks</u> has a similar behavior [Ya1].

Some of the deepest results on concurrency control concerns <u>locking policies</u>, that is, rules for inserting P and V steps in transactions so as to make the whole system of transaction safe. Such policies are the popular <u>two-phase locking</u> [EGLT], and the very different <u>tree policy</u> [SK]. A surprising result [Ya1] is that there is a <u>single universal safe locking policy</u>, special cases of which are all possible safe locking policies. Finally, it can be shown [Ya3] that locking policies cannot realize the full power of serializability: They can only produce conflict-serializable schedules. The reader is reffered to these papers and [Pa4] for an exposition of those results.

5. Distributed Concurrency Control

The most challenging practical problems in concurrency control arise in connection with distributed databaces |BG|. Researchers in the field soon discovered that, like in most areas, the distributed problem is, conceptually, qualitatively harder than the centralized one. Recently, we gave a complexity-theoretic explanation of this fact |KaP|. It was shown that distributed concurrency control enbodies a universal two- person combinatorial game. As such games are some of the most hard and intricate combinatorial problems known, being complete for PSPACE, this result explains the apparent conceptual complexity of distributed concurrency control.

In a distributed environment we have a number of sites. Transactions are now partial orders of steps occurring at either side, in which all steps at one site must be totally ordered. Likewise, schedules are partial orders with total orders locally. The concept of serializability generalizes readily. A distributed scheduler is a distributed program which grants and delays locally submitted steps. The modules of the scheduler must communicate via messages with undeterministic delays. We say that a distributed scheduler implements a set C of schedules if it outputs only schedules in C, and, moreover, if the delays are zero, then it never delays a step, when the schedule submitted is indeed in C.

In distributed concurrency control, we have three measures of performance. Besides the parallelism of the scheduler, measured by C, and its complexity, which were also present in the centralized case, we also have the communication costs, the number of messages exchanged. Suppose that C is given - in fact, fix it to be the set of serializable schedules. If we do not care about the number of messages expended we can design a polynomial-time scheduler which uses broadcasting to achieve C. However, for minimizing communication costs, we have the following result:

Theorem 7 The following problem is PSPACE-complete: Given a set of transactions, distributed on two sites, and an integer b, can we design a distributed scheduler with a worst - case number of exchanged messages at most b?

References

[BG] P. Bernstein, N. Goodman "Fundamental algorithms for concurrency control", ACM Comp. Surveys, 1981.

[EGLT] K. Eswaran, J. Gray, R. Lorie, I.Traiger "The notions of consistency and predicate locks in database systems" CACM, 1976.

[KaP] P. Kanellakis, C.H.Papadimitriou "The complexity of distributed concurrency control", Proc 1981 FOCS. Also, to apear in SIAM J. Computing, 1983.

[KP] H.T. Kung, C.H. Papadimitriou "An optmality theory of concurrency control", Proc 1979 SIGMOD.

[LP] W. Lipski, C.H. Papadimitriou "Fast algorithm for testing for safety and detecting deadlocks" J. Algorithms, 1981.

[Pa1] C.H. Papadimitriou "The serializability of concurrent database updates", JACM, 1979.

[Pa2] _____ "Conurrency control by locking", to appear in SIAM J. Computing, 1982 .

[Pa3] _____ "A theorem in database concurrency control", to appear in J. ACM, 1982.

[Pa4] _____ The theory of concurrency control, in preparation, 1982.

[SLR] R. Stearns, P. Lewis, D. Rosenkrantz"Concurrency control for database systems", Proc 1976 FOCS.

[SK] A. Silbersatz, Z. Kedem " Consistency in hierarchical database systems", JACM 1980.

[SW] Soisalon-Soininen, D. Wood, Proc PODS Conference, 1982

[Ya1] M. Yannakakis "The theory of safe locking policies in database systems", JACM 1982.

[Ya2] ____ "Freedom from deadlock of safe locking policies", SIAM J. Computing, 1982.

[Ya3] ____ "Issues of correctness in database concurrency control by locking", Proc. 1981 STOC.

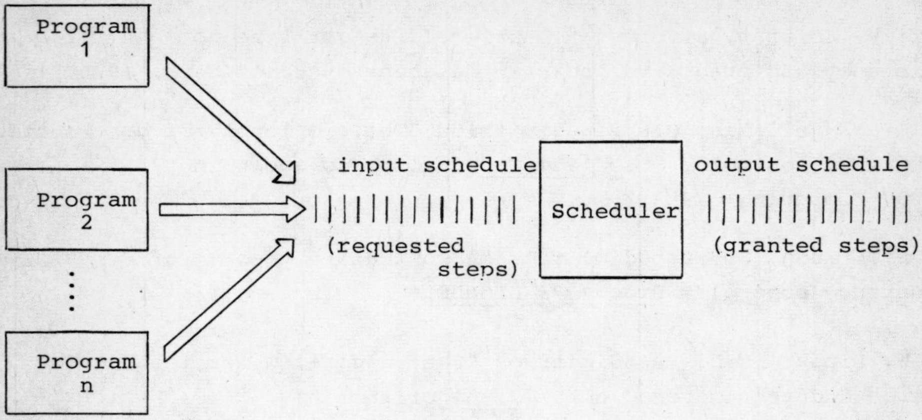
Program 1
Program 2
Program n
input schedule
(requested steps)
Scheduler
output schedule
(granted steps)

Figure 1

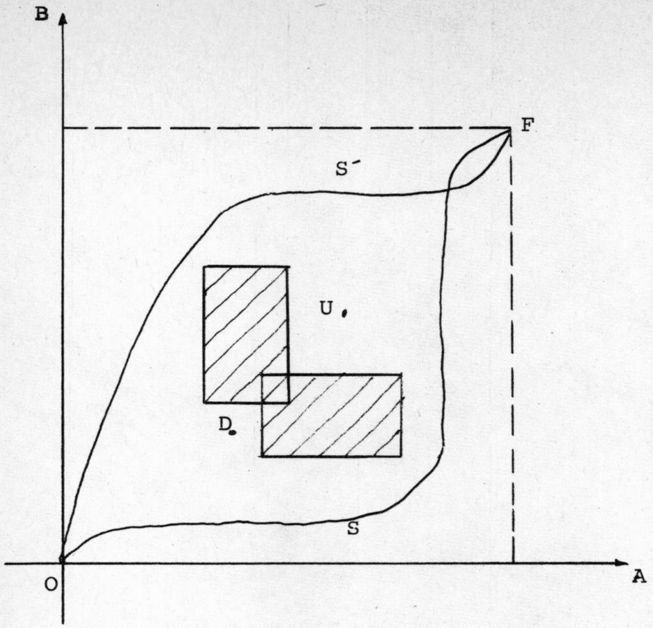

Figure 2

INTERPROCEDURAL DATA FLOW SYSTEMS

Gerhard Barth

Fachbereich Informatik
Universität Kaiserslautern
6750 Kaiserslautern
West Germany

1. Introduction

It will be reported how the iterative approach to data flow analysis can be extended from its intraprocedural to an interprocedural setting. Kildall's work [Ki73] provided the fundamentals to iterative methods and was taken a step further in [KU76]. These two references may be viewed as the starting point for the investigations described in this paper.

The terminology used here resembles the one employed in [He77] and will be briefly summarized in the subsequent paragraph. A program consists of a collection of procedures and is denoted by PROG = $(P_o, P_1, \ldots, P_m)$, P_o being the start procedure. Flow graphs G_i of procedures P_i, $o \leq i \leq m$, are given as quadruples (N_i, A_i, s_i, e_i), where s_i and e_i are the single start and exit block of P_i, respectively. Semilattices $(L, \wedge)$ contain both a zero element $\underline{0}$ and a one element $\underline{1}$ and are of finite decreasing length. An intraprocedural data flow system for a procedure P_i is a quintuple $(L, \wedge, F_i, G_i, M_i)$ where

- $(L, \wedge)$ is a semilattice,
- F_i is an operation space associated with L [see He77, p.165],
- G_i is P_i's flow graph
- $M_i : N_i \rightarrow F_i$ is a mapping which assigns an operation from F_i to each basic block of P_i.

Depending on whether F_i contains monotone or distributive functions over L only, the data flow system is called monotone or distributive, respectively.

2. Interprocedural Data Flow Systems

In [My81] a simple way is described how to combine flow graphs of procedures calling each other mutually or recursively. Firstly, each block of procedure P_i containing a call of procedure P_j is split in two blocks, hereafter termed call block and return block. Secondly, call arcs from call blocks to P_j's start block s_j and return arcs from P_j's exit block e_j to return blocks are added. Applying this construction to all procedures of a program PROG = $(P_o, P_1, \ldots, P_m)$ results in the super flow graph of PROG. A dominant feature of such graphs is the possibility of modelling each execution sequence of PROG's statements as a path in its super flow graph. Conversely, as can be observed in the case of a procedure being called more than once, either from distinct sites in one procedure or by different procedures, not every path in a super flow graph represents a semantically valid flow of control through PROG.

Definition 2.1 An execution path is a path in a super flow graph which upon exit from a procedure leads to the return block matching the call block in which this procedure was activated last. An execution path is balanced if each procedure P_i entered on it eventually is left again through its exit e_i.

Definition 2.2 Let PROG = $(P_o, P_1, \ldots, P_m)$ be a program. An interprocedural data flow system for PROG is a quintuple $(L, \wedge, F, G, M)$, where

- $(L, \wedge)$ is a semilattice,
- $F = \cup \{F_i \mid 0 \leq i \leq m\}$ is an operation space associated with L,
- $G = (N, A, s_o, e_o)$ is the super flow graph for PROG,
- $M : N \to F$ is a mapping which assigns to each node in N an operation from F.

For each node n in the super flow graph, the operation $M(n) : L \to L$ transforms data flow objects according to the statements associated with n. The overall transformation elements in L are subjected to on an execution path $p = (n_o, n_1, \ldots, n_k, n_{k+1})$ through G is given by the composite effect

$$M_p = M(n_k) \cdot \ldots \cdot M(n_1) \cdot M(n_o)$$

Definition 2.3 Let $(L, \wedge, F, G, M)$ be an interprocedural data flow system for a program PROG = $(P_o, P_1, \ldots, P_m)$. The meet-over-all-paths solution is a mapping $MOP : N \to L$ defined as

$$MOP(n) := \wedge \{M_p(\underline{O}) \mid p \text{ is an execution path in G from } s_o \text{ to } n\}$$

The <u>effect of a procedure P_i</u>, $0 \leq i \leq m$, is a mapping $EFFECT_i : L \to L$ defined as

$$EFFECT_i(\ell) := \wedge\{M_p(\ell) \mid p \text{ is a balanced execution path in } G \text{ from } s_i \text{ to } e_i\}$$

for each $\ell \in L$. Note that both MOP and $EFFECT_i$ are well defined since the bounded decreasing length of L guarantees convergence when applying the meet operator $\wedge$ to a countably infinite set.

3. Interprocedural Data Flow Equations

Having set the proper framework in the preceding chapter, the next step will be to establish a system of equations relating data flow information valid at different nodes of a super flow graph. The prime difficulty is the handling of relationships among call blocks and start blocks, as well as relationships among procedure exits and return blocks. The following figure will expedite the discussion of some heuristics to pick the right choice. There it is assumed

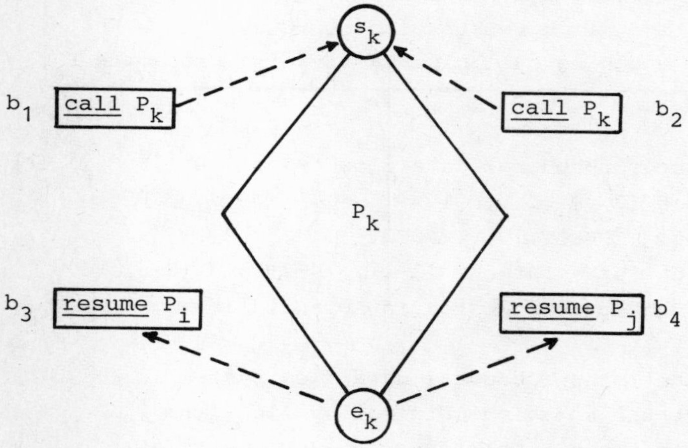

that procedure P_k is called from procedures P_i and P_j. Let INF[n] denote the data flow information valid at node n of a super flow graph. It is sensible to establish an equation

$$INF[s_k] = M(b_1)(INF[b_1]) \wedge M(b_2)(INF[b_2]),$$

since data flow information may be imported into P_k from all calling sites. On the other hand, we do not wish to consider either of the equations

$$INF[b_3] = M(e_k)(INF[e_k]) \text{ or } INF[b_4] = M(e_k)(INF[e_k]).$$

This is because $INF[e_k]$ can be traced back to both $INF[b_1]$ and $INF[b_2]$ and there should be no interaction between $INF[b_1]$ and $INF[b_4]$ or between $INF[b_2]$ and $INF[b_3]$. What we really want is a relationship among $INF[b_1]$ and $INF[b_3]$ and among $INF[b_2]$ and $INF[b_4]$. Hence the proper equations would be

$$INF[b_3] = EFFECT_k \cdot M(b_1)(INF[b_1])$$
$$INF[b_4] = EFFECT_k \cdot M(b_2)(INF[b_2])$$

The generalization of the above heuristics gives rise to the following system of data flow equations for an interprocedural data flow system for $PROG = (P_o, P_1, \ldots, P_m)$.

(3-1) $INF[s_o]$	$= \underline{O}$
(3-2) $INF[n]$	$= \wedge\{M(n')(INF[n']) \mid n' \rightarrow n \text{ is an arc in } G\}$, if n is not a return block in G
(3-3) $INF[n]$	$= EFFECT_k \cdot M(n')(INF[n'])$, if n is a return block in G and n' is the matching call block activating procedure P_k

ALGORITHM 3.1

Input: (1) An interprocedural data flow system $(L,\wedge,F,G,M)$ for $PROG = (P_o,P_1,\ldots,P_m)$

(2) $EFFECT_o, EFFECT_1, \ldots, EFFECT_m$

Output: A solution for equations (3-1), (3-2) and (3-3)

Method: Perform the actions listed in Appendix 1.

THEOREM 3.2 If the interprocedural data flow system is

(a) distributive, the solution obtained by Algorithm 3.1 coincides with the MOP solution

(b) monotone, the solution obtained by Algorithm 3.1 is the maximum fixed point of equations (3-1), (3-2) and (3-3).

Obviously, the main problem with Algorithm 3.1 is that it has to be fed with the entire collection $EFFECT_o, EFFECT_1, \ldots, EFFECT_m$ for the procedures of a program. In order to find a method for their computation we proceed as follows. Any two operations f and g from an operation space F, associated with domain L, may be combined into a new operation $f\wedge g : L \rightarrow L$, specified as

$$f\wedge g(\ell) := f(\ell) \wedge g(\ell)$$

It can easily be verified that if both f and g are distributive or monotone, respectively, so is $f \wedge g$. Let F^* denote the closure of F under $\wedge$ enriched by two functions MIN and MAX, defined as

$$\text{MIN}(\ell) := \underline{0} \quad , \quad \text{MAX}(\ell) := \underline{1} \text{ for all } \ell \in L.$$

F^* is a semilattice, yet not necessarily of finite decreasing length, as demonstrated in Example 3.3.

<u>Example 3.3</u> The natural numbers form a semilattice (without a one element) if the meet operator is defined as $i \wedge j := \min(i,j)$. No function space F, not to say its closure F^*, containing the functions f_i, specified as

$$f_i(j) := \underline{\text{if}}\ j \leq i\ \underline{\text{then}}\ 1\ \underline{\text{else}}\ j$$

is of finite decreasing length, since $f_1 > f_2 > f_3 > \ldots$ is an infinite descending chain in F.

<u>Definition 3.4</u> Let $(L,\wedge,F,G,M)$ be an interprocedural data flow system for PROG = $(P_0,P_1,\ldots,P_m)$. The <u>partial effects</u> of P_i, $0 \leq i \leq m$, and a basic block n are mappings $\text{effect}_i[n] : L \to L$ with the following specification

$$\text{effect}_i[n](\ell) := \wedge\{M_p(\ell) \mid p \text{ is a balanced execution path in G from } s_i \text{ to } n\}$$

Note that EFFECT_i (see Definition 2.3) coincides with $\text{effect}_i[e_i]$.

With this definition and employing heuristics as at the outset of this chapter, another system of equations can be established

(3-4)	$\text{effect}_i[s_i]$	= <u>id</u> (means: identity)
(3-5)	$\text{effect}_i[n]$	$= \wedge\{M(n')\cdot\text{effect}_i[n'] \mid n' \to n \text{ is an arc in } G\}$, if n is neither start block of P_i nor a return block
(3-6)	$\text{effect}_i[n]$	$= \text{EFFECT}_k \cdot M(n') \cdot \text{effect}_i[n']$, if n is a return block in P_i, n' is the matching call block activating procedure P_k

Although being almost identical in structure with equations (3-1), (3-2) and (3-3), the recent equation system bears a totally different semantics. Equations (3-4), (3-5) and (3-6) relate operations from F^*, whereas the former equations put objects of L into proper relationships.

ALGORITHM 3.5

Input: An interprocedural data flow system (L,$\wedge$,F,G,M) for PROG = (P_o,P_1,...,P_m)

Output: A solution for equations (3-4), (3-5) and (3-6)

Method: See Appendix 2.

THEOREM 3.6 Provided the semilattice F^* of the interprocedural data flow system is of finite decreasing length and the data flow system is

(a) distributive, the solution obtained by Algorithm 3.5 coincides with the partial effects as described in Definition 3.4

(b) monotone, the solution obtained by Algorithm 3.5 is the maximum fixed point of equations (3-4), (3-5) and (3-6).

Finite decreasing length of F^* has to be postulated in order to guarantee termination of Algorithm 3.5. In all situations where a finite domain L of data flow objects is involved, as is the case in the majority of data flow problems, this condition is met. Consequently, there is a wide range of data flow problems that can be tackled by the method advocated in this paper.

The results derived so far amount to a two-phase solution of interprocedural data flow systems: Firstly, apply Algorithm 3.5 to compute the mappings $EFFECT_i$, secondly, solve equations (3-1), (3-2) and (3-3) by means of Algorithm 3.1. Yet, there is some waste of resources when proceeding in this way, as we do not fully exploit the results produced by Algorithm 3.5. Only the mappings $effect_i[e_i]$ (=$EFFECT_i$) are used in Algorithm 3.1. Equations of type (3-2) suggest to propagate data flow information in a block-by-block fashion through a super flow graph. We can do much better, however, by recognizing the fact that once data flow information has passed the entry of a procedure P_i, it can be transported to any block n interior to P_i in a single sweep by means of $effect_i[n]$. Hence we replace equations (3-2) and (3-3) by

(3-7)	$INF[s_i]$	$= \wedge\{M(n) \cdot effect_j[n](INF[s_j]) \mid$ n is a call block for P_i in $P_j\}$
(3-8)	$INF[n]$	$= effect_i[n](INF[s_i])$, if $n \neq s_i$ is an interior block of P_i.

In Appendix 3 an Algorithm is described to solve equations (3-1), (3-7) and (3-8), whose behavior is summarized in the following theorem.

THEOREM 3.7 If the interprocedural data flow system is

(a) distributive, the solution computed by the algorithm coincides with the MOP solution

(b) monotone, the solution computed by the algorithm is the maximum fixed point of equations (3-1), (3-7) and (3-8), and is identical with the maximum fixed point of equations (3-1), (3-2) and (3-3).

4. Conclusion

The investigations reported about in this paper were conducted in order to show that Kildall's lattice-theoretic approach to data flow analysis can be extended from its intraprocedural to an interprocedural setting. For this purpose it was mandatory to have a model for describing interprocedural flow of control. Myers' construction for integrating flow graphs of distinct procedures into a single super flow graph proved to be helpful. He, too, relates his work to the theory of data flow analysis frameworks (here called data flow systems). The main difference between his and my strategy stems from the handling of procedure calls and returns. Myers uses a "memory component" to monitor the flow of control as it enters or leaves procedures. The idea used here, namely to capture the effects of procedure calls onto data flow objects by the mappings $EFFECT_i$ and $effect_i[n]$ is a direct and natural extension of the principle to characterize transformations within basic blocks by functions of an associated operation space F. The fact that the required mappings can be computed algorithmically from F is deemed the major contribution of this paper.

To the knowledge of this author, no non-trivial quantitative analysis for work-list versions of iterative data flow analysis algorithms, as to how many iterations are necessary to empty the list, have been published. In contrast, for round-robin strategies it has been shown that d+2 (d stands for the loop connectedness parameter) iterations suffice to achieve stabilization, provided the flow graph of the analyzed procedure is reducible [He77, Section 7.3]. In an empirical study of FORTRAN programs an average value of d = 2.75 was revealed [Kn71]. Hence in "most cases" a round-robin version should terminate after 5 iterations only. All of the algorithms described in this paper can be translated into round-robin implementations. The upper bound d+2 holds then, too. Yet, now it stands for the loop connectedness parameter of super flow graphs and it remains to be verified that for them a reasonably small value may be assumed in practical applications. Corresponding investigations are just being performed.

5. Bibliography

[He77] HECHT, M.S. "Flow Analysis of Computer Programs", Elsevier, North-Holland, 1977

[KU77] KAM, J.B. and ULLMAN, J.D. "Monotone Data Flow Analysis Frameworks", Acta Informatica, 7, 309-317, 1977

[Ki73] KILDALL, G.A. "A Unified Approach to Global Program Optimization", 1st POPL, Boston, Mass., 194-206, 1973

[Kn71] KNUTH, D.E. "An Empirical Study of FORTRAN Programs", Software Practice and Experience, 1:12, 105-134, 1971

[My81] MYERS, E.U. "A Precise Interprocedural Data Flow Algorithm", 8th POPL, Williamsburg, Virginia, 219-230, 1981

Appendix 1: Method for Algorithm 3.1

A first-in-first-out list QUEUE is used to store pairs <n,ℓ>, with n being a basic block and $\ell \in L$. Two operations *top* and *store* serve to remove pairs from QUEUE or to append them to QUEUE, respectively.

```
{initialize}
INF[s_o] := 0;
for all n ≠ s_o do INF[n] := 1 endfor;
for all n ≠ e_i, 0≤i≤m, do
   for each successor n' of n do
        store (<n', M(n)(INF[n])>);
        if n is a call block for procedure P_i then
           store (<n", EFFECT_i·M(n)(INF[n])>), where n"
                 denotes the return block matching n
        endif
   endfor
endfor

{iterate}
while QUEUE not empty do
  x := top(QUEUE); {let x be the pair <n,ℓ>}
  TEMP := ℓ ∧ INF[n];
  if TEMP ≠ INF[n] then
     INF[n] := TEMP;
     if n ≠ e_i, 0≤i≤m, then
        for each successor n' of n do
            store (<n', M(n)(INF[n])>);
            if n is a call block for procedure P_i then
               store (<n", EFFECT_i·M(n)(INF[n])>), where n"
                     denotes the return block matching n
            endif
        endfor
     endif
  endif
endwhile
```

Appendix 2: Method for Algorithm 3.5

A first-in-first-out list QUEUE is used to store pairs <n,f> with n and f denoting a basic block and an operation in F^*, respectively.

```
{initialize}
for i := 0 to m do effect[s_i] := id endfor;
for all basic blocks n ≠ s_i in any P_i, 0≤i≤m, do
    effect_i[n] := MAX
endfor;
for each basic block n ≠ e_i in any P_i, 0≤i≤m, do
    for each successor n' of n do
        store (<n', M(n)·effect_i[n]>);
        if n is a call block for P_j in P_i then
            store (<n", effect_j[e_j]·M(n)·effect_i[n]>), where
                  n" is the return block matching n
        endif
    endfor
endfor

{iterate}
while QUEUE is not empty do
  x := top(QUEUE); {let x denote the pair <n,f>}
  TEMP := f ∧ effect_i[n]; {n is an interior basic block of P_i}
  if TEMP ≠ effect_i[n] then
     effect_i[n] := TEMP;
     if n = e_i for some i,0≤i≤m then
        for each call block n' in any P_j activating P_i do
           store (<n", effect_i[e_i]·M(n')·effect_j[n']>), where
           n" is the return block matching n'
        endfor;
     elseif n is call block in P_i activating P_j then
           store (<n', effect_j[e_j]·M(n)·effect_i[n]>), where
           n' is the return block matching n
     else for each successor n' of n do
           store (<n', M(n)·effect_i[n]>)
          endfor
     endif
  endif
endwhile
```

Appendix 3: Solving Equations (3-1), (3-7), (3-8)

```
{initialize}
INF[s_o] := 0;
for i := 1 to m do INF[s_i] := 1 endfor;
for each call block n in P_j activating P_i do
    store (<s_i, M(n)·effect_j[n] (1)>)
endfor;

{iterate}
while QUEUE not empty do
   x := top(QUEUE); {let x be a pair <s_i,ℓ>}
   TEMP := INF[s_i] ∧ ℓ;
   if TEMP ≠ INF[s_i] then
      INF[s_i] := TEMP;
      for each call block n in P_i activating P_k do
          store (<s_k, M(n)·effect_i[n](INF[s_i])>)
      endfor
   endif
endwhile
```

On the Crossing-free, Rectangular Embedding of Weighted Graphs in the Plane

Bernd Becker
Fachbereich 1o
Universität des Saarlandes
66 Saarbrücken

Abstract:

In [1] M.J.Fischer and M.S.Paterson pointed out that finding the optimal planar layout of a weighted graph with respect to the L_2-metric is NP-hard. We consider this problem with respect to the L_1-city-block metric in the discrete and continuous case and show that it remains NP-hard.

I. Introduction

In various fields of computer science (communication networks, switching circuit theory, VLSI-theory,...) one is often faced with problems, which may be summarized in the following "exercise": "Find the most suitable embedding of a graph in a given space with respect to certain conditions." At this a graph is used as the description of the "abstract structure" of a problem, f.e.: the nodes of the graph symbolize switching elements (processing elements), the edges stand for the wires connecting these elements with each other. To each edge we associate the width of the corresponding wire. The product width.length of a wire then corresponds to the cost of the wire or to the area occupied by the wire. We are interested in a technique that realizes the given "abstract" circuit with cost, resp. space as small as possible. Besides additional restrictions to the routing of the wires (according to the used technology) are possible. There exist a lot of papers dealing with problems of this kind, f.e. [1],[3],[4],[5].

II. Model, Definitions

We use a general model introduced in [1]:

<u>Given</u>: $G=(V,E,w)$ with $G'=(V,E)$ graph and $w:E\to \mathbb{Q}^+$ an edge weight

function, (G is called <u>weigthed graph</u>)

$\chi : L \rightarrow \mathbb{Q}^2$ ($L \subseteq V$) partial embedding of the nodes in the plane

<u>Problem</u>: The nodes of $V \setminus L$ are to place in the plane according to the following points: - the edges of the graph can be realized as paths in the plane in such a way, that the complete length of all paths in consideration of the weight function does not exceed a given number k;

- certain conditions (for routing) have to be fulfilled.

There are given results in [1] for the following additional conditions:

i) The paths must run in vertical or horizontal direction (according to the L_1-metric): There are given efficient algorithms for the construction of the optimal layout.

ii) The paths have to be crossing-free with each other (but may run in arbitrary directions): There is outlined a proof that this problem is NP-hard.

In this paper we consider the problem under the following additional conditions, which are of interest even in classical circuit theory:

<u>The continuous case</u>:

All paths have to run <u>rectangular</u> (according to the L_1-metric) and must be <u>crossing-free</u> with each other.

<u>The discrete case</u>:

There is given a grid Γ in the plane. The embeddings of the graphs have to take place <u>within the grid</u> ($\Rightarrow$ all paths run rectangular), the paths are <u>crossing-free</u>.

We focus on the discussion of the discrete case, the solution of the continuous one will result later from that of the discrete one.

$\Gamma := \{(r_1, r_2) \in \mathbb{R}^2 \mid \exists\, z_1, z_2 \in \mathbb{Z}: (r_1 = z_1\gamma) \vee (r_2 = z_2\gamma)\}$

is called <u>grid</u> of size γ ($\gamma \geq 0, \gamma \in \mathbb{Q}$).

$\Gamma P := \{(r_1, r_2) \in \mathbb{R}^2 \mid \exists\, z_1, z_2 \in \mathbb{Z}: (r_1 = z_1\gamma) \wedge (r_2 = z_2\gamma)\}$

is called the set of <u>grid points</u> in Γ.

Paths, which run in Γ, are called <u>Γ-paths</u>. With the help of these notions we are able to define Γ-realisations of weighted graphs:

Let $G = (V,E,w)$ be a weighted graph;

i) Let $\lambda : V \rightarrow \Gamma P$ be an embedding,

$r = (\lambda, E_\lambda)$ is called <u>crossing-free Γ-realisation of G for λ</u>

$:\Longleftrightarrow$

E_λ is a set of Γ-paths with:

- $\forall (v,w) \in E_\lambda$ there exists exactly one Γ-path in E_λ with end points $\lambda(v), \lambda(w)$,
- these are all the elements of E_λ,
- Γ-paths in E_λ are simple and crossing-free.

$\underline{cost_G(r)} := \sum_{e \in E} w(e).(\text{length of the corresponding path in } E_\lambda)$
is called the <u>cost of the Γ-realisation r</u>.

ii) Let $\chi: L \to \Gamma P$ ($L \subseteq V$) be a partial embedding,
$\underline{\text{Planar-}C_\Gamma(G,\chi)} := \min \{cost_G(r) \mid r \text{ crossing-free } \Gamma\text{-realisation of } G \text{ for } \lambda: V \to \Gamma P \text{ with } \lambda|L = \chi\}$
is called the <u>cost of the optimal layout of G for χ with respect to crossing-free Γ-realisation</u>.
A realisation, whose cost is the above minimum, is called <u>optimal Γ-realisation of G for χ</u>.

III. Results

We are now able to give the exact formulation of the considered problems:

<u>Planar-Γ-Trees Full Layout Problem</u> (notion: P-Γ-TFLP)
Instance: $G = (V,E,w)$ a weighted acyclic graph,
$\chi: V \to \Gamma P$ injective,
$k \geq o$, $k \in \mathbb{Q}$
Question: $\text{Planar-}C_\Gamma(G,\chi) \leq k$

We get the following

<u>Theorem 1</u>:
P-Γ-TFLP is NP-hard with respect to log-space reduction.

<u>Corollary</u>:
If we change the problem in the following way
- $G = (V,E,w)$ is an arbitrary weighted graph and $\chi: L \to \Gamma P$ ($L \subseteq V$)
- or $G = (V,E,w)$ is a weighted tree and $\chi: L \to \Gamma P$ ($L \subseteq V$) is injective and we only consider injective $\lambda: V \to \Gamma P$, $\lambda|L = \chi$,

then the problems remain NP-hard.

In the continuous case we may define the notions of L_1-path, crossing-free L_1-realisation of G for λ, cost, ... similarily to the discrete case. Let P-L_1-TFLP be the problem corresponding to P-Γ-TFLP. Then we have analoguous results:

<u>Theorem 2</u>:
P-L_1-TFLP is NP-hard with respect to log-space reduction.

The corollary holds too, if we substitute the corresponding notions.

IV. Proofs

We take advantage of the "proof-philosophy" outlined in [1]:
The construction of four switching elements (= weighted graphs) and the matching paths makes it possible to represent, transport and change logical values. This way we succeed in the "simulation" of logical circuits. We construct the following four elements:

- bistable element: can store two different values (see appendix figure 1)
- rotation element: rotates the bistable element by 9o degree (see appendix figure 2)
- fanout element: doubles a bistable element (see appendix figure 3)
- or gate: consists of 2 bistable elements as input gates, 1 bistable element as output gate, which contains as value the logical or of the 2 input gates (see appendix figure 4)

In [1] we have a bistable element, a fanout element and an or gate too; but they are of no use for our case and don't have any similarity to to the elements we construct, see appendix figure 6. The desired function of the above elements is prooved by the construction of all optimal Γ-realisations. This is the main difficulty beside the actual design of the elements. In [1] the existence and uniqueness of the minimal solutions for all elements is clear without a detailed proof (see appendix figure 6). In this paper we often have to consider a lot of optimal Γ-realisations (see appendix figure 4). In order to construct and classify all these solutions, we develope topological means: Optimal Γ-realisations, which run "almost the same way", are called "equivalent". (This notion corresponds to that of homotopy of paths (for this see appendix figure 1).) A simple test gives us the possibility to decide the equivalence of two Γ-realisations. With the help of this and exact look at the different cases we are able to find all optimal Γ-realisations and to devide them into equivalence classes, which we call minimal solutions. The different minimal solutions correspond to the different values of the elements above mentioned and guarantee the desired function. (Representatives of all minimal solutions are given in the appendix.)
The elements are used for the construction of a log-space reduction of the satisfiability problem for Boolean expressions to P-Γ-TFLP. To a Boolean expression we assign a circuit consisting of copies of the four elements. These elements are linked together in such a way, that a minimal solution of the whole circuit consisting of minimal solutions

of the single elements exists if and only if the Boolean expression is satisfiable. (In the appendix, figure 5, three bistable elements are linked together in such a way, that the optimal solution of one element determines the minimal solutions for the remaining two; so it is possible to simulate signal lines.) There is no difficulty to choose a log-space reduction fulfilling the above statements. The proof of the corollary is given by the choice of the reduction as well. So we may conclude the discrete case.

The proof of the continuous case can be done in an analoguous way after a very slight modification of the four elements.

Remark:

A more detailed presentation and a complete version of the proofs is given in [2].

References:

[1] M.J.Fischer, M.S.Paterson: Optimal Tree Layout (Preliminary Version); Proc. Twelfth Annual ACM Symposium on Theory of Computing, pp.177-189, 198o

[2] B.Becker: Über die kreuzungsfreie, rechtwinklige Einbettung von gewichteten Graphen in die Ebene; Dissertation, Saarbrücken 1982

[3] M.Tompa: An Optimal Solution to a Wire-routing Problem; Proc. Twelfth Annual ACM Symposium on Theory of Computing, pp.2o1-21o, 198o

[4] A.S.LaPaugh: A Polynomial Time Algorithm for Optimal Routing around a Rectangle; Proc. Twenty-first Annual IEEE Symposium on Foundations of Computer Science, pp.282-293, 198o

[5] D.Dolev, K.Karplus, A.Siegel, A.Strong, J.D.Ullman: Optimal Wiring between Rectangles; Proc. Thirteenth Annual ACM Symposium on Theory of Computing, pp.312-317, 1981

Appendix:

The connections emphasized by heavier lines in the following figures correspond to edges whose weights are so big, that they must be realized as straight lines in any optimal solution. The pairs at each figure denote, which points (except the above mentioned) have to be joined by minimal paths.

Figure 1

(a_1, a_2)

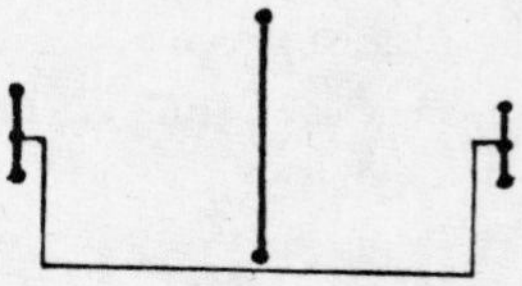

solution 1 = value 'o'
— and --- give two
equivalent realisations

solution 2 = value '1'

Figure 2

(a_1, a_2) , (a_5, a_6) , (c_1, c_2)

solution 1

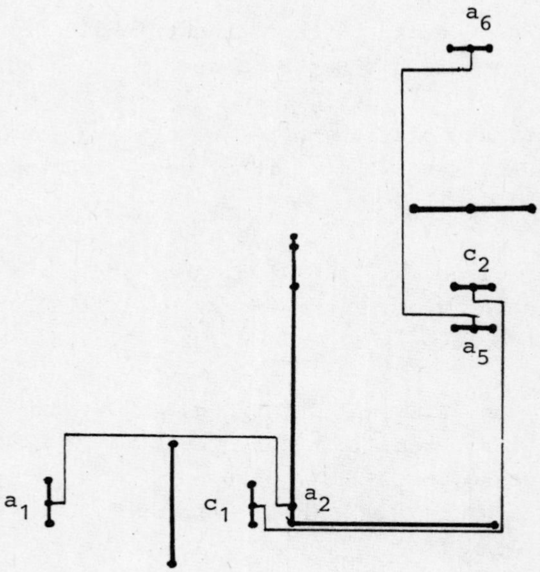

solution 2

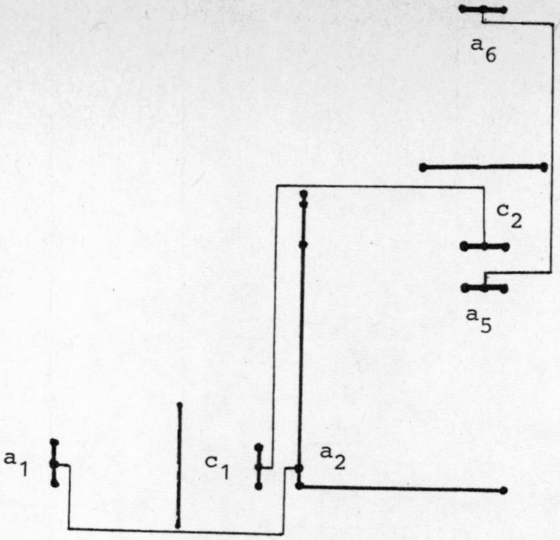

function of the element:
it rotates a bistable element by 9o degree and conserves its value 'o' or '1'.

<u>Figure 3</u>
(a_1,a_2) , (a_5,a_6) , (a_9,a_{1o}) , (c_1,c_2) , (c_1,c_3)

solution 1

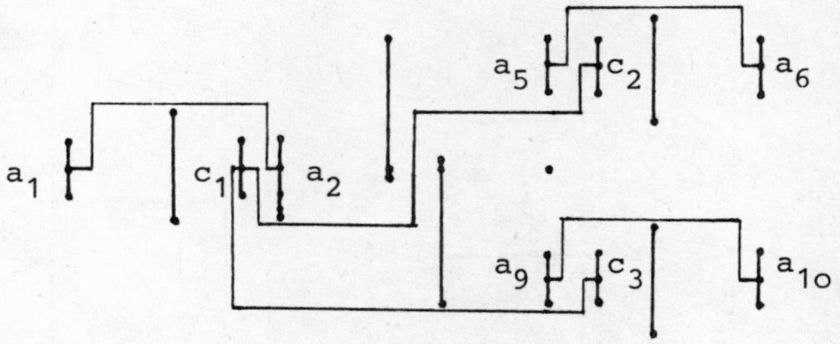

solution 2

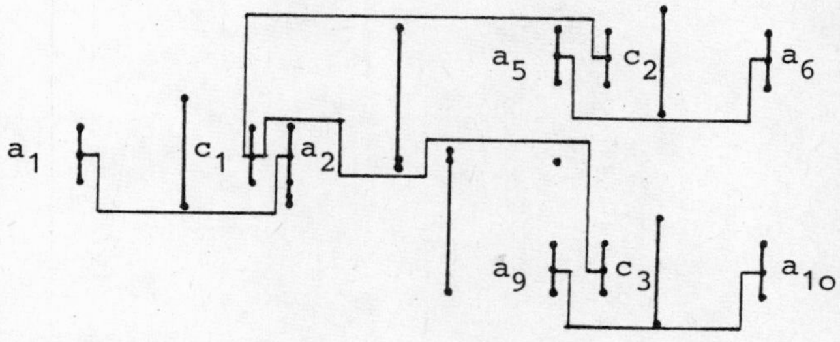

function of the element:
it doubles a bistable element and conserves its value.

Figure 4

(c_1,c_2) , (c_9,c_{10}) , (c_{18},c_{19}) , (a_1,a_2) , (a_3,a_4) , (a_5,a_6)

solution 1

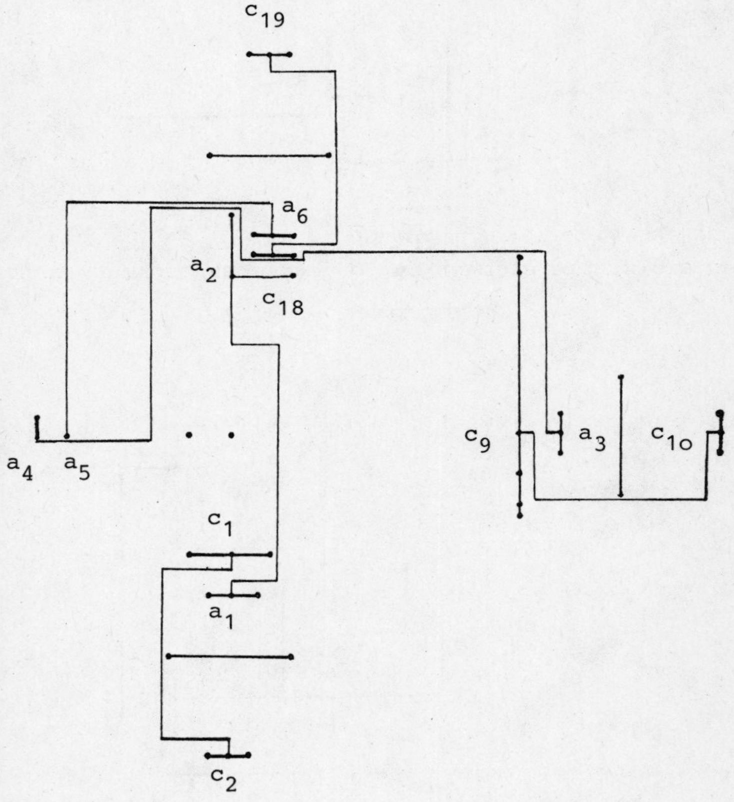

solution 2

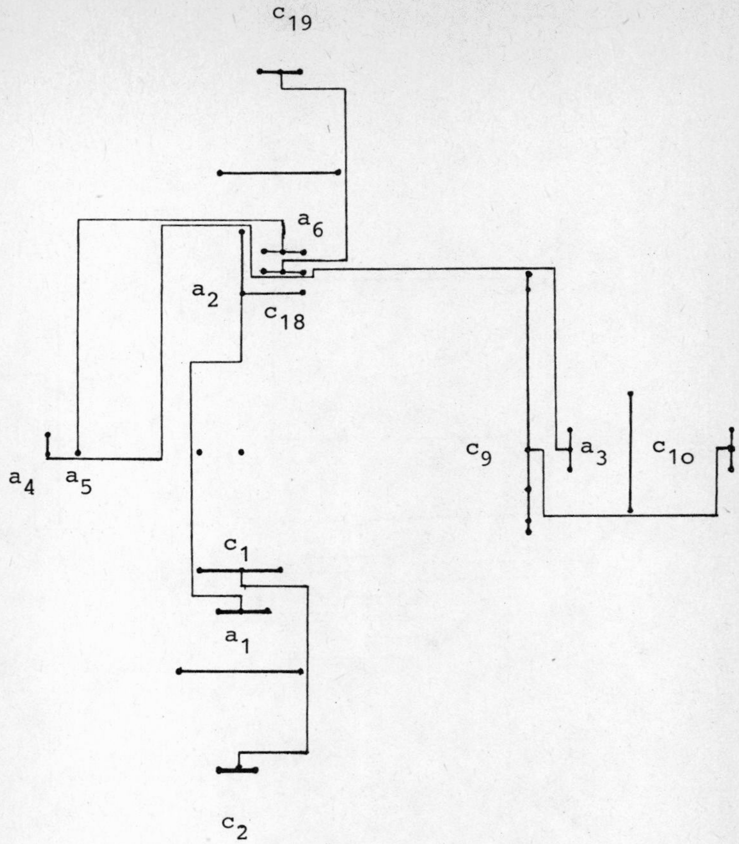

solution 3

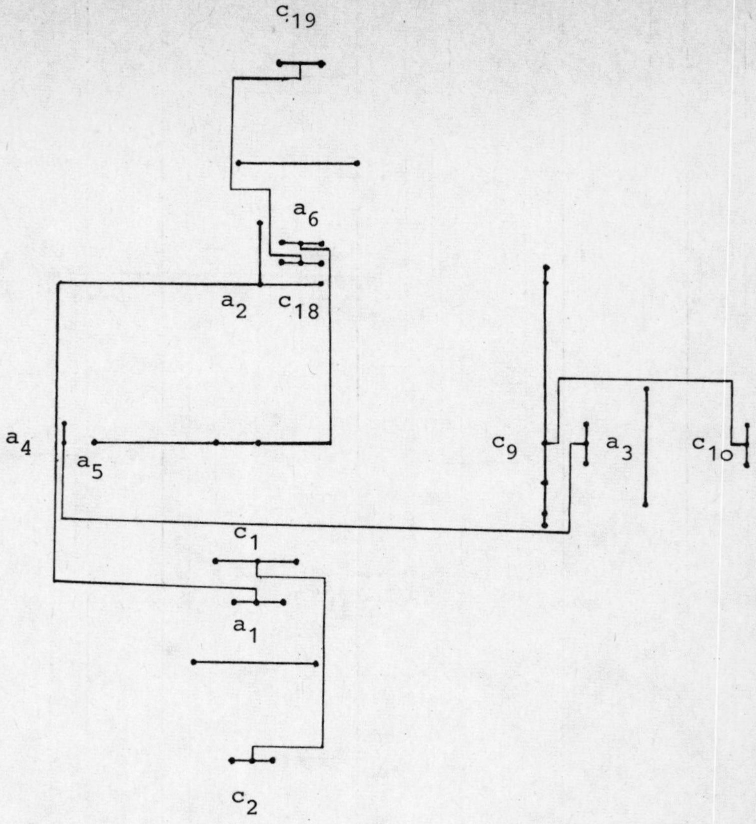

solution 4

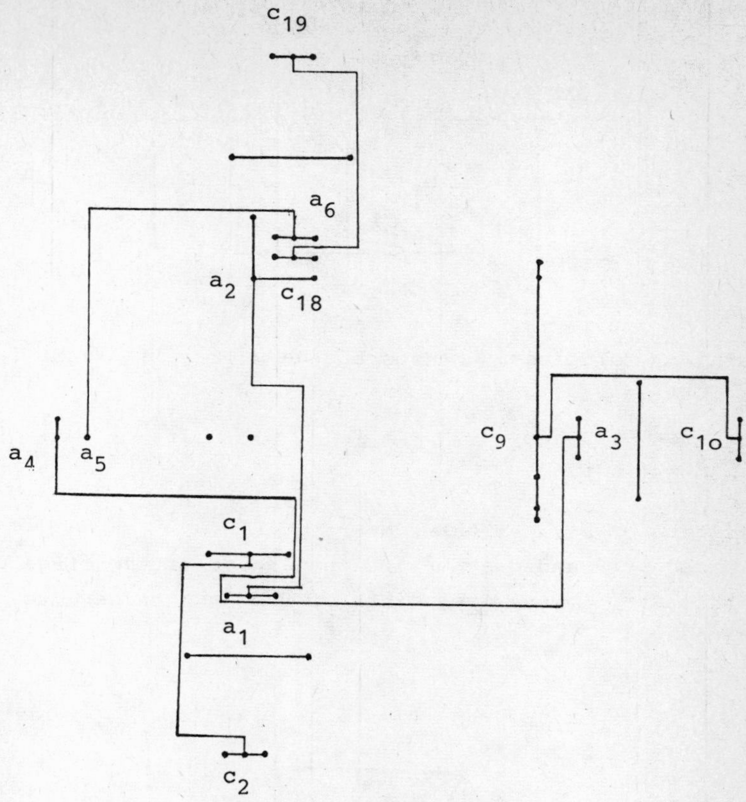

function of the element:
Four possible input values of the lower and the left bistable element create the value '1' three times and the value 'o' once at the upper bistable element. In this sense this element may be interpreted as an or-gate.

Figure 5

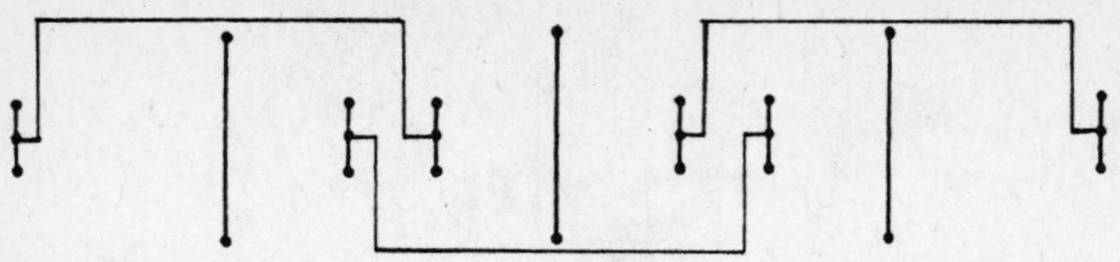

The minimal solutions "transport" the values '1' resp. 'o'.

Figure 6

The or-gate of Fischer/Paterson:
The rhombs at P and Q symbolize the inputs of the or-gate, the rhomb at R the output. Opposite points of the hexagon have to be joined.

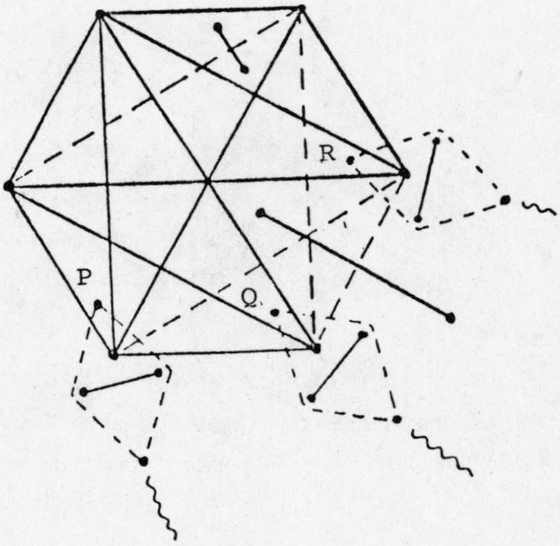

DISCRETENESS, K-DENSITY AND D-CONTINUITY OF OCCURRENCE NETS

Eike BEST and Agathe MERCERON
GMD-ISF
Schloß Birlinghoven
Postfach 1240
5205 St. AUGUSTIN 1, F.R.G.

ABSTRACT

This paper is devoted to the study of occurrence nets as models of non-sequential processes, and of some of their properties. We characterise the properties known as discreteness, K-density and D-continuity which have been proposed in the literature as meaningful properties of processes. We show that they are closely related to each other.

INDEX TERMS: Continuity, Density, Discreteness, Non-Sequential Processes, Occurrence Nets, Partially Ordered Sets, Petri Nets.

1. INTRODUCTION

In a seminal paper by Petri [P1], occurrence nets[1)] have been proposed as a mathematical model of non-sequential processes. Occurrence nets might, for example, be used to describe the processes arising in a Petri net [GLT] or the executions of a concurrent program [BR]. Occurrence nets feature the following characteristic properties: alternation between events and conditions; a partial (i.e. not necessarily linear) ordering of events and conditions; and the absence of branching and looping. By abstracting from the particular system that may generate the processes, they provide a framework for the study of some interesting properties inherent in the process model itself.

The aim of the present paper is to characterise three such properties, called discreteness, K-density and D-continuity, and to study their relationships. Discreteness can be motivated by the intuitive idea that between any two subsequent events of a process there should not be any infinite chain of intermediate events. K-density which has been introduced in [P1], has been motivated in [P1,B1,B2] by the idea that every sequential subprocess of a process should always be in a well-defined state. A similar motivation has been put forward in [FT1-3] for the property of D-continuity which has first been defined in [P2] as a generalisation of Dedekind's notion of the continuity of the real numbers. For further motivation we refer to the literature.

The paper is organised as follows. Section 2 contains basic definitions. In section 3 we define discreteness and prove a characterisation of it in terms of the sequential subprocesses of an occurrence net. Section 4 contains the definition of K-density and a characterisation of it in terms of discreteness. In section 5 we present a characterisation of D-continuity in terms of discreteness which is analogous to the previous characterisation of K-density. As a corollary we obtain a direct relationship between D-continuity and K-density. In section 6 we show that this result can be generalised to partially ordered sets. In section 7 a summary and a brief discussion of our results can be found. We also review related work in more detail.

---

1) We use the term occurrence net as defined in [GS]. This coincides with the definition of causal net in [P1].

Because of space limitations, only the proofs of the main results of this paper can be given. However, for each missing proof we indicate a location where it can be retrieved.

2. OCCURRENCE NETS

2.1 Definition.

A triple $N = (B,E;F)$ is called a net [GS] iff

(i) $B \cap E = \emptyset$, $B \cup E \neq \emptyset$; (B is the set of conditions, E is the set of events)

(ii) $F \subseteq B \times E \cup E \times B$; (F is the flow relation)

(iii) $dom(F) \cup cod(F) = B \cup E$.

In diagrams, conditions are drawn as circles, events as boxes, and a pair $(x,y) \in F$ as an arrow leading from x to y.

2.2 Definition.

Let $N = (B,E;F)$ be a net.

(i) $X = B \cup E$; (X is the set of elements of N)

(ii) For $x \in X$, ${}^\bullet x = \{y \in X \mid (y,x) \in F\}$ and $x^\bullet = \{y \in X \mid (x,y) \in F\}$.

(iii) $\leq\ = F^*$, $<\ = (\leq \setminus id)$, $\lessdot\ = (< \setminus <^2)$, $li = (\leq \cup \geq)$, $co = \overline{li} \cup id$, where $\overline{li} = (X \times X \setminus li)$.

If two events, say $e_1 \in E$ and $e_2 \in E$, share a condition (i.e. ${}^\bullet e_1 \cap {}^\bullet e_2 \neq \emptyset$ and/or $e_1^\bullet \cap e_2^\bullet \neq \emptyset$) then they are said to be in conflict. An occurrence net is a net without repetitions and without conflicts; formally:

2.3 Definition.

A net $N = (B,E;F)$ is called an occurrence net [GS] iff

(i) $\forall x,y \in X$: $x<y \Rightarrow$ not $y<x$;

(ii) $\forall b \in B$: $|{}^\bullet b| \leq 1 \wedge |b^\bullet| \leq 1$.

Throughout the paper we assume $N = (B,E;F)$ to be an occurrence net. Note that as a consequence of 2.3(i), the structure $(X,\leq)$ defined as in 2.2 is a partially ordered set (poset). Many of our subsequent definitions apply to (and, with a view to section 6, will be phrased in terms of) posets in general. Since we always assume a poset $(X,\leq)$ to be associated with N as given in 2.2, all definitions are equally applicable to occurrence nets.

2.4 Definition.

(i) $l \subseteq X$ is a li-set (chain) iff $\forall x,y \in l$: $x\ li\ y$;

(ii) $l \subseteq X$ is a line (maximal chain) iff l is a li-set and $\forall z \in X \setminus l\ \exists x \in l$: $z\ co\ x$;

(iii) The set of lines of N will be denoted by L;

(iv) $c \subseteq X$ is a co-set (antichain) iff $\forall x,y \in c$: $x\ co\ y$;

(v) $c \subseteq X$ is a cut or slice (maximal antichain) iff
c is a co-set and $\forall z \in X \setminus c\ \exists x \in c$: $z\ li\ x$;

(vi) The set of cuts of N will be denoted by C.

The axiom of choice is assumed to hold. As a consequence, for every li-set l_0 (co-set c_0) there exists a line l (a cut c) with $l_0 \subseteq l$ ($c_0 \subseteq c$, respectively).

2.5 Definition.

(i) For $A \subseteq X$, $\downarrow A = \{x \in X \mid \exists z \in A: x \le z\}$ and $\uparrow A = \{x \in X \mid \exists z \in A: z \le x\}$;

(ii) For $x \in X$, $\downarrow x = \downarrow\{x\}$ and $\uparrow x = \uparrow\{x\}$.

3. DISCRETENESS

3.1 Definition.

Let $x,y \in X$ and let $l \in L$ be a line.

(i) $[x,y] = \{z \in X \mid x \le z \le y\}$ (the interval between x and y);

(ii) $[x,y;l] = [x,y] \cap l$ (the path along l between x and y).

3.2 Definition.

N will be called

(i) discrete (same as E-discrete in [B2]) iff $\forall x,y \in X\ \forall l \in L: |[x,y;l]| < \infty$;

(ii) line-normal iff $\forall l \subseteq X: l \in L \Rightarrow (\forall x \in l: {}^\bullet x \neq \emptyset \Rightarrow |{}^\bullet x \cap l| = 1 \wedge x^\bullet \neq \emptyset \Rightarrow |x^\bullet \cap l| = 1)$;

(iii) line-connected iff

$\forall l \subseteq X: (\emptyset \neq l \wedge l \text{ li-set} \wedge \forall x \in l: {}^\bullet x \neq \emptyset \Rightarrow |{}^\bullet x \cap l| = 1 \wedge x^\bullet \neq \emptyset \Rightarrow |x^\bullet \cap l| = 1) \Rightarrow l \in L$.

Discreteness 3.2(i) states that all li-sets between x and y must be finite, though not necessarily boundedly so. Line-normality 3.2(ii) states that every line must be a sequence of alternations of events and conditions. Line-connectedness 3.2(iii) states that all li-sets of this form must be lines. For counterexamples, we refer to the following net defined in [P1]: $E = \mathbb{R}$ (the set of reals), B is the set of open intervals $\langle r_1, r_2 \rangle$ ($r_1, r_2 \in \mathbb{R}$), and $r\ F\ \langle r_1, r_2 \rangle\ F\ r'$ iff $r = r_1$ and $r_2 = r'$. We remark, however, that nets violating all or part of 3.2 need not necessarily be uncountable [B2,FT1-3].

3.3 Theorem.

N is discrete iff it is line-normal and line-connected.

Proof:

($\Rightarrow$)(i): Let N be discrete and let $l \in L$.
We prove that $\forall x \in l: ({}^\bullet x \neq \emptyset \Rightarrow |{}^\bullet x \cap l| = 1 \wedge x^\bullet \neq \emptyset \Rightarrow |x^\bullet \cap l| = 1)$.
Let $x \in l$ such that ${}^\bullet x \neq \emptyset$.
Of course $|{}^\bullet x \cap l| \le 1$, so it suffices to prove ${}^\bullet x \cap l \neq \emptyset$.
If $x \in B$ then $|{}^\bullet x| = 1$, say ${}^\bullet x = \{e\}$; clearly, $e \in l$.
If $x \in E$ then consider $b \in {}^\bullet x$.
Since $b < x'$ for all $x' \ge x$, either $b \in l$ or $y < x$ for some $y \in l$.
In the latter case, $[y,x;l]$ is finite by discreteness.
Hence in this set there must be a maximal element below x, say $b' \in {}^\bullet x \cap l$.

(ii): Let N be discrete and let $\emptyset \neq l \subseteq X$ be a li-set such that
$\forall x \in l: ({}^\bullet x \neq \emptyset \Rightarrow |{}^\bullet x \cap l| = 1 \wedge x^\bullet \neq \emptyset \Rightarrow |x^\bullet \cap l| = 1)$.
We prove that l is a line.
Consider any $z \notin l$; we wish to show that z co y for some $y \in l$.
Define $l_1 = \{x \in l \mid x < z\}$, $l_2 = \{x \in l \mid z < x\}$.
Suppose $l_1 = l_2 = \emptyset$; then since $l \neq \emptyset$, z co y for some $y \in l$.
W.l.o.g. suppose $l_1 \neq \emptyset$ and take any $x \in l_1$, i.e. $x \in l \wedge x < z$.
By discreteness, $[x,z;l]$ is a finite set.
Hence there exists a maximal element, say x', in $[x,z] \cap l$.
Suppose $x' \in B$.
By $x' < z$, $x'^\bullet \neq \emptyset$; say, $x'^\bullet = \{e\}$.
By $|x'^\bullet \cap l| = 1$, $e \in l$, and also $e < z$, which contradicts the maximality of x'.
Hence $x' \in E$.
Again because $|x'^\bullet \cap l| = 1$, there exists a $y \in x'^\bullet$ such that $y \in l \cap B$.

y<z would contradict the maximality of x'; z<y would imply z<x', contradicting $x' \in [x,z]$.
Hence y co z, which was to prove. □(⇒)

(⇐): Let N be line-normal and line-connected.
We prove that N is discrete.
Let $x,y \in X$ and $l \in L$; we show that $|[x,y;l]| < \infty$.
W.l.o.g. assume $x,y \in l$; otherwise one can find a line l' with $x,y \in l'$ and $|[x,y;l]| \le |[x,y;l']|$. (Conduct the proof for l' and then apply the inequality.)
W.l.o.g., assume further that x<y.
Define $x_0 = x$, $x_i^{\bullet} \neq \emptyset \Rightarrow x_{i+1} \in x_i^{\bullet} \cap l$ ($\neq\emptyset$ by line-normality)
$^{\bullet}x_{-i} \neq \emptyset \Rightarrow x_{-i-1} \in {}^{\bullet}x_{-i} \cap l$ ($\neq\emptyset$ by line-normality).
By line-connectedness, the set $\{\ldots x_{-i} \ldots x_i \ldots\}$ so constructed is a line, hence y must be contained in it.
Hence $\exists j>0$: $y = x_j$, whence $|[x,y;l]| = j+1 < \infty$. □(⇐)□3.3

Theorem 3.3 states that an occurrence net is discrete iff all lines are of the form shown in Figure 1 below.

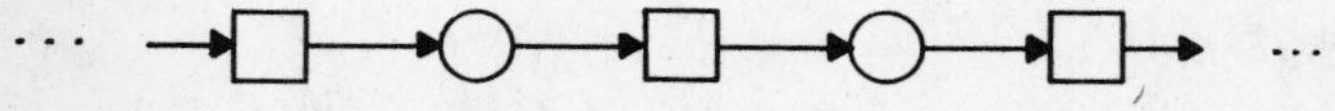

Figure 1

4. K-DENSITY

4.1 Definition.

(i) N is called K-dense [P1] iff $\forall l \in L\ \forall c \in C$: $|c \cap l| = 1$.
(ii) N will be said to have the cut-cross property iff $\forall l \in L\ \forall c \in C$: $\downarrow c \cap l \neq \emptyset \neq \uparrow c \cap l$.

For the proof of 4.3 and for later purposes we need the following lemma, the proof of which is left to the interested reader; or consult [BM], lemma 3.8.

4.2 Lemma.

Let $l \in L$ and $x,y \in l$ such that x<y and $(x,y) \notin F$. Then $\exists z \in l$: x<z<y.

4.3 Theorem.

N is K-dense iff N is discrete and has the cut-cross property.

Proof:

(⇒): K-dense ⇒ discrete: the proof of this is not obvious and can be found in [B1].
K-dense ⇒ cut-cross property is immediate.

(⇐): Let $l \in L$, $c \in C$.
Let $x \in \downarrow c \cap l$, $y \in \uparrow c \cap l$ (x,y exist by the cut-cross property).
By discreteness, $|[x,y;l]| < \infty$.
Hence there exists a maximal element $x' \in \downarrow c \cap l$ and a minimal element $y' \in \uparrow c \cap l$.
Assume $x' \neq y'$; then clearly x'<y'.
If $(x',y') \in F$ then w.l.o.g. $x' \in B$;
$x' \in \downarrow c \Rightarrow \exists z \in c$: $x' \le z$;
if x'=z then the result is proved;
if x'<z then $x' < y' \le z$, contradicting the maximality of x'.
If $(x',y') \notin F$ then, by 4.2, x'<z<y' for some $z \in l$.
$z \in \downarrow c$ contradicts the maximality of x',
$z \in \uparrow c$ contradicts the minimality of y',
but no other cases remain because $X = \downarrow c \cup \uparrow c$.
Hence $x' = y' \in \downarrow c \cap \uparrow c = c$. □4.3

5. D-CONTINUITY

Throughout this section, for $A \subseteq X$ let $\overline{A} = X \setminus A$.

5.1 Definition.

$A \subseteq X$ will be called a Dedekind cut (abbreviated D-cut) [P2,FT1-3] iff $\emptyset \neq A \neq X$ and $A = \downarrow A$.

5.2 Definition.

(i) The set of D-cuts of N will be denoted by D;

(ii) For $A \subseteq X$, $Max(A) = \{x \in A \mid \underline{not}\ \exists z \in A: x<z\}$ and $Min(\overline{A}) = \{x \in \overline{A} \mid \underline{not}\ \exists z \in \overline{A}: z<x\}$;

(iii) $M(A) = Max(A) \cup Min(\overline{A})$.

5.3 Definition.

Let $A \in D$.

(i) $Obmax(A) = \{x \in Max(A) \mid \forall A' \in D\ \forall l \in L: x \in Max(A' \cap l) \Rightarrow x \in Max(A')\}$;

(ii) $Obmin(\overline{A}) = \{x \in Min(\overline{A}) \mid \forall A' \in D\ \forall l \in L: x \in Min(\overline{A'} \cap l) \Rightarrow x \in Min(\overline{A'})\}$;

(iii) $c(A) = Obmax(A) \cup Obmin(\overline{A})$.

Definition 5.3 is as given in [P2,FT1-3]. The next result serves to characterise the sets Obmax(A) and $Obmin(\overline{A})$ for occurrence nets; its proof can be found in [BM] (proposition 6.4). It generalises a result of [FT1] (theorem 1.3).

5.4 Proposition.

Let $A \in D$ and let $x \in Max(A)$, $y \in Min(\overline{A})$. Then

(i) $x \in Obmax(A)$ iff $|x^{\bullet}| \leq 1$;

(ii) $y \in Obmin(\overline{A})$ iff $|{}^{\bullet}y| \leq 1$.

5.5 Definition.

N will be called D-continuous [P2,FT1-3] iff $\forall A \in D\ \forall l \in L: |c(A) \cap l| = 1$.

5.6 Proposition.

Let N be D-continuous. Then N is K-dense.

Again, the proof of 5.6 must be left to the reader; or consult theorem 1.2 of [FT1] of which 5.6 is a special case.

We now come to our characterisation of D-continuity.

5.7 Definition.

N will be called of non-single degree iff $\forall e \in E: |{}^{\bullet}e| \neq 1 \neq |e^{\bullet}|$.

5.8 Definition.

N will be said to possess the D-cut cross property iff $\forall A \in D\ \forall l \in L: \downarrow c(A) \cap l \neq \emptyset \neq \uparrow c(A) \cap l$.

5.9 Theorem.

N is D-continuous iff it is discrete, of non-single degree, and possesses the D-cut cross property.

Proof:

($\Rightarrow$): D-continuous $\Rightarrow$ discrete: by 5.6 and 4.3.

D-continuous $\Rightarrow$ of non-single degree:

Suppose $|{}^{\bullet}e|=1$ for some $e\in E$; say, ${}^{\bullet}e=\{b\}$;

define $A={\downarrow}b$ and let $l\in L$ such that $b\in l$ and $e\in l$.

A is a D-cut and both $b\in c(A)$ and $e\in c(A)$ by 5.4; hence $|c(A)\cap l|=2$.

D-continuous $\Rightarrow$ D-cut cross property: immediate.

To prove 5.9($\Leftarrow$) we need the following lemma for whose proof we refer the reader to [BM], 6.10 and 6.11.

5.10 Lemma.

Let N be of non-single degree. Then $\forall A\in D\ \forall l\in L$: $|c(A)\cap l| \le 1$.

We continue with the proof of 5.9.

($\Leftarrow$): Let $A\in D$ and $l\in L$.
The non-single degree property, together with 5.10, implies $|c(A)\cap l|\le 1$.
Thus it suffices to show $c(A)\cap l\neq\emptyset$.
By the D-cut cross property, $\exists x,y\in l$: $x\in{\downarrow}c(A)$, $y\in{\uparrow}c(A)$.
If $x\in c(A)$ or $y\in c(A)$ then the result is proved.
Assume $x\in A\backslash c(A)$, $y\in\overline{A}\backslash c(A)$ and $x<y$.
By discreteness, $[x,y]\cap l$ is a finite set.
Hence there exists a x' which is maximal on l in A and a y' which is minimal on l in $\overline{A}$.
Furthermore, $(x',y')\in F$, otherwise $x'<z<y'$ for some $z\in l$ by 4.2, and both $z\in A$ and $z\in\overline{A}$ would give a contradiction.
W.l.o.g. assume $x'\in B$ and $y'\in E$.
By 5.4 we have $x'\in Obmax(A)$, hence $x'\in c(A)\cap l$. □5.9

The non-single degree property should not be regarded as an essential part of this characterisation of D-continuity. This is because whenever the non-single degree property is not satisfied in some net then some redundant (in the sense of not changing the original partial order) conditions can be added such that it is satisfied in the extended net.

Thus far, we have seen that both D-continuity and K-density are equivalent to discreteness plus a set of other properties, mainly the D-cut cross property versus the cut-cross property. To make the connection explicit we characterise the former in terms of the latter and obtain a characterisation of D-continuity in terms of K-density. The key role played in this will be that of the boundedness property defined next.

5.11 Definition.

N will be said to be

(i) bounded iff $\forall A\in D$: $A\subseteq{\downarrow}M(A) \wedge \overline{A}\subseteq{\uparrow}M(A)$;

(ii) strongly bounded iff $\forall A\in D$: $A\subseteq{\downarrow}c(A) \wedge \overline{A}\subseteq{\uparrow}c(A)$.

For example, the net shown in Figure 2 below is not bounded since $A\not\subseteq{\downarrow}M(A)$.

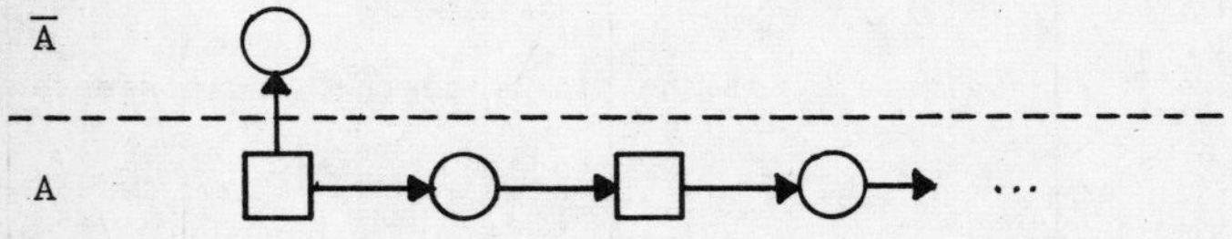

Figure 2

5.12 Proposition.

N is bounded iff it is strongly bounded.

For the proof of 5.12 the reader is referred to [BM], proposition 6.13. We remark that the non-obvious part of 5.12, namely the implication "bounded ⇒ strongly bounded", relies on the occurrence net properties; thus, 5.12 fails to hold for posets in general.

5.13 Theorem.

N has the D-cut cross property iff it has the cut-cross property and is bounded.

Proof:

(⇒)(i): D-cut cross property ⇒ cut-cross property.
Let $c \in C$ and consider the set $A = \downarrow c$; we have $A \neq \emptyset$ and $c = Max(A)$.
Case 1: $A \neq X$.
Pick $x \in \downarrow c(A) \cap l$ ($\neq \emptyset$ by hypothesis).
If $x \in A$ then $\downarrow c \cap l \neq \emptyset$ and we are done.
Assume $x \in \overline{A}$; this means that $x \in Obmin(\overline{A})$.
By 5.4, $|{}^{\bullet}x| \leq 1$.
If ${}^{\bullet}x = \emptyset$ then $\forall y \in A$: x co y, which contradicts c being a cut.
If ${}^{\bullet}x = \{y\}$ then clearly $y \in A \cap l$.
Case 2: $A = X$.
Since $|X| \geq 2$ as a consequence of 2.1(iii), the re-definition $\overline{A} = \uparrow c$, $A = X \setminus \overline{A}$ suffices.

(ii): D-cut cross property ⇒ bounded.
Let $x \in A$; we show $\exists z \in Max(A)$: $x \leq z$.
Define $l \in L$ such that $x \in l$.
By the D-cut cross property, $x \leq y$ for some $y \in l \cap \uparrow c(A)$.
If $y \in A$ then $y \in Obmax(A)$ and all is proved.
For $y \in \overline{A}$, let $x = x_0, \ldots, x_n = y$ be a path from x to y.
There exists i such that $(x_i, x_{i+1}) \in F$, $x_i \in A$, $x_{i+1} \in \overline{A}$.
If $x_i \in B$ then $x_i \in Max(A)$; if $x_i \in E$ then $x_{i+1} \in Min(\overline{A})$.

For the other direction of 5.13 we need a lemma for whose proof see lemma 6.15 of [BM].

5.14 Lemma.

Let N be bounded and $A \in D$.

Then $c = B \cap c(A) \cup \{x \in Obmax(A) \mid x^{\bullet} = \emptyset\} \cup \{x \in Obmin(\overline{A}) \mid {}^{\bullet}x = \emptyset\}$

is a slice contained in c(A).

(⇐): Cut-cross property and boundedness ⇒ D-cut cross property.
Let $A \in D$, $l \in L$.
By 5.14, $\exists c \in C$: $c \subseteq c(A)$; clearly, $\downarrow c \subseteq \downarrow c(A)$ and $\uparrow c \subseteq \uparrow c(A)$.
By the cut-cross property, $\downarrow c \cap l \neq \emptyset \neq \uparrow c \cap l$; the fact that $\downarrow c(A) \cap l \neq \emptyset \neq \uparrow c(A) \cap l$ is then immediate. □5.13

From 5.9, 5.13 and 4.3 we can now deduce the following corollaries which complete our characterisation of D-continuity for occurrence nets.

5.15 Corollary.

N is D-continuous iff it is discrete, of non-single degree, bounded, and possesses the cut-cross property.

5.16 Corollary.

N is D-continuous iff it is K-dense, of non-single degree, and bounded.

Keeping in mind what has been said above about the non-single degree property, it thus turns out that for occurrence nets, D-continuity is, essentially, K-density plus the boundedness property.

6. A GENERALISATION TO PARTIALLY ORDERED SETS

We show that theorem 5.16 can be generalised to partially ordered sets if boundedness is replaced by strong boundedness.

6.1 Definition.

Let $(X,\leq)$ be a poset.

(i) $(X,\leq)$ is nsd iff $\forall x,y\in X$: $x \lessdot y \Rightarrow \exists z\in X,\ z\neq x,y$: $(x < z \text{ co } y) \vee (x \text{ co } z < y)$;

(ii) $(X,\leq)$ is dense iff $\lessdot = \emptyset$; (see 2.2(iii) for $\lessdot$)

(iii) $(X,\leq)$ is linear iff co = id.

K-density, D-continuity and (strong) boundedness have already been defined for posets in general. On the other hand, the nsd property 6.1(i) is intended to generalise the non-single degree property 5.7. 6.1(ii) and 6.1(iii) correspond to usual terminology. Note that there are no dense occurrence nets according to definition 6.1(ii).

6.2 Theorem.

$(X,\leq)$ is D-continuous iff it is K-dense, strongly bounded and nsd.

The proof of theorem 6.2, which can be found in [B3], closely follows the lines of argument expounded in 5.9 through to 5.16. We have the following corollary:

6.3 Corollary.

Let $(X,\leq)$ be dense.

Then $(X,\leq)$ is D-continuous iff it is K-dense and strongly bounded.

Proof: Immediate from 6.2 and the fact that dense $\Rightarrow$ nsd. □6.3

Finally in this section we specialise theorem 6.2 to dense linear posets, thereby retrieving the connection [P2] to the completeness properties of the real numbers.

6.4 Proposition.

Let $(X,\leq)$ be linear. Then,

(i) $(X,\leq)$ is K-dense;

(ii) $(X,\leq)$ is strongly bounded iff $\forall A\in D$: $M(A) \neq \emptyset$.

Proof:

(i): Since $(X,\leq)$ is linear, $L = \{X\}$ and $C = \{\{x\} \mid x\in X\}$, i.e. there is only one line and all cuts have a single element.

(ii): First we note that $\forall A\in D$: $c(A) = M(A)$, as a consequence of $(X,\leq)$ being linear.
($\Rightarrow$): Suppose $A\in D$.
Pick $x\in A$ ($\neq \emptyset$ by definition); strong boundedness $\Rightarrow \exists z\in c(A)$: $x\leq z$;
hence $\emptyset \neq c(A) = M(A)$.
($\Leftarrow$): Suppose $A\in D$ and $x\in A$.
By $M(A) \neq \emptyset$, $\exists z\in X$: $z\in M(A)$;
$x\leq z$ since $(X,\leq)$ is linear and $z<x$ is impossible. □6.4

6.5 Corollary.

Let $(X,\leq)$ be dense and linear.

Then $(X,\leq)$ is D-continuous iff $\forall A\in D$: $M(A) \neq \emptyset$.

Proof: Immediate from 6.3 and 6.4. □6.5

We give an example, pointed out by C.Fernández, of the significance of 6.5. The poset

$(\mathbb{Q},\leq)$ of the rational numbers with their usual ordering is dense and linear, whence 6.5 applies. However $(\mathbb{Q},\leq)$ is K-dense but not D-continuous: for example, the subset $A = \{x\in\mathbb{Q} \mid x^2<2\}$ satisfies $M(A) = \emptyset$ (in $\mathbb{Q}$!). By contrast, $M(A) \neq \emptyset$ for any D-cut in $\mathbb{R}$, whence by 6.5, $\mathbb{R}$ is (not only K-dense but also) D-continuous.

7. CONCLUDING REMARKS

7.1 Summary and Outlook

The diagram shown in Figure 3 (which is, hopefully, self-explanatory) summarises the main results proved in this paper.

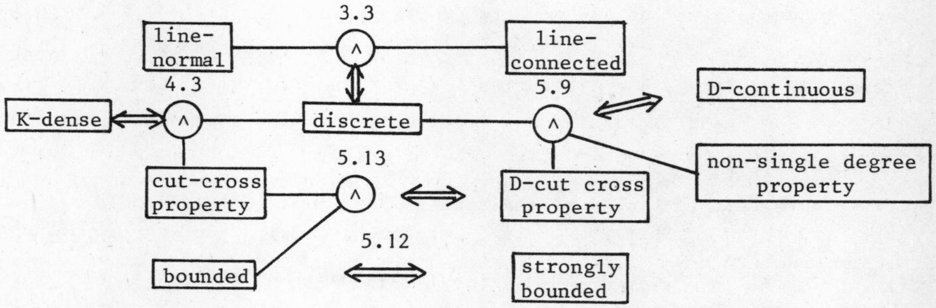

Figure 3

Amongst other things, these results reveal a close relationship between K-density and D-continuity, manifesting itself in the analogy between the definitions 4.1(i) and 5.5, in the similarity of the corresponding characterisations 4.3 and 5.9, and in the connections 5.16 and 6.2. The latter show that the essential property distinguishing K-density and D-continuity is strong boundedness which for occurrence nets is equivalent to boundedness. Boundedness may be an interesting property by itself; it is characterised further in [BM], propositions 6.20 and 6.21, where we show that for a large class of infinite occurrence nets, boundedness is equivalent to the property that every two elements have a common predecessor and a common successor.

An obvious question to be asked is which of the above results can be generalised to partial orders. Though section 6 contains an answer, strong boundedness remains a rather "awkward" property which calls for further characterisation.

Regarding interpretation, we would be slightly more hesitant than [P2,FT1-3] in proposing any particular set of properties as axioms to be satisfied by occurrence nets (or posets, for that matter) as "reasonable" models of non-sequential processes. Nonetheless, it seems that some properties can be motivated more easily than others. For example, the imposition of discreteness certainly seems to be a good idea. On the other hand, it seems less obvious whether the non-single degree property (and therefore, D-continuity as a whole) should be required. The non-single degree property would exclude, for example, lines such as shown in Figure 1 (section 3), which would appear to create difficulties in interpreting sequential processes as special cases of concurrent processes. We would hope, however, that our results may help in eventually coming up with an agreed set of axioms for non-sequential processes.

7.2 History and Related Work

This work falls into a line of research, exemplified by [P1,P2,B1,B2,FT1,FT2,FT3,P11], where interest has mainly been concentrated on the "density" and "discreteness versus continuity" aspects of concurrency structures (with occurrence nets as a special case thereof). In [P2], Petri offers a number of properties of concurrency structures as axioms of concurrency, without fully clearing up the interdependencies between these axioms. D-continuity, being one of them, has since been investigated for a restricted class of occurrence nets called causal nets (CN) in [FT1-3][2]. In [FT1,FT2] it is proved that D-continuous CNs satisfy almost all other axioms put forward in [P2]. [FT3] contains, in addition, a characterisation of D-continuity for CNs. In [P11], Plünnecke proves some general results which partly generalise some of the results in [B1,B2,FT1], especially those on K-density in [B1,B2].

The present authors felt that many of the results described in [FT1] could be generalised by relaxing the CN restriction; indeed, that the restriction on D-continuous CNs tends to obscure some of these results, in the sense that it is not always clear which properties enter in what way. We also considered it desirable to obtain a characterisation of D-continuity and of the remaining axioms of [P2] for occurrence nets in terms of other properties, and then to see how all of these properties fit together. The result of this effort is described in [BM] which, in addition to the material contained in the present paper (excluding section 6), contains sufficient (weaker than D-continuity) and necessary conditions for many of the axioms defined in [P2] to hold.

Theorem 3.3 of the present paper, characterising discreteness, generalises theorem 1.4 of [FT1] which states that D-continuous CNs satisfy line-normality and line-connectedness. This latter result now appears as a consequence of 3.3 and 5.9. Theorem 4.3 is implicit in the discussion in [B2], and is also a consequence of theorem 3.14.5 of [P11] which generalises it to combinatorial partial orders. Theorem 5.9, characterising D-continuity for occurrence nets, began to take shape when various cut-cross properties were brought into connection with D-continuity in discussions between C.Fernández and the authors. The characterisation of D-continuity for CNs described in [FT3] has been conjectured independently by Fernández and Thiagarajan [F]; their result can be derived from 5.16 as shown in [BM], corollary 6.24. H.Plünnecke has obtained a similar result independently [P12], but this is not contained in [P11].

ACKNOWLEDGEMENTS

We had many valuable discussions with C.Fernández and with P.S.Thiagarajan, especially with the former.

---

2) CNs in the sense of [FT1-3] are a subclass of the set of causal nets defined in [P1]; see footnote 1) in the introduction.

REFERENCES

[B1] E.Best: A Theorem on the Characteristics of Non-Sequential Processes. Fundamenta Informaticae, Vol. 3, No. 1, pp.77-94 (1980).

[B2] E.Best: The Relative Strength of K-Density. Lecture Notes in Computer Science, Vol. 84, pp.261-276, Springer Verlag (1980).

[B3] E.Best: A Characterisation of D-Continuity For Partially Ordered Sets. GMD-ISF, Internal Memorandum BEGRUND-12 (September 1982).

[BM] E.Best and A.Merceron: Some Properties of Non-Sequential Processes. GMD-ISF Technical Report 82.06 (August 1982).

[BR] E.Best and B.Randell: A Formal Model of Atomicity in Asynchronous Systems. Acta Informatica, Vol. 16, pp.93-124 (1981).

[F] C.Fernández: Private Communication.

[FT1] C.Fernández and P.S.Thiagarajan: Some Properties of D-Continuous Causal Nets. GMD-ISF Technical Report 81.02 (November 1981).

[FT2] C.Fernández and P.S.Thiagarajan: Some Properties of D-Continuous Causal Nets. Proc. ICALP'82, Lecture Notes in Computer Science, Vol. 140, pp.225-238. Springer Verlag (1982).

[FT3] C.Fernández and P.S.Thiagarajan: D-Continuous Causal Nets: A Model of Non-Sequential Processes. GMD-ISF Technical Report 82.05 (July 1982).

[GLT] H.J.Genrich, K.Lautenbach and P.S.Thiagarajan: Elements of General Net Theory. Lecture Notes in Computer Science, Vol. 84, pp.21-163, Springer Verlag (1980).

[GS] H.J.Genrich and E.Stankiewicz-Wiechno: A Dictionary of Some Basic Notions of Net Theory. Lecture Notes in Computer Science, Vol. 84, pp.519-531, Springer Verlag (1980).

[P1] C.A.Petri: Non-Sequential Processes. GMD-ISF Technical Report 77.05 (1977).

[P2] C.A.Petri: Concurrency. Lecture Notes in Computer Science, Vol. 84, pp.251-260, Springer Verlag (1980).
(See also: C.A.Petri: State-Transition Structures in Physics and in Computation. Int. Journal of Theoretical Physics, Vol. 21, Nos. 10/11, 1982.)

[Pl1] H.Plünnecke: Schnitte in Halbordnungen. GMD-ISF Technical Report 81.09 (April 1981).

[Pl2] H.Plünnecke: Private Communication.

CONTROLLED RELATIVIZATIONS OF P AND NP[†]

(Abstract)

Ronald V. Book

Department of Mathematics
University of California at Santa Barbara
Santa Barbara, California 93106, U.S.A.

Timothy J. Long

Department of Computer Science
New Mexico State University
Las Cruces, New Mexico 88003, U.S.A.

Alan L. Selman

Department of Computer Science
Iowa State University
Ames, Iowa 50010, U.S.A.

Baker, Gill, and Solovay [1] argue on the basis of their relativization results that traditional methods, diagonalization in particular, will not settle questions such as "P =? NP" or "NP =? co-NP." On the one hand, ordinary diagonalization methods appear to be inadequate for showing $P \neq NP$ since one might expect that such a method would apply equally well to all relativized classes so that for all A, $P(A) \neq NP(A)$, contradicting the existence (shown in [1]) of a set B such that $P(B) = NP(B)$. On the other hand, a general method for simulating nondeterministic machines by deterministic machines running in polynomial time should apply to relativized classes so that for all A, $P(A) = NP(A)$, contradicting the existence (shown in [1]) of a set C such that $P(C) \neq NP(C)$.

Much of the work on complexity-bounded reducibilities, their reduction classes, and relativizations of complexity classes has been carried out by researchers with backgrounds in recursive function theory. Thus, it has been natural to look for recursion theoretic arguments, that is, arguments that relativize. But the results of Baker, Gill, and Solovay (and many others) show that some questions about P-degrees of sets in

---

[†]This research was supported in part by the National Science Foundation under Grants MCS80-11979 and MCS81-20263.

NP cannot be answered by such arguments. Let us consider two examples. First, consider the lattice of NP sets (where set-theoretic union and intersection are the operations). This lattice does not have a maximal element. This result is due to Breidbart [8] who showed that for every recursive set A that is infinite and co-infinite, there is a set B such that B can be recognized deterministically by a machine that uses real time and log space simultaneously, and each of $A \cap B$, $A \cap \overline{B}$, $\overline{A} \cap B$, and $\overline{A} \cap \overline{B}$ are infinite--thus, no "reasonable" notion of complexity class can have a maximal element in its lattice. In contrast, the lattice of recursively enumerable sets does have a maximal element. Second, Bennett and Gill [2] showed that, with probability one, for a random oracle A there is an infinite set in NP(A) that has no infinite subset in P(A). Homer and Maass [9] and, independently, Schöning [13] showed that there is a recursive set A such that there is an infinite set in NP(A) with no infinite subset in P(A), and also there is a recursive set B such that every infinite set in NP(B) has an infinite subset in P(B). Contrast these results with the fact that every infinite recursively enumerable set has an infinite recursive subset.

The results cited above suggest that one must be careful about conclusions drawn from relativization results. This paper reports on some recent contributions to the analysis of the computational power of oracle machines with emphasis on the "P =? NP" and "NP =? co-NP" problems. These contributions have arisen in the context of a long-term project that is being pursued by the authors individually and jointly.

Consider the problems "P =? PSPACE" and "NP =? PSPACE." For any set A, let PQUERY(A) (NPQUERY(A)) be the class of languages L such that $L \in$ PSPACE(A) is witnessed by a deterministic (resp., nondeterministic) oracle machine that operates in polynomial space and is restricted so that it can make at most a polynomial number of oracle queries in any computation. The following result was established in [3]: NP = PSPACE if and only if for all sets A, NP(A) = NPQUERY(A). Later, using somewhat different techniques, the corresponding result for the "P =? PSPACE" problem was established in [14]. (Similar results regarding the union of the polynomial-time hierarchy can be found in [7] and results regarding classes such as NTISP(poly,lin) can be found in [6,14].) These results lead us to the notion of a "positive relativization" of a question. We shall formally define this notion in the context of the "P =? NP" and "NP =? co-NP" problems.

A <u>positive relativization of the</u> "P =? NP" <u>problem</u> is a restriction R placed on both the deterministic and the nondeterministic polynomial time-bounded oracle machines such that the following is true:

$P = NP$ if and only if for all sets A, $P_R(A) = NP_R(A)$.

A <u>positive</u> <u>relativization</u> <u>of</u> <u>the</u> "NP =? co-NP" <u>problem</u> is a restriction R placed on the nondeterministic polynomial time-bounded oracle machines such that the following is true: $NP = \text{co-}NP$ if and only if for all sets A, $NP_R(A) = \text{co-}NP_R(A)$.

Suppose that we have a positive relativization R of "P =? NP." It is clear that a proof of the existence of a set A such that $P_R(A) \neq NP_R(A)$ results in a proof that $P \neq NP$. Similar statements can be made for the "NP =? co-NP" problems as well as those mentioned above.

What type of restriction of the polynomial time-bounded oracle machines leads to positive relativizations of the "P =? NP" or "NP =? co-NP" problems? This report announces partial answers to this question.

For the most part our notation is standard. The length of a string x is denoted $|x|$ and the cardinality of a set S is denoted $|S|$. It is assumed that all sets of strings are taken over some fixed alphabet, say $\Sigma = \{0,1\}$. If $A \subseteq \Sigma^*$, then $\overline{A} = \Sigma^* - A$.

Let M be an oracle machine. For any set A and any input string x to M, let $Q(M,A,x)$ be the set of strings queried by M during any of M's computations relative to A on input x. For any input string x to M, let $Q(M,x) = \cup_A Q(M,A,x)$.

For any set A, let $P\#Q(A)$ $(NP\#Q(A))$ be the class of languages L such that L is accepted relative to A by a deterministic (resp., nondeterministic) polynomial time-bounded oracle machine M with the additional property that for some polynomial p and all input strings x to M, $|Q(M,x)| \leq p(|x|)$.

It is clear that for every set A, $P\#Q(A) \subseteq NP\#Q(A)$, $P\#Q(A) \subseteq P(A)$, and $NP\#Q(A) \subseteq NP(A)$. We are interested in the existence of oracle sets that separate classes and so we first consider the inclusions $P\#Q(A) \subseteq P(A)$ and $NP\#Q(A) \subseteq NP(A)$.

Using a modification of a construction due to Ladner, Lynch, and Selman [10] in their study of deterministic truth-table reducibilities computed in polynomial time, we can establish the existence of a set C such that $P(C) - NP\#Q(C)$ is not empty. Since $P(C) \subseteq NP(C)$, this means that $NP\#Q(C) \neq NP(C)$. Further, $P\#Q(C) \subseteq NP\#Q(C)$ so that $P(C) - NP\#Q(C)$ being nonempty implies that $P\#Q(C) \neq P(C)$. Thus we have the following result.

<u>Lemma 1</u>. There is a recursive set C such that $P\#Q(C) \subsetneq P(C)$ and $NP\#Q(C) \subsetneq NP(C)$.

In Lemma 1 we have said nothing about the relationship between P#Q(C) and NP#Q(C). This is the subject of the first theorem.

Theorem 1. The following are equivalent:

(a) P = NP;

(b) for every set A, P#Q(A) = NP#Q(A).

Thus we have a positive relativization of the "P =? NP" problem. This relativization is "quantitative" in the sense that the restriction "polynomial bound on the number of strings queried by any computation relative to any oracle set" bounds the size of a set.

Consider the oracle property "x is in L(A) if and only if A contains at least one string of length $|x|$." A nondeterministic oracle machine can accept L(A) relative to A because it can nondeterministically guess a string y of length $|x|$ and then query the oracle regarding y's membership in A. Without restrictions on the machine, $2^{|x|}$ different guesses can be made. Intutition says that no deterministic oracle machine can perform this search in polynomial time, and the proof in [1] bears this out. Our quantitative restrictions lead to positive relativizations because they allow nondeterministic oracle machines to search sets of size at most a polynomial in the length of the input.

This restriction also yields a positive relativization of the "NP =? co-NP" problem. (Also, see [12].)

Theorem 2. The following are equivalent:

(a) NP = co-NP;

(b) for every set A, NP#Q(A) = co-NP#Q(A).

A sketch of the proof of Theorem 2 is given in the Appendix.

There are a number of other results of this type. Here we have restricted our attention to the simplest quantitative relativization that we have studied. The full development of this approach to the "P =? NP" problems, as well as the other problems indicated above, can be found in [4,5].

Appendix

This appendix is devoted to a sketch of the proof of Theorem 2. The overall outline is based on arguments in [11].

If for every set A, NP#Q(A) = co-NP#Q(A), then NP = NP#Q(ϕ) = co-NP#Q(ϕ) = co-NP. Conversely, suppose that NP = co-NP. It suffices to show that for every set A and every $L \in$ NP#Q(A), the complement

$\overline{L}$ of L is in NP#Q(A).

Let M witness $L \in$ NP#Q(A) and let p be a polynomial such that $|Q(M,x)| \leq p(|x|)$ for all x. We show that "tables" $T_Y = Q(M,x) \cap A$ and $T_N = Q(M,x) \cap \overline{A}$ can be constituted and then M can be simulated. To accomplish this we need certain notations.

Assume some lexicographic ordering on Σ that extends to a total ordering of Σ^*. For a finite set $S \subset \Sigma^*$, say $S = \{y_1, \ldots, y_n\}$ where $i < j$ implies $y_i < y_j$, let $c(S) = \% y_1 \% \ldots \% y_n \%$ where % is not in Σ. We consider c to be an encoding function. Notice that if $S \subset \Sigma^*$ is a finite set and $y \in \Sigma^*$, then the predicate "y is in S" can be computed in time polynomial in $|y| + |c(S)|$.

We assume the existence of an effective enumeration of clocked nondeterministic oracle machines that run in polynomial time, say $M(0), M(1), \ldots$.

Let f be the multi-valued function such that for all x, $\{y \mid y$ is a value of f on $x\} = Q(M,x)$; denote this set as set-f(x). Since for all x, $|Q(M,x)| \leq p(|x|)$ and M operates nondeterministically in polynomial time, the assumption NP = co-NP allows one to conclude that the partial function defined by $g(x) = c(\text{set-f})$ can be computed nondeterministically in polynomial time.

Let $K = \{\langle M(i), x, c(T_Y), c(T_N), 0^k\rangle \mid$ some computation of $M(i)$ on input x accepts x in at most k steps, and if y is a string that is queried in this computation, then $y \in T_Y \cup T_N$ and the answer to the query is "yes" if and only if $y \in T_Y\}$. It is clear that $K \in$ NP so that under the hypothesis NP = co-NP, $\overline{K}$ is in NP. Let t be a polynomial bounding M's running time. Consider the following oracle procedure.

<u>Begin</u>

$T_Y := T_N := \phi$;

(1) <u>for</u> each y in set-f(x) <u>do</u>

  <u>if</u> $y \in$ oracle set

    <u>then</u> $T_Y \leftarrow T_Y \cup [y]$

    <u>else</u> $T_N \leftarrow T_N \cup [y]$;

(2) <u>if</u> $\langle M, x, c(T_Y), c(T_N), 0^{t(|x|)}\rangle \in \overline{K}$

  <u>then</u> accept x

<u>end</u>.

Since $g(x) = c(\text{set-f}(x))$ can be computed in polynomial time, the control of the for-loop at line 1 can be accomplished in polynomial time. Since $c(\text{set-f}) = Q(M,x)$ and $|Q(M,x)| \leq p(|x|)$, the body of the for-loop executes at most a polynomial number of times. When A is used as oracle set, $T_Y = Q(M,x) \cap D$ and $T_N = Q(M,x) \cap \overline{D}$ upon execution of line 2. Thus, this procedure witnesses $\overline{L} \in NP\#Q(D)$. □

The proof of Theorem 1 is similar to that of Theorem 2. The hypothesis $P = NP$ yields both the fact that g can be computed deterministically in polynomial time, and also the fact that K and $\overline{K}$ are in P.

References

1. Baker, T., Gill, J. and Solovay, R., Relativizations of the P =? NP question. SIAM J. Computing, 4(1975), 431-442.

2. Bennett, C. and Gill, J., Relative to a random oracle A, $P^A \neq NP^A \neq co\text{-}NP^A$ with probability 1. SIAM J. Computing, 10(1981), 96-113.

3. Book, R., Bounded query machines: on NP and PSPACE. Theoret. Comput. Sci., 15(1981), 27-39.

4. Book, R., Long, T. and Selman, A., Qualitative relativizations of complexity classes, in preparation.

5. Book, R., Long, T. and Selman, A., Quantitative relativizations of complexity classes, submitted for publication.

6. Book, R., Wilson, C. and Xu Mei-rui, Relativizing time, space, and time-space. SIAM J. Computing, 11(1982), 571-581.

7. Book, R. and Wrathall, C., Bounded query machines: on NP( ) and NPQUERY( ). Theoret. Comput. Sci., 15(1981), 41-50.

8. Breidbart, S., Splitting recursive sets. J. Comput. Syst. Sci., 17(1978), 56-64.

9. Homer, S. and Maass, W., Oracle dependent properties of the lattice of NP sets. Theoret. Comput. Sci., to appear.

10. Ladner, R., Lynch, N. and Selman, A., A comparison of polynomial-time reducibilities. Theoret. Comput. Sci., 1(1975), 103-123.

11. Long, T., Relativizing nondeterministic time, unpublished manuscript, 1981.

12. Long, T., Strong nondeterministic polynomial-time reducibilities. Theoret. Comput. Sci., 21(1982), 1-25.

13. Schöning, U., Relativization and infinite subsets of NP sets, unpublished manuscript, 1982.

14. Selman, A., Xu Mei-rui and Book, R., Positive relativizations of complexity classes. SIAM J. Computing, 12(1983), to appear.

THE COMPUTATIONAL COMPLEXITY OF CERTAIN GRAPH GRAMMARS

Franz J. Brandenburg

Institut für Informatik, Universität Bonn
Wegelerstr. 6, 53oo Bonn
Federal Republic of Germany

ABSTRACT:

This paper contributes to the theory of graph grammars, studying the generated languages of graphs from the viewpoint of complexity theory. To this respect we naturally bridge the gap between graphs and strings. A string is identified with a graph which is an oriented chain, and conversely, a representation of a graph, e.g., by its adjacency matrix, is a well-structured string. Our main result states that context-free respectively monotone graph grammars in the approach developed by Nagl [5] precisely have the computational power of n^2-space-bounded nondeterministic Turing machines, and for this result there is no difference between directed and undirected graphs respectively graph grammars.

INTRODUCTION:

The theory of graph grammars constitutes a well-motivated and developing area within theoretical computer science. It has substantial applications in various fields of computer science including pattern recognition, two-dimensional programming languages, data flow analysis, incremental compilers, semantics, abstract data types, data bases, software specification, and problems of concurrency and consistency. See, e.g. [1] and [5].

It is clear that the mathematical theory of string grammars, i.e. formal language theory, is widely used as a guide-line for the development of a theory of graph grammars. This is partly due to the fact that strings can naturally be identified with graphs which are oriented chains. So the theory of graph grammars is an extension of formal language theory. Conversely, a graph is a well-structured string, if it is formally represented, e.g., by its adjacency matrix. From this perspective graph grammars are string grammars with a complex, non-local rewriting mechanism, and the theory of graph grammars can be seen as part of formal language theory.

In this paper we study the generative capacity of graph grammars, using the notion of graph grammars developed by Nagl [5]. This approach is characterized by a general and powerful embedding mechanism, and seems to include all other existing notions of graph grammars as a special case. In particular, we prove that each monotone graph grammar can be simulated by an n^2-space-bounded nondeterministic Turing machine, which uses the representation of graphs by their adjacency matrices. Conversely, each n^2-space-bounded nondeterministic Turing machine can be simulated by a context-free graph grammar, which generates the strings accepted by the Turing machine as oriented chains. These results are independent of the use of directed or undirected graphs. Note that for a string of length n, such a graph grammar may use only intermediate graphs with n vertices. Thus the working space of the Turing machine of size $O(n^2)$ is encoded into the $O(n^2)$ edges of complete graphs with n vertices. This encoding is a crucial step and is based on a simple enumeration of the edges of complete, loop-free graphs.

The computational equivalence of context-free graph grammars and n^2-space-bounded nondeterministic Turing machines reveals an interesting property of graph grammars. Context-free graph grammars primarily rewrite single vertices. Thus they operate on the vertices of graphs. However, in doing so they define computations that are executed on the edges, and so they exploit their full computational capacity.

GRAPHS AND GRAPH GRAMMARS:

We assume familiarity with the basic concepts from graph theory, most of which are evident by a graphical representation. As far as graphs and graph grammars are concerned we give all definitions that are necessary for an understanding of this paper. We shall omit an exact definition of a graph grammar and of a derivation by a graph grammar, which can be found in [5].

DEFINITION. A (directed) graph over the alphabets A_V and A_E is a system $\Gamma = (V,E,A_V,A_E,f)$, where A_V and A_E are the sets of labels for the vertices and the edges of Γ, V is a finite nonempty set of vertices, f is a function from V into A_V, called the vertex labelling function, and E is a finite subset of $V \times A_E \times V$, called the set of edges. Each $(u,\alpha,v) \in E$ is called an edge with edge label α from vertex u to vertex v, and is denoted by $\underset{u}{\bullet}\xrightarrow{\alpha}\underset{v}{\bullet}$. A graph Γ is undirected, if $(u,\alpha,v) \in E$ implies $(v,\alpha,u) \in E$, in which case we denote edges as lines.

DEFINITION. The size of a graph Γ is defined by the number of its vertices and is denoted by $|\Gamma|$.

Note that there may be multiple edges between any two vertices of a graph which, however, must differ by their direction or by their labels. Hence, a graph of size n has at most $c \cdot n^2$ edges, where $c = |A_E|$.

<u>DEFINITION.</u> Two graphs $\Gamma = (V,E,A_V,A_E,f)$ and $\Gamma' = (V',E',A_V,A_E,f')$ are <u>isomorphic</u>, if there is a bijection h from V into V' such that $f' = f \circ h$ and $E' = \{(h(u),\alpha,h(v)) \mid (u,\alpha,v) \in E\}$.

<u>DEFINITION.</u> A <u>Σ-hamiltonian</u> <u>circuit</u> of a graph Γ is a sequence of vertices $v_o, v_1, \ldots, v_{n-1}, v_n$ and edges (v_{i-1}, α_i, v_i), such that $\alpha_i \in \Sigma$, $v_o = v_n$, $v_i \neq v_j$ for $o \leqq i,j < n$, and $\{v_o, \ldots, v_{n-1}\} = V$ is the full set of vertices of Γ.

Hence, a Σ-hamiltonian circuit defines a round trip through all vertives of Γ using only edges with labels from Γ. Moreover, it induces an ordering of the vertices, once the starting vertex is chosen.

<u>DEFINITION.</u> An <u>oriented</u> <u>chain</u> is a directed graph of the form

$$\underset{a_1}{\overset{v_1}{\bullet}} \xrightarrow[\alpha_1]{} \underset{a_2}{\overset{v_2}{\bullet}} \xrightarrow[\alpha_2]{} \underset{a_3}{\overset{v_3}{\bullet}} \cdots\cdots \underset{a_{n-1}}{\overset{v_{n-1}}{\bullet}} \xrightarrow[\alpha_{n-1}]{} \underset{a_n}{\overset{v_n}{\bullet}}$$

or an undirected graph of the form

$$\underset{¢a_1}{\overset{v_1}{\bullet}} \xrightarrow[\alpha_1]{} \underset{a_2}{\overset{v_2}{\bullet}} \xrightarrow[\alpha_2]{} \underset{a_3}{\overset{v_3}{\bullet}} \cdots\cdots \underset{a_{n-1}}{\overset{v_{n-1}}{\bullet}} \xrightarrow[\alpha_{n-1}]{} \underset{a_n}{\overset{v_n}{\bullet}}$$

, where ¢ is a left-boundary marker.

<u>DEFINITION.</u> For an oriented chain Γ as depicted above let $w(\Gamma) = a_1 a_2 \ldots a_n$ be the (<u>vertex</u>) <u>string</u> of Γ.

Hence, we can identify a string w with a graph Γ which is an oriented chain with $w = w(\Gamma)$. Conversely, we treat graphs as strings via their representation by adjacency matrices.

<u>DEFINITION.</u> For a graph Γ over A_V and A_E with vertices $v_1, \ldots, v_n$ (in that order) let $\mathrm{mat}(\Gamma)$ be its <u>string</u> <u>representation</u> formed by a concatenation of the rows of the augmented adjacency matrix. Here, the <u>adjacency</u> <u>matrix</u> of Γ is an $n \times n$ matrix whose (i,j)th entry contains the labels of all edges from v_i to v_j, and the augmented adjacency matrix of Γ has an additional initial row containing the labels of the vertices.

Note that $\mathrm{mat}(\Gamma)$ is a well-structured string over the alphabet $A_V \cup A_E \cup A$, where A contains some delimiters, e.g., "{},;". The length of $\mathrm{mat}(\Gamma)$ is proportional to the square of the size of Γ, and by results from [2] this is asymptotically the shortest possible representation for arbitrary graphs.

DEFINITION. A (directed) graph grammar is a system $G = (N,T,S_o,P)$, where $N = N_V \cup N_E$ and $T = T_V \cup T_E$ are the alphabets of nonterminal and terminal labels of vertices and edges, $S_o = \overset{\bullet}{S}$ is the start graph and P is a finite set of productions of the form (x,y,β), where x and y are graphs over N and T, and β is the embedding relation.

DEFINITION. A graph grammar G is monotone resp. context-free, if for each production (x,y,β), $|x| \leq |y|$ resp. $|x| = 1$.

As regards the vertices, these definitions are in analogy with a classification of string grammars in the Chomsky hierarchy. However, these properties do not hold for the edges, and thus for the graphs as a whole. This is made precise by the Proposition below.

DEFINITION. Let G be a graph grammar, and let Γ and Γ' be graphs. Then Γ derives Γ' by using the production (x,y,β), denoted $\Gamma \Rightarrow \Gamma'$, if Γ' is obtained by selecting a subgraph x' of Γ which is isomorphic to x, replacing it by an isomorphic subgraph y' of y, and embedding y' into the host graph $\Gamma - x'$ according to the embedding relation β.

The language of G, denoted $L(G)$, is the set of graphs $L(G) = \{\Gamma \mid S_o \overset{*}{\Rightarrow} \Gamma$ and Γ is a graph over $T_V \cup T_E\}$. The language of strings generated by the graph grammar G is $L_w(G) = \{w(\Gamma) \mid \Gamma$ is in $L(G)$ and is an oriented chain$\}$.

Clearly these definitions are incomplete since the embedding is not specified. Its definition in all details does beyond the scope of this article and can be found in [5] and in Nagl's paper in [1]. Using monotone graph grammars in Theorem 3 and Theorem 4 we need only restricted embeddings of inheriting type. I.e., for each production (x,y,β) and each edge label α there is a mapping h_α from the set V_y of vertices of y into the set of vertices of x such that each $v \in V_y$ inherits the in-going and out-going α-edges from $h_\alpha(v)$. Thus there is an α-edge from/to the vertex v of y to/from the vertex u in the host graph $\Gamma - x'$ if and only if there is an α-edge from/to $h_2(v)$ to/from u in Γ. Embeddings in their full generality are used in the proof of the following fundamental result concerning Nagl's graph grammars.

PROPOSITION. (see [5], I. 3.17)
For each monotone graph grammar G there exists a context-free graph grammar G' such that $L(G) = L(G')$, and conversely.

Hence, in Nagl's approach, monotone and context-free graph grammars are equivalent in their graph generating power.

OUR COMPLEXITY RESULTS :

We assume that the reader is familiar with the notion of a space-bounded non-deterministic Turing machine [3].

First we define functions f_n which induce a simple enumeration and ordering of the edges of complete, loop-free graphs with n vertices.

<u>DEFINITION.</u> For each $n \geq 1$ define the function f_n by:
$f_n : \{o,1,\dots,n^2-n-1\} \to \{(i,j) \mid o \leq i,j \leq n-1,\ i \neq j\}$ with $f_n(k) = (i,j)$ if and only if $k = (l-1)\cdot n+r$, $o \leq r < n$, $i = s\cdot l+p \pmod n$ and $j = i+1 \pmod n$, where $r = p\cdot q+s$ with $q = n/\gcd(n,l)$, $o \leq p < \gcd(n,l)$, and $o \leq s < q$.

The following properties of f_n can easily be established.

<u>LEMMA.</u>

(i) f_n is a well-defined function, and is bijective.

(ii) For $o \leq k < n$, $f_n(k) = (k,k+1 \pmod n)$ and $f_n(n^2-n-1-k) = (k+1 \pmod n),k)$

(iii) $f_n(k) = (O,l)$ if and only if $k = (l-1)\cdot n$.

(iv) For $o \leq k < n^2-n-1$, if $f_n(k) = (i,j)$ and $f_n(k+1) = (i',j')$, then

a) $j'-i' \pmod n = 1+j-i \pmod n$ iff $k+1 = n\cdot((j-i) \pmod n)$ iff $i' = o$, and $j'-i' \pmod n = j-i \pmod n$, otherwise.

b) $i'=j$ iff $\gcd(n,j-i \pmod n) = 1$ or $i < j$, iff $k = (l-1)\cdot n+r$ and $\gcd(n,l) = 1$ or $\gcd(n,l) \neq 1$ and $r+1 = m \cdot n/\gcd(n,l)$ with $1 \leq m \leq \gcd(n,l)$.

c) If $i' \neq j$ then $i' = j+1$ or $i' = o$ and $i = n-1$.

Let Γ be a graph with n vertices $v_o,\dots,v_{n-1}$ and with an edge between any two district vertices. Then Γ is a complete, loop-free graph with n^2-n edges. Based on the chosen ordering of the vertices, the function f_n induces an ordering of the edges, such that e_k is the edge from v_i to v_j if and only if $f_n(k) = (i,j)$.

To illustrate the ordering of the edges, let $v_o,\dots,v_{n-1}$ be written clockwise, and let l mean the length of an edge. Then edges are ordered firstly according to their length, and then clockwise as a round trip, which must be shifted, if $\gcd(n,l) > 1$ and the edge passes v_o. The following example will make the concept clear.

EXAMPLE. Ordering of edges for graphs with n=5 and n=6 vertices.
Overlay the figures to get the full picture.

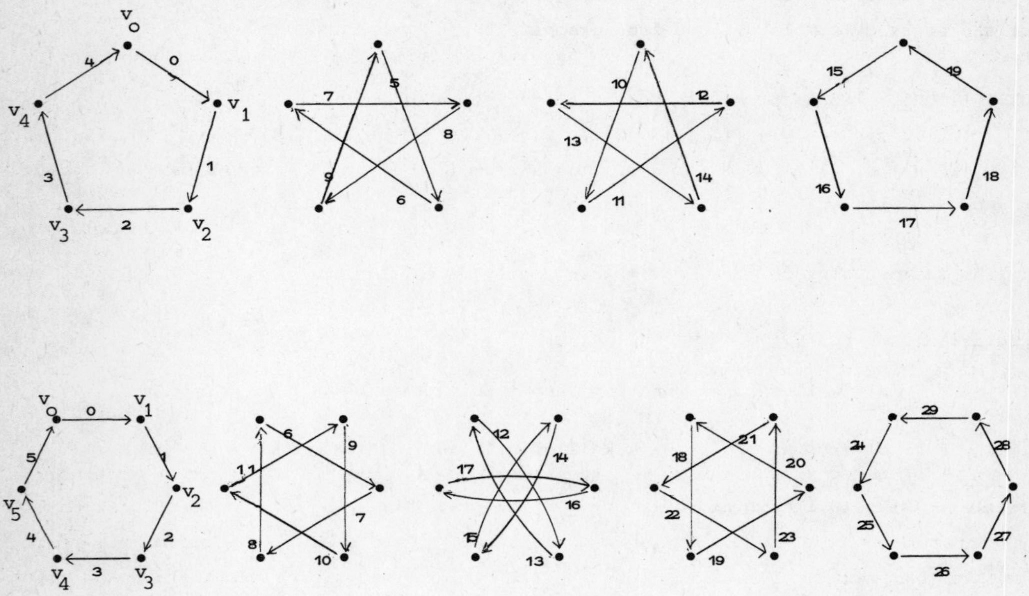

THEOREM 1. For each monotone resp. context-free graph grammar G there exists a nondeterministic Turing machine M such that $T(M) = \{mat(\Gamma) \mid \Gamma \text{ is a graph in } L(G)\}$, and M operates in space bounded by $O(|\Gamma|^2)$.

More intuitively, $L(G) \equiv T(M)$, and M is $O(n^2)$-space bounded, where n is the size of the graphs, whose adjacency matrix is given as input to M. Note that M is linearly-space bounded with respect to the length of its input $mat(\Gamma)$. The discrepancy between linear and quadratic space bounds disappears for chain graphs.

THEOREM 2. For each monotone resp. context-free graph grammar G there exists an n^2-space-bounded nondeterministic Turing machine M such that $T(M) = L_w(G)$.

<u>Proof.</u> The proof covers Theorem 1 and Theorem 2. Let Γ be a graph in $L(G)$ having n vertices and let $\Gamma_o \Rightarrow \Gamma_1 \Rightarrow \ldots \Rightarrow \Gamma_t = \Gamma$ be a derivation in G. From the monotony of G each Γ_i has at most n vertices and thus at most $c \cdot n^2$ edges, where c is the size of G's edge-label alphabet. Hence, $mat(\Gamma_i)$ is a string of length $O(n^2)$. For $i=o,1,\ldots,t-1$, M stores $mat(\Gamma_i)$ on a separate working tape and simulates the derivation step $\Gamma_i \Rightarrow \Gamma_{i+1}$ of G calculating $mat(\Gamma_{i+1})$ from $mat(\Gamma_i)$. To this effect M proceeds in a nondeterministic manner. It guesses the relevant production and the position of its left-hand side, verifies the guess on $mat(\Gamma_i)$ and executes the production. Clearly all these tasks can be done on $O(n^2)$ space. Finally, M matches its working tape against its input tape.

[]

Surprisingly, the converse of the previous theorems holds, too, which undoubtedly is the more valuable result.

<u>THEOREM 3.</u> For each n^2-space-bounded nondeterministic Turing machine M there exists a context-free resp. monotone graph grammar G such that $T(M) = L_w(G)$ and $L(G)$ contains only oriented chains.

<u>Proof.</u> Without loss of generality suppose that M is a one-tape Turing machine. Moreover, suppose that for each input w of length n and each accepting computation M first marks off n^2-n squares as its working space. Then M performs its real computation leaving the working space unchanged. M accepts by final state and empty storage, i.e., with all squares holding a dummy symbol, say δ. Hence, there is a sequence of instantaneous descriptions $ID_o,\ldots,ID_s,\ldots,ID_t$ with $ID_o = (q_o,a_1)a_2\ldots a_n$, $ID_s = ID_o\,\gamma^m$, and $ID_t = q_f\,\delta^r$, where $w = a_1a_2\ldots a_n$, γ and δ are new symbols, $m = n^2-2n$, and $r = n^2-n-1$. q_o is an initial state, q_f is a final state, and q_o and q_f do not appear elsewhere. Moreover, $|ID_{i-1}| \leq |ID_i|$ for $1 \leq i \leq s$ and $|ID_i| = n^2-n$ for $s \leq i \leq t$. These assumptions simplify the construction of G. Note that any two successive ID's differ in at most two neighbored places indicated by a symbol of the form (q,a), where q is a state of M. Namely, if (q,A,q',A',R) is the instruction at the pth step, then $ID_p = u(q,A)Bv$ and $ID_{p+1} = uA'(q',B)v$. And if M moves left by (q,A,q',A',L) then $ID_p = uB(q,A)v$ and $ID_{p+1} = u(q',B)A'v$.

Let $s \leq p \leq t$. Each ID_p is encoded into the edges of a graph Γ_p. Γ_p has n vertices $v_o,\ldots,v_{n-1}$, whose labels are used for auxiliary calculations. For a specification of the ordering of the vertices, Γ_p has a clockwise $\{\alpha,\overline{\alpha}\}$-hamiltonian circuit, i.e., edges (v_i,α,v_{i+1}) for $o \leq i < n-1$ and $(v_{m-1},\overline{\alpha},v_o)$, where $\alpha,\overline{\alpha}$ are new edge-labels. Similarly, it has an anti-clockwise $\{\beta,\overline{\beta}\}$-hamiltonian circuit. Now the subgraph

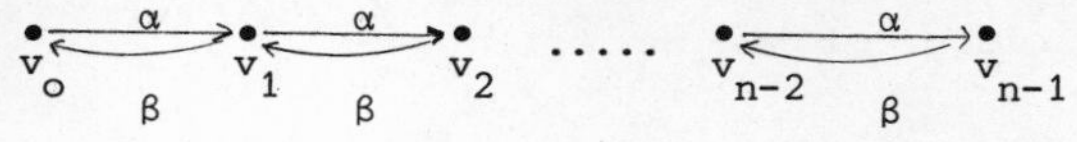

can be used as

a string of length n or as a Turing tape with n squares. Additionally, there are n^2-n new edges between any two vertices, and the edge from v_i to v_j is labelled by b_k if and only if $f_n(k) = (i,j)$ and $ID_p = b_o \ldots b_k \ldots b_r$ with $r = n^2-n-1$.

The graph grammar G simulates the Turing machine backwards. For each string $w = a_1 \ldots a_n$, G first generates the graph Γ_t corresponding to ID_t, using context-free productions and inheriting embeddings. Thus Γ_t has n vertices $v_o, \ldots, v_{n-1}$, a clockwise $\{\alpha,\overline{\alpha}\}$- and an anti-clockwise $\{\beta,\overline{\beta}\}$- hamiltonian circuit, δ-edges (v_i,δ,v_j) for $i \neq j$ and $(i,j) \neq (o,1)$ and the edge $(v_o,(q_f,\delta),v_1)$, which signals acceptance. For $s < p \leq t$, Γ_{p-1} is obtained from Γ_p by relabelling the distinguished edge with a state-label and the predecessor respectively successor edge according to the instruction which leads from ID_{j-1} to ID_j. To this effect, G labels the vertices v_ν and v_μ of the state-labelled edge by special markers, and guesses and labels the vertices v_ξ and v_η of the relevant predecessor resp. successor edge. Next G verifies the guess. To this effect it uses the orientation given by the $\{\alpha,\overline{\alpha}\}$-hamiltonian circuit and acts like a monotone string grammar or a Turing machine along this circuit, calculating $(\xi,\eta) = f_n(k\pm 1)$ from $(\nu,\mu) = f_n(k)$. Observe that in most cases $\eta = \nu$ and $\eta-\xi \pmod n = \mu-v \pmod n$, so that $v_\nu = v_\eta$ and the distance from v_μ to v_ν along the $\{\alpha,\overline{\alpha}\}$-hamiltonian circuit equals that from v_η to v_ξ.

Finally, G deletes all edges with labels from $\{\alpha,\overline{\alpha},\beta,\overline{\beta},\gamma\}$, shifts the labels of the remaining edges to their left vertices, deletes the edge from v_{n-1} to v_o, and removes the components that do not belong to the string $a_1 \ldots a_n$ from the labels of its vertices.

By construction, the resulting graph is an oriented chain whose (vertex) string is w if and only if $w \in T(M)$. Hence, $L(G) = \{\Gamma \mid w(\Gamma)$ is in $T(M)\}$. As outlined above, G is a monotone graph grammar, which by the Proposition can be made to be context-free.

[]

The graph grammars introduced by Nagl are based on directed graphs. Clearly, one may vary this concept to undirected graph grammars, which operate on undirected graphs and with undirected embeddings in the sense defined above. By the symmetry of the edges and embeddings undirected graph grammars are a special case of directed graph grammars. Thus Theorem 1 and Theorem 2 hold accordingly. For an undirected analogue to Theorem 3 we simulated the directed $\{\alpha,\overline{\alpha}\}$-hamiltonian circuit by an undirected $\{\alpha,\overline{\alpha}\}$-hamiltonian circuit and additional labels on the vertices, such that each v_i has $i \pmod 3$ as a new component of its label, with v_o also having the left-marker ¢. The remaining part of the proof will then go through. Since the Proposition can be carried over to the undirected case we obtain:

<u>THEOREM 4.</u> For each n^2-space-bounded Turing machine M there exists a context-free respectively monotone undirected graph grammar G such that $T(M) = L_w(G)$ and $L(G)$ contains only oriented chains.

Clearly, an undirected graph grammar cannot generate any (purely) directed graph. So the graph generating capacity of undirected graph grammars is weaker than that of directed graphs. However, there is no difference, when the generation of languages of strings or the computational power are concerned.

<u>COROLLARY.</u> For each context-free respectively monotone (directed) graph grammar G there exists a context-free respectively monotone undirected graph grammar G' such that $L_w(G) = L_w(G')$, and conversely.

CONCLUSION:

Our main theorem should be seen as the first step towards a classification of the different notions of graph grammars in the framework of complexity theory. We hope that these investigations will increase our understanding of graph grammars and will help finding graph grammars with efficient parsing algorithms. The types of graph grammars studied here are bad from that point of view, since complexity theory actually provides the time bound c^{n^2} for the simulation of n^2-space-bounded nondeterministic Turing machines.

REFERENCES:

[1] V. Claus, H. Ehrig, and G. Rozenberg (Eds.)
Graph grammars and their application to computer science and biology.
Lecture Notes in Computer Science, Vol. 73 (1979).

[2] F. Harary, and E.M. Palmer
Graphical Enumeration.
Academic Press, New York, 1973.

[3] J.E. Hopcroft, and J.D. Ullman
Introduction to Automata Theory, Languages and Computation.
Addison Wesley, Reading, 1979.

[4] D. Janssens, and G. Rozenberg
A characterization of context-free string languages by directed node label controlled graph grammars.
Acta Inform. 16 (1981), 63-85.

[5] M. Nagl
Graph-Grammatiken.
Vieweg, Braunschweig, 1979.

Inconsistencies of pure LISP

Andreas Eick Elfriede Fehr
Lehrstuhl für Informatik II
RWTH Aachen

Abstract

In a first informal section we shall discuss some problems with definitions of list functions. In particular we motivate the restrictions of pure LISP with respect to list expressions using the full lambda definability.

In sections two and three we formally define the lambda-semantics of the pure LISP language as well as the denotational description of the original semantics of pure LISP as defined by the interpreter EVALQUOTE. In the last section, we show that even for this restricted language the interpreter does not work correctly with respect to the laws of the λ-calculus.

These results sharpen previous results by Perrot [6], Simon [7] and others, which point out that the usage of functional arguments in extended LISP destroys the α- and β-convertibility of LISP-expressions.

1. Introduction

Many algorithms can be formulated as string or list transformations. Either the underlying data structure corresponds immediately to lists or a suitable list representation was found because most machines require sequential input and output. The question in which (programming) language to express a list transformation is easy to answer for mathematicans: Take the lambda notation for defining functions and use some basic list operations as additional atoms in your expressions! This clearly gives a powerful tool for defining programs, and the mathematical theory which is well developed provides a sound basis for verification systems. Furthermore, it is well known that all lambda-definable functions are computable and there exists a number of strategies to compute the value of a lambda-expression, which are based on the laws of α- and β-conversion. These are the ideas some people developing applicative programming languages have in mind and Mc Carthy et.al. were the first to design a real language, namely LISP, on this base.
Unfortunately it turns out that α- and β-reduction cannot be efficiently performed on a machine. The main reasons for this are: 1. Searching for free variables in the arguments

which are bound in the body, finding new names and renaming variables accordingly, is highly inefficient and 2. The literal substitution of arguments for formal parameters is expensive.

A first idea to overcome these problems is to introduce a stack which holds pairs of formal and actual parameters and then evaluate procedure bodys refering to the stack whenever a variable occurs. It is easy to see that this approach works satisfactory in some cases but causes parasitic bindings in others. Consider the following example, where A and B denote constants:

$$t = (\lambda x.(\lambda y.(\lambda x.\ y\ B)\ x\ )\ A) \underset{\beta}{\longrightarrow} (\lambda y.(\lambda x.\ y\ B)\ A\ ) \underset{\beta}{\longrightarrow} (\lambda x.\ A\ B) \underset{\beta}{\longrightarrow} A$$

Hence, the intended meaning of the expression t is the value A . On the other hand a simple stack implementation would work as follows:

To compute t compute the value of

$(\lambda y.(\lambda x.yB)x)$ with entry $[x \mid A]$ on the stack. Next compute $(\lambda x.y\ B)$ with respect to the stack $[x \mid A]$. $[y \mid x]$ and finally take the value of y with respect to the stack $[x \mid A]$. $[y \mid x]$. $[x \mid B]$ which yields B .

This example shows, that when the value of x is evaluated in the innermost block, then the actual environment is used rather than the static one given by the programmer. This defect is called 'dynamic binding' or "most recent" error (Mc Gowan [5]) . It causes problems because it is not consistent with the mathematical theory underlying the lambda-calculus.

Another idea to overcome these problems is to disallow local declarations of globally defined variables. It would be an unpleasant restriction though, because it would distroy the full modularity. Anyhow it can be shown by an example that this method does not work in general either. Consider the following expression together with two reductions:

$$(\lambda z.(zz)\ \lambda x.\lambda y.(xy)) \underset{\beta}{\longrightarrow} (\lambda x.\lambda y.(xy)\ \lambda x.\lambda y.(xy)) \underset{\beta}{\longrightarrow} \lambda y.(\lambda x.\lambda y.(xy)y)\ .$$

Although there were no redefined variables in the original expression, we find that after two reductions y is globally and locally defined.

The next idea to solve the problem is trying to completely evaluate arguments before they are put onto the stack. Of course one knows that this corresponds to the call-by-value strategy and is thus not always defined when a safe strategy terminates, but it seems to be possible to program in a style which tolerates call-by-value execution.

One positive aspect comes in with this idea, namely call-by-value increases efficiency because arguments are evaluated exactly once, even if they occur more often.

This method works correctly for our first example:

$(\lambda y.(\lambda x.\ y\ B)x)$ with entry $[x \mid A]$ would continue evaluating $(\lambda x.\ y\ B)$ with respect to the stack $[x \mid A]\ .\ [y \mid A]$ and then finish up by computing the value of y with respect to the stack $[x \mid A]\ .\ [y \mid A]\ .\ [x \mid B]$ which yields A .

Unfortunately, the suggested method does not work correctly for all expressions. Functional arguments can spoil the idea of reducing arguments completely before storing them. A stepwise reduction of our second example with corresponding stacks would work as follows:

	expression	stack
1.	$(\lambda z.(zz)\quad \lambda x.\lambda y.(xy))$	$[\ ]$
2.	(zz)	$[z \mid \lambda x.\lambda y.(xy)]$
3.	$(\lambda x.\lambda y.(xy)z)$	$[z \mid \lambda x.\lambda y.(xy)]$
4.	$\lambda y.(xy)$	$[z \mid \lambda x.\lambda y.(xy)].[x \mid \lambda x.\lambda y.(xy)]$
5.	$\lambda y.(\lambda x.\lambda y.(xy)y)$	$[z \mid \lambda x.\lambda y.(xy)].[x \mid \lambda x.\lambda y.(xy)]$
6.	$\lambda y.\lambda y.(xy)$	$[z \mid \lambda x.\lambda y.(xy)].[x \mid \lambda x.\lambda y.(xy)].[x \mid y]$
7.	$\lambda y.\lambda y.(yy)$	

Observe that in step 2 the argument of z cannot be further evaluated. The conflict with β-reduction occurs in step 6, when x is associated to y which in the last step gets erroneously bound to the second declaration of y , instead of the intended first declaration.

The last idea we want to discuss here is to put a strict type system onto the language such that expressions are built up from functions which take a certain number of arguments of base type and produce a value of base type too. In order to obtain a sufficiently wide class of definable list functions a recursion operator is added to the language which is not necessary in the type-free case because then the Y-operator of the λ-calculus can be used instead. One can expect that the usage of base typed closed expressions allows a correct stack-implementation by the following considerations: If the expression is of base type (and closed) then the outermost arguments are also closed and of base type and hence one can inductively reduce the arguments to a constant value and then bind them on the stack to continue the execution. As constant values cannot be captured by other bindings, this seems to be a correct strategy.

The language we have arrived at is exactly the meta-language of pure LISP as introduced by Mc Carthy et.al. in [1] .

Now, in order to compare the operational semantics of LISP with the mathematically intended semantics of the LISP-expressions we shall develop a more formal framework in the next sections.

2. Syntax and static semantic specification of pure LISP

We shall use the method of denotational descriptions of programming language semantics in the Scott-Strachey style [8]. Our domains will be complete partial orders (cpo's), where a cpo is a partially ordered set containing a minimal element and least upper bounds of directed subsets.
The standard syntactic domains are flat cpo's for list structures and identifiers, where we obtain from an arbitrary set S the flat cpo $S_\perp$ by adjoining a minimal element $\perp$ and defining the order by $\perp \sqsubseteq s$ for all $s \in S$.
We shall fix an infinite denumerable set X of variables and let f,x,y,z denote elements of X.

Definition 1 (the domains Id and L, and the set Σ)

(i) $Id := X_\perp$ is the syntactic domain of identifiers

(ii) $L := \underline{List}_\perp$ is the domain of lists, where the set List is given by the following grammer:

List ::= err | Atom | (List *)
Atom ::= Word | Bool | Integer
Word ::= $\{A,\dots,Z\}^+$
Bool ::= tt | ff
Integer ::= $\{0,\dots,9\}^+$

(iii) Σ denotes the set of base functions, given explicitely by

$\Sigma := \{\underline{car}^{(1)}, \underline{cdr}^{(1)}, cons^{(2)}, \underline{eq}^{(2)}, \underline{atom}^{(1)}, +^{(2)}, *^{(2)}, \dot{-}^{(2)}, \underline{Zero}^{(1)}, \dots\}$,

where (n) denotes the functional arity n.

The meanings of base functions are exactly as they are defined for LISP, and can be looked up in Mc Carthy et. al [1]. For LISP-expressions one defines two syntactic categories, namely Form and Function with metavariables e and fn respectively. 'Forms' define objects of base type whereas 'Functions' define functional objects of type 1, i.e. they expect a finite number of arguments of base type and produce an answer of base type. These domains are specified by the following syntactic clauses:

Definition 2 (forms and functions)

$e ::= \underline{List} \mid X \mid fn[e_1;\dots;e_n] \mid [e_{11} \to e_{12};\dots;e_{n1} \to e_{n2}]$

$fn ::= \Sigma \mid X \mid \lambda\,[[x_1;\dots;x_n];e] \mid \underline{label}\,[f;fn]$

Corresponding to the syntactic categories, there are two semantic functions for each denotational specification. Let us first formalize the static semantics, which is consistent with the conversion rules of the λ-calculus (see Fehr [3]).

Let in general for a domain D with subdomain E $d_{|E}$ denote the projection of $d \in D$ onto E .

Defintion 3 ($[\![\ ]\!]^s$, the static semantics of pure LISP) :

(i) $U := [Id \to [L+[L^* \to L]]]$ is the set of environments with metavariable σ .

(ii) E : Form $\to U \to L$ is the semantic function for 'Forms', where we denote $E(e)(\sigma)$ by $E[\![e]\!]^s\sigma$. E is given by the following equations:

a) $E[\![L]\!]^s\sigma = L$ for each $L \in$ List

b) $E[\![x]\!]^s\sigma = \sigma(x)_{|L}$ for each $x \in X$

c) $E[\![fn[e_1;\ldots;e_n]]\!]^s\sigma = F[\![fn]\!]^s\sigma(E[\![e_1]\!]^s\sigma,\ldots,E[\![e_n]\!]^s\sigma)$

d) $E[\![[e_{11} \to e_{12};\ldots;e_{n1} \to e_{n2}]]\!]^s\sigma =$ if $E[\![e_{11}]\!]^s\sigma$ then $E[\![e_{12}]\!]^s\sigma$ else if ... else if $E[\![e_{n1}]\!]^s\sigma$ then $E[\![e_{n2}]\!]^s\sigma$.

(iii) F : Function $\to U \to L^* \to L$ is the semantic function for 'Functions', where again we denote $F(fn)(\sigma)$ by $F[\![fn]\!]^s\sigma$. F is given by the following equations, where we use $\underline{\lambda}$ in the metalanguage to denote strict and rank free functions:

a) $F[\![f]\!]^s\sigma = \underline{\lambda}\, x_1\ldots x_n .\ f(x_1,\ldots,x_n)$ for each $f \in \Sigma^{(n)}$

$= \sigma(f)_{|L^* \to L}$ for $f \in X$

b) $F[\![\lambda[[x_1;\ldots;x_n];e]]\!]^s\sigma = \underline{\lambda}\, l_1\ldots l_n .\ E[\![e]\!]\sigma[x_1 \mid l_1]\ldots[x_n \mid l_n]$

c) $F[\![$label $[f; fn]]\!]^s\sigma = \mu a.(\lambda F.F[\![fn]\!]^s\sigma[f / F])(a)$, where $\mu a.\ f(a)$ denotes the minimal fixed point of f .

We state now two results which derive from Scott's theory of lambda-calculus, and are formally proved for this restricted language over the list interpretation in Eick [2] .

Lemma 1 (α-consistency)
Let fn be an expression of the form $\lambda[[x_1;\ldots;x_n];e]$. Assume that the variable z does not occur in fn . Then $F[\![fn]\!]^s = F[\![\lambda[[x_1;\ldots;x_{i-1};z;x_{i+1};\ldots;x_n];\ \$_z^{x_i}\ e]]\!]^s$ holds for all $1 \leq i \leq n$, where $\$_t^x\, e$ denotes the result of substituting t for all free occurences of x in e .
This Lemma is the semantic pendant to the α-conversion in λ-calculus. Analoguous theorems can be proved for the β-conversion and value reduction:

Theorem 2 (β-consistency)
Let e be an expression of the form $\lambda[[x_1;\ldots;x_n];e'][e_1;\ldots;e_n]$. Assume that no variable occurs both free in $e_1;\ldots;e_n$ and bound in e' . Then

$\mathcal{E}[\![e]\!]^s = [\![\$^{x_1 \ldots x_n}_{e_1 \ldots e_n} e']\!]^s$ holds.

Theorem 3 (δ-consistency) :
Let e be an expression of the form $f[L_1;\ldots;L_n]$, where $L_i \in \underline{List}$ for $1 < i < n$ and $f \in \Sigma$.
Then $\mathcal{E}[\![f[L_1;\ldots;L_n]]\!]^s = L$, where $L = f(L_1,\ldots,L_n)$ holds.

The next theorem formalizes an important property of this semantic defintion:

Theorem 4 (substitutivity of equivalence):

Let $e_1,e_2 \in \underline{Form}$ be expressions such that $\mathcal{E}[\![e_1]\!]^s = \mathcal{E}[\![e_2]\!]^s$. If e is another form which contains e_1 as a subexpression, then $\mathcal{E}[\![e]\!]^s = \mathcal{E}[\![\$^{e_1}_{e_2} e]\!]^s$.

The essential idea of the proof of this theorem strongly depends on the fact that closed expressions are independant from the environment.

Theorem 5 (expansion rule):

$\mathcal{F}[\![\underline{label}[f;fn]]\!]^s\sigma = \mathcal{F}[\![fn]\!]^s\sigma[f \mid [\![fn]\!]^s\sigma]$

3. Dynamic semantic specification

In this section we shall present the original LISP-semantics in a denotational style as suggested by Gordon in [4]. He also proved in the same paper that this semantic description is equivalent to the operational definition given in Mc Carthy et. al. [1] by the interpreter function EVALQUOTE.

Definition 4 ($[\![\ ]\!]^d$ the dynamic (original) semantics of LISP):

(i) Env : Id → [Env → [$\mathcal{L}$+[$\mathcal{L}$* → $\mathcal{L}$]]] is the set of recursive environments with meta-variable ρ . This is needed to model the fact that the meaning of free variables is not explicitely determined by an environment but rather as a function from (the calling) environment into values.

(ii) $\mathcal{E}'$: Form → Env → $\mathcal{L}$ is the dynamic semantic function for forms, where we denote $\mathcal{E}'(e)(\rho)$ by $[\![e]\!]^d\rho$. $\mathcal{E}'$ is given by the following equations:

a) $[\![L]\!]^d\rho = L$

b) $[\![x]\!]^d\rho = \rho(x)\rho_{\mid \mathcal{L}}$

c) $[\![fn[e_1;\ldots;e_n]]\!]^d\rho = [\![fn]\!]^d\rho([\![e_1]\!]^d\rho,\ldots,[\![e_n]\!]^d\rho)$

d) $[\![[e_{11} \to e_{12};\ldots;e_{n1} \to e_{n2}]]\!]^d\rho = \underline{if}\ [\![e_{11}]\!]^d\rho\ \underline{then}\ [\![e_{12}]\!]^d\rho$

$\underline{else}\ \underline{if}\ \ldots\ \underline{else}\ \underline{if}\ [\![e_{n1}]\!]^d\rho\ \underline{then}\ [\![e_{n2}]\!]^d\rho$

(iii) F' : $\underline{\text{function}} \to \text{Env} \to L^* \to L$ is the dynamic semantic function for 'functions' where again we denote $F'(\text{fn})(\rho)$ by $[\![fn]\!]^d\rho$. F' is given by the following equations:

a) $$[\![f]\!]^d\rho = \begin{cases} \underline{\lambda}\ x_1\ldots x_n.\ f(x_1,\ldots,x_n) & \text{for each } f \in \Sigma^{(n)} \\ \rho(f)\rho \mid_{L^* \to L} & \text{for } f \in X \end{cases}$$

b) $[\![\lambda[[x_1;\ldots;x_n];e]]\!]^d\rho = \underline{\lambda}\ l_1\ldots l_n\ .\ [\![e]\!]^d\rho[^{x_1}/\lambda\rho.l_1]\ldots[^{x_n}/\lambda\rho.l_n]$

c) $[\![\underline{label}[f;fn]]\!]^d\rho = [\![fn]\!]^d\rho[f/[\![fn]\!]^d]$

This dynamic semantics looks quite similar to the static one: In iii(b) we see that abstraction yields bindings of constant functions to variables, together with definition ii(b) for the semantics of variables this yields exact equivalence for the λ-abstraction to the static case.
Furthermore, the definition iii(c) for label looks like one expansion of the recursive definition of f . Note however that in the updated environment f is not bound to $[\![fn]\!]^d\rho$, but to the function $[\![fn]\!]^d$ which expects a new environment first. How this fact can cause danger is demonstrated in the final section.

4. The difference between static and dynamic binding for pure LISP

Consider the following LISP-expression:

$e := \lambda[[x];\ \underline{label}[f;\ \lambda[[z];[z = 0 \to x;\ \underline{tt} \to \lambda[[x];f[x \dot{-} 1]][1]]]]][1]][0]$

This example is a definition of the constant function 0 , when considered with static semantics, applied to the argument 0 . In the sequel we shall omit E and F , when it is clear from the context.

Fact 1 $\quad [\![e]\!]^s\sigma = 0$ for all environments σ

Proof $\quad [\![\lambda[[x];\ldots][0]]\!]^s\sigma = [\![\underline{label}[\ldots][1]]\!]^s\sigma[^x/0]$ by Def. 3.ii(c) and iii(b)

$= [\![\lambda[[z];\ldots]]\!]^s\sigma[^x/0][^f/[\![\ldots]\!]^s\sigma[^x/0]](1)$ by theorem 5 and 3.ii(c)

$= [\![\lambda[[x];f[x \dot{-} 1]][1]]\!]^s\sigma[^x/0][^f/\ldots][^z/1]$ by Def. 3.ii(c), iii(b), ii(d)

$= [\![f[x \dot{-} 1]]\!]^s\sigma[^x/0][^f/\ldots][^z/1][^x/1]$ by Def. 3.ii(c) and iii(b)

$= [\![\lambda[[z];\ldots]]\!]^s\sigma[^x/0](0)$ by Def. 3.ii(c)

$= [\![[z = 0 \to x; tt \to \ldots]]\!]^{s} \sigma[^{x}/0][^{z}/0]$ by Def. 3.ii(c) and iii(b)

$= 0$ by Def. 3.ii(b)

Fact 2 $[\![e]\!]^{d}\rho = 1$ for all environments ρ

Proof $[\![\lambda[[x];\ldots][0]]\!]^{d}\rho = [\![\underline{label}[f;\ldots][1]]\!]^{d}\rho[^{x}/\lambda\rho.0]$ by 4.iii(b), ii(c), ii(a)

$= [\![\lambda[[z]\ldots]]\!]^{d}\rho[^{x}/\lambda\sigma.0][^{f}/[\![\lambda[[z]\ldots]]\!]^{d}](1)$ by Def. 4.iii(c), ii(c)

$= [\![\lambda[[x];f[x \dot{-} 1]][1]]\!]^{d}\sigma[^{x}/\ldots][^{f}/\ldots][^{z}/\lambda\rho.1]$ as above

$= [\![f[x \dot{-} 1]]\!]^{d}\rho[^{x}/\ldots][^{f}/\ldots][^{z}/\ldots][^{x}/\lambda\rho.1]$ as above

$= [\![\lambda[[z];\ldots]]\!]^{d}\rho[^{x}/\ldots][^{f}/\ldots][^{z}/\ldots][^{x}/\lambda\rho.1](0)$ by Def. 4.ii(c) et. al.

$= [\![x]\!]^{d}\rho[^{x}/\ldots][^{f}/\ldots][^{z}/\ldots][^{x}/\lambda\rho.1]$ by Def. 4.iii(b) and ii(d)

$= 1$ by 4.ii(b)

Fact 3 For any LISP-function fn and arguments arg 1,...,arg n , the following holds: $[\![fn[arg\ 1;\ldots;arg\ n]]\!]^{d}\rho$ = EVALQUOTE[fn;(arg 1...arg n)] for arbitrary ρ .

Proof see Gordon [4]

From these facts we can easily conclude the following theorems:

Theorem 6 The semantics of pure LISP is inconsistent with the static semantics.

Theorem 7 The semantics of pure LISP is inconsistent with α-conversion.

Proof Rename the second declaration of x in the above example into y . Compute the value analoguously as before. The result is 0 , which is different from 1.

Theorem 8 The semantics of pure LISP is inconsistent with β-conversion.

Proof Reduce in the above example the innermost redex. You obtain the form: $\lambda[[x]\ ;\ \underline{label}\ [f;\lambda[[z];[z = 0 \to x\ ;\ tt \to f[0]]]][1]][0]$.

This equals again to 0 , contradicting the value of e which was 1 .

Simon claims ([7] page 20):
"We have the strong opinion that the Church-Rosser property still holds for λ-calculus if the only operation of λ-terms is β-reduction on proper redexes", where a λ-term $(\lambda z.MN)$ is called a proper redex, if N is closed. He further claims that LISP fits to this restricted calculus, in the sense that the LISP interpreter works correctly with respect to this restriction. A corollary of theorem 8 contradicts his conjecture:

Corollary The semantics of pure LISP is inconsistent with β-reduction of proper redexes.

Proof Remark that the contracted redex in the proof of theorem 8 was proper.

These results are not only surprising, but also violate the mathematical theory underlying the lambda notation. Mc Carthy et. al. were wrong when they claimed in [1] p. 7:
"The variables in a lambda expression are dummy or bound variables because systematically changing them does not alter the meaning of the expression."

Proving properties of programs works usually by applying reduction rules. No valid reduction rules can be formulated for pure LISP on the expressions alone, but at least a simulation of the a-list has to be developed together with the reduction of expressions, as Gordon shows in [4] .
One question that arises now is, can pure LISP be further restricted in order to be safely evaluated by EVALQUOTE ?
The answer is not formally presented in this paper, but we show in Eick [2] that the answer can be positive if redeclaration of globally declared identifiers is forbidden. This restriction is equivalent to Mc Gowans sufficient condition for the correctness of his Interpreter I_{MR} , which performs the "most recent" evaluation strategy for block structured languages [5] . His condition is the following:
"A program must have no potentially recursive procedure R which contains the declaration of a procedure P(a label L) and a call of some procedure Q having P(L) as one of its arguments, where Q can call-*R".

References

[1] Mc Carthy, J. et. al.: "LISP 1.5 Programmer's Manual" M.I.T. Press (1965)

[2] Eick, A.: "Semantische Analyse des LISP-Interpreters" Diplomarbeit RWTH Aachen (1982)

[3] Fehr, E.: "The lambda-semantics of LISP" Schriften zur Informatik und Angewandten Mathematik, Bericht Nr. 72, RWTH Aachen (1981)

[4] Gordon, M.: "Operational reasoning and denotational semantics" Stanford Artificial Intelligence Laboratory, Memo AIM-264, (1975)

[5] Mc Gowan, C.L.: "The "most recent" error: its causes and correction" SIGPLAN Notices, Vol. 7, Nr. 1 (1972)

[6] Perrot, J.-F.: "LISP et λ-Calcul" Ecole de Printemps d'Informatique Théorique, Le Châtre 1978

[7] Simon, F.: "Lambda Calculus and LISP", Bericht Nr. 8006, Institut für Informatik und Praktische Mathematik, Universität Kiel (1980)

[8] Strachey, C.: "Towards a Formal Semantics" in Formal Language Description Languages for Computer Programming (ed. Steele, T.B.), North-Holland (1966)

FIFO NETS: A NEW MODEL OF PARALLEL COMPUTATION

by A. FINKEL and G. MEMMI

Thomson-CSF
Laboratoire Central de Recherches
Domaine de Corbeville
BP 10 - 91401 ORSAY CEDEX
France

ABSTRACT :

We introduce a new model of parallel computation, namely the FIFO nets. First, we introduce some basic definitions. A restriction of this model has the power of the Turing machine. Monogeneous Fifo nets are then introduced. The coverability tree is a procedure to decide whether a monogeneous net is bounded or not. At last, regularity is decidable for monogeneous nets.

INTRODUCTION

In our methodology [*** 81], we wanted to model and analyze sequential processes communicating by FIFO channels. In a first approach, each process is modelled by a state machine (i.e. a specific class of Petri nets), each channel by a place. The whole system is then represented by a Petri net. But this modelling is not precise enough anymore, when channels must contain different kinds of messages, involving different kinds of treatments. If the length of the FIFO channel is known, we can substitute a place by a subgraph; or introduce some powerful (in the descriptive sense) abbreviation like coloured Petri net [Jen 81] or predicate/transition net [Gel 79]. In our work, came out the problem of modelling such FIFO channel without knowing its length.

Then, we have constructed our own model of parallel computation namely: the FIFO nets. Starting from Petri nets, we have distinguished tokens in order to model different kinds of messages. Then, we have transformed the firing rules for modelling FIFO mechanisms easily.

After giving some basic definitions, we recall that it is possible to simulate effectively Petri nets and coloured Petri nets. In addition, one abbreviation is given, increasing the descriptive power of our model of parallel computation. Then we show how a class of FIFO nets: the alphabetic FIFO nets, can simulate a program machine [Min 67]. We prove, by this way, that FIFO nets have the same algorithmic power as Turing machine.

This last result is rather negative when regarding our aim of analyzing concurrent systems. This leads to the construction of the class of monogeneous Fifo nets which at least contains Petri nets and where the coverability tree [KaM 69] gives a procedure for deciding if a monogeneous Fifo net is bounded or not. At last, we prove that regularity is decidable for monogeneous FIFO nets.

I - INTRODUCTION OF FIFO NETS

I.1. Basic definitions

A FIFO net is a triplet $< R;M_0;A >$ where R is a finite valuated bipartite graph. R describes the topology of the net as in a Petri net [Bra 82]; M_0 is the initial marking which defines the initial state of the net; A is a finite alphabet associated with messages.

Formally, we have :

Definition : A FIFO net is a triplet $< R; M_o; A >$ where :

i) $R = < F, T; \Gamma ; V >$ is a finite valuated bipartite graph where F is the set of fifo (represented by circles), T the set of transitions (represented by bars) $(F \cap T = \emptyset)$; Γ is the corresponding between F and T giving for each node the set of its successors; V is a valuation on A^*; V is a function from $(T \times F) \cup (F \times T)$ into A^* with : $V(x, y) \neq \lambda$ iff $y \in \Gamma(x)$.

ii) M_o, the initial marking, is a function from F in A^*

iii) A is a finite alphabet. Each letter is called a message.

A FIFO net is often shortly denoted by $< R; M_o >$ without mentionning the name of the alphabet.

As in Petri net or any system of transitions, the marking of a FIFO net changes by firing transitions.

Definition: A transition t of T is fireable from the marking M iff:

$\forall f \in F : V(f,t) < M(f)$ (i.e. $V(f,t)$ is a prefix of $M(f)$) t fireable from M is denoted by $M(t>$.

Let $g(\alpha, x)$ be a function that removes α in the word x iff α is a prefix of x.

The firing of a transition creates a new marking M' from M with the following rule (where $(A^*)^F$ denotes the set of the functions from F into A^*)

Definition: The firing of a transition t is a partial function δ_t from $(A^*)^F$ into $(A^*)^F$ such that :

$$\forall M \in (A^*)^F : \forall f \in F : \delta_t(M)(f) = g(V(f,t), M(f)).V(t, f)$$

where g is the partial function from $A^* \times A^*$ into A^* such that :

$$g(\alpha, x) = y \text{ iff } x = \alpha y$$

$$g(\alpha, x) \text{ is undefined otherwise}$$

$\delta_t(M)$ is defined iff $\delta_t(M)(f)$ is defined for any f of F.

$M' = \delta_t(M)$ is denoted by $M(t> M'$.

We have $M(t>$ iff $\delta_t(M)$ is defined.

The firing of a transition t consists for each fifo f in input of t (i.e. $t \in \Gamma(f)$) to remove $V(f,t)$ which is then prefix of $M(f)$ and for each fifo f' in output of t (i.e. $f' \in \Gamma(t)$) to append $V(t,f')$ to $M(f')$; then $V(t, f')$ is a suffix of $M'(f')$. So, the simulation of FIFO mechanisms becomes quite natural.

Example 1 :

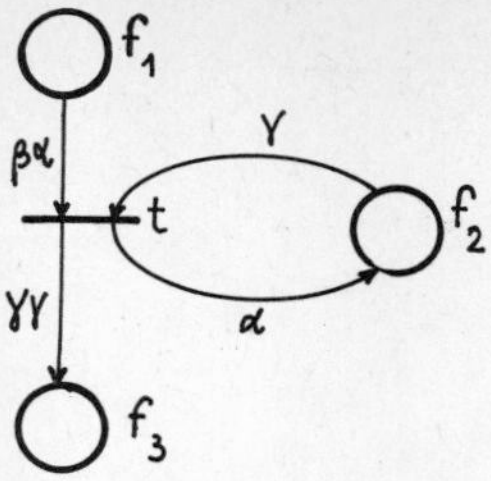

$A = \{\alpha,\beta,\gamma\}$. $M(f_1) = \beta\ \alpha\ a$ where $a \in A^*$; $M(f_2) = \gamma\ \gamma$; $M(f_3) = c$ where $c \in A^*$. t is fireable from M. M(t>M' with: $M'(f_1) = a$; $M'(f_2) = \gamma\ \alpha$; $M'(f_3) = c\ \gamma\ \gamma$ □

Figure 1

The firing notion is extended to words.

Definitions: A firing sequence x from a marking M, is defined by :

$x = x_1 \ldots x_k$ is a finite sequence of transitions and :

i) $x = \lambda$ then x is always defined which is denoted by M (λ> and we do not change of marking : M (λ> M.

ii) $x = x_1 \ldots x_k$ then x is defined iff :

- $x_1 \ldots x_{k-1}$ is defined and reach a marking M' from M: M($x_1 \ldots x_k$ > M'

- M' (x_k > is defined, we reach a marking M" and write: M'(x_k > M"

A marking M' is said to be reachable from M if :

$\exists\, w \in T^*$: M (w > M' .

This is also denoted by M (* > M'

I.2. Basic properties

Like for any transition system, we want to prove that a net has essentially two kinds of properties. On the one hand, a fifo must not accumulate an infinite number of letters (or messages). On the other hand, it is sometimes critical that a transition may become fireable from any reachable marking. These properties can be checked by analyzing two sets associated with a FIFO net.

Definitions: For a FIFO net N = < R; M_o; A >, the language of firing sequences is defined by F (N) = { $x \in T^*$ | M_o (x > }.

The reachability set from M is denoted by $A_{CC}(N)$ = {M'| M_o (* > M' }.

In a concurrent system, processes are generally defined by sequences of actions. In a net, an action may be modelled by several transitions. The firing of some transitions may be either ignored or not observable. Instead of firing sequences, we are more generally interested by sequences of actions. In other words, we label a transition by a letter or by the empty word.

Definitions: A labelled FIFO net is a couple N_1 = < N; h > where N is a FIFO net, h is a labelling function h: $T \to X \cup \{\lambda\}$ where X is a finite alphabet. h is naturally extended to words.

When $h : T \to X$, we say that the labelling is <u>λ-free</u>

$L(N_1) = \{h(x) \mid x \in F(N)\}$ denotes the <u>language of the labelled net.</u>

Then we refind the same properties as for Petri nets.

<u>Definition</u>: A fifo f is <u>bounded</u> in a FIFO net $N = \langle R; M_o; A \rangle$

iff : $\exists k \in N, \forall M \in Acc(M_o) : |M(f)| \leq k.$

where $|x|$ denotes the length of the word x.

N is bounded iff each file is bounded.

A transition is pseudo-live from M_o if it is possible to fire it from some reachable marking. A transition is live if it is pseudo-live from any reachable marking.

<u>Definitions</u>: Let $N = \langle R; M_o; A \rangle$ be a FIFO net, the transition t is said <u>to be pseudo-live</u> from M_o iff $\exists M \in Acc(M_o) : M(t >$. N is pseudo-live iff each transition is pseudo-live from M_o.

I.3. Abbreviation

FIFO nets have been created in order to model and analyze concurrent systems. Then it is interesting to increase the descriptive power of the model in adding some abbreviations. In this paper, we introduce one abbreviation which has been of some usefulness when practicing in modelling sequential processes communicating by FIFO channels [***81]. This abbreviation consists in modelling a subset of transitions by only one transition under some conditions: if $t_1, \ldots, t_k$ have the same inputs and the same outputs, then a unique transition t can represent them. t is fireable iff there exists a transition t_j fireable. The firing of t then corresponds to the firing of a transition t_j.

Paradigm: let $Q = \{q_1, \ldots, q_k\}$ be a finite set of A^* and $a \in A^*$. In particular for decoding the marking of a fifo, subgraphs of the type of the Figure 2a are often designed. This type of subgraphs can then be substituted by the one of the figure 2b.

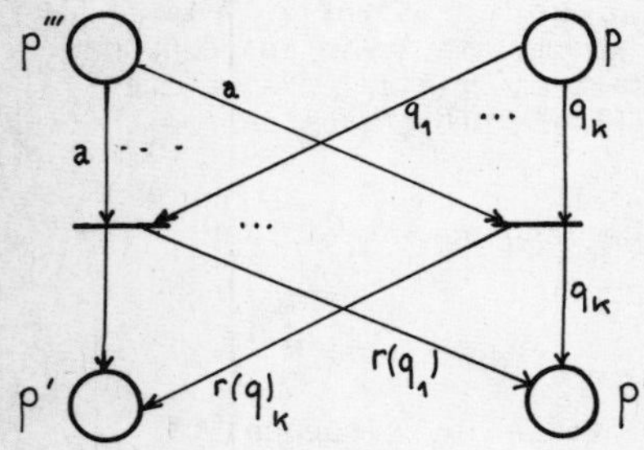

Figure 2a

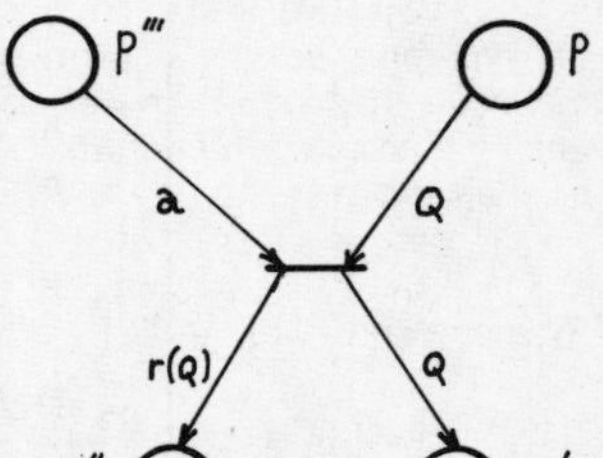

Figure 2b

This abbreviation partially takes into account the ones used for coloured Petri nets [Jen 81].

II - POWER OF THE MODEL

We are going to show that FIFO nets have the algorithmic power of the Turing Machine. Before, we show how to simulate effectively Petri nets and coloured Petri nets.

II.1. Petri nets and coloured Petri nets

Let $N = \langle\langle P,T;\Gamma;V\rangle;\ M_o\rangle$ a Petri net, then the simulation of this net by a FIFO net is straightforward. It suffices to construct the FIFO net $\langle\langle P,T;\Gamma;\overline{V}\rangle;\ \overline{M}_o;\ \{m\}\rangle$ where $\overline{V}(x,y)$ is the word of $\{m\}^*$ of length $V(x,y)$. $\overline{M}(p)$ is the word of length $M(p)$.

For a coloured Petri net,(see [Jen 81]), the set C of colours is used as the alphabet of the net. The problem is then to lose the order of arriving of messages.

For proving this, it suffices to number from 1 to n all the tokens in M(p),(differently coloured or not) and to show that we can generate the permutation group S_n in $\{1,\dots,n\}$ ([MaM 81]).

II.2. Alphabetic FIFO nets

We show that a class of FIFO nets has the power of the Turing machine, in simulating a program machine [Min 67], [VaV 81].

Definition: $\langle R;\ M\rangle$ is an alphabetic FIFO net iff $\forall\ x,y\ |V(x,y)| \leq 1$. Each edge is valuated by a letter of A.

We simulate a program machine by an alphabetic FIFO net $\langle R;\ M_o;\ A\rangle$ such that :

A = {0, 1}. Each register r_i is associated with a fifo r_i .

An integer n is coded by the word $0\underbrace{1\dots1}_{n\ \text{times}}0$

Each label q_i is associated with a fifo q_i .

The increment of a register (q_s: $r_i := r_i + 1$ goto q_m ;)is simulated by the following subgraph :

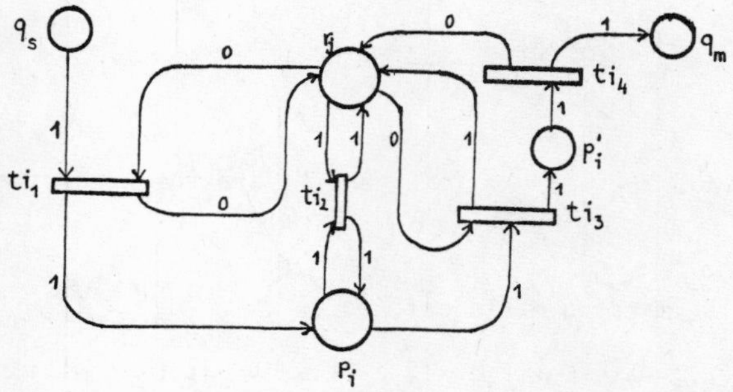

Figure 3

r_j contains $0\underbrace{1 \ldots. 1}_{n \text{ times}}0$. The firing of ti_1 is the beginning of the instruction, r_j contains now $1 \ldots 100$; then we fire ti_2 n times which permutes the 1: r_j contains now $001 \ldots 1$; ti_3 is then fireable and adds one 1 in r_j; ti_4 ends the instruction suffixing r_j by 0.

The test and decrement instruction (q_s : if r_i := o then goto q_m else r_i := r_i - 1 goto q_1 endif) is simulated by the following subgraph :

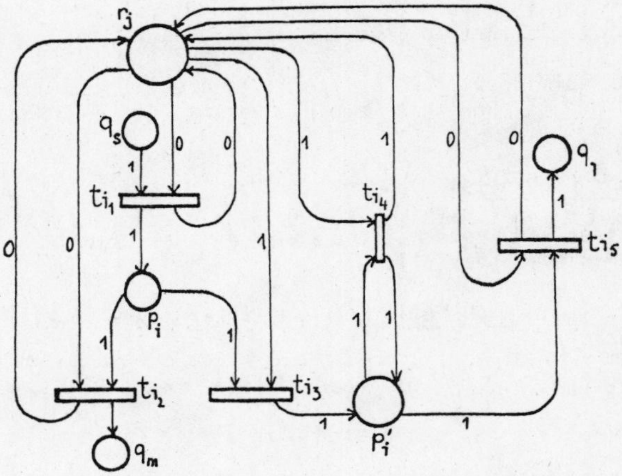

Figure 4

r_j contains $0\underbrace{1 \ldots. 1}_{n \text{ times}}0$. The firing of t_{i_1} is the beginning of the instruction, r_j contains now $1 \ldots 100$; t_{i_2} tests if $r_j = 0$; if $r_j \neq 0$ t_{i_3} is the only transition fireable. Then t_{i_4} permutes all the 1. After that t_{i_5} fires, r_j contains $0\underbrace{1 \ldots. 1}_{n-1 \text{ times}}0$.

Fifos q_i and auxiliary fifo P_i and P_i' are the support of a state machine S.

The initial marking M_o is defined by : $M_o(q_o) = 1$, $\forall f \in S$; $M_o(f) = \lambda$; $M_o(r_i) = 0\underbrace{1 \ldots. 1}_{n \text{ times}}0$ if r_i contains n in the program machine.

From these two subgraphs we have :

Theorem 1 : The alphabetic FIFO nets have the power of the Turing machine.

It is enough to invoke Church's thesis, to deduce that FIFO nets have the power of the Turing machine. We have also constructed [Mem 82] the effective homomorphism allowing to simulate any FIFO net by an alphabetic FIFO net. Homomorphism and simulation notions are then taken in [KsM 79]. Another method [Fin 82b] consists in showing that the family of the languages associated to the labelled Fifo nets is closed by rational transduction and contains a generator (the anti Dyck) of the family of the R.E. languages [Va F-Z 80].

III MONOGENEOUS FIFO NETS

Our aim was to construct a class of FIFO nets containing at least a class isomorphic to Petri nets, and for which the boundedness problem is decidable. The Karp and Miller's procedure [KaM 69], used for Petri nets, is mainly based upon two considerations:

(1) : if $M \geq M'$ then $Acc(\langle R ; M' \rangle) \subseteq Acc(\langle R ; M \rangle)$ i.e. if a marking M is greater than or equal to M', then each sequence fireable from M' is also fireable from M.

(2) : Koenig - Dückson Lemma : From each infinite sequence of vectors (here of markings) in $(\mathbb{N} \cup \{\omega\})^r$ one can extract a nondecreasing subsequence.

First, we have constructed an order on a set of markings as large as possible. This relation verifies the two considerations we mentionned. We then convinced ourself that the valuation of the input edges of a fifo had to be restricted. Otherwise it was hopeless to get sure that the reachability set of a net be contained in the set in which our order is defined. These reflexions led us to the definition of "monogeneous FIFO nets". More precisely, a FIFO net is monogeneous if each input edge of a fifo is valuated by a power of the same word.

At last, we show that regularity is decidable for monogeneous FIFO net.

III.1. Boundedness is decidable for monogeneous FIFO nets

Definition : A FIFO net $\langle\langle F, T, \Gamma, V \rangle ; M_0 \rangle$ is a Monogeneous net iff

$$(\forall f_i \in F)(\exists u_i \in A^*)(\forall t \in T)(V(t, f_i) \in u_i^*)$$

A word $u \in A^+$ is primitive iff $\forall v \in A^+ \ \forall n \geq 2 \quad u \neq v^n$. We denote by u_i the unique primitive word associated to the fifo f_i.

Let $\omega = \text{card}\,\mathbb{N}$ and A^ω the set of infinites words on A. We have $A^\infty = A^* \cup A^\omega$.

Theorem 2 : Let $N = \langle R; M_0 \rangle$ be a Monogeneous FIFO net. Then the boundedness of Acc(N) is a decidable problem.

Sketch of the proof : see [Fin 82b]

We define an ordering relation, denoted >> on $E=\{\overset{|F|}{\underset{i=1}{X}} (\mathrm{Suffix}(u_{iU}M_\circ(f_i)))u_i^\infty\}$ such that :

$\forall M, M' \in E \quad M' \gg M \quad \Leftrightarrow \quad \forall i = 1,\dots,|F| \quad M'(f_i) \in M(f_i)\, u_i^\infty$.

This ordering relation satisfies our considerations (1) and (2) in (E, >>). For a monogeneous FIFO net, Acc (N) $\subseteq$ E. Then "Acc (N) is infinite" is equivalent to " there exists a firing sequence x such that if M(x > M' then M' >> M and M' ≠ M."

This equivalence allows us to extend the construction of the coverability tree ([KaM 69],[VaV 81]) from Petri nets to monogeneous FIFO nets.

The coverability tree CT (N) of a monogeneous net N = < R, $M_\circ$ > is defined by CT (N) = < S, X > where :

S is a set of nodes labelled by elements of E

X is a set of edges labelled by elements of T.

CT(N) is defined by the following conditions :

1) the root r is labelled by $M_\circ$.

2) if s is a node labelled by Q, then s has no successor when either :

   (a) on a path from r to s there is a node $s_1 \neq s$, also labelled by Q, or,

   (b) there is no transition t such that $Q > V(\circ,t)$

3) if s is labelled by Q and s does not satisfy conditions (a) or (b), then for each $t \in T$ such that $Q > V(\cdot,t)$, let $Q_1(f_i) = g(V(f_i,t),Q(f_i))V(t,f_i)$,there is a successor s' labelled by Q' with:

   (i) $Q'(f_i) = Q_1(f_i)\, u_i^\omega$ for any fifo $f_i \in F$, for which there is a node s_2 on the path from r to s (inclusing s) labelled by Q_2 with $Q_2 \ll Q_1$ and $Q_2(f_i) \neq Q_1(f_i)$.

   (ii) Q' (fi) = Q_1 (fi) otherwise;

   the edge from s to s' is labelled by t.

In assuming the opposite and applying the Koenig-Dücksons's Lemma on (E, >>) we prove that CT (N) is finite. We show, with the definition of CT (N), that "Acc (N) is infinite" is equivalent to "there exists a node s in CT (N), labelled by Q such that $|Q(fi)| = \omega$ for a fifo $f_i \in F$".

Thus we have found an effective procedure which decides the boundedness of Acc (N).

We also can extend the definition of the coverability graph as given in [VaV 81], [Bra 82]. Then almost all the results of a theorem in [VaV 81] are extended to monogeneous nets [Fin 82a].

Example 2 : $N = \langle R; M_o \rangle$

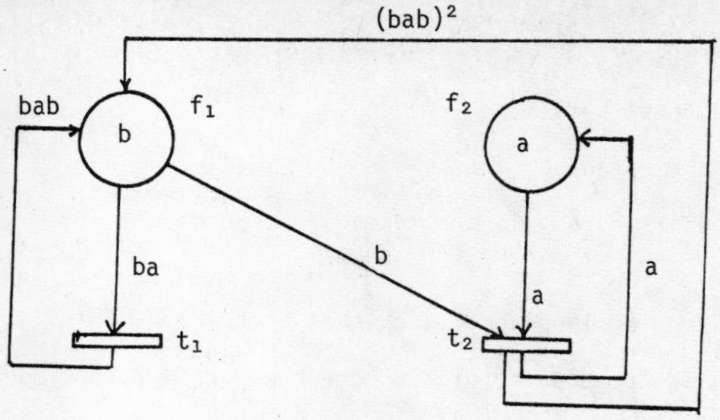

$$N = \langle R; M_o \rangle \quad M_o = (b, a)$$

Figure 5

CT (N)

$$Q_o = (b, a)$$

$\downarrow t_2$

$$Q_1 = ((bab)^2, a)$$

$t_1 \swarrow \qquad \searrow t_2$

$$Q_2 = (b (bab)^\omega, a) \qquad (ab (bab)^3, a) = Q_5$$

$t_2 \downarrow$

$$Q_3 = ((bab)^\omega, a)$$

$t_1 \swarrow \qquad \searrow t_2$

$$Q_2 = (b (bab)^\omega, a) \qquad (ab (bab)^\omega, a) = Q_4$$

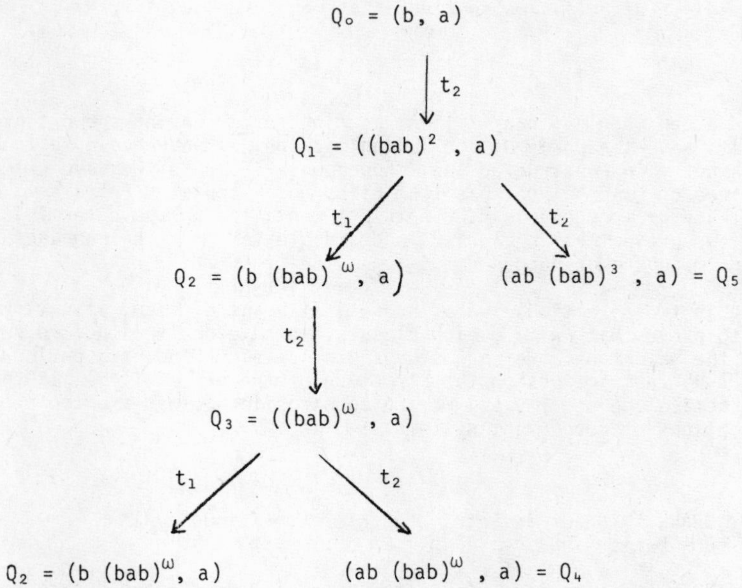

Figure 6

III.2. Regularity in F_m is decidable

Definition : [Vid 81] A labelled Petri net <N; h > is deterministic when

$\forall M \in Acc(M_\circ)\ \forall t, t' \in T\ [(M(t> \text{ and } M(t'>) \Rightarrow (t=t' \text{ or } h(t) \neq h(t'))]$

The classes of languages F_p, F_m, D_p^c and Pref (Rat) are then defined by :

F_p = {F(N) | N is a Petri net}

F_m = {F (N) | N is a monogeneous net}

D_p^c = { L (< N, h >) | < N; h > is a deterministic Petri net and h is λ-free}.

Pref(Rat) is the set of regular language L such that Pref (L) = L

Theorem 4:[Fin 82b] The regularity of a monogeneous net N is decidable.

Proof: We first show that $F_m \subseteq F_p \cap$ Pref(Rat). Pref(Rat) $\subseteq D_p^c$ is proved in [ViD 81]. Then :

$$F_m \subseteq D_p^c. \quad (1)$$

The regularity in F_p is decidable [VaV 81], and for each word u of $(h(T))^*$ there exists at most a marking M such that $M_\circ$ (W > M with h (W) = u. Then the regularity is also decidable in D_p^c. With (1), we conclude that we can decide if F(N) is regular or not □

IV - CONCLUSION

We have introduced a new model of parallel computation. After having shown that the alphabetic FIFO nets have the power of the Turing machine, we have again restricted the valuation of a net then constructed the monogeneous FIFO nets. We have extended the coverability tree of [KaM 69] to this last class which contains Petri nets. At last, in showing that the monogeneous FIFO nets are contained in the deterministic, λ-free Petri nets, we prove that regularity is decidable for F_m, the languages of firing sequences of monogeneous nets.

We are now working in two directions. On a theoretical point of view, it will be very interesting to prove that $F_p \subsetneq F_m$. The classes, we have dealt with, are defined by restriction on the valuation. We are studying classes of FIFO nets defined like Petri nets [Bra 82] by restrictions on the structure of the graph of the FIFO net [Fin 82b]. On a practical point of view, we are constructing a software tool for analyzing specifications of concurrent systems.

V - BIBLIOGRAPHY

[Bra 82] : G.W. BRAMS "Réseaux de Petri: théorie et pratique" (tome 1) Masson - Paris (1982).

[Fin 82a] : A. FINKEL "Monogeneous FIFO Petri nets" - 3rd European Workshop on applications and theory of Petri net - Varenna - Italy (September 1982)

[Fin 82b] : A. FINKEL - "Deux Classes de Réseaux à files: Les Réseaux Monogènes et les Réseaux Préfixes" - Thèse de 3ème cycle - Paris VII (Octobre 1982).

[GeL 79] : H.J. GENRICH & K. LAUTENBACH "The analysis of distributed systems by means of predicate/transition nets". Semantics of Concurrent Computation (G. KAHN ed.) L.N.C.S. 70 pp 123 - 146 - Springer Verlag - (1979).

[Jen 81] : K. JENSEN "Coloured Petri nets and the invariant method". T.C.S. Vol. 14, n° 3, pp. 317-336 (June 1981).

[KaM 69] : R.M. KARP & R.E. MILLER "Parallel program schemata" J. Comput. System Sci. 3 (4), pp. 167-195 (1969).

[KaM 79] : T. KASAI & R.E. MILLER "Homomorphisms between models of parallel computation". Research Report IBM - RC 7796 (33742) (1979).

[MaM 81] : R. MARTIN & G. MEMMI "Spécification et validation de système temps réel à l'aide de réseaux de Petri à files". Revue Technique THOMSON-CSF, Vol. 13, n° 3, pp. 635-653 (September 1981).

[Mem 82] : G. MEMMI - Thèse d'Etat - Paris VI - to appear.

[Min 67] : M. MINSKY "Computation: finite and infinite machines" Prentice-Hall, Englewood Cliffs N.J. (1967).

[VaF-Z 80]: B. VAUQUELIN & P. FRANCHI-ZANNETTACCI "Automates à files" TCS 11 pp. 221-225 (1980).

[VaV 81] : R. VALK & G. VIDAL-NAQUET "Petri nets and regular languages" J.C.S.S. Vol. 23, n° 3, pp. 299-325 (december 1981).

[Vid 81] : G. VIDAL-NAQUET "Rationalité et déterminisme dans les réseaux de Petri". Thèse d'Etat - Paris VI - (1981).

[*** 81] : "Méthodologie d'analyse et de programmation des systèmes" Rapport final du marché d'études DAII n° 79-35-059 (1981).

UNE EXTENSION AUX MOTS INFINIS DE LA NOTION DE TRANSDUCTION RATIONNELLE

F.Gire,

LITP et Université de PARIS 7

2, place Jussieu , 75221 Paris cedex 05.

ABSTRACT :

Here is introduced an extension for infinite words of the classical notion of rational transduction . We prove that this extension has the important property of mapping the adherence of a language of finite words into the adherence of an other language of finite words .The set of such extensions is closed by composition and is exactly the family of the compositions of an inverse faithful sequential mapping and of a faithful sequential mapping .

Then we study the stability and principality with respect to these extensions , of a family of languages of infinite words , Adh($\mathcal{L}$) , defined as the set of the adherences of languages of finite words wich belong to a given family $\mathcal{L}$.

0 _ INTRODUCTION _ RAPPELS -

Le but de ces pages est d'étudier les propriétés d'une extension aux mots infinis de la notion classique de transduction rationnelle . Une telle extension a déjà été proposée dans le cas des applications séquentielles fidèles ,[2] , et il a été prouvé que cette extension laisse stable la famille des adhérences de langages de mots finis . L'extension proposée ici est plus générale; dans une première partie nous montrons qu'elle laisse aussi stable la famille des adhérences de langages de mots finis , qu'elle constitue une notion stable par composition , et qu'elle coïncide avec la notion de composée d'une application séquentielle fidèle inverse et d'une application séquentielle fidèle ; dans une seconde partie , nous étudions les problèmes de stabilité et de principalité relativement à cette extension d'une famille de langages de mots infinis , Adh $\mathcal{L}$, définie , à partir d'une famille, $\mathcal{L}$, de langages de mots finis , comme la famille des adhérences des éléments de $\mathcal{L}$.

- On note X^* le monoide libre engendré par X et X^ω l'ensemble des mots infinis sur X ; on pose $X^\infty = X^* \cup X^\omega$. $|f|$ désigne la longueur du mot f .
- Soit $L \subset X^*$, l'adhérence de L est le sous ensemble de mots infinis , noté AdhL , défini par :

  $$\text{AdhL} = \{ u \in X^\omega \;/\; \forall n \in N^+ \; u[n] \in FG(L) \} .$$

  L'ensemble $\{ u[n] \;,\; n \in N^+ \;,\; u \in \text{AdhL} \}$ des facteurs gauches de mots de AdhL est appelé centre du langage L et est noté C(L) .
- Nous prenons comme définition des transductions rationnelles , la caractérisation qu'en a donné M.Nivat , [5] :

  une application τ de X^* dans l'ensemble , $\mathcal{P}(Y^*)$, des parties de Y^* , est une transduction rationnelle si et seulement si il existe un alphabet Z , un rationnel K de Z^*, et deux morphismes φ et ψ de Z^* dans X^* et dans Y^* respectivement , tels que :

  $$\forall u \in X^* , \; \tau(u) = \psi(\varphi^{-1}(u) \cap K)$$

  Une telle application est notée $\tau = (\varphi, \psi, K)$.

- Enfin , on appelle morphisme étendu de Z^{∞} dans X^{∞} toute application φ de Z^{∞} dans X^{∞} vérifiant :

-1- La restriction φ_1 , de φ à Z^* , est un morphisme de Z^* dans X^* ;

-2- $\forall u \in Z^{\omega}$, $\varphi(u) = \begin{cases} .\text{Sup } \{\varphi_1(u[n]) , n \in N^+\} \text{ si } \{\varphi_1(u[n]) , n \in N^+\} \text{ est infini} \\ .\ \varphi_1(u[n_o]) \text{ s'il existe } n_o \in N^+ \text{ tel que : } \\ \quad \forall n > n_o , \varphi_1(u[n]) = \varphi_1(u[n_o]) \end{cases}$.

I – DEFINITION ET PROPRIETES –

Nous nous proposons d'étudier les applications τ de X^{ω} dans $\mathcal{P}(Y^{\omega})$ pour lesquelles il existe un alphabet Z , un rationnel K de Z^* et deux morphismes étendus φ et ψ de Z^{∞} dans X^{∞} et dans Y^{∞} respectivement vérifiant:

-1- φ et ψ sont ε-limités sur K

-2- $\forall u \in X^{\omega}$, $\tau(u) = \psi(\varphi^{-1}(u) \cap \text{AdhK})$

où $\varphi^{-1}(u) = \{ v \in Z^{\omega} / \varphi(v) = u \}$

On notera $\tau = [\varphi, \psi, \text{AdhK}]$, toute application vérifiant toutes les conditions ci-dessus , et $\mathcal{C}$ la famille de toutes ces applications .

- Remarques :

-1- Le caractère ε-limité de ψ sur K assure que l'image par τ d'un mot infini sur X est un mot infini sur Y .

-2- Soit $\tau = [\varphi, \psi, \text{AdhK}]$; on vérifie sans peine que l'application τ^{-1}, de Y^{ω} dans $\mathcal{P}(X^{\omega})$, définie par :

$\forall v \in Y^{\omega}$, $\tau^{-1}(v) = \{ u \in X^{\omega} / v \in \tau(u) \}$

satisfait l'égalité : $\tau^{-1} = [\psi, \varphi, \text{AdhK}]$.

Nous établissons ci-dessous l'importante propriété suivante :

l'image par un élément de $\mathcal{C}$, de l'adhérence d'un langage de mots finis est l'adhérence d'un langage de mots finis .

- PROPRIETE 1 :

Soit $\tau = [\varphi, \psi, \mathrm{Adh}K]$ et $L \subset X^*$.

On a : $\tau(\mathrm{Adh}L) = \mathrm{Adh}(\bar{\tau}(C(L)))$

où $\bar{\tau}$ est la transduction rationnelle de X^* dans $\mathcal{P}(Y^*)$

définie par : $\forall f \in X^*, \quad \bar{\tau}(f) = \psi(\varphi^{-1}(f) \cap FG(K))$.

preuve :

- L'inclusion $\tau(\mathrm{Adh}L) \subset \mathrm{Adh}(\bar{\tau}(C(L)))$ ne pose pas de difficultés .

- Etablissons l'inclusion inverse : soit $v \in \mathrm{Adh}(\bar{\tau}(C(L)))$; $\forall n \in N^+, \exists k_n \in FG(K)$ tel que $\varphi(k_n) \in C(L)$ et $v[n] \leqslant \psi(k_n)$.

Posons $E_n = \{ kx \in FG(K) \ / \ x \in Z , \ \psi(k) < v[n] \leqslant \psi(kx) \ \text{ et } \ \varphi(kx) \in C(L) \}$.

En appliquant le lemme de Koenig on obtient une suite $(k_n)_{n \in N^+}$ vérifiant :

$\forall n \in N^+, \quad k_n \in E_n$ et $k_n \leqslant k_{n+1}$.

On en déduit que la suite $(k_n)_{n \in N^+}$ définit un mot infini $k = \mathrm{Sup}\{ k_n, \ n \in N^+\}$ tel que : $k \in \mathrm{Adh}K$, $\psi(k) = v$ et $\varphi(k) \in \mathrm{Adh}L$. Donc $v \in \tau(\mathrm{Adh}L)$. □

- Remarque : il est important de noter que si ψ n'est pas ε-limité sur K , ou si φ n'est pas ε-limité sur K , la propriété 1 n'est plus vraie comme le montre les exemples suivants :

.exemple 1 :

$X = \{a,b,c\}$; $Y = \{b,c\}$; $\psi : X^\infty \longrightarrow Y^\infty$ défini par $\psi(a) = \varepsilon, \psi(b)=b, \psi(c)=c$.

$\forall u \in X^\omega$, posons $\tau(u) = \psi(u)$.

Soit $L = \{a^n b^p , \ n \geqslant 1 , \ p \leqslant n\} c^+$; $\psi(\mathrm{Adh}L) = \{\varepsilon\} \cup b^* c^\omega$ et on montre facilement que $b^* c^\omega$ ne peut être l'adhérence d'un langage de mots de Y^*.

.exemple 2 :

$X = \{a\}$; $Y = \{a,b\}$; $\varphi : Y^\infty \longrightarrow X^\infty$ défini par $\varphi(a)=a$, $\varphi(b)=\varepsilon$;

$\forall u \in X^\omega$, posons $\tau(u) = \varphi^{-1}(u)$.

Soit $L=a^*$; $\varphi^{-1}(\mathrm{Adh}L) = \{ u \in Y^\omega \ / \ |u|_a \text{ est infini}\}$ donc $\tau(\mathrm{Adh}L)$ n'est pas l'adhérence d'un langage de mots de Y^* .

Nous étudions maintenant la stabilité de $\mathcal{C}$ par composition :

si τ est une application de X^ω dans $\mathcal{P}(Y^\omega)$ et τ' une application de Y^ω dans $\mathcal{P}(Z^\omega)$ nous notons $\tau' \circ \tau$ la composée de ces deux applications :

$\tau' \circ \tau : X^\omega \longrightarrow \mathcal{P}(Z^\omega)$

$$\forall u \in X^\omega , \quad \tau' \circ \tau(u) = \{ v \in Z^\omega / \ \exists u_1 \in Y^\omega \text{ tel que } u_1 \in \tau(u) \text{ et } v \in \tau'(u_1) \}$$

Nous utilisons les lemmes suivants que l'on établit sans peine :

- LEMME 1 :

Soit $\tau = [\varphi, \psi, \mathrm{AdhK}]$ une application de X^ω dans $\mathcal{P}(Y^\omega)$; il existe un alphabet Z_1 , un rationnel K_1 de Z_1^* , deux morphismes étendus alphabétiques φ_1 et ψ_1 de Z_1^∞ dans X^∞ et dans Y^∞ respectivement tels que : $\tau = [\varphi_1, \psi_1, \mathrm{AdhK}_1]$.

-LEMME 2 :

Soit $\tau = [\varphi, \psi, \mathrm{AdhK}]$ une application de X^ω dans $\mathcal{P}(Y^\omega)$;il existe un alphabet Z_2 , un rationnel K_2 de Z_2^* , deux morphismes étendus φ_2 et ψ_2 de Z_2^∞ dans X^∞ et dans Y^∞ respectivement , avec ψ_2 strictement alphabétique , tels que : $\tau = [\varphi_2, \psi_2, \mathrm{AdhK}_2]$.

-PROPRIETE 2 :

Si τ et τ' sont deux éléments de $\mathcal{C}$, alors $\tau' \circ \tau$ appartient à $\mathcal{C}$.

preuve :

Soit $\tau = [\varphi, \psi, \mathrm{AdhK}]$ avec $\varphi : T^\infty \longrightarrow X^\infty$, $\psi : T^\infty \longrightarrow Y^\infty$ et K rationnel de T^*, et soit $\tau' = [\varphi', \psi', \mathrm{AdhK}']$ avec $\varphi' : V^\infty \longrightarrow Y^\infty$, $\psi' : V^\infty \longrightarrow Z^\infty$ et K' rationnel de V^* . D'aprés les lemmes 1 et 2 , on peut supposer ψ strictement alphabétique et φ' alphabétique .

Soit $U_1 = \{ (t,v) \in T \times V \ / \ \psi(t) = \varphi'(v) \}$

Soit $U_2 = \{ (\varepsilon,v) \,/\, v \in V$ et $\varphi'(v) = \varepsilon \}$; on pose $U = U_1 \cup U_2$

Soit p_1 la première projection de U^∞ sur T^∞ et p_2 la deuxième projection de U^∞ sur V^∞ ; on note k le nombre maximum de lettres consécutives effacées par φ' dans un mot de K' , et on pose :

$$K'' = p_1^{-1}(FG(K)) \cap p_2^{-1}(FG(K')) \cap U_2^{(k)}(U_1U_2^{(k)}) \quad \text{où} \quad U_2^{(k)} = \bigcup_{i=0}^{k} U_2^i$$

on a alors :

$$AdhK'' = p_1^{-1}(AdhK) \cap p_2^{-1}(AdhK') \cap U_2^{(k)}(U_1U_2^{(k)})^\omega .$$

et si l'on pose : $\varphi'' = \varphi \circ p_1$ et $\psi'' = \psi' \circ p_2$, on vérifie sans peine que φ'' et ψ'' sont ε-limités sur K" et que $\tau'' = [\varphi'', \psi'', AdhK''] = \tau' \circ \tau$. □

Si l'on compare la famille $\mathcal{C}$ à la famille des applications séquentielles fidèles on obtient les résultats suivants :

-1- Clairement , la famille des applications séquentielles fidèles est incluse dans $\mathcal{C}$;

-2- Si φ est un morphisme étendu ε-limité sur K , la composée du morphisme inverse φ^{-1} et de l'intersection avec AdhK est une application séquentielle fidèle inverse ;
- d'autre part tout morphisme étendu strictement alphabétique est une application séquentielle fidèle .

-3- En utilisant 1 et 2 et la stabilité de $\mathcal{C}$ par composition et inversion , on en déduit que $\mathcal{C}$ coïncide avec la famille constituée des composées d'une application séquentielle fidèle inverse et d'une application séquentielle fidèle .

II – ADHERENCES ET $\mathcal{C}$ -STABILITE –

Nous étudions dans cette partie la stabilité et la principalité relativement à $\mathcal{C}$, de familles d'adhérences de langages de mots finis .

DEFINITION :

Soit $\mathcal{F}$ une famille de langages de mots infinis .

$\mathcal{F}$ est dite $\mathcal{C}$-stable si et seulement si :

pour tout couple d'alphabets X et Y , pour toute application τ de X^ω dans $\mathcal{P}(Y^\omega)$ appartenant à $\mathcal{C}$, on a :

$$(L \subset X^\omega \text{ et } L \in \mathcal{F}) \Longrightarrow \tau(L) \in \mathcal{F} .$$

La propriété 1 a pour corollaire immédiat :

COROLLAIRE 1 :

Soit $\mathcal{L}$ un cône rationnel de langages de mots finis , stable par passage au centre i.e. : $\forall\ L \in \mathcal{L},\ C(L)$ appartient à $\mathcal{L}$.

La famille Adh$\mathcal{L}$ de langages de mots infinis , définie par :

$$\mathrm{Adh}\mathcal{L} = \{ \mathrm{Adh}L\ ,\ L \in \mathcal{L} \},$$

est $\mathcal{C}$-stable .

Ce résultat nous conduit à nous poser les questions suivantes :

-1- Soit $\mathcal{L}$ une famille de langages de mots finis , constituant un cône rationnel stable par passage au centre , Adh$\mathcal{L}$ est-elle principale relativement à $\mathcal{C}$, i.e existe-t-il un élément AdhL$_0$ de Adh$\mathcal{L}$ vérifiant :

$$\forall\ L \in \mathcal{L},\ \exists\ \tau \in \mathcal{C} \text{ tel que } \tau(\mathrm{Adh}L_0) = \mathrm{Adh}L \quad ?$$

Un tel élément , s'il existe , sera appelé générateur de Adh$\mathcal{L}$.

-2- Si la réponse à la question précédente est positive , quels liens existe-t-il entre les générateurs de Adh$\mathcal{L}$ et les générateurs de $\mathcal{L}$, dans le cas où $\mathcal{L}$ est un cône principal ?

La propriété 1 nous permet d'exhiber une condition suffisante pour que Adh$\mathcal{L}$ soit principale relativement à $\mathcal{C}$:

Soit L un langage de mots finis , nous notons $\Gamma(L)$ l'ensemble des langages qui sont images de L par une transduction rationnelle bifidèle définie au moyen d'un rationnel stable par facteur gauche :

$$\Gamma(L) = \{ \tau(L) \text{ où } \tau = (\varphi, \psi, K) \text{ avec } K = FG(K) \text{ et } \varphi \text{ et } \psi\ \varepsilon\text{-limités sur } K \}$$

COROLLAIRE 2 :

Si $\mathcal{L}$ est un cône rationnel de langages de mots finis , stable par passage au centre et pour lequel il existe un élément $L_\circ$ de $\mathcal{L}$ tel que

$$\{ C(L) , L \in \mathcal{L} \} \subset \Gamma(C(L_\circ))$$

alors $AdhL_\circ$ est un générateur de Adh $\mathcal{L}$.

EXEMPLE :

Examinons le cas où $\mathcal{L}$ est le cône rationnel , ALG , formé des langages algébriques; les résultats suivants ont étés prouvés dans [2] et [4] :

PROPRIETE 3 :

Pour tout langage algébrique L , il existe une application séquentielle fidèle s telle que $AdhL = s(Adh(D_2^*))$

(où D_2^* désigne le langage de Dyck à deux types de parenthèses engendré par la grammaire : $S \longrightarrow \varepsilon + z_1 S \bar{z}_1 S + z_2 S \bar{z}_2 S$) .

PROPRIETE 4 :

Pour tout langage algébrique L , il existe une application séquentielle fidèle s telle que $AdhL = s(AdhE)$

(où E désigne le langage engendré par la grammaire : $S \longrightarrow aSbSc + d$).

Il en résulte donc que la famille Adh(ALG) , qui est $\mathcal{C}$ -stable , est principale relativement à $\mathcal{C}$, admettant pour générateurs : $Adh(D_2^*)$ et AdhE .

D_2^* et E étant des générateurs de ALG , une question se pose :

l'adhérence de tout générateur de ALG est-elle un générateur de Adh(ALG) ?

La réponse négative à cette question est apportée par le fait suivant :

FAIT 1 :

Soit $X = \{a,b,c,d\}$ et $\# \notin X$; on pose $L_1 = X^* \cup C(E)\#^+$

L_1 est un langage central générateur de ALG ;

$Adh(L_1)$ n'est pas un générateur de Adh(ALG) .

D'autre part , C(E) étant générateur de ALG , si la réciproque du corollaire 2 était vraie , tout générateur de Adh(ALG) serait l'adhérence d'un langage algébrique de mots finis dont le centre dominerait C(E) et donc serait générateur de ALG ; or le fait suivant montre que ceci **est faux et donc** que la **réciproque du corollaire** 2 est fausse :

Soit $\mathcal{A}$ l'automate à pile sans états ni ε-transition associé de manière canonique à la grammaire ($S \longrightarrow aSBSC + d$; $B \longrightarrow b$; $C \longrightarrow c$) et qui reconnait E par pile vide . Pour tout h $\in$ FG(E) , on note $\rho(h)$ la hauteur de la pile de $\mathcal{A}$, lorsque $\mathcal{A}$ a lu h ; pour tout f $\in X^*$, on note $\alpha(f)$ le plus long facteur gauche de f qui appartienne à FG(E) ; on pose alors :

$$L_p = \{ f = \alpha(f)g \ / \ \rho(\alpha(f)) \leqslant 2|g| \text{ et } |g| \leqslant 2\,\rho(\alpha(f)) \} .$$

on a : $C(L_p) = C(E)$ et on sait ,[1] , que L_p n'est pas générateur de ALG .

FAIT 2 :

Soit $L_2 = FG(L_p \#^+)$, $Adh(L_2)$ est générateur de Adh(ALG) mais $C(L_2)$ n'est pas générateur de ALG .

L'examen de la famille Adh(ALG) nous fait donc entrevoir que la résolution du problème proposé n'est pas aisée . Les difficultés proviennent des faits suivants , mis en évidence dans les deux exemples précédents : si L et L' sont deux langages de mots finis , il peut exister un élément τ de $\mathcal{C}$ tel que τ(AdhL) = AdhL' sans que C(L) ne domine C(L') et inversement C(L) peut dominer C(L') sans qu'il existe d'élément τ de $\mathcal{C}$ tel que τ(AdhL) = Adh(L') .

Nous allons maintenant étudier une sous famille de $\mathcal{C}$, associée à un langage L de mots finis donné , pour laquelle ces difficultés n'existent pas :

Soit $L \subset X^*$ et $\tau = [\varphi, \psi, \text{AdhK}]$ une application de X^ω dans $\mathcal{P}(Y^\omega)$.

On dit que τ vérifie la condition (C) vis à vis de L si et seulement si :

il existe un entier M tel que , pour tout élément f de C(L) et k de FG(K) vérifiant $\varphi(k) = f$, on a :

$$(\exists g \in X^* \text{ et } k_1 \in Z^* \ / \ |g| \geq M \ , \ fg \in C(L) \ , \ kk_1 \in FG(K) \text{ et } \varphi(kk_1) = fg \ )$$

$$\Downarrow$$

$$(\exists u \in X^\omega \text{ et } l \in Z^\omega \ / \ fu \in \text{AdhL} \ , \ kl \in \text{AdhK} \text{ et } \varphi(kl) = fu \ )$$

La condition (C) vis à vis de L exprime donc le fait que , si f et k sont deux éléments de C(L) et de FG(K) respectivement tels que $\varphi(k) = f$, pour que f ait un prolongement dans l'adhérence de L ayant dans son image réciproque par φ un mot de AdhK qui soit un prolongement de k , il suffit que f ait un prolongement dans C(L) de longueur plus grande que $|f| + M$ ayant , dans son image réciproque par φ , un mot de FG(K) qui soit un prolongement de k .

Nous définissons également une sous-famille de transductions rationnelles de mots finis , attachée à un langage L :

soit $L \subset X^*$ et $\tau = (\varphi, \psi, K)$ une transduction rationnelle bifidèle de X^* dans $\mathcal{P}(Y^*)$; on dit que τ vérifie la condition (CC) vis à vis de L si et seulement si les conditions suivantes sont réalisées :

-1- L'élément $[\varphi, \psi, \text{AdhK}]$ de $\mathcal{C}$ vérifie la condition (C) vis à vis de L

-2- Il existe un entier M tel que pour tout élément f de C(L) et k de FG(K) vérifiant $\varphi(k) = f$ on a :

$$(\exists g \in X^* , \ k_1 \in Z^* / \ |g| \geq M \ , \ fg \in C(L) \ , \ kk_1 \in FG(K) \text{ et } \varphi(kk_1) = fg \ )$$

$$\Downarrow$$

$$(\exists f' \in X^* \text{et } k' \in Z^* \ / \ ff' \in C(L) \ , \ kk' \in K \text{ et } \varphi(kk') = ff' \ ).$$

Nous établissons alors la propriété suivante :

<u>PROPRIETE 5</u> :

Soient $L \subset X^*$ et $L' \subset Y^*$ deux langages de mots finis ; soit $\tau = [\varphi, \psi, \text{AdhK}]$ un élément de $\mathcal{C}$ vérifiant la condition (C) vis à vis de L et tel que $\tau(\text{AdhL}) = \text{Adh}(L')$.

Il existe alors une transduction rationnelle de mots finis bifidèle , $\hat{\tau}$, vérifiant la condition (CC) vis à vis de L et telle que :

$$\hat{\tau}(C(L)) = C(L') .$$

preuve :

Soit $\tau = [\varphi, \psi, \mathrm{AdhK}]$ vérifiant la condition (C) vis à vis de L et tel que $\tau(\mathrm{AdhL}) = \mathrm{Adh}(L')$ .La transduction rationnelle $\hat{\tau}$ est construite comme suit : pour toute lettre z de Z , si $|\psi(z)| = p$, on associe à z,p+1 copies $z_0, z_1, \ldots, z_p$ et on pose $T_z = \{z_0, z_1, \ldots, z_p\}$.

Soit $T = \bigcup_{z \in Z} T_z$ et $V = T \cup Z \cup \bar{Z}$ où $\bar{Z} = \{\bar{z} , z \in Z\}$.

On note $Z_1 = \{z \in Z \,/\, \varphi(z) \neq \varepsilon\}$ et $Z_2 = Z / Z_1$.

Soit χ le morphisme étendu de V^∞ dans Z^∞ défini par :

$\forall z \in Z , \ \chi(z) = z ; \ \forall z_i \in T_z , \ \chi(z_i) = z ; \ \forall \bar{z} \in \bar{Z} , \ \chi(\bar{z}) = z$.

Onpose : $\hat{K} = \chi^{-1}(FG(K)) \cap Z^*T(\bar{Z}_2^*\bar{Z}_1 \ \bar{Z}_2^*)^M$

Les deux morphismes étendus $\hat{\varphi}$, et $\hat{\psi}$ sont définis par :

$\hat{\varphi} = \varphi \circ \chi$

$\hat{\psi} : V^\infty \longrightarrow Y^\infty$: $\forall z \in Z , \ \hat{\psi}(z) = \psi(z) ; \ \forall \bar{z} \in \bar{Z} , \ \hat{\psi}(\bar{z}) = \varepsilon ;$

$\forall z_i \in T_z , \ \hat{\psi}(z_i)$ est le facteur gauche de $\psi(z)$ de longueur i.

Soit $\hat{\tau} = (\hat{\varphi}, \hat{\psi}, \hat{K})$; on vérifie sans peine que $\hat{\varphi}$ et $\hat{\psi}$ sont ε-limités sur $\hat{K}$; les lettres barrées dans les mots de $\hat{K}$ permettant de réaliser un "look ahead" , et τ vérifiant la condition (C) vis à vis de L , on est assuré que : pour tout élément k de $\hat{K}$ tel que $\hat{\varphi}(k) \in C(L)$, si k_1 est le facteur gauche de k appartenant à Z^*T , $\chi(k_1)$ admet un prolongement dans AdhK dont l'image par φ est un mot de AdhL ; ceci assure l'inclusion : $\hat{\tau}(C(L)) \subset C(L')$. L'inclusion inverse , ainsi que le fait que $\hat{\tau}$ vérifie la condition (CC) vis à vis de L , n'offrent pas de difficultés . □

Inversement on a le résultat suivant :

PROPRIETE 6 :

Soient $L \subset X^*$ et $L' \subset Y^*$ deux langages de mots finis ; soit $\tau = (\varphi, \psi, K)$ une transduction rationnelle de mots finis bifidèle telle que $\tau(C(L)) = C(L')$ et vérifiant la condition (CC) vis à vis de L . Si l'on pose $\mu = [\varphi, \psi, \mathrm{AdhK}]$,on a:

-1- $\mu(\mathrm{AdhL}) = \mathrm{Adh}(L')$

-2- μ vérifie la condition (C) vis à vis de L .

preuve :

Le 2 est clair ; l'inclusion $\mathrm{Adh}(L') \subset \mu(\mathrm{AdhL})$ se prouve en remarquant que $\tau(C(L)) \subset \bar{\mu}(C(L))$ où $\bar{\mu} = (\varphi, \psi, FG(K))$; on a donc :

$$\mathrm{Adh}(L') = \mathrm{Adh}(\tau(C(L))) \subset \mathrm{Adh}(\bar{\mu}(C(L))) = \mu(\mathrm{AdhL}) .$$

La condition (CC) vérifiée vis à vis de L par τ assure que tout facteur gauche d'un mot de $\mathrm{AdhK} \cap \varphi^{-1}(\mathrm{AdhL})$ se prolonge en un mot de K dont l'image par φ appartient à C(L) ; ceci permet de prouver l'inclusion inverse: $\mu(\mathrm{AdhL}) \subset \mathrm{Adh}(L')$.□

Ainsi si Adh $\mathcal{L}$ est $\mathcal{C}$-stable , les propriétés 5 et 6 nous permettent de donner une caractérisation d'une sous famille de générateurs de Adh $\mathcal{L}$:

Soit L_0 un élément de $\mathcal{L}$; le langage $\mathrm{Adh}(L_0)$ sera appelé (C)-générateur de Adh $\mathcal{L}$ si et seulement si : $\forall L \in \mathcal{L}$, il existe **un élément** τ de $\mathcal{C}$ vérifiant la condition (C) vis à vis de L_0 tel que $\tau(\mathrm{Adh}(L_0)) = \mathrm{AdhL}$.

De même , si l'on note $C(\mathcal{L})$ la famille de langages : $C(\mathcal{L}) = \{ C(L) , L \in \mathcal{L} \}$

On dira que $C(L_0)$ est un (CC)-générateur de $C(\mathcal{L})$ si et seulement si :

$\forall L \in \mathcal{L}$, il existe une transduction rationnelle τ bifidèle de mots finis vérifiant la condition (CC) vis à vis de L_0 telle que : $\tau(C(L_0)) = C(L)$.

On a alors :

COROLLAIRE 3 :

Soit $\mathcal{L}$ une famille de langages de mots finis , telle que Adh $\mathcal{L}$ soit $\mathcal{C}$ -stable ; les (C)-générateurs de Adh $\mathcal{L}$ coïncident avec les adhérences des (CC)-générateurs de $C(\mathcal{L})$.

Si nous reprenons le cas particulier de ALG , nous obtenons les deux faits suivants:

FAIT 3 :

$\mathrm{Adh}(D_2^*)$ est un (C)-générateur de Adh(ALG)

schéma de la preuve :

Soit L un langage algébrique et G une grammaire engendrant L dont toutes les règles sont de l'une des 4 formes :

-1- $v_i \longrightarrow xv_jv_k$ avec $x \in X$ et $v_i,v_j,v_k \in V$

-2- $v_i \longrightarrow xv_j$ avec $x \in X$ et $v_i,v_j \in V$

-3- $v_i \longrightarrow x$ avec $x \in X$

-4- $v_i \longrightarrow \varepsilon$

(V est l'ensemble des variables , X l'alphabet terminal , et P l'ensemble des productions de la grammaire G).

On note $V_\infty = \{ v \in V \ / \ L(G,v) \text{ est infini} \}$; soit $\overline{V_\infty} = \{ \bar{v} \ , \ v \in V_\infty \}$ et $\bar{G}$ la grammaire $\bar{G} = \langle X, V \cup \overline{V_\infty} \ , \ \bar{P} \rangle$ où $\bar{P} = P \cup P_1$, P_1 étant défini comme suit :

$(\ (v_i \rightarrow xv_jv_k) \in P \ , \ v_j \in V_\infty \ ) \implies (\ \bar{v}_i \rightarrow x\bar{v}_j \ ) \in P_1$

$(\ (v_i \rightarrow xv_jv_k) \in P \ , \ v_k \in V_\infty \ ) \implies (\ \bar{v}_i \rightarrow xv_j\bar{v}_k) \in P_1$

$(\ (v_i \rightarrow xv_j) \in P \ , \ v_j \in V_\infty \ ) \implies (\ \bar{v}_i \rightarrow x\bar{v}_j) \in P_1$

$v_i \in V_\infty \implies (\bar{v}_i \rightarrow \varepsilon \ ) \in P_1$.

On a alors le résultat suivant ([3]) : $C(L(G,v)) = FG(L(\bar{G},\bar{v})) \quad \forall v \in V$;

et donc , si $v_\circ$ est l'axiome de G : $\mathrm{Adh}L = \mathrm{Adh}(L(\bar{G},\bar{v}_\circ))$.

On fait alors à partir de $L(\bar{G},\bar{v}_\circ)$ la construction utilisée en [2] pour prouver que $\mathrm{Adh}(D_2^*)$ est un générateur de Adh(ALG) , et on vérifie sans peine que la condition (C) est satisfaite avec la constante M=0 .

FAIT 4 :

AdhE est un (C)-générateur de Adh(ALG) .

schéma de la preuve :

Soit L un langage algébrique de X^* et $G = \langle X,V,P \rangle$ une grammaire engendrant L dont les règles sont de l'une des trois formes :

-1- $(v \longrightarrow f v_1 v_2 g)$ avec $f , g \in X^+$ et $v_1 , v_2 \in V$

-2- $(v \longrightarrow f v_1 g)$ avec $f , g \in X^+$ et $v_1 \in V$

-3- $(v \longrightarrow f)$ avec $f \in X^+$.

On suppose , en outre , que les variables les plus à droite des membres droits des règles de type 1 ou 2 engendrent un langage infini .

On numérote les règles de G de façon telle que les n_1 premières , $r_1,\dots,r_{n_1}$,sont du premier type , les règles $r_{n_1+1},\dots,r_{n_2}$ sont du second type et les règles $r_{n_2+1},\dots,r_n$ sont du troisième type .

Soit $Z = \{ d, a_i, b_i, c_i,\ i \in [1,n] \}$ et $G' = \langle Z , V , P' \rangle$ où P' est constitué des n éléments $\rho_1, \rho_2, \dots, \rho_n$ définis comme suit :

$\forall k \in [1,n_1]$, si la règle n° k de P est $(v \longrightarrow f v_1 v_2 g)$

alors $\rho_k = (v \longrightarrow a_k v_1 b_k v_2 c_k)$

$\forall k \in [n_1+1 , n_2]$, si la règle n°k de P est $(v \longrightarrow f v_1 g)$

alors $\rho_k = (v \longrightarrow a_k d b_k v_1 c_k)$

$\forall k \in [n_2+1 , n]$, si la règle n° k de P est $(v \longrightarrow f)$

alors $\rho_k = (v \longrightarrow a_k d b_k d c_k)$

La construction d'un élément de $\mathcal{E}$ envoyant AdhE sur AdhL , et vérifiant la condition (C) vis à vis de E , se fait alors comme suit :

-1- Utilisant la correspondance entre les règles (r_i) de G et les règles (ρ_i) de G' , on construit un morphisme ψ de Z^∞ dans X^∞ vérifiant :

si $v_\circ$ est l'axiome de G , $\psi(L(G',v_\circ)) = L$ et $\psi(Adh(L(G',v_\circ)) = AdhL$.

-2- On met en évidence , $\forall v \in V$, l'existence d'un rationnel K_v sur lequel ψ est ε-limité , vérifiant :

$L(G',v) = E_n \cap K_V$ et $Adh(L(G',v)) = AdhE_n \cap AdhK_v$.

où E_n est le langage engendré par la grammaire : $\langle S \longrightarrow \sum_{i=1}^{n} a_i S b_i S c_i + d \rangle$.

-3-On modifie le rationnel $K_{v_\circ}$ de façon à pouvoir mettre en évidence la décomposition sur $\{ a_i E_n b_i , a_i , i \in [1,n] \}$ d'un mot de $AdhE_n \cap Adh(K_{v_\circ})$.

On procède pour cela comme suit :

Soit $T = Z \cup \{ \alpha_i, \beta_i , i \in [1,n_2] \}$

On pose $R = \{ \alpha_i, \alpha_i K_{v(i)} \beta_i , i \in [1,n_1] \} \cup \{ \alpha_i d \beta_i , i \in [n_1+1 , n_2] \}$

où $\forall\, i \in [1,n_1]$ v(i) désigne la première variable du membre droit de ρ_i .

On note H le rationnel local qui contrôle que les consécutions des lettres α_i et β_i , dans R^* , sont les mêmes que les consécutions des lettres a_i et b_i dans K_{v_o} et on pose : $K = R^* \cap H$.

Si χ est le morphisme de T^∞ dans Z^∞ défini par :

$$\chi|_{Z^\infty} = \text{id} \qquad \text{et} \qquad \forall\, i \in [1,n_2] \quad \chi(\alpha_i) = a_i \ , \ \chi(\beta_i) = b_i$$

on vérifie que : $\text{Adh}(L(G',v_o)) = \chi\left[\text{Adh}(M^* \cap H)\right]$

$$\text{où } M = \left\{\alpha_i (K_{v(i)} \cap E_n) \beta_i \ , \ i \in [1,n_1]\right\} \cup \left\{\alpha_i d\, \beta_i , i \in [n_1+1,n_2]\right\}$$

-4- On choisit un morphisme φ de Z^* dans $\{a,b,c,d\}^*$ codant E_n dans E , vérifiant $\varphi^{-1}(E) = E_n$ et $\varphi^{-1}(FG(E)) = FG(E_n)$, ainsi que deux mots $\mathcal{A}$ et $\mathcal{B}$ sur $\{a,b,c,d\}^*$ satisfaisant la propriété (a) suivante :

(a) | Soit f un élément de $(\varphi(Z))^*$; s'il existe un élément u de $\{\mathcal{A} \ , \ \mathcal{A}(\varphi(Z))^* \mathcal{B}\}^*$ tel que u $\mathcal{A} f \mathcal{B} \in FG(E)$ (resp. u $\mathcal{A} f \in FG(E)$) alors $f \in E$ (resp. à FG(E)) .

On définit $\Phi : T^\infty$ dans $\{a,b,c,d\}^\infty$ comme suit :

$$\Phi|_{Z^\infty} = \varphi \qquad \text{et} \qquad \Phi(\alpha_i) = \mathcal{A} \quad \Phi(\beta_i) = \mathcal{B} \ , \forall\, i \in [1,n_2] .$$

On vérifie alors sans peine que : $\Phi^{-1}(\text{AdhE}) \cap \text{AdhK} = \text{Adh}(M^* \cap H)$.

-5- L'élément de $\mathcal{C}$ cherché est le suivant :

$$\tau = \left[\Phi , \Psi = \psi \circ \chi \ , \ \text{AdhK}\right] .$$

De façon claire : $\text{AdhL} = \Psi\left[\Phi^{-1}(\text{AdhE}) \cap \text{AdhK}\right]$

De plus la propriété (a) assure que la condition (C) est satisfaite avec la constante M=0 .

Les deux générateurs classiques , AdhE et $\text{Adh}(D_2^*)$, de Adh(ALG) sont donc des (C)-générateurs , avec une constante M=0 .

Une question se pose : la constante M intervenant dans la condition (C) peut-elle toujours être réduite à 0 ?

La réponse est non :

soit $L_3 = \left\{ a^n b^p \text{ , } p < n \right\} d^+ \cup \left\{ a^n b^n \text{ , } n \in N^+ \right\} d^M c^+$

et $L'_3 = \left\{ a^n b^n \text{ , } n \in N^+ \right\} d^M c^+$

FAIT 5 :

-Il existe $\tau \in \mathscr{C}$ vérifiant la condition (C) avec une constante non nulle telle que $\tau(\text{Adh}(L_3)) = \text{Adh}(L'_3)$.

- On ne peut trouver $\tau' \in \mathscr{C}$ vérifiant la condition (C) avec une constante nulle telle que $\tau'(\text{Adh}(L_3) = \text{Adh}(L'_3)$.

Nous terminons en exhibant dans Adh(ALG) un langage qui est générateur de Adh(ALG), dont le centre est générateur de ALG mais qui n'est pas un (C)-générateur de Adh(ALG) ; ainsi , pour un langage , Adh(L∘) , générateur d'une famille Adh $\mathscr{L}$, être (C)-générateur est donc une condition suffisante mais non nécessaire pour que C(L∘) soit générateur de C($\mathscr{L}$) .

$L_4 = E\#_1^+ \cup L'_p\#_2^+$ où $L'_p = \left\{ f = \alpha(f)g \ / \ |g| \leq \rho(\alpha(f)) \right\}$

(les notations étant celles utilisées dans la définition du langage L_p qui intervient dans L_2)

$C(L_4) = FG(L'_p) \cup E\#_1^+ \cup L'_p\#_2^+$

FAIT 6 :

- ADH(L_4) est un générateur de Adh(ALG) ;
- C(L_4) est générateur de ALG ;
- Adh(L_4) n'est pas un (C)-générateur de Adh(ALG) .

-REFERENCES-

-[1]- Boasson L. , "Un langage algébrique particulier " , publication L.I.T.P n° 78-7 .

-[2]- Boasson L. et Nivat M. , "Adherences of languages " , J. of Comp. Syst. Sciences , vol.20 , No.3 , Juin 1980 , p.285-309 .

-[3]- Gabarro J. , "Index rationnel , centres et langages algébriques " , Thèse de troisième cycle , Juin 1981 , Paris 6 .

-[4]- Latteux M. , "Générateurs algébriques et linéaires " , Acta Informatica 13 , 347-363 (1980) .

-[5]- Nivat M. , "Transductions des langages de Chomsky " , Annales de l'institut Fourier 18 , p. 339-456 .(1968) .

ALGEBRAIC AND OPERATIONAL SEMANTICS OF EXCEPTIONS AND ERRORS

M.Gogolla, K.Drosten, U.Lipeck
Abteilung Informatik, Universität Dortmund
Postfach 500500, D-4600 Dortmund 50

H.D.Ehrich
Lehrstuhl B für Informatik, TU Braunschweig
Postfach 3329, D-3300 Braunschweig

Abstract

The specification of abstract data types requires the possibility to treat exceptions and errors. We present an approach allowing all forms of error handling : error introduction, error propagation and error recovery. The algebraic semantics of our method and a new correctness criterion is given. We also introduce an operational semantics of a subclass of our specifications which coincides with the algebraic semantics.

Key Words

Specification of abstract data types, error and exception handling, algebraic semantics , correctness of specifications , operational semantics.

1. Introduction

Abstract data types offer promising tools for the specification and implementation of programs. Research in this field has been initiated by [Gu 75, LZ 74]. Pleasant features of the method are that it is well-founded algebraically [ADJ 78, Eh 79, EKTWW 81, WPPDB 80] and operationally [Ro 73, Hu 77, O'D 77, Wa 77] and that it is a sound basis for specification languages.
The problem of handling exceptions and errors in abstract data types has been studied in [GHM 77, ADJ 78, Go 78.1, Go 78.2, Ma 79, Bl 80] and an operational treatment has been given in [EPE 81].
We here modify the approach of [EPE 81] and study the algebraic and operational semantics of specifications allowing error and exception handling. We distinguish syntactically between error introducing and normal functions and allow two different types of variables for the same sort. Thus all forms of error and exception handling, i.e. error introduction, error propagation and error recovery, may be treated. We avoid the strict propagation of errors as in [ADJ 78,Go 78.1,Ma 79], the transformation of axioms via new operations as in [ADJ 78] and the introduction of a semi-lattice structure on the set of sorts as in [Go 78.2].
Section 2 gives an informal introduction to our method. In sections 3 and 4 we present the algebraic semantics of our specifications. Section 5 gives a new correctness criterion and section 6 introduces the operational semantics of a subclass of our specifications and shows that it coincides with the algebraic semantics. Because of space limitations, we omit the proofs.

2. The basic idea

The natural numbers are an example of a simple data type, which needs error and exception handling. We are going to use the natural numbers in different versions throughout the paper.

Example 2.1

To specify the natural numbers we need the following functions :

```
    0 : ---> nat
    pred, succ : nat ---> nat
    add, times : nat x nat ---> nat
```

The axioms are given by :

```
    pred(succ(n))=n                           ( 1 )
    pred(0)=error                             ( 2 )
    add(0,n)=n                                ( 3 )
    add(succ(n),m)=succ(add(n,m))             ( 4 )
    times(0,n)=0                              ( 5 )
    times(succ(n),m)=add(times(n,m),n)        ( 6 )
```

But what is the semantics of an axiom like pred(0)=error ? If we treat 'error' as an extra constant in nat, we will find times(0,pred(0)) = times(0,error) = 0 and so the introduced error has been forgotten by axiom (5). This might suggest the idea that errors should propagate and so we could add the following axioms :

```
    succ(error)=error        ( E1 )
    pred(error)=error        ( E2 )
    add(error,n)=error       ( E3 )
    add(n,error)=error       ( E4 )
    times(error,n)=error     ( E5 )
    times(n,error)=error     ( E6 )
```

But unfortunately we didn't really specify what we had intended, because unwanted contradictions occur. 0 = times(0,error) = error holds due to equations (5) and (E6) and so $succ^n(0)$ = error for every $n \in N_0$ due to (E1).

There are other reasons which don't support the idea of strict error propagation. For example consider a straightforward specification of the factorial function on the natural numbers :

```
    fac(n) = if(eq(n,0),succ(0),times(n,fac(pred(n))))
```

With the error propagation idea in mind we will find :

```
    fac(0) = if(eq(0,0),succ(0),times(0,fac(pred(0))))
           = if(true,succ(0),times(0,fac(error)))
           = if(true,succ(0),times(0,error))
           = if(true,succ(0),error) = error                        ***
```

We present an approach which allows all forms of error handling, i.e. error introduction, error propagation and error recovery, to be treated in an easy way and which avoids difficulties like the above. Our main instruments are :

- the partition of the carrier sets into a normal and an error part,
- the syntactical classification of functions into those which introduce errors in normal situations and those which preserve ok states and
- the introduction of two types of variables. The first type will serve for non error situations only, the other for ok and exceptional states as well.

Example 2.2

We give a specification for the intended natural number algebra including an error constant.

```
    0 : ---> nat
    succ : nat ---> nat
    pred : nat ---> nat : unsafe
    add , times : nat x nat ---> nat
    error : ---> nat : unsafe
```

Functions, which might introduce errors and error constants, unsafe functions as we call them, are indicated in the signature by ': unsafe'. The other functions are called ok functions.
The signature gives a classification for all terms t. If an unsafe function occurs in t, it is not known whether an error might be introduced or not and so t is viewed as a possible error and called unsafe term. If only ok functions occur in t, we know t corresponds to a natural number. In this case t is called an ok term.
We mark pred as an unsafe function, because it introduces an error when applied to the ok value 0. For the functions succ, add and times we know that they will return ok values when they are applied to such ones.
The ok part of the intended carrier set are terms of the form $succ^n(0)$ with $n \in N_0$ corresponding to the natural numbers. The error part of the carrier set are terms in which the function symbol 'error' occurs. These terms can be seen as error messages informing about illegal application of pred to 0.
We now use ok variables n and m which means they serve for non error situations only, i.e. only for ok terms. The axioms are exactly (1) - (6) of example 2.1, but there are semantical differences. It is not allowed to substitute for example the term 'error' for variable n in axiom (5) and therefore the difficulties described in example 2.1 do not occur.
Now the following identities hold :

- pred(succ(succ(pred(succ(0))))) = pred(succ(succ(0))) = succ(0)
  Please note it is not allowed to substitute succ(pred(succ(0))) into the ok variable n in axiom (1), but we may substitute the semantically equivalent term succ(0). This will be clarified later.
- times(0,pred(0)) = times(0,error)
  No further simplifications can be made on the last term, because axiom (5) cannot be applied. The term can be seen as an error message within its environment. ***

3. Algebras with ok predicates

In this and the following two sections we show how the results of [ADJ 78] carry over to our notion of algebra. The syntax of our many-sorted algebras with ok predicates is defined via a signature, which gives names corresponding to the sorts of the carrier sets and to the operations on these sets. Our carrier sets are not homogeneous, because we want to distinguish between normal situations and exceptions. For this reason we already mark in the signature those function symbols, which correspond to operations introducing errors in normal situations.

Definition 3.1

A signature (with ok predicate) is a quintupel $(S,\Sigma,arity,sort,ok_\Sigma)$, where

(1) S is a set (of sorts) , Σ is a set (of function symbols) and
(2) arity , sort and ok_Σ are mappings :
$arity : \Sigma \text{ ---> } S^*$, $sort : \Sigma \text{ ---> } S$ and $ok_\Sigma : \Sigma \text{ ---> } BOOL$.

- A signature $(S,\Sigma,arity,sort,ok_\Sigma)$ will often be denoted by Σ only.
- Given a function symbol σ, $arity(\sigma)=s1...sn$ denotes the sorts of the arguments, $sort(\sigma) = s$ gives the result sort. This is written as $\sigma : s1 \times ... \times sn \text{ ---> } s$.

- $ok_\Sigma(\sigma)$=TRUE means σ is an <u>ok function symbol</u>, while $ok_\Sigma(\sigma)$=FALSE indicates an <u>unsafe function symbol</u>. The notion of ok and unsafe functions will be made clear by the following definition.

<u>Definition 3.2</u>

Let signature Σ be given. A <u>Σ-algebra</u> (with ok predicates) is a triple (A,F,ok_A), where

(1) $A=\langle A_s\rangle_{s\varepsilon S}$ is an S-indexed family of sets,

(2) $F=\langle \sigma_A\rangle_{\sigma\varepsilon\Sigma}$ is a Σ-indexed family of functions, for every function symbol σ : s1 × ... × sn ---> s we have a function $\sigma_A : A_{s1} \times \ldots \times A_{sn} \text{ ---> } A_s$ and

(3) $ok_A=\langle ok_s\rangle_{s\varepsilon S}$ is an S-indexed family of predicates, $ok_s : A_s$ ---> BOOL such that

(4) for every function symbol σ : s1 × ... × sn ---> s with $ok_\Sigma(\sigma)$= TRUE and (a1,...,an) ε $A_{s1} \times \ldots \times A_{sn}$ with $ok_{si}(ai)$=TRUE for i=1,...,n, we have $ok_s(\sigma_A(a1,\ldots,an))$=TRUE.

- A Σ-algebra (A,F,ok_A) will often be denoted by A only. Whenever no ambiguity arises, we will omit indices of the predicates : for a function symbol σ ok(σ) means $ok_\Sigma(\sigma)$ and for aεA_s ok(a) means $ok_s(a)$. If ok(σ)=TRUE holds, we call σ_A an <u>ok function</u>, otherwise an <u>unsafe function</u>.
- For aεA_s $ok_s(a)$=TRUE will mean a is an <u>ok element</u> of A_s, otherwise it is called <u>error element</u>. The ok predicates split the carrier sets into an ok part A_{ok} and an error part A_{err}.
  $A_{ok} =\langle A_{ok,s}\rangle_{s\varepsilon S}$, $A_{ok,s}$ = { aεA_s | $ok_s(a)$=TRUE } .
  $A_{err}=\langle A_{err,s}\rangle_{s\varepsilon S}$, $A_{err,s}$= { aεA_s | $ok_s(a)$=FALSE } .
  For the application we have in mind the ok elements correspond to normal situations, while the error elements indicate exceptional states.
- Part (4) of the definition requires that <u>ok functions yield ok values for ok arguments</u>, or in other words, only unsafe functions may introduce errors when applied to normal situations. Because we have to treat these unsafe functions carefully, we already distinguish them syntactically from ok functions. This garantees that whenever an expression consisting only of ok functions is applied to ok arguments, this will result in an ok element. For expressions including unsafe functions this is not known.
- Every algebra with ok predicates can also be interpreted as a conventional <u>algebra without ok predicates</u> by just omitting the predicates. On the other hand every conventional algebra without ok predicates can be made into an algebra with ok predicates by demanding all functions to be ok functions and all elements to be ok elements. The same holds for signatures.

<u>Example 3.3</u>

We describe the <u>natural numbers</u> together with an extra error element, which is introduced because we want to apply the predecessor function to 0. Let S = { bool,nat } be the set of sorts. Unsafe function symbols will be indicated by ': unsafe'.

```
false,true : ---> bool
0 : ---> nat
succ : nat ---> nat
pred : nat ---> nat : unsafe
negative : ---> nat : unsafe
if : bool x nat x nat ---> nat
```

The carrier sets and the ok predicates on them are given by :

$A_{bool} = \{ f , t \}$ $\quad$ $ok_{bool}(b) = TRUE$

$A_{nat} = N_0 + \{ e_{nat} \}$ $\quad$ $ok_{nat}(n) = (n \varepsilon N_0)$

The functions corresponding to the function symbols are defined by :

$false_A : |---> f$ $\quad$ $0_A : |---> 0$

$true_A : |---> t$ $\quad$ $negative_A : |---> e_{nat}$

$$succ_A : n \mid ---> \begin{cases} n+1 & \text{if } n \varepsilon N_0 \\ e_{nat} & \text{if } n = e_{nat} \end{cases}$$

$$pred_A : n \mid ---> \begin{cases} n-1 & \text{if } n \varepsilon N \\ e_{nat} & \text{if } n=0 \text{ or } n = e_{nat} \end{cases}$$

$$if_A : (b, n1, n2) \mid ---> \begin{cases} n1 & \text{if } b=t \\ n2 & \text{if } b=f \end{cases}$$

$pred_A$ is an unsafe function, because only for some ok arguments it yields ok results, for the ok value 0 it returns the error element e_{nat}. ***

For every signature Σ we define the term algebra with ok predicates in the following way.

Definition 3.4

Let signature Σ be given. The Σ-term algebra $(T_\Sigma, F_\Sigma, ok_T)$ is defined by :

(1) (T_Σ, F_Σ) is the usual term algebra. $T_\Sigma = \langle T_s \rangle_{s \varepsilon S}$. $F_\Sigma = \langle \sigma_T \rangle_{\sigma \varepsilon \Sigma}$.

(2) $ok_T = \langle ok_s \rangle_{s \varepsilon S}$. For $t \varepsilon T_s$ ok_s is given by :

$$ok_s(t) = \begin{cases} \text{FALSE} & \text{if an unsafe function symbol occurs in } t \\ \text{TRUE} & \text{otherwise} \end{cases}$$

- A term is an ok term, if and only if all function symbols occurring in the term are ok function symbols.
- Our term algebras are well defined, that means T_Σ is a Σ-algebra with ok predicates satisfying part (4) of definition 3.2.

Example 3.5

Looking at the signature in example 3.3 we find if(true,0,succ(0)) is an ok term and pred(succ(0)), pred(0) or if(true,0,negative) are error elements in the term algebra. ***

Σ-algebras with ok predicates may be compared by structure preserving mappings called Σ-algebra morphisms.

Definition 3.6

Let Σ-algebras $(A1, F1, ok_{A1})$, $(A2, F2, ok_{A2})$ be given. An S-indexed family of functions $h = \langle h_s \rangle_{s \varepsilon S}$, $h_s : A1_s ---> A2_s$ is called Σ-algebra morphism, if

(1) h is a morphism from A1 to A2 taken without ok predicates and

(2) for $s \varepsilon S$ and $a \varepsilon A1_s$ $ok_{A1}(a)$ implies $ok_{A2}(h_s(a))$.

A morphism is called injective respectively surjective, if every h_s is injective respectively surjective.

A morphism is called strict, if for $s \varepsilon S$ and $a \varepsilon A1_s$ $ok_{A1}(a) = ok_{A2}(h_s(a))$.

- Because of the additional predicate structure on signatures and algebras we require in part (2) that no ok element may be mapped onto an error element or in other words that the ok property for elements is preserved by our morphisms.
- The isomorphisms are the injective, surjective and strict morphisms. The strictness property is necessary, because we do not only want the operational structure but also the predicate structure to be respected by isomorphisms.

- h_{ok} and h_{err} denote the restrictions of h to ok and error elements.
  $h_{ok} = \langle h_{ok,s} \rangle_{s \varepsilon S}$, $h_{ok,s} : A1_{ok,s} \dashrightarrow A2_{ok,s}$.
  $h_{err} = \langle h_{err,s} \rangle_{s \varepsilon S}$, $h_{err,s} : A1_{err,s} \dashrightarrow A2_{s}$.
  For strict morphisms we can denote $h_{err,s}$ of course by :
  $h_{err,s} : A1_{err,s} \dashrightarrow A2_{err,s}$.

Example 3.7

The following is an example of a morphism between algebras with ok predicates and a motivation for the freedom of allowing error elements to be mapped to ok elements. We give a morphism from the term algebra of example 3.5 into the algebra of example 3.3. It is the uniquely determined morphism between these algebras taken without ok predicates.

$h_{bool} : T_{bool} \dashrightarrow A_{bool}$
- false |---> f
- true |---> t

$h_{nat} : T_{nat} \dashrightarrow A_{nat}$
- 0 |---> 0
- negative |---> e_{nat}
- succ(t) |---> $succ_A(h_{nat}(t))$
- pred(t) |---> $pred_A(h_{nat}(t))$
- if(b,t1,t2) |---> $if_A(h_{bool}(b), h_{nat}(t1), h_{nat}(t2))$

Obviously, h respects the operations and h preserves ok elements. It sends each term to the result of the corresponding evaluation in A. So succ(succ(0)) will naturally be mapped to 2 and of course the error (or unsafe) terms pred(succ(succ(0))), if(true,0,negative) and pred(0) will result in 1, 0 and e_{nat}, respectively.
The next theorem confirms that this morphism is the only morphism between such algebras, i.e. our term algebras are initial. ***

Theorem 3.8

Let signature Σ, term algebra T_Σ and Σ-algebra A be given. Then there exists a unique morphism $h : T_\Sigma \dashrightarrow A$, or in other words, T_Σ is initial in the class of all Σ-algebras.

4. Specifications

An important difference between our specification technique and the usual algebraic specification without error handling is that we introduce two different types of variables for the same sort. Variables of the first type will serve for the ok part of the corresponding carrier set only, variables of the second type for the whole carrier set.

Definition 4.1

Let signature Σ be given. A pair (V, ok_V) is called a set of variables (with ok predicates) for Σ, if

(1) $V = \langle V_s \rangle_{s \varepsilon S}$ is an S-indexed, pairwise disjoint family of sets (of variables) , each V_s disjoint from Σ and

(2) $ok_V = \langle ok_{V,s} \rangle_{s \varepsilon S}$, $ok_{V,s} : V_s \dashrightarrow BOOL$ is an S-indexed family of predicates.

- Again, a set of variables (V, ok_V) is often denoted by V only.
- When no ambiguity arises, ok(v) means $ok_{V,s}(v)$ for $v \varepsilon V_s$. In analogy to ok and unsafe functions we use the notions of ok and unsafe variables.

Definition 4.2

Let signature Σ, Σ-algebra A and variables V be given. An assignment to (or interpretation of) the variables is an S-indexed family of functions $I=\langle I_s\rangle_{s\in S}$, $I_s : V_s \text{--->} A_s$ such that $ok_{V,s}(v)$ implies $ok_s(I_s(v))$ for $s\in S$ and $v\in V_s$.

- If ok(v)=TRUE holds, it is not allowed to assign an error element to v, ok(v)=FALSE indicates that v may hold ok or error values.

Also, for our notions of algebra and morphism there always exist free algebras.

Lemma 4.3

Let signature Σ, variables V, Σ-algebra A and assignment I : V ---> A be given. Then there exists a Σ-algebra $T_\Sigma(V)$, such that there is a unique Σ-algebra morphism $\underline{I}$: $T_\Sigma(V)$ ---> A, extending I in the sense that $I_s(v)=\underline{I}_s(v)$ for $s\in S$ and $v\in V_s$.

The notions of Σ-equation, of equations satisfied by a Σ-algebra and of congruence relation on an algebra are defined as usual.
But please note, our definition of assignment implies that there is a restriction to the substitution of variables. An equation may be valid although it does not hold for error elements substituted for ok variables.

Example 4.4

Let n, n1+ and n2+ be variables of sort nat with ok(n)=TRUE and ok(n1+)=ok(n2+)=FALSE. Then the algebra of example 3.3 satisfies the following equations (among others).

pred(succ(n))=n	(1)	pred(0)=negative	(2)
if(false,n1+,n2+)=n2+	(3)	if(true,n1+,n2+)=n1+	(4)
succ(negative)=negative	(5)	pred(negative)=negative	(6)

But, for example the equation

succ(pred(n))=n

does not hold, because $succ_A(pred_A(0))=succ_A(e_{nat})=e_{nat}$. ***

Given a Σ-algebra A and a congruence relation $\equiv$ on it, the quotient $A/\equiv$ of A by $\equiv$ can be made into a Σ-algebra with ok predicates by defining the carrier sets and operations in the usual way and by letting a class be ok, if and only if there is an ok element of the algebra in it. In this sense TRUE dominates FALSE with respect to the ok predicate of a class.

Defintion 4.5

Let signature Σ, Σ-algebra A and congruence $\equiv = \langle\equiv_s\rangle_{s\in S}$ be given.

(1) ($A/\equiv$, $F_{A/\equiv}$) denotes the usual quotient of an algebra by a congruence relation on it.

(2) $ok_{A/\equiv}=\langle ok_{\equiv,s}\rangle_{s\in S}$ is an S-indexed family of predicates.

$$ok_{\equiv,s}([a])=\begin{cases}\text{TRUE} & \text{if there is a } b\in[a] \text{ with } ok_{A,s}(b)=\text{TRUE}\\ \text{FALSE} & \text{otherwise}\end{cases}$$

- $(A/\equiv, F_{A/\equiv}, ok_{A/\equiv})$ is a Σ-algebra with ok predicates satisfying part (4) of our definition for algebra.

For a given set of equations E with variables the induced set of constant equations $E(T_\Sigma)$ and the generated least congruence relation denoted by $\equiv_E = \langle \equiv_{E,s} \rangle_{s\in S}$ are defined in the usual way. There always exists such a $\equiv_E$, since we know that there always is a least congruence generated by a given relation, if we deal only with algebras without ok predicates and our congruence definition didn't involve the predicates. For brevity we often denote $\equiv_E$ by $\equiv$ and $a \equiv_{E,s} b$ by $a \equiv b$, if no ambiguities arise.

Example 4.6

If we look at the equations of example 4.4, we find the following pairs are in $E(T_\Sigma)_{nat}$ due to the first equation :

<pred(succ(0)),0>

<pred(succ(succ(0))),succ(0)>

But the following pairs are not in $E(T_\Sigma)_{nat}$:

<pred(succ(negative)),negative>

<pred(succ(pred(succ(0)))),pred(succ(0))>

On the other hand, the last pair is in the congruence relation generated by $E(T_\Sigma)$:

<pred(succ(0)),0> ε $E(T_\Sigma)_{nat}$ ===> pred(succ(0)) $\equiv$ 0 ===>
succ(pred(succ(0))) $\equiv$ succ(0) ===>
pred(succ(pred(succ(0)))) $\equiv$ pred(succ(0)) $\equiv$ 0 ***

The pleasant thing about our approach to error and exception handling is that the fundamental initiality result of [ADJ 78] is still valid.

Theorem 4.7

$T_\Sigma/\equiv_E$ is initial in the class of all Σ-algebras satisfying E, i.e. given a Σ-algebra A, which satisfies E, we have a unique morphism $g : T_\Sigma/\equiv_E \text{ ---> } A$.

Remark

$T_\Sigma/\equiv_E$ is denoted by $T_{\Sigma,E}$ and called the quotient term algebra.

Example 4.8

The quotient of T_Σ in example 3.5 by the equations in example 4.4 is isomorphic to the algebra of natural numbers in example 3.3. ***

We now know that for given signature Σ, variables V and equations E, there always exists an initial Σ-algebra which can be chosen as a standard semantics. So we put together signatures, variables and equations as usual, getting a specification.

Definition 4.9

A specification is a triple (Σ,V,E), where Σ is a signature with ok predicate, V is a set of variables with ok predicates and E is a set of Σ-equations.

5. Correctness of specifications

The usual notion of correctness of specifications - the isomorphism between the specified algebra and the given model - is somewhat too strong for our purpose. Our main interest lies in the ok part of the carrier sets. The cruical point is that terms like succ(error) and pred(error) in example 2.2 are error elements, but it is not important here that they are different. So we allow different error elements of the specified algebra to be identified in our model.

Definition 5.1

Let specification (Σ,V,E) and Σ-algebra A be given. (Σ,V,E) is called correct with respect to A, if

(1) there is a strict morphism $h : T_{\Sigma,E} \text{ ---> } A$ such that
(2) $h_{ok} : T_{\Sigma,E,ok} \text{ ---> } A_{ok}$ is bijective and
(3) $h_{err} : T_{\Sigma,E,err} \text{ ---> } A_{err}$ is surjective.

(Σ,V,E) is strongly correct with respect to A, if it is correct with respect to A and the morphism h is an isomorphism.

- The conventional notion of correctness of specifications for algebras without ok predicates may be embedded into this correctness criterion, because then we only deal with ok functions and ok elements and so $T_{\Sigma,E,err} = A_{err} = \emptyset$.

Example 5.2

We give a correct specification for the algebra A defined in example 3.3. The axioms E are identical to equations (1) - (4) of example 4.4. $T_{\Sigma,E}$ is described by a canonical term algebra using the context-free languages defined by the following productions.

```
<bool>     ::= false | true
<nat>      ::= <nat-ok> | <nat-err>
<nat-ok>   ::= 0 | succ( <nat-ok> )
<nat-err>  ::= negative | succ( <nat-err> ) | pred( <nat-err> )
```

$T_{\Sigma,E,bool}$ = L (<bool>) $ok_{bool}(b)$=TRUE

$T_{\Sigma,E,nat}$ = L (<nat>) $ok_{nat}(n)$=($n\varepsilon$L(<nat-ok>))

The operations in $T_{\Sigma,E}$ are defined in the usual way, e.g.

$$pred_{\Sigma,E} : t \mid\!\!---> \begin{cases} succ^{n-1}(0) & \text{if } t=succ^n(0) \text{ and } n>0 \\ negative & \text{if } t=0 \\ pred(t) & \text{if } t\varepsilon L(\text{<nat-err>}) \end{cases}$$

We now define a mapping h : $T_{\Sigma,E}$ ---> A.

h_{bool} : $T_{\Sigma,E,bool}$ ---> A_{bool}
  true |---> t
  false |---> f

h_{nat} : $T_{\Sigma,E,nat}$ ---> A_{nat}

$$t \mid\!\!---> \begin{cases} n & \text{if } t\varepsilon L(\text{<nat-ok>}),\ t=succ^n(0) \\ e_{nat} & \text{if } t\varepsilon L(\text{<nat-err>}) \end{cases}$$

To prove that h is a strict morphism, we have to show :

(1) $h(\sigma_{\Sigma,E}(a1,...,an))=\sigma_A(h(a1),...,h(an))$ holds for every $\sigma\varepsilon\Sigma$.

(2) $ok_{\Sigma,E}(a)=ok_A(h(a))$ for $s\varepsilon S$ and $a\varepsilon A_s$.

It is easy to see that the mapping h respects the operations. The strictness of h, its bijectivity on the ok part and its surjectivity on the error part can be seen directly from its definition. The specified algebra is correct with respect to the algebra A of example 3.3 , although all error elements are mapped to the one error element in A. If we want to get a strongly correct specification, we have to add equations (5) and (6) of example 4.4. ***

6. Operational semantics of specifications

A set of equations can be viewed as a set of rewrite rules interpreting equations from left to right. By substituting constant terms for the variables we get a set of constant rewrite rules. These rules determine a reduction process on terms which stops if none of the axioms can be applied further. In this way we give an operational semantics for specifications which is well-defined if the set of constant rewrite rules has the finite church-rosser property.

Definition 6.1

Let specification (Σ,V,E) and the set of constant equations $E(T_\Sigma)$ be given.

$-->_E = < -->_s >_{s\varepsilon S}$ is the family of relations on T_Σ defined by :

(1) If $<t,t'> \varepsilon E(T_\Sigma)_s$, then $t -->_s t'$.

(2) If σ : s1 x ... x sn ---> s, $ti\varepsilon T_{si}$ for i = 1,...,n and
j ε { 1,...,n } with $tj -->_{sj} tj'$ are given, then
$\sigma(t1,...,tj,...,tn) -->_s \sigma(t1,...,tj',...,tn)$

$-->^{*}_{E} = < -->^{*}_{s} >_{s\varepsilon S}$ is the reflexive and transitive closure of $-->_{E}$ and called the family of <u>subterm replacements</u> induced by E.
A term t of sort s has the <u>normal form</u> t', if t $-->^{*}_{s}$ t' and there is no t' $-->_{s}$ $\overline{t}$. This is denoted by <u>nf(t)=t'</u>.

<u>Example 6.2</u>
The normal forms of example 5.2 are identical to the elements of the carrier set of the given canonical term algebra. ***

<u>Definition 6.3</u>
$-->^{*}_{E}$ is called <u>finite church-rosser</u>, if every term t of sort s has a normal form, and if t $-->^{*}_{s}$ $\overline{t}$ and t $-->^{*}_{s}$ $\overline{t}'$, then there is a t' with $\overline{t}$ $-->^{*}_{s}$ t' and $\overline{t}'$ $-->^{*}_{s}$ t'.

- If $-->^{*}_{E}$ is finite church-rosser, <u>each term has a unique normal form</u>.

<u>Example 6.4</u>
For the specifications in examples 2.2 and 5.2 the families of subterm replacements $-->^{*}_{E}$ are finite church-rosser. ***

<u>Definition 6.5</u>
Let specification (Σ,V,E) with finite church-rosser $-->^{*}_{E}$ be given. The <u>normal form algebra</u> (NF, F_{NF}, ok_{NF}) is defined by :
(1) $NF = < NF_{s} >_{s\varepsilon S}$. NF_{s} are the normal forms of sort s.
(2) $F_{NF} = < \sigma_{NF} >_{\sigma\varepsilon\Sigma}$. For σ : s1 x ... x sn ---> s and normal forms ti of sort si for i=1,...,n , the function σ_{NF} is given by : $\sigma_{NF}(t1,...,tn) = nf(\sigma(t1,...,tn))$.
(3) $ok_{NF} = < ok_{NF,s} >_{s\varepsilon S}$. For a normal form t of sort s $ok_{NF,s}$ is defined by :

$$ok_{NF,s}(t) = \begin{cases} \text{TRUE} & \text{if there is an ok term t' with nf(t')=t} \\ \text{FALSE} & \text{otherwise} \end{cases}$$

- (NF, F_{NF}, ok_{NF}) is a Σ-algebra with ok predicates satisfying part (4) of our definition for algebra.
- A normal form t is ok in the normal form algebra if and only if there is an ok term t' which has t as its normal from. In this sense the ok terms dominate the error terms, or in other words if an error term is equivalent to an ok term this 'heals' the error term. If the rules are <u>ok term preserving</u>, which means there is no $<t,t'> \varepsilon E(T_{\Sigma})$ with ok(t)=TRUE and ok(t')=FALSE, the ok predicates in the normal form algebra are determined by the normal forms themselves.

<u>Example 6.6</u>
If we compare the normal form algebra and the quotient term algebra of example 5.2, we find they are isomorphic. ***

<u>Theorem 6.7</u>
Let specification (Σ,V,E) with finite church-rosser $-->^{*}_{E}$ be given. Then the quotient term algebra $T_{\Sigma,E}$ and the normal form algebra NF are isomorphic.

<u>Acknowledgements</u>

We thank Udo Pletat and especially Gregor Engels for their earlier work in the field and many fruitful discussions.

References

ADJ 78 Goguen,J.A./Thatcher,J.W./Wagner,E.G. : An Initial Algebra Approach to the Specification, Correctness and Implementation of Abstract Data Types. Current Trends in Programming Methodology, Vol. IV (R.T.Yeh, ed.). Prentice Hall, Englewood Cliffs, 1978, pp. 80-149.

Bl 80 Black,A.P.: Exception Handling and Data Abstraction. IBM Research Report RC 8059, 1980.

Eh 79 Ehrich,H.-D.: On the Theory of Specification, Implementation and Parametrisation of Abstract Data Types. Journal ACM, Vol.29, 1982, pp. 206 - 227.

EKTWW 81 Ehrig,H./Kreowski,H.-J./Thatcher,J.W./Wagner,E.G./Wright,J.B.: Parameter Passing in Algebraic Specification Languages. Proc. Workshop on Algebraic Specification, Aarhus, 1981.

EPE 81 Engels,G./Pletat,U./Ehrich,H.-D.: Handling Errors and Exceptions in the Algebraic Specification of Data Types. Osnabrücker Schriften zur Mathematik, Reihe Informatik, Heft 3, Univ. Osnabrück, 1981.

GDLE 82 Gogolla,M./Drosten,K./Lipeck,U./Ehrich,H.D. : Algebraic and Operational Semantics of Specifications Allowing Exceptions and Errors. Forschungsbericht Nr. 140, Abteilung Informatik, Univ. Dortmund, 1982. [Long Version of this Paper including the Proofs].

GHM 77 Guttag,J.V./Horowitz,E./Musser,D.R.: Some Extensions to Algebraic Specifications. SIGPLAN Notices, Vol. 12, No. 3, March 1977, pp. 63-67.

Go 78.1 Goguen,J.A.: Abstract Errors for Abstract Data Types. Proc. Conf. on Formal Description of Programming Concepts (E.J. Neuhold, ed.), North-Holland, Amsterdam, 1978.

Go 78.2 Goguen,J.A.: Order Sorted Algebras : Exception and Error sorts, Coercions and Overloaded Operators. Semantics and Theory of Computation Report No. 14, University of California, Los Angeles, Dec. 1978.

Gu 75 Guttag,J.V.: The Specification and Application to Programming of Abstract Data Types. Techn. Report CSRG-59, Univ. of Toronto, 1975.

Hu 77 Huet,G.: Confluent Reductions: Abstract Properties and Applications to Term Rewriting Systems. Proc. 18th IEEE Symp. on Foundations of Computer Science, 1977, pp. 30-45.

LZ 74 Liskov,B./Zilles,S.: Programming with Abstract Data Types. SIGPLAN Notices Vol. 9, No. 4, April 1974, pp. 50-59.

Ma 79 Majster,M.E.: Treatment of Partial Operations in the Algebraic Specification Technique. Proc. Specifications of Reliable Software, IEEE, 1979, pp. 190-197.

O'D 77 O'Donnell,M.J.: Computing in Systems Described by Equations. LNCS 58, Springer Verlag, New York, 1977.

Ro 73 Rosen, B.K. : Tree-Manipulating Systems and Church-Rosser Theorems. Journal ACM, Vol. 20, 1973, pp. 160-187.

Wa 77 Wand,M.: Algebraic Theories and Tree Rewriting Systems. Technical Report No. 66, Indiana Univ., Bloomington, Indiana, July 1977.

WPPDB 80 Wirsing,M. / Pepper,P. / Partsch,H. / Dosch,W./ Broy,M. : On Hierachies of Abstract Data Types. Bericht TUM-I8007,Institut für Informatik, Technische Univ. München, Mai 1980.

THE EXPECTED NUMBER OF NODES AND LEAVES AT LEVEL K IN ORDERED TREES

R. Kemp
Johann Wolfgang Goethe-Universität
Fachbereich Informatik (20)
D-6000 Frankfurt a. M.

Abstract. In this paper the average number of nodes (nodes of degree t) appearing at some level k in a n-node ordered tree is computed. Exact enumeration formulae for the number of all n-node trees with r nodes (r nodes of degree t) at level k are derived. Assuming all n-node trees to be equally likely, it is shown that the expected number $n_1(n,k)$ of nodes ($n_1^{(t)}(n,k)$ of nodes of degree t) at level k is given by

$$n_1(n,k) = n\,\frac{2k-1}{2n-1}\binom{2n-1}{n-k}\Big/\binom{2n-2}{n-1}$$

and

$$n_1^{(t)}(n,k) = n\,\frac{2k+t-2}{2n-t-2}\binom{2n-t-2}{n-t-k}\Big/\binom{2n-2}{n-1}\,.$$

Furthermore, asymptotic equivalents for these expected values and exact expressions for the higher moments about the origin are computed.

I. Introduction

The knowledge of the average shape of trees can be carried over to Computer Science, because the performance of several algorithms can be described by trees [5]. Furthermore, there are many one-to-one correspondences between ordered trees and other mathematical objects, such as ballot sequences, random walks, binary trees or Dyckwords. This paper deals with the expected number of nodes and the expected number of nodes of degree t at some level k in ordered trees. The number of nodes at some level k plays a part in problems dealing with search trees, path length, parallel evaluation of expressions or generally with tree-structured deterministic models of processor scheduling.
In [6] there is given a general approach to the computation of the expected number of nodes at some level k for simply generated families of trees. This method does not work in the case of the average number of nodes of degree t at level k; furthermore, it does not give any approach to enumeration results. Therefore, the methods given in this paper are different from those in [6]; on the other hand, they work only in the case of ordered trees or certain subclasses of ordered trees which can be described by "context-free schemes".
Before we present some enumeration results, let us give some basic definitions. An *ordered tree* T is a rooted tree which has been embedded in

the plane so that the relative order of subtrees at each branch is part of its structure. The *level of a node* x appearing in T is the number of nodes on the simple path from the root to node x including the root and node x. The *degree* of a node x is the number of all subtrees of T with root x. The *height* of an ordered tree T is the maximum level of a node appearing in T. The tree has a *height of order r*, $r \in \mathbb{N}$, if there are exactly r nodes in T with maximum level.

II. Enumeration Results

Let t(n) be the number of all ordered trees with n nodes. It is well-known ([5]) that t(n) is the Catalan number

$$t(n) = \frac{1}{n}\binom{2n-2}{n-1} \tag{1}$$

and that the ordinary generating function C(z) is given by

$$C(z) = \sum_{n\geq 1} t(n)z^n = \tfrac{1}{2}(1 - \sqrt{1-4z}). \tag{2}$$

Note that $C^2(z)-C(z)+z=0$. The Taylor coefficients of the powers of C(z) are also well-known ([7]). We have in general

$$C^m(z) = \sum_{\mu\geq 0}\left[\binom{2\mu+m-1}{\mu} - \binom{2\mu+m-1}{\mu-1}\right]z^{\mu+m} \ , \ m\geq 1. \tag{3}$$

It is not hard to see that the coefficient of z^n in the expansion of $zC^m(z)$ can be interpreted as the number $t_m(n)$ of all n-node ordered trees with a root of degree m ([3]).

Now let Q(n,k,r) be the number of all ordered trees with n nodes and a height k of order r. In [4] there is shown that the ordinary generating function of the numbers Q(n,k,r) is given by $(r\geq 1)$

$$Q_{k,r}(z) = \sum_{n\geq 1} Q(n,k,r)z^n = A_{k-1}^{r-1}(z)\left[A_{k-1}^2(z) - A_{k-1}(z) + z\right], \tag{4}$$

where $A_k(z) = \sum_{n\geq 0} A(n,k)z^n$ is the ordinary generating function of the numbers A(n,k) of all ordered trees with n nodes and height less than or equal to k. An explicit expression for $A_k(z)$ is computed in [2]; there is shown that

$$A_k(z) = 2z\,\frac{(1+u)^k - (1-u)^k}{(1+u)^{k+1} - (1-u)^{k+1}} \ , \ u = \sqrt{1-4z} \ , \ k\geq 0, \tag{5}$$

which is the solution of the recurrence

$$A_0(z) = 0, \quad A_k(z) = z/(1-A_{k-1}(z)), \ k\geq 1. \tag{6}$$

Note that $A_k(z)$ is the k-th approximant of the continued fraction

$$C(z) = \frac{z|}{|1} + \frac{-z|}{|1} + \frac{-z|}{|1} + \frac{-z|}{|1} + \ldots \ ; \tag{7}$$

solving the linear recurrences induced for the numerator and denominator of the k-th approximant, we find $A_k(z) = z\,P_k(z)/P_{k+1}(z)$, where

$$P_k(z) = 2^{-k}u^{-1}\left[(1+u)^k - (1-u)^k\right]. \tag{8}$$

The polynomials $P_k(z)$ are related to the Chebyshev polynomials $U_{k-1}(z)$ of the second kind by $P_k(z) = z^{k/2}U_k(2^{-1}z^{-1/2})$.

Let us now study the numbers $N_t(n,k,r)$ and $N(n,k,r)$ of all n-node ordered trees with r nodes of degree t at level k and r nodes at level k, respectively. For this purpose, let

$$N_{k,r}^{(t)}(z) = \sum_{n\geq 1} N_t(n,k,r)z^n$$

and

$$N_{k,r}(z) = \sum_{n\geq 1} N(n,k,r)z^n$$

are the corresponding ordinary generating functions of these numbers. We prove the following

<u>Lemma 1.</u>

(a) $N_{k,0}(z) = A_{k-1}(z),\ k\geq 1$

$$N_{k,r}(z) = z^{-r}\left[A_{k-1}^2(z) - A_{k-1}(z) + z\right] A_{k-1}^{r-1}(z)\ C^r(z),\ r\geq 1,\ k\geq 1.$$

(b) $N_{k,0}^{(t)}(z) = A_{k-1}(z),\ k\geq 1,\ t\geq 0$

$$N_{k,r}^{(t)}(z) = \frac{\left[A_{k-1}^2(z) - A_{k-1}(z) + z\right] A_{k-1}^{r-1}(z)\ C^{tr}(z)}{\left[1 - z^{-1}A_{k-1}(z)\{C(z)-zC^t(z)\}\right]^{r+1}},\ r\geq 1,\ k\geq 1, t\geq 0.$$

Proof. Obviously, the number of all n-node trees with no node at level k is equal to the number of all trees with n nodes and height less than k. Hence $N_{k,0}(z)=N_{k,0}^{(t)}(z)=A_{k-1}(z)$. Next let us consider the cases $r\geq 1$.

(a) We obtain the number of all n-node ordered trees with r nodes at level k by

(i) taking a tree with height k of order r (giving the contribution $Q_{k,r}(z)$)

and by

(ii) attaching r ordered trees to the nodes appearing at level k (giving the contribution $\{z^{-1}C(z)\}^r$).

Therefore, $N_{k,r}(z)=z^{-r}Q_{k,r}(z)C^r(z)$. An application of (4) leads to part (a) of our lemma.

(b) We obtain the number of all n-node ordered trees with λ nodes at level k, where r of these nodes have the degree t, by

(i) taking a tree with height k of order λ (giving the contribution $Q_{k,\lambda}(z)$)

and by

(ii) choosing r of the λ nodes appearing at level k (giving the contribution $\binom{\lambda}{r}$)

and by

(ii1) attaching ordered trees with a root of degree t to these r nodes (giving the contribution $[z^{-1}\{zC^t(z)\}]^r$) and

(ii2) attaching ordered trees with a root of degree unequal to t to the remaining $(\lambda-r)$ nodes (giving the contribution $[z^{-1}\{C(z)-zC^t(z)\}]^{\lambda-r}$).

Hence by (4)

$$N^{(t)}_{k,r}(z) = \sum_{\lambda\geq 0}\binom{\lambda}{r} Q_{k,\lambda}(z)\ C^{tr}(z)\ [z^{-1}\{C(z)-zC^t(z)\}]^{\lambda-r}$$
$$= \left[A^2_{k-1}(z)-A_{k-1}(z)+z\right]\ C^{tr}(z)\ A^{r-1}_{k-1}(z)\ \times$$
$$\times\ \sum_{\lambda\geq 0}\binom{\lambda+r}{r}\ [z^{-1}A_{k-1}(z)\{C(z)-zC^t(z)\}]^{\lambda}\ .$$

In general, we have $\sum_{\lambda\geq 0}\binom{\lambda+r}{r} z^{\lambda} = (1-z)^{-r-1}$. Using this relation, we find immediately the expression for $N^{(t)}_{k,r}(z)$ given in part (b) of our lemma. This completes the proof. □

The results of Lemma 1 can also be derived by an alternative, more elegant method. A *context-free scheme* G is a 4-tuple $G=(N,T,P,S)$, where N and T are countable disjoint sets of *nonterminals* and *terminals*, respectively; $S\in N$ is the *start symbol* and P is a countable subset of $N\times(N\cup T)^*$, the set of *productions*. Note that context-free schemes are a generalization of context-free grammars; the notions "derivation", "generated language", "unambiguous scheme" etc. are defined as in the case of context-free grammars. It is well-known ([8]) that the productions of a context-free grammar $G=(N,T,P,X_1)$ with $N=\{X_1,X_2,\ldots,X_n\}$ define a system E_G of formal equations given by

$$X_i = \sum_{(X_i,u)\in P} u \in \mathbb{N}_0\langle(N\cup T)^*\rangle\quad ,\ 1\leq i\leq n,$$

where $\mathbb{N}_0\langle(N\cup T)^*\rangle$ is the subsemiring of all polynomials in the semiring $\mathbb{N}_0\langle\langle(N\cup T)^*\rangle\rangle$ of all formal power series with variables in $(N\cup T)$ and coefficients in $\mathbb{N}_0$. If G has no ε-rules and no chain rules, then the system E_G has exactly one solution $\vec{\sigma} = (\sigma(X_1),\ldots,\sigma(X_n))\in[\mathbb{N}_0\langle\langle T^*\rangle\rangle]^n$ satisfying the condition that the coefficient $(\sigma(X_i),\varepsilon)$ of the empty word ε is zero, $1\leq i\leq n$; the solution $\vec{\sigma}$ is obtained by successive approximations. The set of all words $w\in T^+$ appearing in $\sigma(X_i)$ with a coefficient $(\sigma(X_i),w)\neq 0$ is identical to the set L_i of all words $w\in T^+$ which can be derived from X_i by means of the productions of G, $1\leq i\leq n$. Furthermore, if G is *unambiguous*, then all coefficients appearing in $\sigma(X_i)$ are zero or one, $1\leq i\leq n$. In this case, substituting the characteristic series $car(L_i) = \sum_{w\in L_i} w$ for each occurence of $X_i\in N$, $1\leq i\leq n$, in the set of equation E_G, we get a set of identities in the corresponding semiring $\mathbb{N}_0\langle\langle T^*\rangle\rangle$. It is easy to see that all these relations are also valid in the case of context-free schemes.

Now let $N=\{X_i\,|\,i\geq 0\}$ and $T=\{g_{i,j}\,|\,i\geq 0\wedge j\geq 1\}$ are two disjoint sets and let

L be the set of all words w which can be derived from X_0 using the following unambiguous context-free scheme $G=(N,T,P,X_0)$, where

$$P = \{X_i \to g_{0,i+1} \mid i \geq 0\} \cup \{X_i \to g_{\lambda,i+1} \underbrace{X_{i+1} X_{i+1} \dots X_{i+1}}_{\lambda\text{-times}} \mid i \geq 0\}.$$

It is not hard to see that each $w \in L \cap T^n$ is a coding of an ordered tree T with n nodes. T is essentially the tree structure induced be the derivation tree of w. For example, Figure 1 shows an ordered tree with 18 nodes together with the corresponding word $w \in L \cap T^{18}$. The broken line is not part of the tree; it only designates the root. Obviously, each $g_{i,j}$ appearing in $w \in L \cap T^n$ corresponds to a node of degree i at level j.

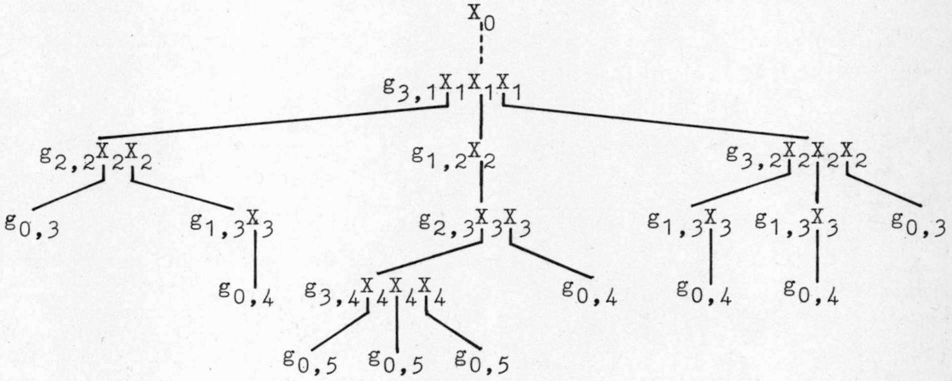

w =

$g_{3,1}g_{2,2}g_{0,3}g_{1,3}g_{0,4}g_{1,2}g_{2,3}g_{3,4}g_{0,5}g_{0,5}g_{0,5}g_{0,4}g_{3,2}g_{1,3}g_{0,4}g_{1,3}g_{0,4}g_{0,3}$

Fig.1: The representation of an ordered tree by the word $w \in L$.

The above scheme induces the formal equations

$$X_i = g_{0,i+1} + \sum_{\lambda \geq 1} g_{\lambda,i+1} \underbrace{X_{i+1} X_{i+1} \dots X_{i+1}}_{\lambda\text{-times}}, \quad i=0,1,2,3,\dots$$

Let now $k \in \mathbb{N}$, $t \in \mathbb{N}_0$ and Θ be the homomorphism defined by

$$\Theta(g_{\lambda,i}) = \begin{cases} z & \text{if } \lambda \in \mathbb{N}_0 \setminus \{t\} \wedge i \in \mathbb{N} \setminus \{k\} \\ zy & \text{if } \lambda = t \wedge i = k \end{cases}.$$

Hence

$$\Theta(\mathrm{car}(L)) = \Theta\Big(\sum_{w \in L} w\Big) = \sum_{w \in L} \Theta(w) = \sum_{n \geq 1} \sum_{w \in L \cap T^n} \Theta(w) =$$

$$= \sum_{n \geq 1} \sum_{w \in L \cap T^n} z^n y^{m(w)}$$

where m(w) is the number of occurences of $g_{t,k}$ in w, i.e. the number of nodes of degree t at level k appearing in the ordered tree encoded by w.

Thus

$$\Theta(\mathrm{car}(L)) = \sum_{n \geq 1} \sum_{r \geq 0} N_t(n,k,r) z^n y^r .$$

Since G is unambiguous, $X_0=\mathrm{car}(L)$ is the solution for the variable X_0 appearing in the above system of equations. Taking the image, these equations imply

$$\Theta(X_i) = \sum_{\lambda\geq 0} \Theta(g_{\lambda,i+1})\ \Theta(X_{i+1})^{\lambda} = z/[1 - \Theta(X_{i+1})]$$

for $0\leq i\leq k-2$ or $i\geq k$ and

$$\Theta(X_{k-1}) = \sum_{\lambda\geq 0} \Theta(g_{\lambda,k})\ \Theta(X_k)^{\lambda} = zy\ \Theta(X_k)^t + z \sum_{\substack{\lambda\geq 0\\ \lambda\neq t}} \Theta(X_k)^{\lambda} =$$

$$= z(y-1)\ \Theta(X_k)^t + z/[1 - \Theta(X_k)]\ .$$

Obviously, by (7)

$$\Theta(X_i) = \frac{z|}{|1} + \frac{-z|}{|1} + \frac{-z|}{|1} + \frac{-z|}{|1} + \dots = C(z)$$

for $i\geq k$. Hence

$$\Theta(X_{k-1}) = z(y-1)\ C^t(z) + z/[1 - C(z)] = z(y-1)\ C^t(z) + C(z).$$

Therefore,

$$\Theta(X_0) = \underbrace{\frac{z|}{|1} + \frac{-z|}{|1} + \frac{-z|}{|1} + \frac{-z|}{|1} + \dots + \frac{-z|}{|1}}_{(k-1)\text{-times}} + \frac{-\Theta(X_{k-1})|}{|1}\ .$$

An inspection of (7) and (8) shows that the (k-1)-th approximant of this continued fraction is $A_{k-1}(z)=zP_k(z)/P_{k+1}(z)$. Using the linear recurrences induced for the numerator and denominator of the k-th approximant, we find $\Theta(X_0) = Q_k(z)/H_k(z)$, where $Q_k(z)=zP_k(z)-z\Theta(X_{k-1})P_{k-1}(z)$ and $H_k(z)= P_{k+1}(z)-\Theta(X_{k-1})P_k(z)$. Hence

$$\Theta(X_0) = A_{k-1}(z)\ \frac{1 - z^{-1}\ [z(y-1)C^t(z)+C(z)]\ A_{k-2}(z)}{1 - z^{-1}\ [z(y-1)C^t(z)+C(z)]\ A_{k-1}(z)}\ . \tag{9}$$

An elementary computation shows that the coefficient of y^r in the expansion of $\Theta(X_0)$ is identical to $N_{k,r}^{(t)}(z)$ given in part (b) of our Lemma 1. Choosing the homomorphism

$$\Psi(g_{\lambda,i}) = \begin{cases} z & \text{if } i\in \mathbb{N}\setminus\{k\} \\ zy & \text{if } i=k \end{cases}\ ,$$

the same technique leads to an expression for the double generating function of the numbers $N(n,k,r)$; we find

$$\Psi(X_0) = \sum_{n\geq 1}\ \sum_{r\geq 0} N(n,k,r)z^n y^r$$

$$= A_{k-1}(z)\ \frac{1 - z^{-1}yC(z)A_{k-2}(z)}{1 - z^{-1}yC(z)A_{k-1}(z)}\ . \tag{10}$$

It should be obvious that similar results for certain subclasses of ordered trees can be derived in the same way; we have only to change the homomorphism and/or the context-free scheme G.

The following theorem presents explicit expressions for the numbers $N_t(n,k,r)$ and $N(n,k,r)$. The abbreviation $<z^n>f(z)$ denotes the coefficient in the expansion of $f(z)$.

Theorem 1.

(a) $N(n,k,0) = \langle v^n\rangle \left[v(1-v)(1+v)^{2n-2}(1-v^{k-1})/(1-v^k)\right]$

$$t(n) - \sum_{\lambda\geq 1}\left[\binom{2n-2}{n-2-\lambda k} - 2\binom{2n-2}{n-1-\lambda k} + \binom{2n-2}{n-\lambda k}\right]$$

and for $r\geq 1$

$$N(n,k,r) = \langle v^n\rangle\left[v^{k+r-1}(1-v)^3(1+v)^{2n-2}(1-v^{k-1})^{r-1}/(1-v^k)^{r+1}\right]$$

$$= \sum_{\lambda\geq 0}\sum_{i\geq 0}\binom{r+\lambda}{r}\binom{r-1}{i}(-1)^{r-i-1}\times$$

$$\times\left[T_0(\lambda,i)-3T_1(\lambda,i)+3T_2(\lambda,i)-T_3(\lambda,i)\right],$$

where $T_a(\lambda,i)=\binom{2n-2}{n-k(r+\lambda-i)-i-a}$.

(b) $N_t(n,k,0) = N(n,k,0)$

and for $r\geq 1$

$$N_t(n,k,r) = \langle v^n\rangle\left[v^{k+r(t+1)-1}(1-v)^3(1-v^{k-1})^{r-1}(1+v)^{2n-1+t}\times\right.$$

$$\left.\times\{(1-v)(1+v)^{t+1}+v^{t+1}(1-v^{k-1})\}^{-r-1}\right]$$

$$= \sum_{\lambda\geq 0}\sum_{s\geq 0}\sum_{j\geq 0}\binom{r+\lambda}{r}\binom{r+\lambda+s}{s}\binom{\lambda+r-1}{j}(-1)^{r-j-1}\times$$

$$\times\left[R_0(\lambda,s,j)-3R_1(\lambda,s,j)+3R_2(\lambda,s,j)-R_3(\lambda,s,j)\right],$$

where $R_a(\lambda,s,j)=\binom{2n-2-r-t(r+\lambda)-\lambda}{n-k(\lambda-j+r)-t(r+\lambda)-s-j-a}$.

Proof. By Lemma 1, $N_{k,0}(z)=N_{k,0}^{(t)}(z)=A_{k-1}(z)$. The expression for $N(n,k,0)=N_t(n,k,0)=A(n,k)$ is computed in [2].

The substitution $z:=v/(1+v)^2$ yields by (2), (5) and part (a) of Lemma 1

$$N_{k,r}(z) = v^{k+r-1}(1-v)^2(1-v^{k-1})^{r-1}/[(1+v)(1-v^k)^{r+1}],\ r\geq 1,\ k\geq 1. \quad (11)$$

Hence

$$N(n,k,r) = \frac{1}{2\pi i}\int^{(0_+)}\frac{dz}{z^{n+1}}N_{k,r}(z) = \frac{1}{2\pi i}\int^{(0_+)}\frac{dv}{v^{n+1}}f(v),$$

where $f(v) = v^{k+r-1}(1-v)^3(1+v)^{2n-2}(1-v^{k-1})^{r-1}/(1-v^k)^{r+1}$. In other words, $N(n,k,r)=\langle v^n\rangle f(v)$. Using the binomial theorem and the expansion of $(1-z)^{-r-1}$, we get our explicit expression for $N(n,k,r)$ by an elementary computation. The result given in part (b) can be proved in an analogous way. □

III. The average number of nodes (of degree t) at level k

Assuming that all n-node ordered trees are equally likely, this section is devoted to the computation of the average number of nodes (of degree t) appearing at level k.

Theorem 2.

Let $s\in\mathbb{N}$ *and assume that all n-node ordered trees are equally likely.*

(a) The s-th moments about the origin $n_s(n,k)$ of the random variable which takes the value r with probability $t^{-1}(n)N(n,k,r)$ is given by

$$n_s(n,k) = t^{-1}(n) \sum_{1\leq j\leq s} \sum_{\lambda\geq 0} \sum_{p\geq 0} \sum_{\nu\geq 0} \binom{\lambda+s-3}{\lambda}\binom{s-j}{p}\binom{j-1}{\nu} (-1)^{s-p-\nu-1} \times$$
$$\times \binom{2n-2}{n-\nu-k(s-p-\nu)-\lambda} B(s,j) ,$$

where the $B(s,j)$ are the Eulerian numbers.

(b) The s-th moments about the origin $n_s^{(t)}(n,k)$ of the random variable which takes the value r with probability $t^{-1}(n)N_t(n,k,r)$ is given by

$$n_s^{(t)}(n,k) = t^{-1}(n) \sum_{1\leq j\leq s} \sum_{\lambda\geq 0} \sum_{p\geq 0} \sum_{\nu\geq 0} \binom{\lambda+s-p-3}{\lambda}\binom{s-j}{p}\binom{s-p-1}{\nu} \times$$
$$\times (-1)^{s-p-\nu-1} \binom{2n-2-(t+1)(s-p)}{n-t(s-p)-k(s-p-\nu)-\nu-\lambda} B(s,j),$$

where the $B(s,j)$ are the Eulerian numbers.

Proof.

(a) We have by definition

$$n_s(n,k) = t^{-1}(n) \sum_{r\geq 1} r^s N(n,k,r). \tag{12}$$

Let now

$$M_{s,k}(z) = \sum_{n\geq 1} n_s(n,k)\ t(n)\ z^n$$

be the ordinary generating function of the numbers $n_s(n,k)t(n)$. We obtain with Lemma 1(a), (11) and (12)

$$M_{s,k}(z) = \sum_{r\geq 1} r^s N_{k,r}(z) = \frac{v^{k-1}(1-v)^2}{(1+v)(1-v^{k-1})(1-v^k)} \sum_{r\geq 1} r^s \left[\frac{v(1-v^{k-1})}{1-v^k}\right]^r .$$

Using the general identity ([1])

$$\sum_{r\geq 0} r^s\ u^r = (1-u)^{-s-1}\ B_s(u),$$

where $B_s(u)$ is the s-th Eulerian polynomial, we get further

$$M_{s,k}(z) = \frac{v^{k-1}(1-v^k)^s}{(1+v)(1-v)^{s-1}(1-v^{k-1})}\ B_s(v\ \frac{1-v^{k-1}}{1-v^k}) .$$

Thus

$$n_s(n,k)\ t(n) = \frac{1}{2\pi i} \int^{(0_+)} \frac{dz}{z^{n+1}} M_{s,k}(z) = \frac{1}{2\pi i} \int^{(0_+)} \frac{dv}{v^{n+1}} f(v) ,$$

where $f(v) = v^{k-1}(1-v^k)^s(1+v)^{2n-2}B_s(v\ \frac{1-v^{k-1}}{1-v^k}) / [(1-v)^{s-2}(1-v^{k-1})]$.

Hence $n_s(n,k)\ t(n) = \langle v^n\rangle f(v)$. Since $B_s(x) = \sum_{1\leq j\leq s} B(s,j)\ x^j$, where the $B(s,j)$ are the Eulerian numbers, we find

$$n_s(n,k)\ t(n) = \langle v^n\rangle \sum_{1\leq j\leq s} B(s,j)v^{k+j-1}(1-v^k)^{s-j}(1-v^{k-1})^{j-1} \times$$
$$\times (1+v)^{2n-2}/(1-v)^{s-2} .$$

An application of the binomial theorem leads to the result given in part (a). The expression for $n_s^{(t)}(n,k)$ can be derived in an analogous way. □

Choosing s=1 and s=2, Theorem 2 implies the following

Corollary 1.

Assuming that all n-node trees are equally likely, the average number of nodes appearing at level k is given by

$$n_1(n,k) = n \frac{2k-1}{2n-1} \binom{2n-1}{n-k} \Big/ \binom{2n-2}{n-1} .$$

The average number of nodes of degree t at level k is

$$n_1^{(t)}(n,k) = n \frac{2k+t-2}{2n-t-2} \binom{2n-t-2}{n-t-k} \Big/ \binom{2n-2}{n-1} .$$

The second moments about the origin are

$$n_2(n,k) = n \left[\binom{2n-1}{n-k} - 2\binom{2n-2}{n-2k}\right] \Big/ \binom{2n-2}{n-1}$$

and

$$n_2^{(t)}(n,k) = n \left[\binom{2n-t-3}{n-t-k} - \binom{2n-t-3}{n-k-t-1} + 2\binom{2n-2t-4}{n-2t-k-1} - 2\binom{2n-2t-4}{n-2t-2k}\right] \Big/ \binom{2n-2}{n-1} .$$

□

The numbers $n_1(n,k)$ are also computed in [6] by a different method. Note that $n_1^{(0)}(n,k)$ is the average number number of leaves appearing at level k in a n-node ordered tree. Since there is only the root at level k=1, $n_1^{(t)}(n,1)$ is equal to the probability that an ordered tree with n nodes is a t-tuply rooted tree ([4]).

It is not hard to see that the sequences $n_1^{(t)}(n,k)$ and $n_1(n,k)$ are unimodal: we have $n_1(n,k+1) \geq n_1(n,k)$ for $k \leq \lfloor\sqrt{n/2}\rfloor$ and $n_1(n,k+1) \leq n_1(n,k)$ for $k \geq \lfloor\sqrt{n/2}\rfloor$; similarly, $n_1^{(t)}(n,k+1) \geq n_1^{(t)}(n,k)$ for $k \leq \lfloor(1-t)/2 + \sqrt{n/2-(t+1)/4}\rfloor$ and $n_1^{(t)}(n,k+1) \leq n_1^{(t)}(n,k)$ for $k \geq \lfloor(1-t)/2+\sqrt{n/2-(t+1)/4}\rfloor$. Therefore, we have the following

Corollary 2.

The level k which contains most nodes in all n-node ordered trees is given by $k = \lfloor\sqrt{n/2}\rfloor + 1$. *The level k which contains most nodes of degree t in all n-node ordered trees is equal to* $k = \lfloor(1-t)/2 + \sqrt{n/2 - (t+1)/4}\rfloor + 1$.

□

Corollary 3.

Assuming that all n-node trees are equally likely, the average number $n_1(n,k)$ *of nodes and the average number* $n_1^{(t)}(n,k)$ *of nodes of degree t appearing at level k are asymptotically given for all* $\varepsilon > 0$ *by*

$$n_1(n,k) = \left[2k-1+\frac{2k^2}{n} + O(n^{-1/2+\varepsilon})\right] \exp(-k^2/n)$$

$$n_1^{(t)}(n,k) = 2^{-t}\left[k+\frac{t}{2}-1+\frac{(2k+t)(7t+8k)}{8n} - \frac{t(2k+t)^3}{16n^2} + O(n^{-1/2+\varepsilon})\right] \times$$
$$\times \exp(-(k+\tfrac{t}{2})^2/n) ,$$

where $k+\frac{t}{2} \leq n^{1/2+\varepsilon}$. *For* $k+\frac{t}{2} > n^{1/2+\varepsilon}$, $n_1(n,k) = n_1^{(t)}(n,k) = O(\exp(-n^{2\varepsilon}))$.

The second moments $n_2(n,k)$ and $n_2^{(t)}(n,k)$ about the origin are for all $\varepsilon>0$

$$n_2(n,k) = \left[2n+2k-1+\frac{3k^2}{n}-\frac{k^4}{3n^2}+O(n^{-1/2+\varepsilon})\right]\exp(-k^2/n) -$$

$$-2\left[n+4k-1+\frac{10k^2}{n}-\frac{8k^4}{3n^2}+O(n^{-1/2+\varepsilon})\right]\exp(-4k^2/n)$$

$$n_2^{(t)}(n,k) = 2^{-t}\left[k+\frac{t}{2}-1+\frac{(2k+t)(7t+8k)}{8n}-\frac{t(2k+t)^3}{16n^2}+O(n^{-1/2+\varepsilon})\right] \times$$

$$\times \exp(-(k+\tfrac{t}{2})^2/n) \quad +$$

$$+2^{-2t}\left[\frac{n}{2}+k+\frac{5t}{4}-\frac{1}{4}+\frac{4(1-2t)(t+k)^2+3t(8k+9)}{16n} -\right.$$

$$\left.-\frac{(k+t)^4+12t(k+t)^3+9t^2(k+t)^2}{12n^2}+\frac{t^2(t+k)^4}{4n^3}+O(n^{-1/2+\varepsilon})\right]$$

$$\times \exp(-(k+t)^2/n) \quad -$$

$$-2^{-2t}\left[\frac{n}{2}+4k+\frac{9t}{4}-\frac{7}{4}-\frac{t(t+2k)^2-117t^2-38kt-26k^2}{2n} -\right.$$

$$-\frac{17t^4+94t^3k+174t^2k^2+112tk^3+8k^4}{6n^2}+\frac{t^2(2k+t)^4}{4n^3}+$$

$$\left.+O(n^{-1/2+\varepsilon})\right] \quad \exp(-(2k+t)^2/n) \ ,$$

where $k+\frac{t}{2}\leq n^{1/2+\varepsilon}$. For $k+\frac{t}{2}>n^{1/2+\varepsilon}$, $n_2(n,k)=n_2^{(t)}(n,k)=O(\exp(-n^{2\varepsilon}))$.

Proof.

A similar computation as in [2], [3] leads to the following approximation for fixed a and all $\varepsilon>0$:

$$\binom{2n-t}{n-k-t+a}\Big/\binom{2n}{n} = \begin{cases} 2^{-t}\exp(-(k+\frac{t}{2})^2/n)\,[f_a(n,k)+O(n^{-3/2+\varepsilon})] & \text{if } k+\frac{t}{2}\leq n^{1/2+\varepsilon} \\ O(\exp(-n^{2\varepsilon})) & \text{if } k+\frac{t}{2}>n^{1/2+\varepsilon} \end{cases},$$

where

$$f_a(n,k) = 1+\frac{t(4a+1)+8ka-4a^2}{4n}-\frac{t(t+2k)^2}{8n^2}+$$

$$+\frac{t^2(16a^2+24a+7)+16tk(4a^2+3a+1)+16k^2(4a^2+1)}{32n^2}-$$

$$-\frac{t^4(6a+5)+2t^3k(18a+11)+6t^2k^2(12a+5)+16tk^3(3a+1)+8k^4}{48n^3}+$$

$$+\frac{t^2(2k+t)^4}{128n^4} \ .$$

Using this approximation and Corollary 1, we obtain our results by a lengthy, but elementary computation. □

Choosing t=0, we find that the average number $n_1^{(0)}(n,k)$ of leaves at level k is asymptotically given by $[k-1+2k^2/n+O(n^{-1/2+\varepsilon})]\exp(-k^2/n)$ for all $\varepsilon>0$. Furthermore, by Stirling's formula and by Corollary 1

$$\frac{n_1^{(t)}(n,k)}{n_1(n,k)} = (n+k-1)\,\frac{2k+t-2}{2k-1}\,\frac{(2n-t-3)!}{(2n-2)!}\,\frac{(n-k)!}{(n-t-k)!} \sim 2^{-t-1}\left(1+\frac{k}{n}\right)\left(1-\frac{k}{n}\right)^t$$

for fixed $t \in [0:n-1]$. In other words, if k/n tends to zero, about 50% (25%, 12.5%, etc.) of all nodes at level k are leaves (nodes of degree 1,2, etc.). Figure 2 shows the graph of $n_1(n,k)$ and $n_1^{(t)}(n,k)$ for n=100 and $t \in \{0,1,2\}$.

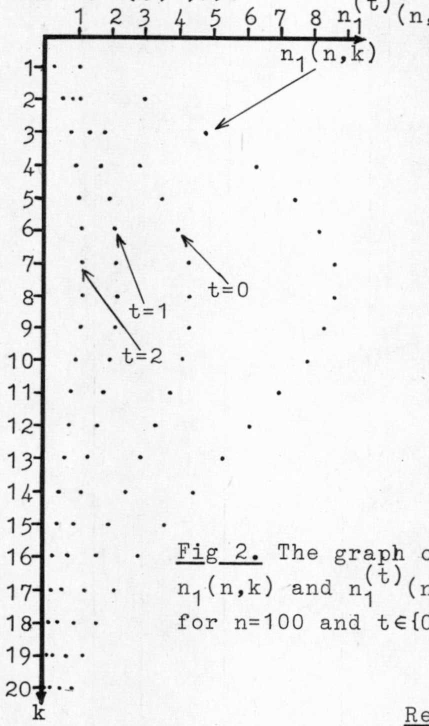

<u>Fig 2.</u> The graph of $n_1(n,k)$ and $n_1^{(t)}(n,k)$ for n=100 and $t\in\{0,1,2\}$.

k	$n_1^{(2)}(n,k)$		$n_1^{(1)}(n,k)$		$n_1^{(0)}(n,k)$		$n_1(n,k)$	
1	0.25	0.27	0.25	0.27	0.00	0.02	1.00	1.01
2	0.49	0.51	0.75	0.77	1.00	1.04	2.94	2.96
3	0.70	0.71	1.19	1.23	1.94	1.99	4.71	4.73
4	0.87	0.89	1.57	1.61	2.77	2.83	6.21	6.24
5	0.99	1.01	1.87	1.90	3.44	3.51	7.37	7.40
6	1.07	1.08	2.06	2.09	3.93	3.99	8.15	8.18
7	1.09	1.10	2.16	2.18	4.22	4.28	8.54	8.56
8	1.07	1.08	2.16	2.18	4.32	4.37	8.56	8.58
9	1.01	1.02	2.08	2.10	4.24	4.28	8.27	8.28
10	0.93	0.93	1.94	1.95	4.02	4.05	7.71	7.72
11	0.82	0.82	1.75	1.75	3.69	3.70	6.98	6.98
12	0.71	0.71	1.53	1.53	3.29	3.29	6.13	6.13
13	0.60	0.60	1.31	1.30	2.84	2.84	5.23	5.24
14	0.49	0.49	1.08	1.09	2.39	2.38	4.35	4.36
15	0.39	0.39	0.88	0.87	1.96	1.95	3.53	3.53
16	0.30	0.30	0.69	0.69	1.57	1.56	2.79	2.79
17	0.23	0.23	0.53	0.53	1.22	1.21	2.15	2.16
18	0.17	0.17	0.40	0.39	0.93	0.92	1.61	1.62
19	0.12	0.12	0.29	0.29	0.69	0.68	1.19	1.20
20	0.09	0.09	0.21	0.21	0.50	0.49	0.85	0.86

<u>Table 1.</u> Some values of $n_1(100,k)$ and $n_1^{(t)}(100,k)$. The first columns give the exact values (Cor. 1), the second columns give the asymptotic values (Cor. 3).

<u>References</u>

[1] Comtet,L.: Advanced Combinatorics. Dordrecht-Boston:Reidel 1974

[2] de Bruijn,N.G.,Knuth,D.E.,Rice,S.O.: The Average Height of Planted Plane trees.In:Graph Theory and Computing, New York-London:Ac.Press 1972

[3] Kemp,R.: The Average Height of R-tuply Rooted Planted Plane Trees. Computing <u>25</u>, 209-232, (1980)

[4] Kemp,R.: On the Number of Deepest Nodes in Ordered Trees. preprint, Johann Wolfgang Goethe-Universität, Fachbereich 20, Frankfurt (M),1982

[5] Knuth,D.E.: The Art of Computer Programming, Vol.1,2nd ed., Reading, Mass.: Addison-Wesley 1973

[6] Meir,A.,Moon,J.W.: On the Altitude of Nodes in Random Trees. Can. J.Math.<u>30</u>, 997-1015 (1978)

[7] Riordan,J.: Combinatorial Identities. New York: Wiley 1968

[8] Salomaa,A.,Soittola,M.: Automata-Theoretic Aspects of Formal Power Series. New York: Springer 1978

Complexity Theory on Real Numbers and Functions

by Christoph Kreitz and Klaus Weihrauch

FERNUNIVERSITÄT Hagen
Fachbereich Mathematik und Informatik
Postfach 940, D-5800 Hagen 1

1. Introduction

Since Turing [17] introduced the concept of computable real numbers in 1937, many authors have studied computability of real numbers and functions (see for example, [1,2,6,10,11,12,13,14,16]). The next subject to be studied is now computational complexity.

The goal of our paper is to present a natural concept for computational complexity of real numbers and functions.

First we develop a complexity theory on $\mathbb{R}$ corresponding to Blum's [3] complexity theory on the recursive functions. (A generalization of his theory to cpo's has already been formulated by Weihrauch [18]). In order to abtain a successful definition of complexity we represent real numbers by Cauchy-sequences of dyadic numbers having a normed convergence. We define the set of computable real numbers ($\mathbb{R}_c$) and an effective numbering η of $\mathbb{R}_c$. Complexity classes of real numbers are introduced and it is shown, that the most interesting statements of abstract complexity theory hold analoguously in $\mathbb{R}_c$.

Our investigation of computational complexity of real functions is based on the computability concept of Grzegorczyk [5]. Improving a corresponding computation model of Ko & Friedman [7], that uses a rather restrictive requirement, we introduce a computation mechanism for real functions, which enables us to define complexity. Studying topological properties of computable functions we observe an important relation between continuity and complexity of a function.

Exploring problems concerning a recursion-theoretic complexity theory on real functions we show, that some computable functions cannot have a complexity bound because of their complicated domains. On the other hand a complexity bound of a function f does exist, if the domain of f is an effective K_σ-set. We prove, that a hierarchy-theorem and a speedup-theorem hold for computable functions too. Finally it is shown, that a computable function may have a high complexity even if its domain is simple and it has simple values at simple arguments.

We shall denote the set of all total (partial) recursive k-ary functions by $R^{(k)}$ ($P^{(k)}$). Let φ be a standard numbering of $P^{(1)}$ and let $W_i := \mathrm{dom}(\varphi_i)$ for all i. Let <,> be the standard pairing function on $\mathbb{N}$

and D_i denote the i-th finite subset of $\mathbb{N}$ (see Rogers [15]).

2. Complexity theory on real numbers

Let $\mathbb{Q}_D := \cup \{\mathbb{Q}_n \mid n \in \mathbb{N}\}$ be the set of all dyadic (rational) numbers, where $\mathbb{Q}_n := \{m \cdot 2^{-n} \mid m \in \mathbb{Z}\}$ for fixed $n \in \mathbb{N}$, and $\nu_D : \mathbb{N} \to \mathbb{Q}_D$ be defined by $\nu_D\langle k,l,n\rangle := (k-l) \cdot 2^{-n}$. We define the set PNC of all partial normed Cauchy-sequences in $\mathbb{Q}_D$ by

$PNC := \{\psi : \mathbb{N} \dashrightarrow \mathbb{Q}_D \mid (\forall k \in Def(\psi))\ (\psi(k) \in \mathbb{Q}_k \wedge (\forall n \leq k)\ |\psi(n) - \psi(k)| < 2^{-n})\}$

and denote the set of all total normed Cauchy-sequences by NC.
A representation $\delta : PNC \dashrightarrow \mathbb{R}$ can be defined by

$$dom(\delta) := NC \quad \text{and} \quad \delta(\psi) := \lim_{n\to\infty} \psi(n) .$$

Sometimes we call a sequence $\psi \in NC$ an oracle for $\delta(\psi)$.
A sequence $\psi \in PNC$ is computable, iff $\psi(n) = \nu_D f(n)$ for some $f \in P^{(1)}$.

<u>Definition</u> A real number x is computable iff there is a computable Cauchy-sequence $\psi \in \delta^{-1}\{x\}$.
$\mathbb{R}_c$ is the set of all computable real numbers.

An effective (partial) numbering η of $\mathbb{R}_c$ can defined as follows.
There is some $p \in R^{(1)}$ with

$$\nu_D\varphi_{p(i)}(k) := \begin{cases} a & \text{, if } a := \nu_D\varphi_i(k) \in \mathbb{Q}_k \text{ and } (\forall n < k)\ |\nu_D\varphi_i(n) - a| < 2^{-n} , \\ \text{div} & \text{, otherwise .} \end{cases}$$

Then define $\psi_i := \nu_D\varphi_{p(i)}$ for all $i \in \mathbb{N}$ and $\eta_i := \delta(\psi_i)$. For any $i,n \in \mathbb{N}$ let $\kappa_i(n)$ be the resource (time, tape) for computing $\varphi_{p(i)}(n)$. We assume that the following axioms hold:

$(\forall i)\ dom(\kappa_i) = dom(\psi_i)$ and $\{(i,n,t) \mid \kappa_i(n) = t\}$ is recursive.

For total recursive t let $\mathbb{R}(t) := \{\eta_i \mid \kappa_i(n) \leq t(n)$ for almost all $n\}$ be the complexity class of computable real numbers determined by t .
The following properties can be proved immediately:

Every weakly η-r.e. class of computable real numbers is contained in some complexity class, and complexity class $\mathbb{R}(t)$ is weakly η-r.e., whenever t is sufficiently large.
Also Borodin's [4] <u>Gap-theorem</u>:

$$(\forall g,h \in R^{(1)}, \text{g increasing})\ (\exists f \in R^{(1)})\ [(\forall n)\ (h(n) \leq f(n)) \wedge \mathbb{R}(g \cdot f) = R(f)]$$

is easy to prove.
Some of the most important results of the recursion-theoretic complexity-

theory can be proved only by effective diagonalization. For a diagonalization on $\mathbb{R}_c$ we shall use patterns of intervalls with decreasing diameter. These patterns are inspired by the geometrical approach to the Cantor-discontinuoum.

<u>Example</u> Define $\tau : \{0,1\}^* \to \{[r,s] \mid r,s \in \mathbb{Q}\}$ by $\tau(\varepsilon) = [0,1]$

and $\tau(w0) := [l, \frac{3l+r}{4}]$ $\tau(w1) := [l, \frac{l+3r}{4}]$

if $w \in \{0,1\}^*$ and $\tau(w) = [l,r]$

Note that for $w \in \{0,1\}^n$ and any intervall I with diameter less or equal $2^{-(n+2)}$ $\tau(w0) \cap I = \emptyset$ or $\tau(w1) \cap I = \emptyset$ holds.

Using an intervall-pattern like τ we are able to diagonalize effectively over a weakly-r.e. set Y of real numbers:

Let $Y = \{\eta_{f(n)} \mid n \in \mathbb{N}\}$ for some $f \in R^{(1)}$.

Step 0 Let $w_o := \varepsilon$

Step n+1 Find a word $w_{n+1} \in \{w_n0, w_n1\}$ such that $\eta_{f(n)} \notin \tau(w_{n+1})$.

[Note that $\psi_{f(n)}(2n+3)$ determines an intervall I of diameter $2^{-(2n+2)}$ with $\eta_{f(n)} \in I$.]

By $\{x\} := \bigcap_{n\in\mathbb{N}} \tau(w_n)$ we get a computable real number $x \notin Y$.

By use of effective diagonalization the compression theorem as well as the speedup theorem (Blum [3]) can be proved. The proofs are variations of the original ones. We only formulate the theorems here. Details can be found in the author's technical report [8].

<u>Compression theorem:</u> There is a function $h \in R^{(1)}$ such that for all $m \in \mathbb{N}$ with $\varphi_m \in R^{(1)}$:

(1) $\eta_{h(m)} \in \mathbb{R}_c$

(2) $(\forall i)\ [\eta_i = \eta_{h(m)} \Rightarrow (\kappa_i(n) > \varphi_m(n)$ for almost all $n)]$

Especially $\eta_{h(m)} \in \mathbb{R}(\kappa_{h(m)}) \setminus \mathbb{R}(\varphi_m)$ holds.

<u>Speedup theorem:</u> For every $r \in R^{(2)}$ there is some $x \in \mathbb{R}_c$ with

$(\forall i \in \eta^{-1}\{x\})\ (\exists j \in \eta^{-1}\{x\})\ [r(n,\kappa_j(n)) \le \kappa_i(n)$ for almost all $n]$.

3. Computable real functions

Computable real functions are defined in two different ways.

One approach is to define a computable function as effective operator on the set $\mathbb{R}_c$ (Mazur [13], Aberth [1]) using an effective numbering of $\mathbb{R}_c$ (like η). The other approach considers all real continuous functions on all real numbers (Grzegorczyk [6], Lacombe [10]) and defines a computable function by a recursive functional on all possible names (e.g. Cauchy-sequences) for real numbers. There is a strong relation between these concepts (see Ceitin [5]), but it isn't fully understood till now.

In this paper we shall follow the second approach, since the first one provides some results in formal contradiction to classical analysis and doesn't seem to allow a successful definition of complexity. We use (function-) Oracle-Turing-machines (OTM's) as computing model for (partial) computable real functions. Thus we can apply a complexity measure of Turing-machines for defining the computational complexity of real functions. Our model is inspired by one of Ko & Friedman [7], but our definition of computability is more general and more natural. A function-Oracle-Turing-machine M with oracle $\psi \in NC$ and input $n \in \mathbb{N}$ computes the n-th term $M^{\psi}(n)$ (if it exists) of a sequence $M^{\psi} \in PNC$ asking the oracle for a finite number of values $\psi(n_1),\ldots,\psi(n_k)$ during the computation.

<u>Definition</u> A function $f : \mathbb{R} \dashrightarrow \mathbb{R}$ is computable, iff there is an Oracle-Turing-machine M such that

$$(\forall \psi \in NC) \quad f(\delta(\psi)) = \delta(M^{\psi}) \qquad (*)$$

Let OTM(f) be the set of all OTM's satisfying (*).

Condition (*) is equivalent to the following ones:

(i) $(\forall x \in dom(f))\ (\forall \psi \in \delta^{-1}\{x\})\ (M^{\psi} \in NC$ and $\lim_{n\to\infty} M^{\psi}(n) = f(x))$,

(ii) $(\forall x \notin dom(f))\ (\forall \psi \in \delta^{-1}\{x\})\ (M^{\psi}(n)$ diverges for almost all $n)$.

Condition (ii) makes our definition differ from Ko's [7], because be requires $M^{\psi}(n)$ to diverge for all $n \in \mathbb{N}$ if $\lim_{n\to\infty} \psi(n) \notin dom(f)$. Therefore his machines have to decide wether $\lim_{n\to\infty} \psi(n) \in dom(f)$ or not before computing any value. This requirement is too restrictive.

Many continuous total functions are computable e.g. polynomials with recursive coefficients, elementary functions, the function $x \to |x|$ etc. . Also partial functions may be computable. Examples are

$$f : \mathbb{R} \dashrightarrow \mathbb{R} \text{ defined by } dom(f) := \mathbb{R} \setminus \{0\} \text{ and } f(x) := 1/x$$

and for $y \in \mathbb{R}_c$

$$g_y : \mathbb{R} \dashrightarrow \mathbb{R} \quad \text{defined by} \quad g_y(x) := \begin{cases} 1 & \text{, if } x < y \\ 0 & \text{, if } x > y \\ \text{div} & \text{, if } x = y \end{cases}$$

But g_y has no extension into a total computable function. Therefore, $\{x \mid x \geq y\}$ is not 'decidable'.

For any OTM M let $TM^{\psi} : \mathbb{N} \dashrightarrow \mathbb{N}$ be the step counting function of M^{ψ}. The following lemma can be proved by the fan theorem (Königs Lemma).

Lemma 3.1 For any computable $f : \mathbb{R} \dashrightarrow \mathbb{R}$, $M \in OTM(f)$, $x \in dom(f)$, $n \in \mathbb{N}$ $TM^{x}(n) := \max \{TM^{\psi}(n) \mid \psi \in \delta^{-1}\{x\}\}$ exists.
Forthermore for any computable x, $TM^{x} : \mathbb{N} \dashrightarrow \mathbb{N}$ is a recursive function.

The function TM^{x} can be viewed as complexity bound of f at x. There is an important relationship between this complexity bound and the topological properties of f.

Theorem 3.2 If $f : \mathbb{R} \dashrightarrow \mathbb{R}$ is computable then f is continuous and the modulus of continuity at any point $x \in dom(f)$ is bounded by $\lambda n.TM^{x}(n+1)$ for any machine $M \in OTM(f)$
[i.e. $(\forall y \in dom(f))\ (\forall n)\ (|x-y| < 2^{-TM^{x}(n+1)} \Rightarrow |f(x)-f(y)| \leq 2^{-n})$]

The proof follows from the argument, that if $|x-y| < 2^{-k}$ there are oracles for x and y, which coincide at the first k values, so that the machine cannot distinguish x and y in k steps.

From topology (Kuratowsky [9]) we know a characterization of the domains of partial continuous functions. This characterization has been extended to computable functions on metric spaces (Weihrauch [19]) an holds analogous for partial computable real functions.

Theorem 3.3 A set $S \subseteq \mathbb{R}$ is a domain of some computable real function if and only if S is an effective G_{σ}-set.
(i.e. $S = \bigcap_i \bigcup_j O_{ij}$ where O_{ij} is a computable double-sequence of open basisintervalls.)

The proof is technical and will be omitted. Further details can be found in the author's technical report [8].

We get as corollary from theorem 3.4 that there is a computable function $f : \mathbb{R} \dashrightarrow \mathbb{R}$ whose domain contains only noncomputable real numbers, e.g. only the number $x_K := \sum_{i \in K} 2^{-i}$, where $K \subseteq \mathbb{N}$ is a nonrecursive but r.e. set.

4. Complexity of partial computable real functions

In section 3 we have defined $TM^x : \mathbb{N} \dashrightarrow \mathbb{N}$, the complexity of a machine $M \in OTM(f)$ at $x \in dom(f)$, where $f : \mathbb{R} \dashrightarrow \mathbb{R}$ is computable. We are now interested in machines M computing a real function f such that there is a (computable) function $t : \mathbb{N} \to \mathbb{N}$ with

$$(\forall x \in dom(f)) \quad TM^x(n) \le t(n) \quad \text{for almost all } n .$$

In that case we say : t is a complexity bound of M (respectively of f). But not every computable real function has a complexity bound.

<u>Example</u> Let $f : \mathbb{R} \dashrightarrow \mathbb{R}$ be computable such that $dom(f) = \mathbb{R} \setminus \mathbb{Q}$ (Note, that $R \setminus \mathbb{Q}$ is an effective G_δ-set). Then f has no complexity bound. [i.e. for every machine $M \in OTM(f)$ and any function $t : \mathbb{N} \to \mathbb{N}$ there is an $x \in \mathbb{R} \setminus \mathbb{Q}$ such that $TM^x(n) > t(n)$ for infinitely many n]

To prove this statement we choose an arbitrary (increasing) function $t : \mathbb{N} \to \mathbb{N}$ an arbitrary machine $M \in OTM(f)$ and a standardnumbering $\nu_{\mathbb{Q}}$ of $\mathbb{Q}$. Since the function f is undefined on $\mathbb{Q}$,we can construct by an effective diagonalization (cf. section 2) a point $x \in \mathbb{R} \setminus \mathbb{Q}$ and an increasing sequence of natural numbers n_k such that

$$|x - \nu_{\mathbb{Q}}(k)| \le 2^{-t(n_k)} \quad \text{and} \quad TM^{\nu_{\mathbb{Q}}(k)}(n_k) > t(n_k)$$

for infinitely many $k \in \mathbb{N}$. So the machine cannot distinguish x and $\nu_{\mathbb{Q}}(k)$ in $t(n_k)$ steps and $TM^x(n_k) \le t(n_k)$ doesn't hold for infinitely many k .

Using the relation between complexity of a computable real function and its topological properties we'll now characterize domains, which guarantee the existence of a complexity bound for any computable real function defined on it. For this purpose we formulate the notion of "effective compactness" (cf. Bishop [2], Martin-Löf [12]) and "effective K_σ-set".

<u>Definition:</u> A set $S \subseteq \mathbb{R}$ is effective -compact iff S is compact and

$$U(S) := \{j \in \mathbb{N} \mid S \subseteq \bigcup_{<i,k> \in D_j} (d_i - 2^{-k}, d_i + 2^{-k})\}$$

(the set of all finite open coverings of S) is an r.e. set.

A set $T \subseteq \mathbb{R}$ is an effective K_σ-set if T is an effective union of effective compact sets (i.e. there are effective-compact sets S_j and a recursive function h such that $W_{h(j)} = U(S_j)$ for all j and $T = \bigcup_{j \in \mathbb{N}} S_j$).

<u>Lemma 4.1</u> Let $f : \mathbb{R} \dashrightarrow \mathbb{R}$ be computable, $S \subseteq \mathrm{dom}(f)$, $M \in \mathrm{OTM}(f)$

a) If S is effective-compact, then there is a function $t \in R^{(1)}$ such that $(\forall x \in S)\ \ TM^x(n) \le t(n)$ for every n,

b) If S is an effective K_σ-set, then there is a function $t \in R^{(1)}$ such that $(\forall x \in S)\ \ TM^x(n) \le t(n)$ for almost all n.

<u>Proof</u> a) Since S is bounded, we can arrange all the oracles $\psi \in \delta^{-1}(S)$ in a finite number of trees with a finite degree. Given $n \in \mathbb{N}$, $\psi \in \delta^{-1}(S)$ the computation of $M^\psi(n)$ needs only a finite prefix $OM^\psi(n)$ of the oracle ψ. By the fan theorem the set $\{OM^\psi(n) \mid \psi \in \delta^{-1}(S)\}$ is finite for all $n \in \mathbb{N}$ and hence using the effectiveness of S can construct a recursive function t such that $(\forall n)$ $t(n) = \max\ \{TM^\psi(n) \mid \psi \in \delta^{-1}(S)\}$ for every n.

b) Let $S = \bigcup_{j \in \mathbb{N}} S_j$ be an effective union of effective-compact sets S_j. Then using 4.1 a) the function $t \in R^{(1)}$ with

$$(\forall n)\ \ t(n) = \max\ \{TM^\psi(n) \mid (\exists j \le n)\ \psi \in \delta^{-1}(S_j)\}$$

has the required properties.

We get as a corollary from theorem 3.2 and Lemma 4.1 a) that every computable function defined on an effective-compact set S is uniformly continuous on S and the modulus of uniform continuity is recursive.

Since the existence of a uniform complexity bound for a computable real function f'(as defined in Lemma 4.1 a)) requires the uniform continuity of f, a definition of computational complexity of real functions by uniform complexity bounds - as Ko used in [7] - seems to us to be too restrictive. Here we give a definition applicable to functions like $f(x) := 1/x$ too, which is based on Lemma 4.1 b).

<u>Definition</u> Let $S \subseteq \mathbb{R}$ be an effective K_σ-set, $f : \mathbb{R} \dashrightarrow \mathbb{R}$ be computable where $S \subseteq \mathrm{dom}\ f$.
A function $t \in R^{(1)}$ is a complexity bound of f on S ("$f \in C_S(t)$") iff there is a machine $M \in \mathrm{OTM}(f)$ such that $(\forall \psi \in \delta^{-1}(S))\ \ (TM^\psi(n)) \le t(n)$ for almost all n)

<u>Hierarchy-theorem</u> For every $t \in R^{(1)}$ one can effectively construct a computable real function, which doesn't belong to $C_{\mathbb{R}}(t)$

<u>Speedup-theorem</u> For every $r \in R^{(2)}$ there is a computable function $f : R \to \mathbb{R}$ such that

$$(\forall M \in \mathrm{OTM}(f))\ (\exists \bar{M} \in \mathrm{OTM}(f))\ (\forall \psi, \psi' \in NC)\ [r(n, T\bar{M}^\psi(n)) \le TM^{\psi'}(n) \text{ for almost all } n]$$

These theorems can be proved by considering constant constant functions and using compression- and speedup-theorem of section 2.

So far we have seen, that real functions are hard to compute if their domains or their values are complicated. However there are computable functions which have high complexity, although their domain is not complicated and their values are easy to compute if the argument is simple. We conclude that a notion like "A function $f : R \to \mathbb{R}$ is easy computable (e.g. in polynomial time) if f maps simple arguments into simple values" isn't suitable for a definition of complexity.

Theorem 4.2 Let $X \subseteq [0,1]$ be an unfinite, weakly η-r.e. set, $t \in R^{(1)}$.
Then there is a computable function $f : [0,1] \to \mathbb{R}$ such that $(\forall y \in X)\ f(y) \in \mathbb{Q}_D$ but $f \notin C_{[0,1]}(t)$

Proof We shall enumerate X injective and construct a converging sequence of polygons f_i, which are constant on neighbourhoods of the 'first' i elements of X.
Let p,q be recursive functions, q strictly increasing such that $(\forall i)\ q(i) \geq 2i+3$ and

(1) $\{n_{p(i)} \mid i \in \mathbb{N}\} = \{0,1\} \cup X$

(2) $(\forall n)\ (\psi_{p(0)}(n) = 0 \wedge \psi_{p(1)}(n) = 1)$

(3) $(\forall i \geq 2)\ (\forall j < i)\ |\psi_{p(i)}(q(i)) - \psi_{p(j)}(q(i))| > 2 \cdot 2^{-q(i)}$.

We shall write ψ_{ji} to shorten $\psi_{p(j)}(q(i))$ and

$$\psi^+_{ji}\ (\psi^-_{ji}) \quad \text{instead of} \quad \begin{cases} \psi_{ji}+2^{-q(i)}\ (\psi_{ji}-2^{-q(i)}) & \text{, if } j \geq 2 \\ \psi_{ji} & \text{, otherwise.} \end{cases}$$

The polygons $f_i : [0,1] \to \mathbb{R}$ $(i \geq 1)$ shall be defined by their values at points $z \in \{\psi^+_{ji} \mid j \leq i\} \cup \{\psi^-_{ji} \mid j \leq i\}$. Let

$$f_1(0) := 0 , \qquad f_1(1) := 1$$

and if $i \geq 2$

$$f_i(z) := \begin{cases} f_{i-1}(\psi_{ii}) + (-1)^{g(i)} \cdot 2^{-q(i)} & \text{, if } z \in \{\psi^+_{ii}, \psi^-_{ii}\} \\ f_{i-1}(z) & \text{, otherwise,} \end{cases}$$

where $g \in R^{(1)}$ is a 0/1-valued function, whose properties will be specified afterwards.
Estimating the gradients of the f_i's $(\leq 2^i - 1)$ we can prove

$$(\forall x \in [0,1])\ (\forall i)\ |f_i(x) - f_{i-1}(x)| \leq 2^{-i}$$

Hence the function $f := \lim_{i\to\infty} f_i : [0,1] \to \mathbb{R}$ exists and is computable (cf. Ko [7]). Moreover

$$(\forall y \in X)\ (\exists i)\ (y = \eta_{p(i)} \wedge f(y) = f_i(\psi_{ii}) \in \mathbb{Q}_D)$$

We now show, that the computational complexity of f is virtually the complexity of the function $g \in R^{(1)}$. Therefore we compute g using a machine $M \in OTM(f)$.

INPUT $i \geq 2$

Find $k, j \in \{0, \ldots, i-1\}$ such that $\psi^+_{ji} < \psi^-_{ii} < \psi_{ii} < \psi^+_{ii} < \psi^-_{kj}$ and $(\psi^-_{ki} - \psi^+_{ji})$ is minimal.

Using $f(\eta_{p(j)}) = f_{i-1}(\psi^+_{j\,i-1})$ and $f(\eta_{p(k)}) = f_{i-1}(\psi_{k\,i-1})$ construct an interpolation F of $f_{i-1}(\psi_{ii})$ with error less than $2^{-[q(i)+1]}$.

Compute an interpolation F' of $f_{ii}(\psi_{ii}) = f(\eta_{p(i)})$ such that the error is less or equal to $2^{-[q(i)+1]}$.

OUTPUT 0 if $F - F' > 0$, otherwise 1.

To see that the algorithm works, look at the following drawing.

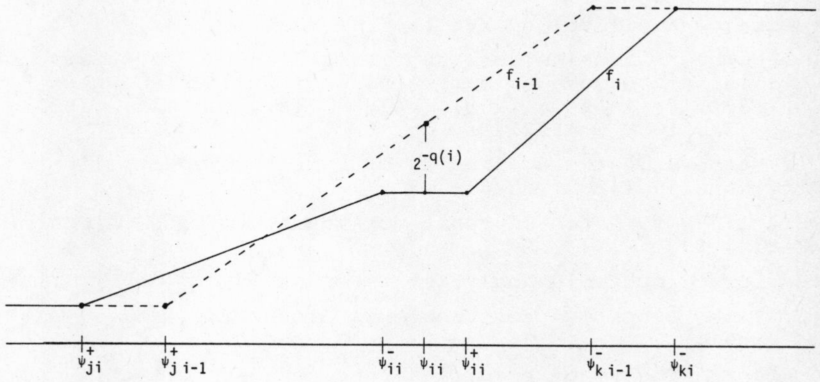

Now let $t \in R^{(1)}$ be a complexity bound for f and $T \in R^{(1)}$ describe the number of steps to compute k and j for given i (only depending on p and q). Then the function $t' \in R^{(1)}$ defined by $t'(i) := 3 \cdot t(q(i) + 3) + T(i)$ is an upper bound for the complexity of g.

Using compression theorem for 0/1-valued recursive functions (Blum [3]), for any $t \in R^{(1)}$ one can construct a function $g \in R^{(1)}$, whose complexity is higher than t', and hence a computable real function f having the desired properties.

In this paper we have introduced a concept for a theory of computation and complexity on $\mathbb{R}$. As a next step the recursion-theoretic complexity theory for functions should be put forewards and extended to sequences of functions and functionals.

References

[1] O. Aberth, Computable Analysis, McGraw-Hill, 1980.

[2] E. Bishop, Foundations of constructive analysis, McGraw-Hill, 1967.

[3] M. Blum, A machine-independant theory of the complexity of recursive functions, J. ACM 14 (1967) 332 - 336.

[4] A. Borodin, Complexity classes of recursive functions and the existence of complexity gaps, Conf. Rec. ACM Symp. on Theory of Computing (1969), 67 - 78.

[5] G.S. Ceitin, Algorithmic operators in constructive complete separable metric spaces (Russian), Doklady Akad. Nauk 128 (1959), 49 - 52.

[6] A. Grzegorczyk, On the definitions of computable real continuous functions, Fundamenta mathematicae 44 (1957), 61 - 71.

[7] K. Ko & M. Friedman, Computational complexity of real functions, TCS 20 (1982), 323 - 352.

[8] C. Kreitz & K. Weihrauch, Komplexitätstheorie auf reellen Zahlen und Funktionen, Informatik Bericht Nr. 28 (1982), Fernuniversität Hagen.

[9] K. Kuratowski, Topology (Vol. 1), Academic Press, 1966.

[10] D. Lacombe, Extension de la notion de function recursive aux functions d'une au plusieurs variables réelles, Comptes Rendus Acad. Sci. Paris 240 (1955), 2478 - 2480, Vol. 241 (1955), 13 - 14, 151 - 153, 1250 - 1252.

[11] A.A. Markov, On the continuity of constructive functions, Uspehi, Math. Nauk. 9 (1954), 226 - 230.

[12] P. Martin-Löf, Notes on constructive mathematics, Almquist & Wiksell, 1970.

[13] S. Mazur, Computable Analysis, Warschau 1963

[14] H.G. Rice, Recursive real numbers, Proc. Amer. Soc. 5 (1954), 784 - 791.

[15] H. Rogers, Theory of recursive functions and effective computability, McGraw-Hill, 1967.

[16] E. Specker, Nicht konstruktiv beweisbare Sätze der Analysis, J. Symb. Logic 14 (1949), 145 - 158.

[17] A.M. Turing, On computable numbers with an application to the entscheidungsproblem, Proc. London Math. Soc. 42 (1937), 230 - 265.

[18] K. Weihrauch, Recursion and complexity theory on cpo's, Proc. 5th GI-Conf. (P. Deussen ed.), LNCS 104, Springer (1981), 195 - 202.

[19] K. Weihrauch, Complexity on metric spaces, Informatik Bericht Nr. 21 (1981), Fernuniversität Hagen.

A MULTIFIT ALGORITHM FOR UNIFORM MULTIPROCESSOR SCHEDULING

Manfred Kunde
Institut für Informatik
und Praktische Mathematik
Universität Kiel
Olshausenstraße 40-60
D-2300 Kiel 1, W. Germany

Abstract

Independent tasks are nonpreemptively scheduled on $m \geq 2$ processors which are assumed to have different speeds. By generalizing ideas of bin packing techniques scheduling algorithms are constructed which have better worst case bounds than the well-known LPT algorithm.

1. Introduction

In this paper we consider the problem of scheduling independent tasks on a nonpreemptive uniform multiprocessor system [1,5,6]. Formally, there is a set $\mathcal{T} = \{T_1,\dots,T_n\}$ of tasks, each having an execution time $\mu(T_i)$ and a set of $m \geq 2$ processors with speeds $s_1 \leq s_2 \leq \dots \leq s_m$. We assume that $s_1 \geq 1$ and abbreviate the m-tuple of speeds with $\sigma_m = (s_1,\dots,s_m)$. A schedule is a partition $\mathcal{P} = \{P_1,\dots,P_m\}$ of $\mathcal{T}$ into m disjoint subsets. P_i, $1 \leq i \leq m$, is that set of tasks, which is executed on the ith processor. For any $X \subseteq \mathcal{T}$ let $\mu(X) = \sum_{T \in X} \mu(T)$. The finishing time or maximum completion time of the schedule $\mathcal{P}$ is given by

$$\omega(\mathcal{P}) = \max_{1 \leq i \leq m} \frac{\mu(P_i)}{s_i} .$$

An optimal m-processor schedule $\mathcal{P}^*$ is one that satisfies $\omega(\mathcal{P}^*) \leq \omega(\mathcal{P})$ for all partitions $\mathcal{P}$ of $\mathcal{T}$ into m subsets. Such an optimal schedule must exist, because there is only a finite number of possible partitions.

The problem of finding an optimal schedule is NP-hard [9,10]. Thus there is only little hope to find a computational tractable algorithm that solvesour problem. These circumstances make us seek efficient algorithms that produce "near optimum" schedules.

For given $\mathcal{T}$ and $\sigma_m = (s_1,\dots,s_m)$ let A be an algorithm that constructs a partition $\mathcal{P}_A[\mathcal{T},\sigma_m]$. Let OP denote an algorithm that produces an optimal schedule and let

$$\omega_A(\mathcal{T},\sigma_m) = \omega(\mathcal{P}_A[\mathcal{T},\sigma_m]) \quad .$$

The m-processor performance ratio (worst case ratio) for A is then defined by

$$R_m(A) = \sup \left\{ \frac{\omega_A(\mathcal{T},\sigma_m)}{\omega_{OP}(\mathcal{T},\sigma_m)} \;\middle|\; \text{all task sets } \mathcal{T}, \text{ all m-tuples } \sigma_m \right\}.$$

In the case of an homogeneous multiprocessor system all speeds are equal. The well-known LPT-algorithm satisfies

$R_m(\mathrm{LPT}) = 4/3 - 1/(3m)$ [4].

An improvement to the LPT is the multifit-algorithm MF which based on the bin-packing algorithm FFD (First-Fit-Decreasing) with worst case ratio

$R_m(\mathrm{MF}) \leq 1.222$ [2] .

If different speeds are allowed the LPT-algorithm [3] fulfills

$$R_m(\mathrm{LPT}) \leq 2 - 2/(m+1) \quad \text{and} \quad \lim_{m\to\infty} R_m(\mathrm{LPT}) \geq 1.5 \quad .$$

If there is only one processor with higher speed $s_m = s > 1$ and $s_1 = s_2 = \dots = s_{m-1} = 1$, then it is shown in [3] that

$R_2(\mathrm{LPT}) = (\sqrt{17} + 1)/4$ and

$4/3 \leq R_m(\mathrm{LPT}) \leq 3/2 - 1/(2m)$ for $m \geq 3$.

In this paper the ideas of the MF-algorithm are generalized for uniform processor systems. It can be shown that for the latter case where only one processor has a higher speed

$$R_2(MF) = \sqrt{6}/2 \quad \text{and}$$

$$R_m(MF) = (\sqrt{17} + 1)/4 \qquad \text{for } m \geq 3.$$

That is, MF is an improvement to LPT for all $m \geq 2$. It is worthwhile to mention that the ratio is independent of the number of processors for $m \geq 3$. The same thing is conjectured for the worse ratio of the LPT-algorithm.

If all speeds are allowed to be different, then it can be shown that $R_m(MF) < 3/2$. But the exact ratio seems to be much better.

2. The multifit algorithm MF

When doing list scheduling [1] the main problem is to generate a list which is then transformed into a schedule by standard techniques. For the packing algorithms beside a list a capacity bound C is needed and one of the problems is to find a good a priori bound.

For the following we assume that the tasks of $\mathcal{T}$ are in decreasing order, that is, $\mu(T_1) \geq \mu(T_2) \geq \ldots \geq \mu(T_n)$. Let $\mathcal{T}$, m, σ_m and a capacity bound C be given. The MF-algorithm tries to put the largest, not yet assigned task on to the slowest processor such that the capacity bound is not violated. We will introduce a boolean function $FFD(\mathcal{T},C,\sigma_m)$ which tells us, if it is possible to assign all of the tasks to the processors within bound C in the above mentioned kind.

<u>boolean function</u> FFD $(\mathcal{T},C,\sigma_m)$

<u>begin</u> $FFD(\mathcal{T},C,\sigma_m) \leftarrow$ <u>true</u> ; $j \leftarrow 0$

    <u>for</u> i <u>from</u> 1 <u>to</u> m <u>do</u> $P_i \leftarrow \emptyset$; $C_i \leftarrow s_i \cdot C$

    $j \leftarrow j + 1$; $i \leftarrow 1$

    <u>if</u> $\mu(P_i) + \mu(T_j) \leq C_i$

```
5        then begin  Pi ← Pi ∪ {Tj}
6                    if j < n then goto 3 else goto END
7             end
8        else begin i ← i + 1
9                    if i ≤ m then goto 4 else FFD(𝒯,C,σm) ← false
10            end
11       END  end
```

Note that the function FFD constructs a partition $\mathcal{P}_{FFD} = \{P_1, \ldots, P_m\}$ of $\mathcal{T}$ with $\omega(\mathcal{P}_{FFD}) \leq C$ iff $FFD(\mathcal{T}, C, \sigma_m)$ = true.

Now we are ready to formulate two basic theorems which will be proved in the next sections.

Theorem 1

Let $m, \mathcal{T}, \sigma_m$ be given. Then for all $r \geq 1.5$

$FFD(\mathcal{T}, r \cdot \omega_{OP}(\mathcal{T}, \sigma_m), \sigma_m)$ = true.

Theorem 2

Let m and $\mathcal{T}$ be arbitrary and $\sigma_m = (s_1, \ldots, s_m)$ with $s_1 = s_2 = \ldots = s_{m-1}$, $s_m > s_1$. Define $r_2 = \sqrt{6}/2$ and $r_m = (\sqrt{17} + 1)/4$ for $m \geq 3$. Then for all $r \geq r_m$

$FFD(\mathcal{T}, r \cdot \omega_{OP}(\mathcal{T}, \sigma_m), \sigma_m)$ = true .

The examples 1 and 2 show that with the preconditions of theorem 2 r_m is the smallest expansion factor, such that FFD guarantees a successful assignment.

The pure multifit algorithm MF works as follows:

Let $C = r_m \cdot \omega_{OP}(\mathcal{T}, \sigma_m)$, apply FFD ,

then $FFD(\mathcal{T}, C, \sigma_m)$ = true and define $\mathcal{P}_{MF} = \mathcal{P}_{FFD}$.

Unfortunately determining $\omega_{OP}(\mathcal{T}, \sigma_m)$ is NP-hard and hence the pure MF is not efficient to our present knowledge. But we will show that with binary search it is possible to construct efficient versions MF(k) of

Examples

1. $\sigma_2 = (1, \sqrt{6}/2)$, $\mathcal{T} = \{ T_1, T_2, T_3, T_4 \}$

$\mu(T_1) = \sqrt{6} - 1$, $\mu(T_i) = 1$ for $i = 2,3,4$

a)

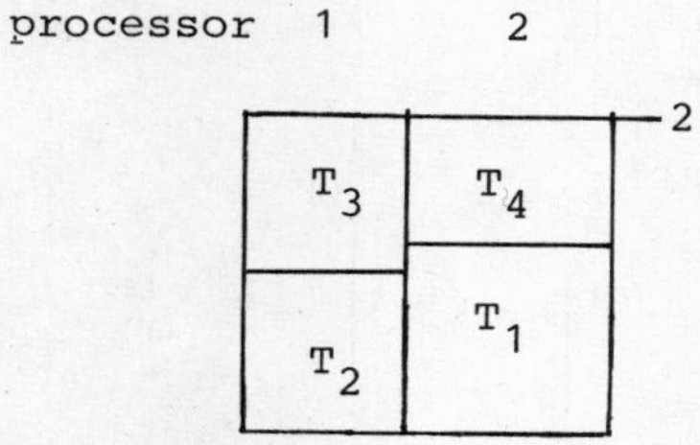

optimal schedule

$\omega_{OP}(\mathcal{T}, \sigma_2) = 2$

b)

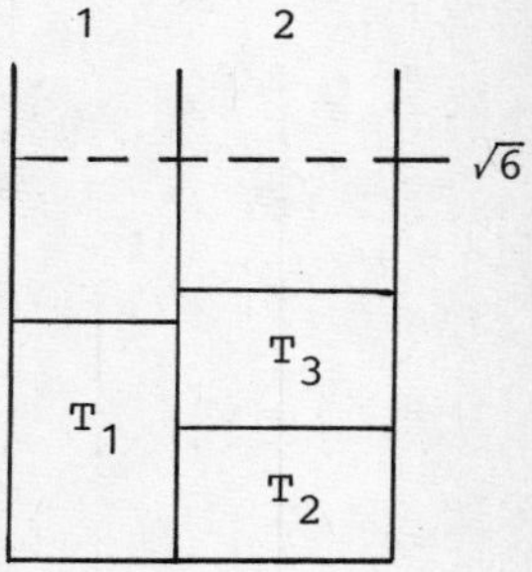

$FFD(\mathcal{T}, C, \sigma_2) =$ false $\forall C < \sqrt{6}$

$FFD(\mathcal{T}, \sqrt{6}, \sigma_2) =$ true

2. $\sigma_3 = (1, 1, (\sqrt{17}-1)/2)$, $\mathcal{T} = \{ T_1, \ldots, T_6 \}$

$\mu(T_1) = \mu(T_2) = (\sqrt{17}-1)/2$

$\mu(T_i) = 1$ for $i = 3,4,5,6$

a)

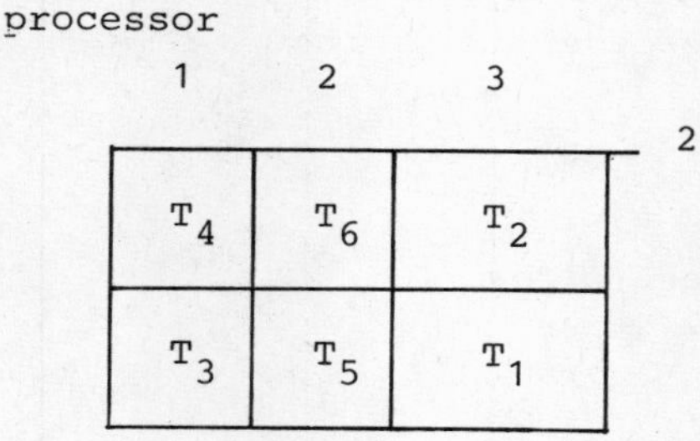

optimal schedule

$\omega_{OP}(\mathcal{T}, \sigma_3) = 2$

b)

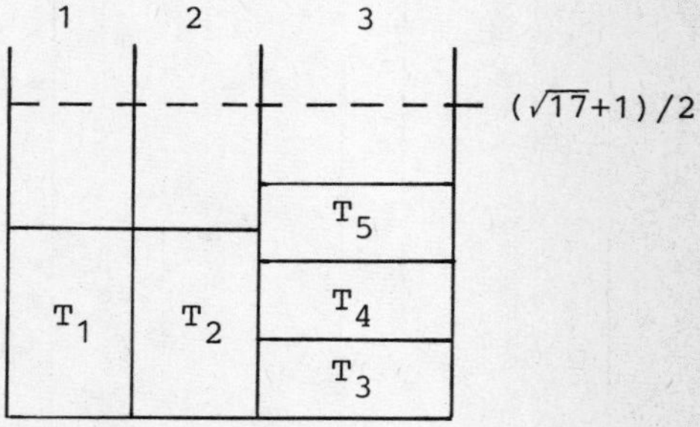

$FFD(\mathcal{T}, C, \sigma_3) =$ false $\forall C < (\sqrt{17}+1)/2$

$FFD(\mathcal{T}, (\sqrt{17}+1)/2, \sigma_3) =$ true

MF with worst case ratios very near to r_m.

For binary search a lower and an upper bound is needed. Let $\mathcal{T} = \{T_1, \ldots, T_n\}$ and $\sigma_m = (s_1, \ldots, s_m)$. Then define

$$C_L[\mathcal{T},\sigma_m] = \max\left\{\left(\sum_{i=1}^{n} \mu(T_i)\right)/\left(\sum_{i=1}^{m} s_i\right),\ \max_{1\le j\le m}\left(\sum_{i=1}^{j} \mu(T_i)\right)/\left(\sum_{i=m+1-j}^{m} s_i\right)\right\}$$

$$C_U[\mathcal{T},\sigma_m] = 2\, C_L[\mathcal{T},\sigma_m] .$$

<u>Lemma 2.1</u> a) For all $C < C_L[\mathcal{T},\sigma_m]$ $\quad FFD(\mathcal{T},C,\sigma_m)$ = <u>false</u>

b) For all $C \ge C_U[\mathcal{T},\sigma_m]$ $\quad FFD(\mathcal{T},C,\sigma_m)$ = <u>true</u>

<u>Proof:</u> Let $C_B = C_B[\mathcal{T},\sigma_m]$ for $B \in \{L,U\}$. If there is a $C < C_L$ with $FFD(\mathcal{T},C,\sigma_m)$ = <u>true</u> , then $\omega_{OP}(\mathcal{T},\sigma_m) \le C < C_L$ in contradiction to a well-known theorem of Liu and Yang [7].

Now assume that there is a set of tasks $\mathcal{T}$, a $\sigma_m = (s_1,\ldots,s_m)$ and a $C \ge C_U$, such that $FFD(\mathcal{T},C,\sigma_m)$ = <u>false</u> . Let $m \ge 2$ be minimal with this property and $\mathcal{T}$ be minimal in the number of tasks. That is, for all $i = 1, \ldots , |\mathcal{T}| - 1 = n - 1$ $FFD(\{T_1,\ldots,T_i\}, C,\sigma_m)$ = <u>true</u> . If $n < m$, then $C_L = \max_{1\le j\le n}\left(\sum_{i=1}^{j} \mu(T_i)\right)/\left(\sum_{i=m+1-j}^{m} s_i\right) > \left(\sum_{i=1}^{n} \mu(T_i)\right)/\left(\sum_{i=1}^{m} s_i\right)$. Hence the pair $(\mathcal{T},\sigma_n)$ with $\sigma_n = (s_{m+1-n}, \ldots, s_m)$ is a counter-example for statement b). But this contradicts the fact that m is minimal.

Thus let $n \ge m$. Let $\{P_1,\ldots, P_m\}$ denote the partition of $\mathcal{T} - \{T_n\}$ constructed by $FFD(\{T_1, \ldots, T_{n-1}\}, C,\sigma_m)$. That means $\sum_{i=1}^{m} \mu(P_i) = \sum_{i=1}^{n-1} \mu(T_i)$. From $FFD(\mathcal{T},C,\sigma_m)$ = <u>false</u> follows that for every i, $1\le i\le m$, $\mu(P_i) + \mu(T_n) > C_i = s_i\cdot C$. Thus

$$\begin{aligned}
\sum_{i=1}^{n} \mu(T_i) &= \sum_{i=1}^{m} \mu(P_i) + \mu(T_n) > \sum_{i=1}^{m} s_i\cdot C - (m-1)\mu(T_n)\\
&\ge \sum_{i=1}^{m} s_i\cdot 2C_L - (m-1)\mu(T_n)\\
&\ge \sum_{i=1}^{m} s_i\left(\left(\sum_{i=1}^{n} \mu(T_i) + \sum_{i=1}^{m} \mu(T_i)\right)/\left(\sum_{i=1}^{m} s_i\right)\right) - (m-1)\mu(T_n)\\
&= \sum_{i=1}^{n} \mu(T_i) + \sum_{i=1}^{m} \mu(T_i) - (m-1)\mu(T_n) > \sum_{i=1}^{n} \mu(T_i) .
\end{aligned}$$

But this is a contradiction and therefore b) must hold.

The following procedure MF(k) is the same one as given in [2] for homogeneous multiprocessor systems. The final value CU(k) gives the smallest C found for which $FFD(\mathcal{T}, C, \sigma_m) = \underline{true}$.

```
procedure MF(k)[𝒯,σ_m]
1     begin  CL(0) ← C_L[𝒯,σ_m]  ; CU(0) ← C_U[𝒯,σ_m] ; i ← 0
2          i ← i + 1
3        if i > k then goto END
4                  else C ← ( CL(i - 1) + CU(i - 1) )/2
5        if FFD(𝒯,C,σ_m) then CU(i) ← C ; CL(i) ← CL(i - 1)
                                goto 2
6                         else CL(i) ← C ; CU(i) ← CU(i - 1)
                                goto 2
7 END end
```

The complexity analysis of MF(k) as given in [2] shows that including the initial sorting of $O(n \log n + knm)$ steps are needed. One application of FFD is comparable to the packing done by LPT. Thus for small n LPT runs at most k times faster than MF(k). But in this case both algorithms are very quick. If n is big enough the time for the initial sorting dominates the running times of both algorithms. Hence the complexity of MF(k) and LPT is comparable.

<u>Theorem 3</u>

Let r_m be a real number, such that $\forall \mathcal{T}$, $\forall \sigma_m$, $\forall r \geq r_m$ $FFD(\mathcal{T}, r \cdot \omega_{OP}(\mathcal{T}, \sigma_m), \sigma_m) = \underline{true}$, then for all $k \geq 0$

$$R_m(MF(k)) \leq r_m + 2^{-k} .$$

<u>Proof</u>: Theorem 3.1 in [2] .

Table 1 shows that in the case where only one processor is faster than the others MF(5) is better than LPT.

Table 1

approximate worst case ratios for $\sigma_m = (s_1, \ldots, s_m)$ with $s_1 = s_2 = \ldots. = s_{m-1} = 1$ and $s_m = s > 1$.

m	2	3	≧ 4
$R_m(LPT) \geq$	1.281	1.333	1.333
$R_m(MF) = r_m$	1.225	1.281	1.281
$R_m(MF(4))$	1.287	1.343	1.343
$R_m(MF(5))$	1.256	1.312	1.312
$R_m(MF(6))$	1.240	1.296	1.296
$R_m(MF(8))$	1.229	1.285	1.285
$R_m(MF(12))$	1.225	1.281	1.281

3. Proofs

We will prove the theorems 1 and 2 by contradiction. That is we assume that there is an $r \geq 1.5$ or $r \geq r_m$, a task set $\mathcal{T}$ and a σ_m, such that $FFD(\mathcal{T}, r \cdot \omega_{OP}(\mathcal{T},\sigma_m),\sigma_m)$ = false. As abbreviations we will use $q = \omega_{OP}(\mathcal{T},\sigma_m)$ and $p = rq$.

For technical reasons it is useful to have standardized forms of counterexamples.

Definition 1 p, q as above. $(\mathcal{T}, m, \sigma_m)$ is called a p/q - counterexample iff

1. $FFD(\mathcal{T},p,\sigma_m)$ = false
2. $\forall \mathcal{T}'$ with $|\mathcal{T}'| < |\mathcal{T}|$, $\forall \sigma'_m$ with $\omega_{OP}(\mathcal{T}',\sigma'_m) \leq q$
   $FFD(\mathcal{T}',p, \sigma'_m)$ = true
3. $\forall m'$, $m' < m$, $\forall \mathcal{T}'$, $\forall \sigma_{m'}$ with $\omega_{OP}(\mathcal{T}',\sigma_{m'}) \leq q$
   $FFD(\mathcal{T}',p,\sigma_{m'})$ = true

That means, a p/q - counterexample is minimal in the number of tasks (condition 2.) and minimal in the numbers of processors (condition 3.).

As before let $\mathcal{T} = \{T_1, \ldots, T_n\}$ and $\mu(T_1) \geq \mu(T_2) \geq \ldots \geq \mu(T_n)$. If $(\mathcal{T}, m, \sigma_m)$ is a p/q - counterexample, then from condition 2. easily follows that $FFD(\{T_1, \ldots, T_{n-1}\}, p, \sigma_m) =$ <u>true</u> . Let $\mathcal{P} = \{P_1, \ldots, P_m\}$ be the partition of $\{T_1, \ldots, T_{n-1}\}$ generated by FFD with bound p and let $\mathcal{P}^+ = \{P_1^+, \ldots, P_m^+\}$ be an optimal partition of $\mathcal{T}$. These notations will be used for the rest of the paper.

<u>Definition 2</u> Let X and Y be subsets of $\mathcal{T}$. X <u>dominates</u> Y iff there is a 1 - 1 mapping $f : Y \to X$, such that $\mu(T) \leq \mu(f(T))$ for all T of Y.

The following three lemmata are due to H. Steppat [8].

<u>Lemma 3.1</u> Let $(\mathcal{T}, m, \sigma_m)$ be a p/q - counterexample. Then a set P_i, $1 \leq i \leq m$, cannot dominate any set P_j^+, $1 \leq j \leq m$, with $s_i \leq s_j$.

<u>Proof</u>: Assume that there is a P_i that dominates P_j^+ and $s_i \leq s_j$. Let $f : P_j^+ \to P_i$ be the involved mapping. Let $\mathcal{T}' = \mathcal{T} - P_i$ and $\sigma'_{m-1} = (s_1, \ldots, s_{i-1}, s_{i+1}, \ldots, s_m)$. Then obviously $FFD(\mathcal{T}', p, \sigma'_{m-1}) =$ <u>false</u> and $FFD(\mathcal{T}' - \{T_n\}, p, \sigma'_{m-1}) =$ <u>true</u> . A new partition $\mathcal{P}'$ is constructed from the optimal partition $\mathcal{P}^+$ by interchanging each $T \in P_j^+$ and its image f(T). Since $\mu(T) \leq \mu(f(T))$ we have $\mu(P_k') \leq \mu(P_k^+)$ for every $k \neq j$. Furthermore $P_j' = f(P_j^+) \subseteq P_i$. For k = 1, ..., m then define

$$\bar{P}_k = \begin{cases} P_k' - P_i & k \neq j \\ P_i' - P_i & k = j \end{cases}.$$

Then

$$\bigcup_{\substack{h=1 \\ h \neq i}}^{m} \bar{P}_h = \bigcup_{\substack{h=1 \\ h \neq j}}^{m} P_h' - P_i = \mathcal{T}' .$$

Thus $\bar{\mathcal{P}} = \{\bar{P}_1, \ldots, \bar{P}_{i-1}, \bar{P}_{i+1}, \ldots, \bar{P}_m\}$ is a partition of $\mathcal{T}'$ into m - 1 sets and for all k, $1 \leq k \leq m$, $k \neq j$, $k \neq i$, $\mu(\bar{P}_k) \leq s_k q$ and $\mu(\bar{P}_j) \leq \mu(P_i^+) \leq s_i q \leq s_j q$. That is, $\omega_{OP}(\mathcal{T}', \sigma'_{m-1}) \leq q$. But then $(\mathcal{T}, m, \sigma_m)$ cannot be a p/q - counterexample.

<u>Lemma 3.2</u> Let $(\mathcal{T}, m, \sigma_m)$ be a p/q - counterexample.

Then $|P_i^+| \geq 2$ for all i = 1, ..., m .

<u>Proof</u>: If for any i $P_i^+ = \emptyset$, then P_i dominates P_i^+ in contradiction to lemma 3.1 .

Now assume that there is a P_i^+ containing only a single task T_k. If T_k is an element of P_j, $j \leq i$, then P_j dominates P_i^+ and this again contradicts lemma 3.1 .

Otherwise, if a P_j, $j > i$, contains T_k or $T_k = T_n$, then FFD must have assigned a task T_h, $h < k$, to P_i. Therefore $\mu(T_h) \geq \mu(T_k)$ and hence P_i dominates P_i^+, giving us a final contradiction.

The next lemma gives a lower bound for the execution times of the tasks.

<u>Lemma 3.3</u> Let $(\mathcal{T}, m, \sigma_m)$ be a p/q - counterexample.

Then $\mu(T_n) > (p - q) \sum_{i=1}^{m} s_i/(m - 1)$.

<u>Proof</u>: From $FFD(\mathcal{T}, p, \sigma_m)$ = <u>false</u> and $FFD(\mathcal{T} - \{T_n\}, p, \sigma_m)$ = <u>true</u> we derive $\mu(P_i) + \mu(T_n) > ps_i$ for all $i = 1, \ldots, m$. Thus

$$\sum_{i=1}^{n} \mu(T_i) = \sum_{i=1}^{m} \mu(P_i) + \mu(T_n) > \sum_{i=1}^{m} s_i p - (m - 1)\mu(T_n) \quad .$$

On the other hand $\sum_{i=1}^{n} \mu(T_i) = \sum_{i=1}^{m} \mu(P_i^+) \leq \sum_{i=1}^{m} s_i q$.

Combining these two inequalities we derive

$$(m - 1)\mu(T_n) > \sum_{i=1}^{m} s_i (p - q) \quad .$$

We are now prepared to prove the first theorem.

<u>Proof of theorem 1 :</u>

Assume that theorem 1 does not hold. That is, for an $r \geq 1.5$ we have a p/q - counterexample $(\mathcal{T}, m, \sigma_m)$ with $q = \omega_{OP}(\mathcal{T}, \sigma_m)$ and $p = rq$. Lemma 3.2 and lemma 3.3 imply

$$s_1 q \geq 2\mu(T_n) > 2(p - q) \sum_{i=1}^{m} s_i/(m-1) \geq 2(p - q) m s_1/(m - 1) \quad .$$

Thus $r = p/q = 1 + (p - q)/q < 1 + (m - 1)/(2m) = 3/2 - 1/(2m)$.

Hence theorem 1 must be true.

Probably the ratio 3/2 - 1/(2m) is not the worst case ratio for the multifit algorithm. Until now we do not know a counterexample with an r near to 1.5, such that $FFD(\mathcal{T}, r\omega_{OP}(\mathcal{T},\sigma_m),\sigma_m)$ = <u>false</u> . But in view of example 2 we can state that

$$(\sqrt{17}+1)/4 \leq R_m(MF) \leq 3/2 - 1/(2m) \quad \text{for } m \geq 3 .$$

For m = 2 we know by theorem 2 that $R_2(MF) = \sqrt{6}/2$.

The proof of theorem 2 is rather lengthy and therefore omitted here. It can be found in [11] .

References

1. COFFMAN, E.G. jr.(ed.): Computer and job/shop scheduling theory, John Wiley and Sons, New York, 1976.
2. COFFMAN, E.G. jr., GAREY, M.R., JOHNSON, D.S.: An application of bin-packing to multiprocessor scheduling, SIAM J. Comp., 7 (1978), 1-17.
3. GONZALEZ, T., IBARRA, O.H., SAHNI, S.: Bounds for LPT schedules on uniform processors, SIAM J. Comput., 6 (1977), 155-166.
4. GRAHAM, R.L.: Bounds on multiprocessing timing anomalies, SIAM J. Appl. Math., 17(1969), 416-429.
5. LAWLER, E.L., LENSTRA, J.K., RINNOOYKAN, A.H.G.: Recent developments in deterministic sequencing and scheduling: a survey, in: M.A.H. DEMPSTER et al. (ed.): Deterministic and stochastic Scheduling, D. Reidel, Dordrecht, 1982, 35-73.
6. LIU, J.W.S. and C.L.: Bounds on scheduling algorithms for heterogeneous computer systems, Information Processing 74, North Holland, Amsterdam 1974, 349-353.
7. LIU, J.W.S., YANG, A.: Optimal scheduling of independent tasks on heterogeneous computing systems, ACM National Conference 1974, 38-45.
8. STEPPAT, H.: Bin-packing-Methoden für das Scheduling in uniformen Mehrprozessorsystemen, Diplomarbeit, Kiel 1982, to appear.
9. ULLMAN, J.D.: NP-complete scheduling problems, J. of Comp. and System Sciences, 10 (1975), 384-393.
10. ULLMAN, J.D.: Complexity of sequencing problems, in [1], 139-164.
11. KUNDE, M.: Bounds for multifit scheduling algorithms on uniform multiprocessor systems, Bericht 8203, Institut für Informatik und Praktische Mathematik, Kiel 1982.

ANALYSIS OF POLYNOMIAL APPROXIMATION ALGORITHMS FOR CONSTRAINT EXPRESSIONS

Karl J. Lieberherr*
Institut für Informatik
ETH Zurich, 8092 Zurich

Stephen A. Vavasis
Dept. of Mathematics, Princeton University
Princeton, NJ 08544

Extended Abstract
(Proofs omitted)

Abstract

The generalized maximum satisfiability problem contains a large class of interesting combinatorial optimization problems. Since most of them are NP-complete we analyze fast approximation algorithms.

Every generalized ψ-satisfiability problem has a polynomial ε_ψ-approximate algorithm for a naturally defined constant ε_ψ, $0\leq\varepsilon_\psi<1$ which is determined here explicitly for several ψ. It is shown that ε_ψ can be approximated by the Soviet Ellipsoid Algorithm. The fraction ε_ψ is known to be best-possible in the sense that the following set is NP-complete: The ψ-formulas S which have an assignment satisfying the fraction $\tau'>1-\varepsilon_\psi$ (τ' rational) of <u>all</u> clauses in S.

Among other results we also show that for many ψ, local search algorithms fail to be ε_ψ-approximate algorithms. In some cases, local search algorithms can be arbitrarily far from optimal.

1. Introduction

The performance of fast approximation algorithms for the maximum ψ-satisfiability problem is investigated. This problem class contains e.g. the following NP-complete problems which are discussed in [Garey/Johnson (1979)]: MAX CUT, EXACT COVER, SET SPLITTING, NOT-ALL-EQUAL SAT, ONE-IN-THREE SAT. An instance of a maximum ψ-satisfiability problem consists of a sequence of constraints and the problem is to find an

---

*) Currently on leave from Princeton University. This research is supported by NSF grant MCS80-04490.

assignment which satisfies as many as possible. These constraint satisfaction problems appear in many practical applications like time table scheduling, minimizing PLA's, decoding messages, designing statistical experiments, etc.

Maximization problems of the type described above are naturally formulated as maximum ψ-satisfiability problems [Schaefer (1978), Lieberherr (1982)]. ψ is a finite set of logical relations $R_1,\ldots,R_m$ which are used to express the constraints. A ψ-formula S with n variables is a finite sequence of clauses each of the form $R_i(x_1,\ldots,x_{r_i})$. r_i is the rank of R_i and $x_1,\ldots,x_{r_i}$ are a subset of the n variables of S. The maximum ψ-satisfiability problem consists of finding, for any ψ-formula S, an assignment to the variables of S satisfying the maximum number of clauses.

It is well-known that for most ψ it is NP-equivalent to find the optimal assignment for a given ψ-formula [Schaefer (1978)]. Therefore it is justified to analyze polynomial heuristics and to determine how close to the optimal solution they come [Garey/Johnson (1979)].

As shown in [Lieberherr (1982)] each maximum ψ-satisfiability problem has an associated constant τ_ψ, which has the following meaning: The fraction τ_ψ of the clauses can be satisfied in polynomial time in any ψ-formula S. However if it can be decided in polynomial time whether at least the fraction $\tau'>\tau_\psi$ (τ' rational, $\tau'<1$) of the clauses can be satisfied, then the maximum ψ-satisfiability problem can be solved in polynomial time. Therefore, if the maximum ψ-satifisfiability problem is NP-equivalent, then the set of ψ-formulas which have an assignment satisfying the fraction $\tau'>\tau_\psi$ (τ' rational, $\tau'<1$) of the clauses is NP-complete. In this case τ_ψ is called a P-optimal threshold.

It is now possible to answer the following question: Is there a polynomial ε_ψ-approximate algorithm for the maximum ψ-satisfiability problem? I.e. is there a polynomial algorithm which for any instance is guaranteed to find an assignment within ε_ψ of the optimal assignment for some constant $\varepsilon_\psi<1$? (For a general definition of an ε-approximate algorithm see e.g. [Papadimitriou/Steiglitz (1981)]. It is well-known that there are maximization problems which do not have a polynomial ε-approximate algorithm for any $\varepsilon<1$ (see e.g. [Sahni/Gonzales (1976)]), however the maximum ψ-satisfiability problem has a polynomial $(1-\tau_\psi)$-approximate algorithm (MAXMEAN* in [Lieberherr (1982)]). This follows directly from the definition of τ_ψ. It is easy to prove that $\tau_\psi>0$ if ψ does not contain the empty relation.

It is in general an open problem whether there are polynomial ε'-approximate algorithms for $\varepsilon'<1-\tau_\psi$ or whether there is even a polynomial approximation scheme for the maximum ψ-satisfiability problem ([Huang/Lieberherr (1981)], see [Papadimitriou/Steiglitz (1981)] for the definition of a polynomial approximation scheme).

The algorithms which we analyze in this paper have the nice property of being "P-optimal". The basic theme of a theory of P-optimal approximation algorithms is the question of determining a threshold that can be satisfied efficiently and showing that satisfying more than the threshold is hard. An algorithm that guarantees to satisfy the threshold is said to be P-optimal. Intuitively, these P-optimal algorithms do the "best possible" of what can be done efficiently. The concept of P-optimal approximation is applicable to any NP-complete problem.

2. Generalized Satisfiability

In this section we define first the generalized satisfiability problem, following [Schaefer (1978)]. However the same concept has been used in artificial intelligence and related areas (see [Freuder (1978)]) under the names "constraint expressions" and "networks of constraints". In the last part of the section we summarize several useful facts about maximum ψ-satisfiability that are special cases of results published in [Lieberherr (1982)].

Let $\psi=\{R_1,\ldots,R_m\}$ be any finite set of logical relations. A logical relation is defined to be any subset of $\{0,1\}^r$ for some integer $r\geq 1$. The integer r is called the rank of the relation. Define a ψ-formula to be any sequence of clauses, each of the form $R_i(\zeta_1,\zeta_2,\ldots)$, where $\zeta_1,\zeta_2,\ldots$ are distinct, non-negated variables, whose number matches the rank of $R_i, i\in\{1,\ldots,m\}$. The ψ-satisfiability problem is the problem of deciding whether a given ψ-formula is satisfiable. The main result in [Schaefer (1978)] characterizes the complexity of the ψ-satisfiability problem for every finite set ψ of logical relations. An interesting feature of this characterization is, that for any such ψ, the ψ-satisfiability problem is either polynomial-time decidable or NP-complete.

The maximum ψ-satisfiability problem consists of finding, for any formula S, an assignment to the variables of S satisfying the maximum number of clauses. The difficulty of approximating the maximum ψ-satisfiability problem is the subject of this paper.

It turns out, that the following question deserves further attention: Given a set ψ of relations, which fraction τ_ψ of the clauses can be satisfied for every ψ-formula S? In other words, we are trying to solve the minimax problem:

$$\tau_\psi = \inf_{\substack{\text{all } \psi\text{-formulas} \\ S}} \max_{\substack{\text{all assignments} \\ J \text{ for } S}} \frac{\text{SATISFIED}(S,J)}{\text{CLAUSES}(S)} .$$

(SATISFIED(S,J) is the number of satisfied clauses in formula S under assignment J. CLAUSES(S) is the number of clauses in formula S.) The following theorem which is proven in [Lieberherr (1982)] (in generalized form) shows that the constant τ_ψ is best possible in an algorithmic sense

Theorem 2.1

Let ψ be a finite set of relations such that the ψ-satisfiability problem is NP-complete.

1.1 There is a polynomial algorithm MAXMEAN* that satisfies the fraction τ_ψ of the clauses.

1.2 For any rational $\tau' > \tau_\psi$ the set of ψ-formulas that have an assignment satisfying at least the fraction τ' of the clauses is NP-complete.

The above theorem claims that algorithm MAXMEAN* (given below) is relative P-optimal.

Algorithm MAXMEAN*
Input: ψ-formula S.
Output: Assignment which satisfies at least τ_ψ clauses.

```
maxassignment := 0;
loop
    compute k such that
     max mean_k'(S)=mean_k(S)
    0≤k'≤n
    {mean_k(S) is the average number of satisfied clauses among all
    assignments having exactly k ones.  mean_k(S) is a polynomial in k
    which can be efficiently computed}
    for all variables x in S do
        if mean_k-1(S_x=1)>mean_k(S_x=0)
        then J[x] := 1; k := k-1; S := S_x=1
        else J[x] := 0; S := S_x=0
        {mean_-1(S)=mean_0(S),mean_n+1(S)=mean_n(S)}
    h := SATISFIED(S,J);
    if h>maxassignment then
    maxassignment := h else exit;
    rename all variables in S which are assigned 1 by J;
end
```

3. Absolute P-optimality of MAXMEAN*

This section improves the results in [Lieberherr (1982)]. Here we show that it is hard to decide whether one can improve on MAXMEAN*. In [Lieberherr (1982)] it was only shown that it is hard to find an assignment which is better than the assignment found by MAXMEAN*. The new insight we gained is that in this context decision and search problems have about the same complexity. Namely we show that the following two problems are polynomially related to each other.

1. Is there an assignment for a given ψ-formula which satisfies more than

$$\mathrm{maxmean}(S) = \max_{0\le k\le n} \mathrm{mean}_k(S)$$

clauses?

2. Find an assignment for a given ψ-formula which satisfies more than maxmean(S) clauses (if such an assignment exists).

This relationship holds since the following two problems are polynomially related.

1. Is there an assignment for a given ψ-formula which is better than the assignment $J_{ALL\ 0}$ (which assigns 0 to all variables).
2. Find an assignment which is better than the assignment $J_{ALL\ 0}$ (if such an assignment exists).

This question is related to the absolute P-optimality of algorithm MAXMEAN*. We first need a few definitions.

Let {S} be the set of instances of an NP-equivalent maximum ψ-satisfiability problem. A polynomial time computable function g: {S} $\to$ R (rational numbers) is said to be absolute P-optimal, if the following two conditions hold

a) there is a polynomial algorithm M which finds for every formula x in {S} an assignment J so that SATISFIED(x,J)$\geq$g(x) and
b) the set of instances x in {S} which have an assignment such that SATISFIED(x,J)>g(x) is NP-complete (by a Turing reduction).

The function g has the following intuitive meaning: There is a polynomial algorithm that finds an assignment which is at least as "good" as g(x), but to do "better" is NP-complete. Algorithm M is said to be absolute P-optimal with respect to function g.

The renaming of a variable with respect to value γ is a substitution of $e(x,\gamma)=(\gamma-x) \bmod 2$ for variable x. The default is "with respect to value 1". Therefore the renaming of variable x is 1-x.

Let J be an assignment for formula S. The renaming R of formula S with respect to J is a substitution of e(x,J(x)) for all variables x in S. The resulting formula R(S) is called the renamed formula S (with respect to J).

Let $Q(x_1,\ldots,x_n)$ be a relation and let J be an assignment for $x_1,\ldots,x_n$. The renamed relation Q with respect to J is the relation L(Q,J) defined by

$$L(Q,J)(e(x_1,J(x_1)),\ldots,e(x_n,J(x_n)))\leftrightarrow Q(x_1,\ldots,x_n) .$$

By definition

$$Q(J(x_1),\ldots,J(x_n))=L(Q,J)(0,\ldots,0) .$$

A set of relations ψ is said to be closed under renaming if all relations that can be generated from relations in ψ by renaming, are in ψ.

Theorem 3.1
Let ψ be a finite set of relations which is closed under renaming. Assume that the maximum ψ-satisfiability problem is NP-equivalent. Then the set of ψ-formulas which have an assignment satisfying more clauses than the assignment $J_{ALL\ 0}$ (which assigns 0 to all variables) is NP-complete (by a Turing reduction).

Lemma 3.2
Let ψ be a finite set of relations.
Let $\Omega(S)$ be a polynomial decision algorithm for deciding whether there is a better assignment than the assignment $J_{ALL\ 0}$ for a given ψ-formla S. Then there is a polynomial algorithm for finding an assignment satisfying more clauses than $J_{ALL\ 0}$.

This Lemma shows that in this context decision and search problems have a polynomially related complexity.

The proof of the following corollary shows the connection between the problem of improving the assignment $J_{ALL\ 0}$ and the absolute P-optimality of MAXMEAN*.

Corollary 3.3
If the maximum ψ-satisfiability problem is NP-equivalent and ψ is closed under renaming, then algorithm MAXMEAN* is absolute P-optimal with respect to the function maxmean(S).

4. Closed Form Analysis of MAXMEAN*

In this section we determine the P-optimal thresholds τ_ψ for various ψ by explicit formulas. It is conjectured that τ_ψ is in general an algebraic number but no efficient method is known to determine (efficiently) an irreducible polynomial which defines τ_ψ ([Demyanov/Malozemov (1974)],[Charalambous/Conn (1978)]).

If ψ contains only one relation then the computation of τ_ψ involves only a maximization of a real polynomial over [0,1] and is therefore straight-forward. We refer the reader to [Lieberherr/Specker (1982)] for examples, how to compute τ_ψ by explicit formulas if ψ contains several relations. In the next section we will show that τ_{ψ} can be approximated efficiently by the Soviet Ellipsoid Algorithm for linear programming.

4.1 Hypergraph coloring

In this and the next subsection we allow the variables to assume c values 0,1,...,c-1 where $c \geq 2$. So far we have only considered logical variables (c=2) in this paper.

Let $R_m(x_1, x_2, \ldots, x_m)$ be the relation that holds, iff $\{0,1,\ldots,c-1\} \subseteq \{x_1, x_2, \ldots, x_m\}$. Let $\psi_m = \{R_m\}, m \geq 3$. A ψ_m-formula S has the following interpretation as a hypergraph coloring problem. Each variable of S corresponds to a node of the hypergraph. Each clause of S corresponds to a hyperedge and the clause expresses that each possible color is assigned to at least one node on the hyperedge. For c=2 this is the regular graph coloring problem (see section 4.2).

Theorem 4.2

$$\tau_{\psi_m} = \frac{c!}{c^m} S_2(m,c)$$

is a P-optimal threshold, if $c \geq 3$ and $m \geq 3$.
τ_{ψ_m} is determined in [Erdös/Kleitman (1968)] ($S_2(m,c)$ are the Stirling numbers of the second kind).

4.2 Graph coloring

Let R(x,y) be the relation that holds, if $x \neq y$. Let $\psi = \{R\}$ and allow c values 0,1,...,c-1 to be assigned to the variables. This maximum ψ-satisfiability problem is a generalization of the graph coloring problem. The c values are intended to be colors. Each clause in a ψ-formula corresponds to an edge and requires that the endpoints have different colors.

Theorem 4.3

$$\tau_{\psi} = \frac{c-1}{c}$$

is a P-optimal threshold, if $c \geq 3$.

([Vitanyi (1981)] and [Sahni/Gonzales (1976)] also determine τ_ψ and give an efficient algorithm to satisfy at least the fraction τ_ψ.

4.3 Exact Cover

We analyze a similar special case of the exact cover problem. Let $R_m(x_1,x_2,\ldots,x_m)$ be the relation that holds iff exactly one of the m variables is 1. Let $\psi_m=\{R_m\}$.

Theorem 4.4

$$\tau_{\psi_m} = \left(\frac{m-1}{m}\right)^{m-1}$$

is a P-optimal threshold, if $m\geq 3$.

5. Efficient Approximation of Performance Bound

The results of this section show that the computation of the performance bound of MAXMEAN* can be done efficiently. This completes our result in [Lieberherr (1982)] that MAXMEAN* can be generated efficiently.

In the last section we expressed the performance bound of MAXMEAN* by giving explicit formulas for the solution of the minimax problems. In general this is not possible since Galois theory proves that the roots of high degree polynomials cannot be expressed by radicals.

However linear programming allows us to compute the performance bound numerically in an efficient way. The Soviet Ellipsoid Algorithm (see e.g. [Papadimitriou/Steiglitz (1981)] will provably solve the problem in polynomial time. The clue to this result is to consider the minimax problem from a different point of view which yields a linear programming interpretation.

Theorem 5.2

Let ψ be a finite set of relations $R_1,\ldots,R_m$. Then the fraction of clauses which can be satisfied in every ψ-formula with n variables (and which will be satisfied by MAXMEAN*) is the solution of a linear program with m+n+2 constraints and m+1 variables. Each number occuring in the program has $O(\log(n))$ bits.

5. Limitations of Local Search

Local search is known to be an excellent heuristic for solving hard combinatorial optimization problems (see e.g. [Papadimitriou/Steiglitz (1982)]. Our empirical observation of the good performance of local search algorithms on the maximum ψ-satisfiability problem motivated us to compare their performance with the known performance of MAXMEAN*.

Our results are negative in the sense that many local search algorithms do not guarantee to satisfy the fraction τ_ψ of the clauses in a given ψ-formula i.e. are not P-optimal. In some cases we even show that local search is arbitrary far from being optimal.

We only give a short summary of our results (for a complete description see [Lieberherr/Vavasis (1982)]). For relations of rank 2 or 3 which are closed under renaming we show that simple local search algorithms are P-optimal. For relations of rank 4 or higher we show that a large class of local search algorithms are not P-optimal. In our reasoning we use ideas from Bernstein's proof of Weierstrass' theorem.

Conclusion

MAXMEAN* is shown to be optimal in several respects: It is relative and absolute P-optimal. It is also bestpossible for the ψ-formulas with a fixed number n of variables in the sense that MAXMEAN* satisfies at least as many clauses as one can satisfy in every ψ-formula with n variables. This last property makes MAXMEAN* superior to previously proposed algorithms with the performance bound τ_ψ. Our relative optimality results depend in a crucial way on the fact that we consider all ψ-formulas. If we restrict our attention to proper subsets of the set of all ψ-formulas, then the above questions may become very hard. The reason is that e.g. the well-known, and now solved, 4-color conjecture can be put into this framework (express the 4-coloring problem as in section 4 and minimize only among formulas which correspond to planar graphs).

References

Charalambous 1978. Charalambous Conn, "An efficient method to solve the minimax problem directly," SIAM J. Num. Anal. 15, pp. 162-187 (1978).

Demyanov 1974. V.F. Demyanov V.N. Malozemov, Introduction to Minimax, John Wiley & Sons, New York (1974).

Erdös 1968. P. Erdös and D.J. Kleitman, "On coloring graphs to maximize the proportion of multicolored k-edges," Journal of Combinatorial Theory 5 (2) pp. 164-169 (Sept. 1968).

Freuder 1978. E.C. Freuder, "Synthesizing Constraint Expressions," Comm. ACM 21 (11) pp. 958-966 (1978).

Garey 1976. M.R. Garey, D.S. Johnson, and L. Stockmeyer, "Some simplified NP-complete graph problems," Theor. Comput. Sci. 1, pp. 237-267 (1976).

Huang/Lieberherr (1982) M.A. Huang, K.J. Lieberherr, "Towards an approximation scheme for generalized satisfiability", Report 292. Dep. EECS, Princeton University (1982).

Lieberherr 1982. K.J. Lieberherr and E. Specker, "Complexity of Partial Satisfaction II," Report 293, Dep. of EECS, Princeton University (1982).

Lieberherr 1982. K.J. Lieberherr, "Algorithmic extremal problems in combinatorial optimization," Journal of Algorithms, September 1982.

Lieberherr/Vavasis (1982). K.J. Lieberherr, Stephen A. Vavasis, "Limitations of Local Search," Report 302, Dep. of EECS, Princeton University (1982).

Papadimitriou 1982. C.H. Papadimitriou K. Steiglitz, Combinatorial Optimization, Prentice Hall (1982).

Sahni 1976. S. Sahni and T. Gonzales, "P-complete approximation problems," J. ACM 23 (3) pp. 555-565 (1976).

Schaefer 1978. T. Schaefer, "The complexity of satisfiability problems," Proc. 10th Annual ACM Symposium on Theory of Computing, pp. 216-226 (1978).

Vitanyi 1981. P.M.B. Vitanyi, "How well can a graph be n-colored?" Discrete Mathematics 34,,pp. 69-80 (1981).

HEURISTICS FOR MINIMUM EDGE LENGTH RECTANGULAR PARTITIONS OF RECTILINEAR FIGURES '

Andrzej Lingas

Massachusetts Institute of Technology
and
Linköping University "

Introduction

Problems of optimally partitioning complex figures into simpler figures belong to the kernel of computational geometry. Besides inherent applications to computational geometry [C80], they have a variety of applications in pattern recognition [OS82], numerical analysis, database systems [LLMPL79], VLSI and architecture design [LPRS82]. In design problems, minimization of the total length of edges of the simpler figures may be more important. In [LPRS82], the following problem has been investigated:

Given a rectilinear figure, partition it into rectangles by drawing edges of the minimum total length.

The authors of [LPRS82] present an $O(n^4)$-time algorithm yielding an optimal solution when the figure is a rectilinear polygon with n corners. They also show that this problem becomes NP-hard when rectilinear polygon holes may appear inside the polygon. Unfortunately, such holes do appear in design problems. The aim of this paper is to complement [LPRS82] by delivering approximation heuristics for the case where the figure is a rectilinear polygon with rectilinear polygon holes.

In Section 1, a heuristic approach to a considerably simplified problem is presented. The simplification consists in assuming that the corners (not edges) of rectangles occuring in the sought partition are given a priori. Such an approach may be efficient if the number of reasonable candidates for rectangle corners, different from concave points of the figure, is very small. By a reduction to maximum weighted matching we obtain a heuristic yielding a solution of length not greater than the double length of an optimal solution. The heuristic runs in time $O(N^3)$, where N is the number of the fixed rectangle corners.

In Section 2, a heuristic for the general case is presented. It transforms the input rectilinear polygon with rectilinear holes into a rectilinear polygon, and then apply the $O(n^4)$-time algorithm optimally partitioning rectilinear polygons The transformation takes only $O(n^2 logn)$ time, and the running time of the entire heuristic is $O(n^4)$. The resulting

---

' This research was supported by NSF grants MCS-8006938 and MCS-7805849.
" Present address : Software Systems Research Center, Linkping University, S-581 83 Linköping, Sweden.

partition is of length not greater than 41 times the length of an optimal partition. If the total length of boundaries of the figure is not greater than the length of an optimal partition than this factor decreases to 4.5. Marginally, a fast "naive" heuristic is mentioned in this section. It yields a solution whose length is within a logarithmic factor of the optimum and the length of boundaries.

Preliminaries

In the course of the entire paper we assume the following conventions. A *polygon* means a simple polygon (see [SH76]), given by a sequence of pairs of integer-coordinate points in the plane, representing its edges. A *rectilinear polygon* is a polygon all of whose edges are either horizontal or vertical. A *rectilinear polygon with holes* is a figure consisting of a rectilinear polygon and a collection of not-overlapping, not degenerate rectilinear polygons lying inside it. The perimeter of the outer polygon and the contours of the inner polygons form *boundaries* of the figure enclosing its inside. A *rectangular partition* (RP for short) of the figure is a set of straight-line segments that lie within its boundaries and partition it into not-overlapping rectangles. By the length of such a rectangular partition we mean the total length of all these segments. A rectangular partition of the figure achieving the smallest length is called a *minimum edge length rectangular partition* (MELRP for short).

A *concave* point of a figure means a corner of its reflex interior angle. The following obvious lemma can be proved analogously to Theorem 1 in [LLMPL].

Lemma 1. In all MELRP of a given rectilinear polygon with holes, each line segment is colinear with a concave vertex of the figure.

The heuristic for MELRP with fixed rectangle corners

Consider a rectilinear polygon with (rectilinear polygonal) holes, F. The horizontal and vertical lines passing through concave vertices of F induce a rectilinear grid. Let us cut this grid along external and internal boundaries of F, throwing away its parts not lying inside F. Let G_F denote the remaining pieces of the grid. In natural way we can view G_F as a planar weighted graph with vertices corresponding to cut points and crossings of grid lines, with edges corresponding to straight-line segments joining neigbhoring vertices, and weights equal to the length of these segments.

By Lemma 1, the problem of finding MELRP of F can be restated as follows. Find a minimum weight subgraph of G_F satisfying:

(a) the subgraph does not contain isolated vertices,

(b) each vertex of G_F corresponding to a concave point of F is included in the subgraph,

(c) if a vertex of the subgraph is adjacent to only one edge then it corresponds to a concave point of F,

(d) if a vertex of the subgraph is adjacent only to two edges then either it corresponds to a concave point of F or these edges correspond to colinear segments.

We may greatly simplify the problem, assuming that all vertices of the subgraph are given by an oracle. Since the concave points are always included in the subgraph, the oracle need only to fix the Steiner points. Suppose that we have an efficient algorithm for the MELRP problem with fixed Steiner points. If the number of candidates for Steiner points is small then we can iterate the the algorithm for all possible oracles. In the proof of the NP-completeness of MELRP, the number of Steiner points is proportional to the number of clauses of the reduced planar formula (see [LPRS82]). The author does not know how to eliminate them to prove the NP-completeness of the simplified problem. It still seems to be difficult. Fortunately, a heuristic approach is more succesfull here.

Let us call a weighted graph on a rectilinear grid *convex* if it does not contain isolated vertices and any of its edges is represented by a straight-line segment. The segments representing edges are allowed to cross. By *terminal* vertices of a convex graph we shall mean all vertices of degree 1, and all vertices of degree 2 adjacent to perpendicular edges. In view of these definitions, the MELRP problem with fixed Steiner points may be generalized as follows:

Given a convex graph, H, find a minimum weight convex subgraph of H such that:
(1) each vertex of H appears in it, and
(2) any non-terminal vertex of H is adjacent to (at least) two its colinear edges.

In other words, the subgraph does not introduce new terminal vertices.

Let us call the above problem SMELRP, and let us call a convex subgraph of H, satisfying (1), (2), *sound*. We shall reduce SMELRP to a minimum weight perfect matching problem [La76]. More precisely:

Let H be a convex graph, and let m be the total weight of a minimum weight sound subgraph of H. We shall construct a weighted graph G such that any minimum weight maximum cardinality matching for G will easily induce a sound convex subgraph of H, of total weight not exceeding $2m$.

The construction of the graph G proceeds as follows. Each edge of H with weight w is replaced by a superedge composed of two edges. Each of these edges has weight of w. Vertices are replaced by junctions of superedges corresponding to original adjacent edges (see Fig.1). Vertices marked by small circles in figures are also vertices in a clique. The clique is edge-disjoint of all superedges and junctions. It may contain one vertex not occurring in junctions in order to make the number of vertices in G even. All edges of G not occuring in superedges have weight of 0. Any matching of G, M, induces a subgraph of H, H_M, as follows:

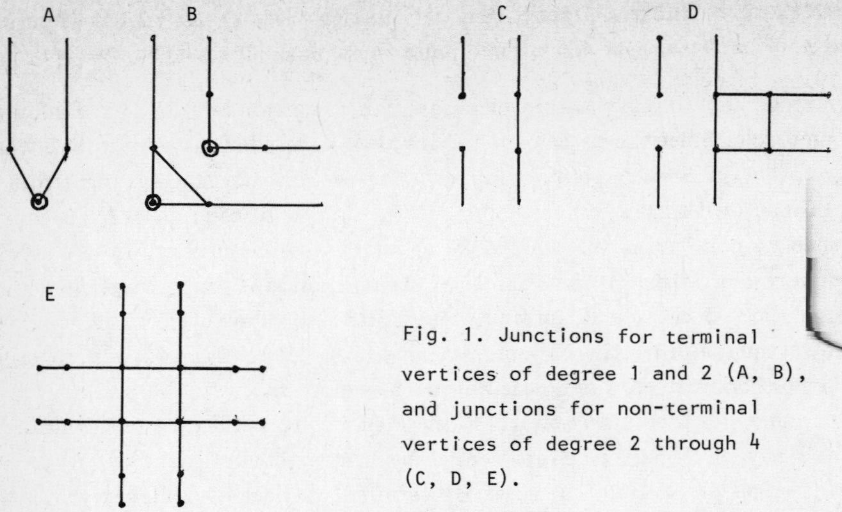

Fig. 1. Junctions for terminal vertices of degree 1 and 2 (A, B), and junctions for non-terminal vertices of degree 2 through 4 (C, D, E).

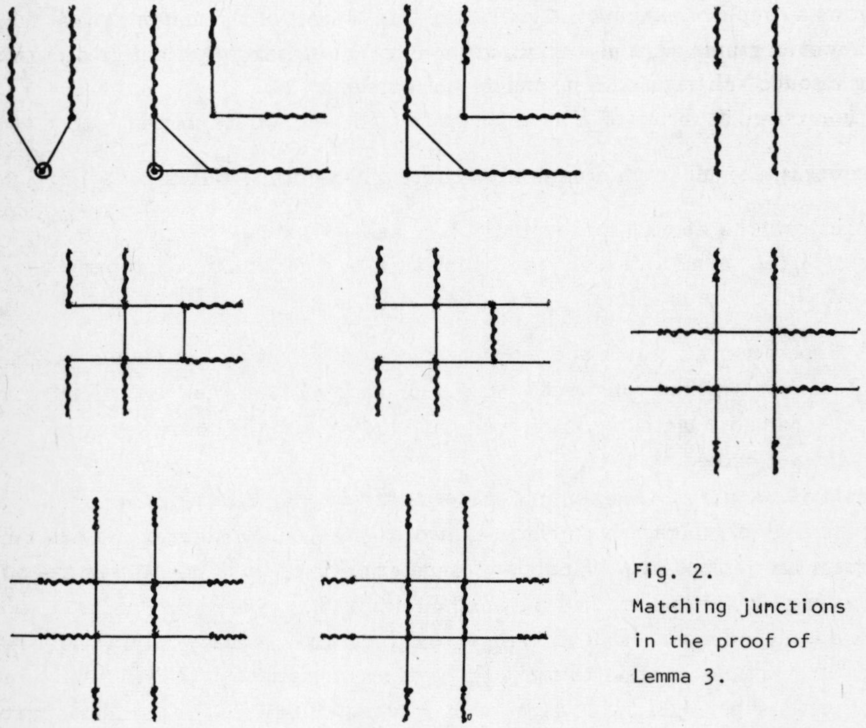

Fig. 2. Matching junctions in the proof of Lemma 3.

(a) each vertex of H is in H_M, and

(b) an edge of H occurs in H_M if and only if at least one of the two edges in the corresponding superedge is matched.

Clearly, the total weight of H_M does not exceed the total weight of M. By inspecting Figure 1 we obtain:

Lemma 2. For any perfect matching of G, M, H_M is a sound subgraph of H.

Let us consider the subgraph of G, G_J, induced by all vertices appearing in junctions. Since the number of vertices of G is even, any matching of G_J that covers all vertices exept perhaps some vertices in the clique, can be extended to a perfect matching of G. Employing this fact we prove:

Lemma 3. For any minimum weight perfect matching of G, M, the total weight of H_M is at most $2m$.

Proof. Consider any minimum weight sound subgraph of H. For each edge of the subgraph match the two edges in the corresponding superedge. The design of superedges, junctions and the clique enables us to complete the preliminary matching to a perfect matching. Fig.2 shows a couple of examples. Clearly, the total weight of the matching is at most $2m$. Hence, any minimum weight perfect matching of G is of total weight not greater than $2m$, inducing a sound subgraph of H of weight not exceeding $2m$.

Given H, the construction of G can be performed in linear time. The number of vertices of G is proportional to that of H. Finding a minimum weight perfect matching in G is easily reducible to finding a maximum weight matching in G with changed weights. It suffices to define the new weight of an edge in G as equal to the triple total weight of G minus its (old) weight. We have an algorithm for maximum weihght matching running in time $O(n^3)$, where n is the number of vertices of the input graph (see [La76]). This all yields:

Theorem 1. We can find a sound subgraph of H of total weight not greater than $2m$ in $O(n^3)$ steps, where n is the number of vertices in H.

In other words, we have an approximation heuristic for SMELRP with the factor 2, taking $O(n^3)$ steps. If H does not contain vertices of degree 4 then by the four color theorem for planar graphs we can show that only edges of total weight $m/3$ need be doubled in the proof of Lemma 3.

The "41" heuristic

The problem of finding a minimum edge length rectangular partition of a rectilinear polygon with holes is NP-complete [LPRS82]. However, if the input figure is just a rectilinear polygon, the problem turns out to be solvable in time $O(n^4)$ [LPRS82].

Let F be a rectilinear polygon with holes, given by a sequence of n edges. To find an approximation of a minimum edge length rectangular partition of F we shall transform F into a rectilinear polygon and then find a minimum edge length rectangular partition of the resulting polygon. The transformation consists in drawing some lines on the grid induced by F (see the previous section). The lines form a Steiner tree connecting the internal and external boundaries of F. To build the Steiner tree we identify each boundary of F with a separate vertex and apply a heuristic for minimum edge length (rectilinear) Steiner tree from [KBM81]. The heuristic runs in time $O(n^2)$ and yields a solution of length within the factor 2 of the optimum.

Clearly, any rectangular partition of F includes a Steiner tree connecting the boundaries of F. Therefore, the length of such a minimum edge length Steiner tree does not exceed that of a minimum edge length rectangular partition of F. The latter will be denoted by $m(F)$. In consequence, the length of transforming lines is at most $2m(F)$.

Unfortunately, new concave corners may be introduced by the transforming lines. So, the problem of estimating the length of a minimum edge length partition of the resulting polygon in terms of $m(F)$ becomes not trivial. To achieve a constant factor in the estimation we refine the transformation. Firstly, we ensure the two following properties of the Steiner tree, preserving the $2m(F)$ bound on its length;

(1) each path in the tree, directly connecting two boundaries, is in the form of one of the two L shape lines shown in Fig. 3,

(2) the L shape lines may overlap but can not intersect.

The above refinement can be obtained by a slightly complicating the heuristic for minimum edge length (rectilinear) Steiner tree from [KMB81]. It takes time $O(n^2)$ as the original heuristic. The resulting polygon has at most $n + \lfloor n/4 \rfloor - 1$ corners. Let us try to estimate the length of a minimum perimeter rectangular partition of this polygon with respect to $m(F)$. One of possible ways is to take an optimal rectangular partition of F, say P, and to try to extend it to a rectangular partition of the polygon. To cancel the new concave corners, i.e. the corners of L shape lines, lying within a rectangle in P, it is sufficient to draw line segments of total length not greater than half of the perimeter of the rectangle (see Fig.4). Let $b(F)$ be the total length of boundaries of F. Summing up over all rectangles in P, and remembering that pieces of its perimeters that overlap with boundaries of F should be counted only once, we conclude that the total length of the extending lines is not greater $m(F) + b(F)/2$. Combining the above bound with that on the length of transforming lines, we obtain the following theorem:

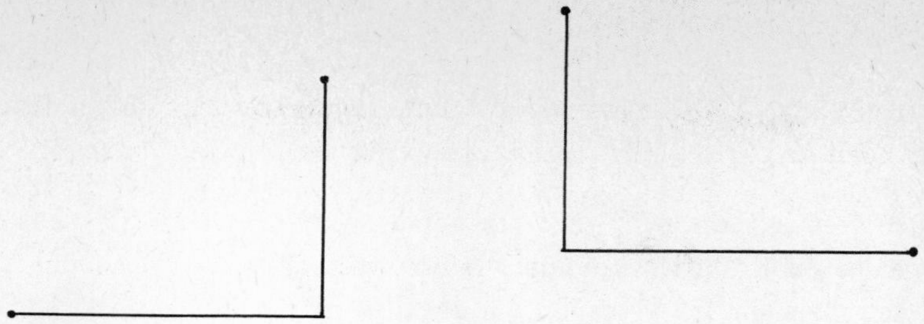

Fig. 3. Two allowed kinds of L-shape lines.

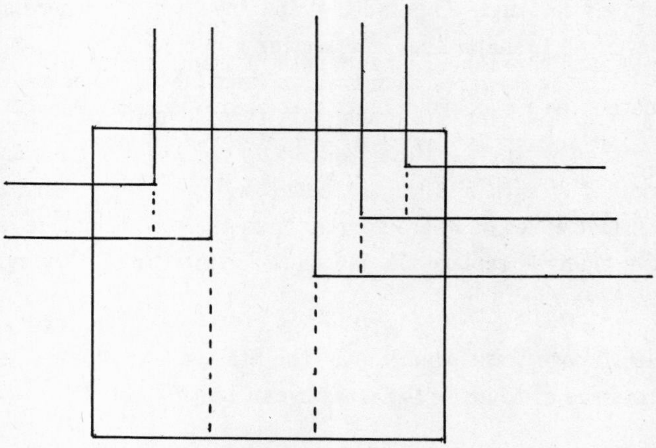

Fig. 4. An example of cancelling corners of L-shape lines inside a rectangle. The cancelling lines are dotted.

Theorem 2. By drawing some edges we can transform F to a rectilinear polygon with at most $n + \lfloor n/4 \rfloor - 1$ corners such that any minimum edge length rectangular partition of the polygon together with the drawn edges form a rectangular partition of F whose length is not greater than $4m(F) + b(F)/2$. The transformation takes $O(n^2)$ time.

If $b(F)$ is much greater than $m(F)$ than the upper bound $4m(F) + b(F)/2$ is of a smaller value. In order to get rid of the boundary factor we shall refine the Steiner tree further. The idea of the refinement is to escape from so called *ugly rectangles* with some corners of L shape lines. The class of ugly rectangles consists of all rectangles r such that:

(a) r lies on the induced grid inside F,
(b) the total length of the perimeter pieces of r that do not overlap with boundaries of F is less than half of the length of a shortest edge of r.

If an ugly rectangle occurs in the partition of F, P, then it may be impossible to cancel the corners of L shape lines within the rectangle, by drawing lines of length proportional to that of the pieces of its perimeter not overlapping with boundaries of F.

Given an ugly rectangle r and an L shape line l whose corner lies inside r, let $imb(r, l)$ be the number of all L shape lines intersecting r and having the corner of l in their inner, convex part. With the corner of each L shape lines l let us associate a rectangle r for which $imb(r, l)$ is largest. Let c be the corner of r that is surrounded by l. If c lies inside any ugly rectangle then with c we associate an ugly rectangle r' such that c lies inside r' and the intersection of r' with r is largest. Also, we associate r' with the corner of l, and r with c. If shortest edges of r' are shorter than these of r, or if c does not lie inside any ugly rectangle, then we replace the pieces of l lying inside r by symmetric pieces of the perimeter of r (see Fig. 5).

Lemma 4. The above transformation of the Steiner tree neither increases its length nor introduces crossings of edges in the tree. It can be performed in time $O(n^2 logn)$.

The implementation of the transformation in time $O(n^2 logn)$ is complicated (the reader is referred for details to [Li81]). It utilizes:

(1) a modification of so called segment tree data structure (see [BW79]) in order to maintain candidates for ugly rectangles,
(2) the Bentley-Wood algorithm for reporting intersections of rectangles [BW79], and
(3) the fact that there are at most n ugly rectangles.

Consider the rectilinear polygon resulting from drawing the transformed tree inside F. As previously, let us try to estimate the minimum length of lines extending the partition of F, P, to a partition of the polygon. Let p be a a rectangle from P.

Lemma 5. To cancel the corners of the transformed Steiner tree that lies inside p it is sufficient to draw edges of total length not greater than 6 times the length of a shortest

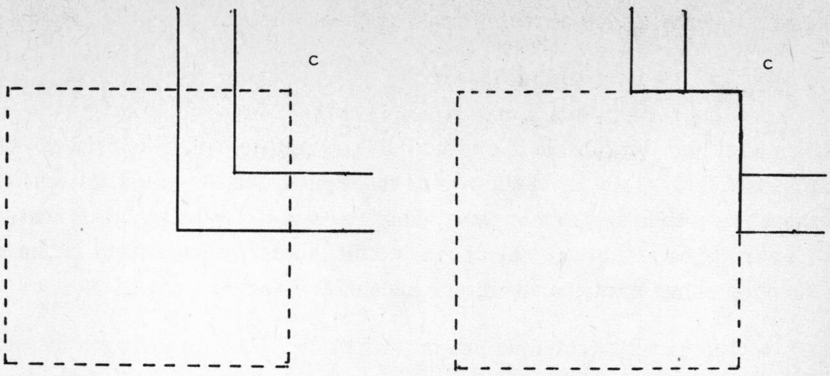

Fig. 5 . An example of transforming L-shape lines.

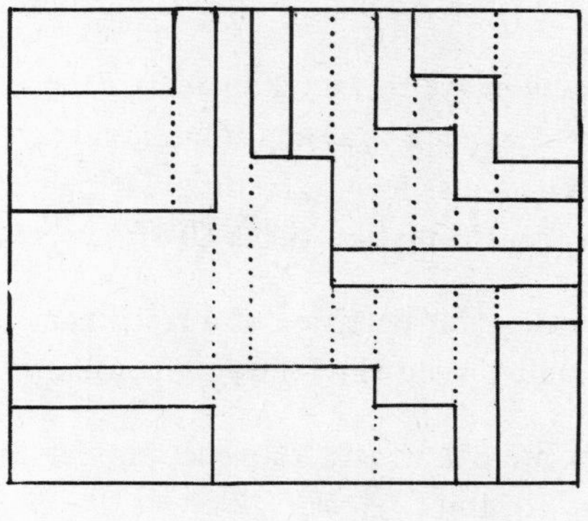

Fig. 6. An example of displacing corners within the rectangle p and their cancellation (dotted lines).

edge of r plus twice the length of transformed L lines lying inside p (see Fig. 6).

If p is ugly then we have to find pieces of P, lying outside of p, to charge them with the cost of cancelling corners within p. Let d be a corner of an L line or the middle corner of a transformed L line lying inside p, and let r be the ugly rectangle associated with d and containing it. It follows from the definition of the transformation and the occurrence of d in r that there is another ugly rectangle r' that is associated with d and intersects r. Let us call r and r' neighbors. At least one of the two neighbors does not occur in the partition P. The following lemma explains the importance of this fact:

Lemma 6. Let q be an ugly rectangle not occuring in P. The total length of pieces of P lying inside q and outside any other ugly rectangle is not less than half of the length of a shortest edge of q.

So, we have a sufficient piece of P in one of the two neighbors to charge with the cost of cancellation. By the definition of neighbor, any ugly rectangle can have at most four neighbors. Putting everything together, we can conclude that the length of the extending lines need not to be greater than $38m(F)$ (see [Li81] for more details). Combining P with the extending lines we obtain a rectangular partition of the polygon whose length is not greater than $39m(F)$. Since the length of the refined Steiner tree is still not greater than $2m(F)$ we have:

Theorem 3. By drawing some edges we can transform F to a rectilinear polygon F' (with at most $n + 3\lfloor n/4 \rfloor - 3$ corners) such that any minimum edge length rectangular partition of F' together with the drawn edges form a rectangular partition of F whose length is not greater than $41m(F)$. The transformation takes $O(n^2 logn)$ time.

A minimum edge length rectangular partition of a rectilinear polygon can be found in time $O(n^4)$. Hence, Theorem 1 and 2 yield the following corollary:

Corollary 1. In time $O(n^4)$, we can construct a rectangular partition of F whose length is not greater than $min\{41m(F), 4m(F) + b(F)/2\}$.

It would be interesting to find a fast heuristic with a constant factor for minimum edge length rectangular partition of rectilinear polygons. Together with our transformations this could give an $O(n^2 logn)$ time heuristic with a greater but still a constant factor. As yet, the author knows merely such a fast heristic yielding solutions within a logarithmic factor of the length of the perimeter of the polygon.

Theorem 4. Suppose that F does not contain holes. In time $O(nlog^2 n)$, we can construct a rectangular partition of F whose length is not greater than $O(b(F)logn)$.

Outline of proof. The idea is to draw from neighboring concave points a pair of perpendicular edges up to their crossing or the polygon perimeter (see Fig. 7). In implementing this idea we meet a difficulty caused by the appearance of sequences of pairs of aligned

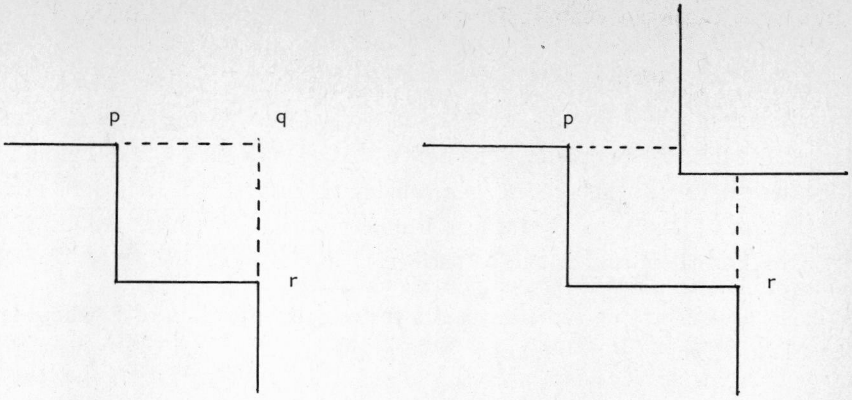

Fig. 7. Two examples of the naive cancellation of concave points.

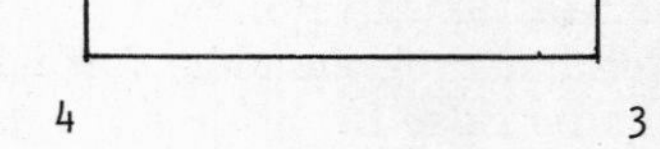

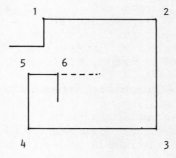

Fig. 8. The cutting of a sequence of pairs of aligned concave points.

concave points. It turns out that if such a sequence contains more than 6 points than it can be cut by drawing an edge of length less that of the piece of perimeter on which the sequence lies. (see Fig. 8) . Therefore, during the first round along the perimeter we can reduce the number of concave points by 1/12 of their number, using edges of total length proportional to that of the perimeter. The new boundary may form a non-simple polygon. Fortunately, we can iterate this process, generalizing the above ideas to include non-simple rectilinear polygons. Hence we have a logarithmic number of rounds. By utilizing ideas from [SH76], each of these rounds can be performed in $O(nlogn)$ time.

Corollary 2. In time $O(n^2)$ we can construct a rectangular partition of F whose length is not greater than $O((m(F) + b(F))logn)$.

Acknowledgements

I would like to express my appreciation to Ron Pinter, Ronald Rivest and Adi Shamir for their encouragments and remarks.

References

[AHU74] Aho,A.V, J.E. Hopcroft and J.D. Ullman, *The Design and Analysis of Computer Algorithms*, Addison-Wesley, Reading, Masss., 1974.
[BW79] Bentley,J.L., D. Wood, *An Optimal Worst-Case Algorithm for Reporting Intersections of Rectangles*, Carnegie-Mellon Report CMU-CS-79-122.
[C80] Chazelle,B., *Computational Geometry and Convexity*, PhD thesis, Yale University, 1980.
[CD79] Chazelle,B. and D. Dobkin, *Decomposing a Polygon into its convex Parts*, Proceedings of the 11th ACM SIGACT symposium, 1979.
[GJ79] Garey,M.R. and D.S. Johnson, *Computers and Intractability: A Guide to the theory of NP-Completeness*, W.H. Freeman and Co., San Francisco, 1979.
[KMB81] Kou,L., G. Markowski and L. Berman, *A fast algorithm for Steiner Trees*, Acta Informatica 15, 1981.
[La76] Lawler, E.L., *Combinatorial Optimization, Networks and Matroids*, Holt, Rinehart and Winston, New York 1976.
[Li82] Lingas,A., *The Power of Non-rectilinear Holes*, Proceedings of 9th International Colloquium on Automata, Languages and Programming, Aarhus, 1982.
[Li81] Lingas,A., *Heuristics for Minimum Edge Length Rectangular Partition*, unpublished manuscript, M.I.T., October 1981.
[LLMP79] Lodi,E., F. Luccio, C. Mugnai, L. Pagli and W. Lipski, Jr., *On Two-dimensional Data Organization 2*, Fundamenta Informatica, Vol. 2, No. 3, 1979.
[LPRS82] Lingas,A., R. Pinter, R. Rivest and A.Shamir, *Minimum Edge Length Decompositions of Rectilinear Figures*, Proceedings of 12th Annual Allerton Conference on Communication, Control, and Computing, Illinois 1982 .
[R82] Rivest,R.,*The PI (Placement and Interconnect) System*, 19th Design Automation Conference, Las Vegas, June 1982.
[P81] Pinter,R., personal communication, December 1981.
[SH76] Shamos,I. and D. Hoey, *Geometric Intersection Problems*, Proc. 17th IEEE Conference on the Foundations of Computer Science, 1976.

AN AXIOMATIC APPROACH

TO SEMANTICS OF SPECIFICATION

LANGUAGES

B.Mahr[1]

Computer Science Department,
The Pennsylvania State University,
University Park, Pennsylvania 16802, USA

J.A.Makowsky[2]

Department of Computer Science,
Technion - Israel Institute of Technology,
Haifa, Israel

Abstract
The paper proposes an axiomatic approach to semantics of specification languages. It introduces the notion of a *semantical system* as a framework to discuss and compare various approaches to specification of (algebraic) data types and to spell out their underlying assumptions. For various of those assumptions we present complete specification languages or show that existing specification languages are complete. Initial and final semantics are characterized as special cases of our unifying concept of semantical systems which admit *D-free* structures.

INTRODUCTION:

Specification of abstract datatypes is widely discussed in the literature of the last decade, and many formalisms and semantical approaches have been proposed. Data types are generally considered to be many sorted structures or algebras, and methods from universal algebra, category theory and model-theory have successfully been applied to study the various questions concerning modularization techniques and expressive power (see for example [ASJ78], [BG80], [Va78], [Ka80], [BBTW81], [EKADJ80], [EKMP82]). While most of the work in this area is intended to contribute to the design of specification techniques of languages, or studies recursiveness in connection with specifications, little is known about the consequences of the implicit assumptions which underly the proposed semantical concepts.

This paper exhibits some of these assumptions common to all of the above mentioned approaches, and shows that, surprisingly, they essentially determine the character of the possible specification languages. Our results confirm the particular choice of specification languages in the literature in the following sense:

Each of the languages we discuss is *complete* for a set of implicit assumptions; in other words, each such language satisfies the assumptions, and any other language which

[1] Supported by th MINERVA Foundation for German-Israeli collaboration while visiting the Computer Science Department at the Technion -Israel Institute of Technology in Haifa, Israel.

[2] Supported by the Swiss National Science Foundation Grant No. 82.820.0.80

satisfies these assumptions has less expressive power.

The results in this paper are inspired by Mal'cev's characterization of free classes [Mal54] and extend our work in [MM82] which is an adaption of this characterization to framework of specification of abstract data types.

The paper is organized as follows: In section 1 we give the axiomatic framework, define reachability and basic compactness. In section 2 we present two complete specification languages, one infinitary and one finitary. The latter is inherently connected with compactness. In section 3 we introduce our key notion of preference systems D and define D-free, a generalization of initial which works unproblematically also in the many-sorted case and in the presence of predicate symbols. This is rather important, for many data structures encountered in practice are of this general form, especially when we have also applications in data bases in mind. In section 4 we prove analoguous theorems as in section 2, but now for specification languages with initial, final or similar semantics, as special cases of our concept introduced in section 3. We conclude the paper with a few general remarks in section 5. Proofs are only sketched and will appear elsewhere, in an expanded version of this paper.

The notions used in this paper are standard in universal algebra and logic and can be found for example in [Mo76]. Explicitly we assume *signatures* to be of the form τ = (S,C,F,R), so including sorts, sorted names for constants, functions and relation symbols. *Finitary signatures* are those where function and relation symbols have finite arity. *Structures* (including relations) and *algebras* are defined in the usual way. *Renaming* $r:\sigma \to \tau$ for signatures σ and τ denotes the bijective assignment of τ to σ which is compatible with the sorting of the components of τ and σ. *Renaming carries over to structures*, and we denote by $A^{(r)}$, with respect to a renaming r , the structure which is identical to A except that its universe, constants, functions and relations are renamed according to r. *Basic formulas* consist of atomic and negated atomic formulas (including equations and inequalities) with free variables. *Basic sentences* are variable free. For a structure A the set of basic sentences holding true in A , is called the *(basic) diagram* of A . If Σ is a set of formulas (possibly infinite) we denote by $\bigwedge B$, $\bigvee B$ the conjunction (resp. disjunction) of all the formulas in B.

1. THE AXIOMATIC FRAMEWORK.

To prove statements about all possible specification languages we have to make precise what we mean by " all possible specification languages ". In this section we give such a definition. The only objection it could provoke is being too general. But since our theorems hold for it, they will a fortiori hold for any narrower concept of specification languages, so we do not have to be bothered by this discussion here.

Definition (Semantical System):
A semantical system is given by a pair (T,φ) consisting of:
- a class T of finitary signatures,
- a family $\varphi=(\mathbf{C}_i)_{i} \subseteq I$ of classes of $type(i)$- structures where $type: I \to T$ associates with each index $i \in I$ a signature $type(i)$ such that the following axioms (1) to (4) hold:

(1) (Closure under isomorphism) Given τ - structures A,B, and a class $\mathbf{C}_i$ from φ. Then $A \cong B$ implies that $A \in \mathbf{C}_i$ iff $B \in \mathbf{C}_i$.
This axiom merely says that we deal with *abstract* data types, i.e. we are only interested in its isomorphism type and not in its particular representation.

(2) (Closure under renaming) Given a renaming $r:\tau \to \sigma$ and a class $\mathbf{C}_i$ with $type(i)=\tau$, then there exists $j \in I$ with $type(j)=\sigma$ such that :
$A \in \mathbf{C}_i$ iff $A^{(r)} \in \mathbf{C}_j$ for all τ-structures A.
This axiom just says that we can change names of relations or functions without affecting the structures. For example we can change from additive to multiplicative notation when dealing with a group without affecting the group itself.

(3) (Closure under intersection) For all indices $i,j \in I$ there is index $k \in I$ such that

$\mathbf{C}_k = \mathbf{C}_i \cap \mathbf{C}_j$.
This axiom ensures that the union of two specifications is again a specification.
(4) (Empty class) For each $\tau \in T$ there is $i \in I$ such that $type(i)=\tau$ and $\mathbf{C}_i=\phi$.
This axiom merely says that we can specify the empty class of τ-structures.

Remark: The definition of a semantical system corresponds exactly to the notion of definability for specification languages, as given in [MM82]. Explicitly: For each semantical system (T,φ) there is a specification language L such that K in φ iff K is L-definable; and conversely, the family of L-definable classes, indexed by the specifications of the specification language L, form a semantical system. Note, the axioms of a semantical system do not predict any syntactical formalism for specification languages, but are meaningful in they own right. They say a semantical system (1) does not differentiate between isomorphic structures, (2) is closed under renaming of the names for sorts, constants, operations and relations, and (3) is closed under refinement by joining specifications. (4) takes care of inconsistent specifications.

The definition of a semantical system is also closely modeled after the abstract definition of a logic, as given in the framework of *generalized model theory*, see the forthcoming book [Higher Model Theory: Logic of Mathematical Concepts, BF83]. What we are doing here is just giving a definition of an abstract logic where the basic notion is not , as usual, the models of a sentence, but the models of sets of sentences. The classes $\mathbf{C}_i$ are just the classes defined by sets of specifications (which we call also specifications).

Definition (Rich Semantical Systems):
A semantical system (T,φ) is *rich enough* if additionally the following axiom (5) holds:
(5) (richness) If $\tau=(S,C,F,R) \in T$, then for all families of constant symbols C over the same sorts S such that $C \subseteq C$ also $\tau'=(S,C,F,R) \in T$; and for all $\tau \in T$ and all sets B of basic τ-sentences $Mod(B) \in \varphi$.
In other words, we can extend a signature by arbitrary sets of constant symbols and every set of basic (variable free) sentences defines a specification.

Definition (Admits Reachable Structures):
Recall that a structure A is *reachable* if every element in a τ-structure A is the interpretation of a term over τ. (Clearly every structure can be made reachable by adding enough constant symbols.)
A semantical system (T,φ) *admits reachable structures* if it is rich enough and additionally the following axiom (6) holds:
(6) (Existence of Reachable Structures) For all indices $i \in I$ there is a reachable structure $A \in \mathbf{C}_i$.

Remark: If (T,φ) is rich enough, then for any reachable τ-structure A with $\tau \in T$ there is an index $i \subseteq I$ with $A \in \mathbf{C}_i$. $\mathbf{C}_i$ can be chosen to be the class of models of the *basic diagram of* A, i.e. the set of atomic and negated atomic (variable free) sentences true in A.

Definition (Basic Compact): Given a class $\mathbf{C}$ of τ-structures. Then $\mathbf{C}$ is *basic compact* if for all sets B of basic τ-sentences $\mathbf{C} \cap Mod(B) \neq \phi$ iff for all finite $B_0 \subseteq B$ $\mathbf{C} \cap Mod(B_0) \neq \phi$.

Definition (Comapct Systems, Systems of Finite Support):
We call a semantical system (T,φ) *basic compact*, if for all $i \in I$ the class $\mathbf{C}_i$ is basic compact.
Note, if $\mathbf{C}$ is first order definable, then $\mathbf{C}$ is basic compact.

Basic compactness just says that if a set of basic sentences makes a specification inconsistent, then there is already a finite subset of basic sentences which makes it inconsistent. Clearly, any system axiomatizable by finitary rules has this property.

Examples:
(1) Let T_E be the class of signatures containing only function symbols and constant symbols and let φ_E be all the equationally definable classes. This gives us a basic compact semantic system which admits reachable structures.
(2) Let T_E be as above and φ_E^f be the all the classes definable by finite sets of equations. This still gives us a basic compact semantic system, but it is not rich enough.
(3) Let T_E be as above and φ_H be the quasi-varieties (i.e. classes definable by sets of finite first order Horn formulas, cf. [Mo76]). This again gives us a basic compact semantic system which admits reachable structures.
(4) Let T be the class of all signatures and φ_ω be the classes definable by first order formulas. Then we get a basic compact semantic system which is rich enough but still does not admit reachable structures. However, if we restrict ourselfs to classes definable by universal formulas, then it does admit reachable structures. If we allow infinitary clauses (cf.section 2) then we destroy compactness, but still get a semantic system which admits reachable structures.
(5) If T_R contains only relation symbols and φ_{DB} consists of classes definable by sets of data base (functional and multivalued) dependencies, the we get a basic compact semantical system which admits reachable structures. For terminology cf [Ul80].
(6) We still get a semantical system which is rich enough if take T as above and let φ_{HL} be the classes definable by sets of statements expressing partial correctness of programs, i.e statements of Hoare Logic. For terminology cf.[Ha79]. But here we loose both compactness and the reachable structures.

2. A COMPLETE SPECIFICATION LANGUAGE FOR RICH SEMANTICAL SYSTEMS ADMITTING REACHABLE STRUCTURES.

In this section we show that the existence of reachable structures together with the axioms of rich semantical systems already determines fairly well, what kind of syntax is appropriate for specification languages.

Definition (Language of Infinitary (Finite) Clauses):
The *language of infinitary clauses* is given by $L_0=(T_0, L_0, \models_0)$ with
- T_0 the class of all finitary signatures,
- $L_0: T_0 \to St_0$, where $L_0(\tau)$ is the class of all τ-formulas of L_0, and $St_0 = \bigcup_{\tau \in T} L_0(\tau)$

defined as follows:
If B is any set of basic τ-formulas (possibly with free variables) , then and only then $\mathbf{V}B \in L_0(\tau)$.
We think of $\mathbf{V}B$ as the infinite disjunction of all the members of B. If B is finite, this definition gives us exactly the clauses in logic.
We now define $\models_0$ *(the satisfaction relation)* $A \models_0 \Phi$ (which we read Φ holds in A), with A a τ-structure and $\Phi \subseteq L_0(\tau)$ if for all $\mathbf{V}B \in \Phi$ the universal closure of $\mathbf{V}B$ (infinite disjunction) holds in A.
We denote by L_f the system which we get from L_0 by restricting it to *finite* sets B of basic formulas and call it *the language of finite clauses*. L_f is logically equivalent to the system given by sets of universal first order sentences (cf. Example (4)).

Our next two theorems show that the language of infinite (finite) clauses is universal for semantic systems which admit reachable structures (and are basic compact). More precisely:

Theorem (Completeness of L_0): Let (T_0, φ_0) be the semantical system of the language L_0 of infinitary clauses, i.e. $\mathbf{C}_i \in \varphi_0$ iff there is $\Phi \subseteq L(type(i))$ with $\mathbf{C}_i = Mod(\Phi)$. Then
(1) (T_0, φ_0) admits reachable structures;
(2) If (T, φ) is a semantical system which admits reachable structures, then φ is a subfamily of φ_0, i.e. for all $\mathbf{C} \in \varphi$ we have $\mathbf{C} \in \varphi_0$, and thus $\mathbf{C}$ is L_0- definable.

Theorem (Completeness of L_f): Let (T_0,φ_f) be the semantical system of the language L_0 of finite clauses, i.e. $\mathbf{C}_i \in \varphi_f$ iff there is $\Phi \subseteq L_f(type(i))$ with $\mathbf{C}_i = Mod(\Phi)$. Then
(1) (T_0,φ_0) admits reachable structures and is basic compact;
(2) If (T,φ) is a semantical system which admits reachable structures and is basic compact, then φ is a subfamily of φ_f, i.e. for all $\mathbf{C} \in \varphi$ we have $\mathbf{C} \in \varphi_f$, and thus $\mathbf{C}$ is L_f- definable.

Proof: The first theorem is proved using the method of diagrams and the second follows from the first using compactness. A reader with no background in model theory should consult [Mo76] , or any other beginning text in model theory. A complete proof may be found in [MM82].

3. TYPICAL MODELS AND INITIAL ALGEBRAS.

The notion of a semantical system is meant to capture the semantics of a specification language and interpretes a class $\mathbf{C}$ in the system as the semantics of a single specification. However, specification of abstract data types often attaches a single structure as semantics to a specification, like the initial algebra approach [ADJ78] or the final algebra approach [Wa78]. In both cases the single structures have a distinguished position in the "specific" class $\mathbf{C}$, which characterizes them uniquely up to isomorphism. On the other side there more possible choices of structures which are unique in their class, so additional arguments should be put forward when one chooses initial or final algebras.

One such argument may be found in the notion of *generic* algebras or, what this really amounts to, the concept of *proof by example*. If we write down a specification Σ of a data structure in some formally defined specification language L, the intended data structure should satisfy Σ, but nothing else. However, this is not possible, since some other statements in L might be logical consequences of Σ. So the best we can hope for is a structure (algebra) A wich satisfies Σ together with all the consequences of Σ, but whenever some statement $\sigma \in L$ is not a consequence of Σ, then it is false in A. In algebra such a structure is called *generic for* Σ . In data base theory such structures are called *Armstrong relations*, (cf.[Fa82]). The usefulness of this concept is that truth in the generic structure (an example) is equivalent to being a logical consequence of Σ, i.e. it formalizes the notion of proof by example.This idea has recently also been exploited for testing programs ,cf [RD81].

What we try to argue for here, is that behind the notion of the *initial algebra* lies a similar concept, and that the uniqueness of the initial algebra is just one of the many nice properties it has. The following notion of *D-free structure* captures the intention behind these two approaches.

Definition (Preference Systems):
Given a class T of signatures, and let P_T and N_T denote the atomic, respectively negated atomic, τ-sentences for $\tau \in T$. Then a class $D \subseteq P_T \subseteq N_T$ is called a *preference system for T* if
(1) D is consistent, i.e. $Mod(D) \neq \phi$,
(2) D is maximal, i.e. any D' with $D \subseteq D' \subseteq P_T \subseteq N_T$ is inconsistent, in other words $Mod(D')=\phi$,
Note that if D contains free variables, then D is consistent if the existential closure of D has a model.

Example: Let A be a τ-structure and D be the set of all basic τ-sentences true in A (the diagram of A). Then D is a preference system. In fact, every preference system can be obtained in this way. To obtain a preference system D with free variables in this way we just look at the free variables as distinct new constant symbols (or generators) and take as A the reachable model described by D and the new constant symbols.

Definition (D-Free Structures):
Given a class T of signatures and a preference system D for T. Let $\mathbf{C}$ be a class of τ-structures with $\tau \in T$ and $A \in \mathbf{C}$, then A *is D-typical in* $\mathbf{C}$ if $A \models \sigma$ implies $\mathbf{C} \models \sigma$ for all $\sigma \in D$.
If σ contains free variables, we mean by $A \models \sigma$ that the universal closure of Σ holds in A and similarily for $\mathbf{C} \models \sigma$.
D-typical structures are a weak form of generic structures, as far as basic, variable free sentences are concerned. If D contains free variables and $D \subseteq P_T$, T has no relation symbols, then they are exactly the generic structures.
A *is D-free in* $\mathbf{C}$ if A is reachable and D-typical in $\mathbf{C}$.

D-free structures combine the requirements of reachability and genericity, as far as they are compatible. For the usual definition of generic algebras, it may well be that there are no reachable generic structures, even if both separately exist. More on generic structures may be found in [Gr79,Appendix 4].

Examples:
(1) (initial) Let T be arbitrary and $D=P_T$. Then A initial in $\mathbf{C}$ iff A D-free in $\mathbf{C}$.
(2) (final) Let T be arbitrary and $D \subseteq N_T$. Then A final in $\mathbf{C}$ iff A D-free in $\mathbf{C}$.
(3) In general , if D is the diagram of some structure A then a D-free structure B in $\mathbf{C}$ is as different from A as $\mathbf{C}$ permits, i.e. for $\sigma \in D$ $B \models \sigma$ only if for all $B' \in \mathbf{C}$ $B' \models \sigma$. This is why we call D a preference system.

Facts:
(1) If A, A' are D-free in $\mathbf{C}$ then $A = A'$.
(2) Let D be an arbitrary preference system for T and $\mathbf{C}$ the class of all τ-structures for given $\tau \in T$, then A is D-free in $\mathbf{C}$ iff the restriction of D to τ is exactly the diagram of A. (Recall that the diagram of A is the set of all basic sentences holding in A).

Definition (Admits D-Free Structures):
A semantical system (T,φ) *admits D-free structures for a given preference system D for T* if (T,φ) is rich enough and additionally satisfies axiom (6'):
(6') (Existence of D-free structures) For all indices $i \in I$ there is a D-free structure in $\mathbf{C}_i$.

4. A COMPLETE LANGUAGE FOR SEMANTIC SYSTEMS WHICH ADMIT INITIAL SEMANTICS.

In this section we show that the existence of D-free structures determines even more, what kind of syntax is appropriate for specification languages.

Definition (Language of infinitary D-Horn Clauses):
Given $T=T_0$, the class of all finitary signatures, and D a preference system for T. Then the *language of infinitary D-Horn clauses* $L_0^D=(T_0, L_0^D, \models_0)$ is defined like L_0, except that for a set B of basic τ-formulas $\mathbf{V} B \in L_0^D(\tau)$ iff there is at most one formula in $B \cap D$.
We denote by L_f^D the set of *finite* Horn clauses.

Note that if B is a set of basic sentences with $B \cap D=\phi$ and $d \in D$ then $\neg d=b_0$ is not in D and the clause $\mathbf{V}(B \cup \{d\})$ is equivalent to the infinitary formulas $\Lambda B \rightarrow b_0$, which is indeed an infinitary Horn formula.

Theorem (Completeness of L_0^D): Let $(T_0, \varphi_0^D$ be the semantical system of the language L_0^D for a given preference system D, i.e. $\mathbf{C}_i \in \varphi_0^D$ iff there is $\Phi \subseteq L(type(i))$ with $\mathbf{C}_i = Mod(\Phi)$. Then
(1) If $D=P_T$ then $L_0, \varphi_0^D)$ admits D-free structures and
(2) If $(T, \varphi^D$ is a semantical system which admits D-free structures, then φ^D is a subfamily of φ_0^D, i.e. for all $\mathbf{C} \in \varphi^D$ we have $\mathbf{C} \in \varphi_0^D$, and thus are L_0^D- definable.

Remark:
(1) of the theorem has an additional assumption, which we conjecture not to be necessary. However, in the case of basic compact semantic systems this additional

assumption is not needed.

Theorem (Completeness of L_f^D): Let $(T_f, \varphi_f^D$ be the semantical system of the language L_f^D for a given preference system D, i.e. $\mathbf{C}_i \in \varphi_f^D$ iff there is $\Phi \subseteq L(type(i))$ with $\mathbf{C}_i = Mod(\Phi)$. Then

(1) $L_f, \varphi_f^D)$ admits D-free structures and

(2) If $(T, \varphi^D$ is a semantical system which admits D-free structures and is basic compact, then φ^D is a subfamily of φ_f^D, i.e. for all $\mathbf{C} \in \varphi^D$ we have $\mathbf{C} \in \varphi_f^D$, and thus are L_f^D-definable.

Proof: Part (2) in both theorems follows from a result due to G.V.Cudnovskii [Cu68] which was independently rediscovered via methods of category theory by H.Andreka and I.Nemeti [AN75] and by B.Banaschewski and H.Herrlich [BH76]. Part (1) in the infinitary case with $D = P_T$ may also be found there. To prove part (1) for general D one has to prove a lemma:

Lemma: Let Σ be a set of finite D-Horn formulas and σ_1, σ_2 two such formulas. Then $\Sigma \cup \{\sigma_1, \sigma_2\}$ is consistent iff for each $i = 1,2$ $\Sigma \cup \{\sigma_i\}$ is consistent.

Proof of lemma: This follows from a close analysis of the resolution method to check satisfiability of sets of clauses, together with compactness. For more details on resolution we recommend [Rob79].

5. RELEVANCE FOR SPECIFICATION OF ABSTRACT DATA TYPES.

The completeness results in the previous sections talk about the limitations in defining classes of structures by specifications. These limitations are not determined by the properties of particular specification languages, but are caused mainly by the assumption of admitting reachable or D-free structures. That such assumptions are reasonable will be discussed below. What should be pointed out here is the *inversion of the usual problem* of finding reasonable semantics for given syntactic approaches. We, on the contrary, have first defined axiomatically how our semantics should look like by extracting some of the key ideas and intuitions behind the [ADJ75]-approach and then we *proved* that this determines, up to logical equivalence, pretty well what kind of a syntax is well suited for specification of abstract data types. For a further discussion of these ideas the reader is referred to [Mak82].

Let us now look, retrospectively, at two special cases, initial and final structures, and discuss the semantic assumptions more closely.

Specificatin of Abstract Data Types with Initial Semantics.

The so-called algebraic approach to data type specification originates in the work of [LZ74], [Gm75] and [ADJ75] and considers specifications to be sets of equations or implicational equations. The definable classes are varieties or quasi-varieties of many-sorted algebras which contain, uniquely up to isomorphism, an initial algebra. Several attempts to extend this approach have been made, namely to use arbitrarty first order formulas (including relation symbols), see [CMPPV80]. The last theorem shows that any extension beyond universal Horn clauses is *unsafe* in the following sense:

A specification language which is rich enough with the property that any specification (set of first order sentences) defines a class of structures which contains an initial structure, must be equivalent to some specification language which uses universal Horn clauses. Otherwise, it cannot guarantee existence of initial structures. Since equivalence to a set of Horn sentences is generally undecidable (see [Ma81]), a specification language which admits initial structures, and which allows syntax analysis, therefore should be the language L_f^D with $D = P_T$. This observation also applies to *Requirement specifications* as introduced in [Eh81]. There a set of requirements (in a typical case a set of first order sentences) is meant to precondition the data type to be specified, or to restrict the class of structures. That such a set of requirements allows initial structures is thus of great importance. A language for such requirements again is bounded in its expressive power by L_f^D with $D = P_T$.

Specification of Abstract Data Types with Final Semantics.

As a reaction to [ADJ75] final semantics is proposed in [Wa78] to determine by a specification not only a single data type, but also its possible implementations. Specification-techniques for the so-called final semantics approach are not equally well developed. See, however, [Ka80] and [HR81]. The possibilities of specifying a class of implementations for the, up to isomorphism, uniquely existing final structure are bounded by L_0^D or L_f^D with $D=N_T$, in a sense just like above.

Acknowledgments: We wish to thank I.Nemeti for his interest in our work and many useful comments.

REFERENCES

[ADJ78]
Goguen, J., Thatcher, J., Wagner, E.; Abstract Data Types as Initial Algebras and Correctness of Data Representations, Current Trends in Programming Methodology, Vol. 4 (R.Yeh, ed.), Prentice Hall, N.Y., 1978, pp. 80-149.

[AN75]
Andreka,H. and Nemeti,I.; Generalisation of variety and quasivariety concepts to partial algebras through category theory, Dissertationes Mathematicae (Rozprawy Math.) 204 (1982)

[BBTW81]
Bergstra, J.A., Broy, M., Tucker, J.W., Wirsing, M.; On the Power of Algebraic Specifications, Proceedings of the MFCS'81, Springer Lecture Notes 118 (1981)

[BF83]
Barwise,J. and Feferman,S.; Higher Model Theory: Logic of Mathematical Concepts, Springer 1983

[BG80]
Burstall, R.M., Goguen, J.A.; The Semantics of CLEAR, a Specification Language, Proc. of 1979 Copenhagen Winter School on Abstract Software Specifications.

[BH76]
Banaschewski,B. and Herrlich,H.; Subcategories defined by implications, Houston Journal of Mathematics 2.2 (1976) pp.149-171

[Cu68]
Cudnovskii,G.V.; Some results in the theroy of infinitely long expressions, Soviet Math.Dokl. 9 (1968) pp.556-559

[CMPPV80]
Carvalho, R.L.de, Maibaum, T.S.E., Pequeno, T.H.C., Pereda, A.A. and Veloso, P.A.S.; A Model Theoretic Approach to the Theory of Abstract Data Types and Data Structures. Research Report CS-80-22, Waterloo, Ontario, 1980.

[Eh81]
Ehrig, H.; Algebraic Theory of Parametrized Specifications with Requirements, Proceedings of the CAAP'81, Springer - Lecture Notes, No.112 (1981)

[EKADJ80]
Ehrig, H., Kreowski, H.J., Thatcher, J.W., Wagner, E.G. and Wright, J.B.; Parametrized Data Types in Algebraic Specification Languages, Proceedings of the 7th ICALP'80, LNCS 85 pp.157-168 ,Springer 1980

[EKMP82]
Ehrig, H., Kreowski, H.J., Mahr, B. and Padawitz, P.; Algebraic Implementation of Abstract Data Types, to appear in TCS, Fall '82.

[Fa82]
Fagin,R.; Armstrong Databases For Functional and Inclusion Dependencies, RJ3500 6.7.1982 IBM Report RJ 3500 (1982)

[Gr79]
Gratzer,G.; Universal Algebra, 2nd ed., Springer 1979

[Gu75]
Guttag, J.V.; The Specification and Application to Programming of Abstract Data Types, TR. CSRG-59, Toronto, 1975.

[Ha79]
Harel,D.; First-Order Dynamic Logic, LNCS 68, Springer 1979

[HR81]
Hornung, G. and Raulefs, P.; Initial and Terminal Algebra Semantics of Parametrized Abstract Data Type Specifications with Inequalities. Proceedings of the CAAP'81, LNCS No. 112, Springer 1981

[Ka80]
Kamin, S.; Final Data Type Specifications: A New Data Type Specification Method, Proc. of the 7th POPL-Conference, 1980.

[LZ74]
Liskov, B.H. and Zilles, S.M.; Programming with Abstract Data Types, Proc. ACM Symp. on Very High Level Languages, SIGPLAN Notices, 9, 1974, pp. 50-9.

[Ma56]
Mal'cev, A.I.; Quasiprimitive Classes of Abstract Algebras,in the Metamathematics of Algebraic Systems, Studies in Logic, Vol. 66. North-Holland, 1971, pp. 27-31.

[Mak81]
Makowsky,J.A.; Characterizing Data Base Dependencies, Proceedings of the 8th ICALP '81, LNCS 115, (1981) pp.86-97

[Mak82]
Makowsky,J.A,; Model theoretic issues in theoretical computer science, to appear in the proceedings of the "Logic Colloquium '82", Florence 1982

[MM82]
Mahr, B. and Makowsky, J.A.; Characterizing Specification Languages with admit Initial Semantics, Tech. Report #232, Technion, Haifa, Israel, February 1982, to appear in TCS.

[Mo76]
Monk,J.D.; Mathematical Logic, Springer 1976

[RD81]
Rowland,J.H. and Davis,P.J.; On the use of transcendentals for program testing, JACM 28.1. (1981) pp.181-190

[Rob79]
Robinson,J.A.; Logic: Form and Function, North Holland 1979

[Ul80]
Ullman,J.D.; Principles of Data Base Systems, Computer Science Press 1980

[Wa78]
Wand,M.; Final Algebra Semantics and Data Type Extensions, Indiana TR65 (1978)

Efficiency of Universal Parallel Computers
(Extended Abstract)

by
Friedhelm Meyer auf der Heide
Johann Wolfgang Goethe-Universität Frankfurt
Fachbereich Informatik
6 000 Frankfurt a.M.
Fed. Rep. of Germany

Abstract:
We consider parallel computers (PC's) with fixed communication network with bounded degree. We construct a universal PC with $n^{1+O(1/\log\log(n))}$ processors which can simulate each PC with n processors with a time loss of $O(\log\log(n))$. This improves a result of [1] where a time loss of $O(\log(n))$ was achieved but only using $O(n)$ processors. Furthermore we prove a time-processor trade-off for a very general type of universal PC's, which includes thatone above. This generalizes a result for a simpler type of simulations presented in [2], where also all results of this paper are included.

Introduction: Galil and Paul dealt in [1] with parallel computers (PC's) with fixed communication network with bounded degree:

A PC M is specified by a graph with bounded degree and by processors which are attached to the vertices of the graph. We suppose that these processors are Random Access Machines (see [3]) which my in addition to their usual instructions read in one step the content of a fixed register - the communication register - of one of its neighbouring processors. M has fixed input - and outputprocessors. We assume M to be syncronized.

A multi-purpose PC (MPC) is a PC whose processors are universal Random Access Machines (see [3]). We say, M_0 can simulate a PC M with time loss k, if there is a program for M_0 (i.e. for every processor of M_0) such that M_0 initialized with this program simulates M and the time it needs to simulate T steps of M is at most $k \cdot T$, i.e. the time for simulating one step is at most k on an average.
M_0 is called n-universal with time loss k, if it can simulate each PC with n processors and degree c with time loss k, where $c>2$ is fixed all over this paper. In [1], a n-universal PC M_0 with $O(n)$ processors and time loss $O(\log(n))$ is constructed.

In the first chapter, we construct a n-universal PC with $n^{1+O(1/\log\log(n))}$ processors but with a time loss of only $O(\log\log(n))$.

In the second chapter, we present a time -processor trade-off for n-universal

PC's M_0, which use simulations with the following property: Let M be simulated for T steps. Then at every time $t \leq T$, each processor of M is simulated by at least one processor of M_0, its representants at time t. If P and Q are neighbouring processors of M, then for every representant of P at time t, there must be a path to some representant of Q at time (t-1) along which the communication is simulated. The maximal length of such a path for some neighbouring processors P and Q let be K_t. Then the time loss of the simulation is

$$\frac{1}{T} \sum_{i=1}^{T} k_t .$$

The simulations of the universal PC from the first chapter are of this type. We prove that every n-universal PC with m processors and time loss k fullfils that $m \cdot k = \Omega(n \log(n)/\log \log(n))$.
In [2] also a trade-off $m \cdot k = \Omega(n \log (n))$ is proved for the case that M_0 only uses simulations in which the representants at time t for some processor are identical for all t. The n-universal PC from [1] fits to this type but not thatone from the first chapter of this paper.

Chapter 1: A fast universal PC.

The basic network of the universal PC we want to construct is a generalization of a permutation nerwork, we call it a distributor.

This is a MPC M_0 with m distinguished processors, its base $B=[1,m]$ $(=\{1,...,m\})$, which are both input -and output- processors. M_0 has the property, that there is a program for M_0 for an arbitrary disjoint partition $A_1,...,A_m$ of B such that M_0 started with $x_i \in N^*$ (*) in processor i of B, $i=1,...,m$, computes y_j in the j-th processor of B with $y_j = x_i$ iff $j \in A_i$ for all $i,j \in [1,m]$. We than say, M_0 distributes $(x_1,...,x_m)$ according to $A_1,...,A_m$.
Note that some A_j's may be empty.
Let G_m be the graph with vertex set $V=\{c_{ij}, i=1,...,m, j=0,...,\lceil \log (m) \rceil -1\}$.
$\{c_{ij}, c_{i'j'}\} \subset V$, $j \leq j'$, is an edge in G_m, if $j'=j+1$ and either $i=i'$ or $|i-i'|=2^{j'}$ or if $j=j'=0$ and $|i-i'|=1$. The MPC W_m is specified by G_m and the base $B=\{c_{i,0}, i=1,...,m\}$. (All its processors are universal Random Access Machines).
Figure 1 shows W_7.

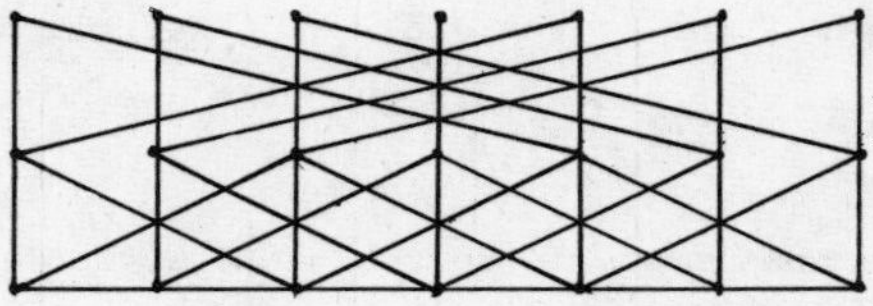

Figure 1: The MPC W_7.

(*) $N^* = \bigcup_{i \geq 0} N^i$, N is the set of non-negative integers.

Because of the similarity of W_m to the Waksman Permutation Network (see [4]) one can prove the following (see [2]):

Theorem 1: W_m is a m-distributor with the properties:

P1: W_m has $m\lceil \log(m) \rceil$ processors and degree 6.

P2: For $a,b \in [1,m]$, $a \leq b$, the MPC whose graph is the subgraph of G_m with vertex set $\{c_{ij},\ i=a, a+1,\ldots,b;\ j=0,\ldots,\lceil \log(b-a+1) \rceil -1\}$ is identical to W_{b-a+1}.

P3: For every disjoint partition $A_1,\ldots,A_m$ of $[1,m]$, $(x_1,\ldots,x_m) \in (N^*)^m$ can be distributed according to $A_1,\ldots,A_m$ in $O(\log(m)+s)$ steps, where s is the maximum length of the x_i's.

Now we shall show how W_m (for a suitable m) can simulate a PC M with n processors $P_1,\ldots,P_n$ and graph G with degree c. (We identify the processors and the corresponding vertices of G). For some P_i and $q \in N$ let $U_q(P_i)$ be the set of all processors of M which can be reached along a path of length at most q from P_i. Let $f,g,h: N \to N$ be functions such that $f(n)<n$ and $g(n) \geq n \cdot g(f(n))$ for all $n>1$ and $\# U_{h(g)}(P_i) \leq q$ for all $q \leq n$ and $\frac{h(n)}{h(f(n))} \in N$ for all $n \geq 1$.

We want to simulate M in $W_{g(n)}$.

For $i=1,\ldots,n$ let M_i be a PC with f(n) processors from $P_1,\ldots,P_n$ including those from $U_{h(f(n))}(P_i)$. The graph of M_i is the restriction of G on the processors of M_i. Let $\overline{W}_1,\ldots,\overline{W}_n$ be n exemplaries of $W_{g(f(n))}$ in $W_{g(n)}$. We can find them because of P2 of theorem 1 and the definition of g.

The following simple lemma is the main observation for our algorithm:

Lemma 1: If for some $i \in [1,m]$, M and M_i execute h(f(n)) steps then the processors P_i in M and M_i resp. have executed the same computation.

The simulation of h(n) steps of M by $W_{g(n)}$ works as follows:

If $n \leq c$, then use any simulation which uses a number of steps only dependent on n. If $n>c$, execute $\frac{h(n)}{h(f(n))}$ times the following three parts: (note that $\frac{h(n)}{h(f(n))} \in N$.)

Part 1: For each $i \in [1,n]$ simulate recursively h(f(n)) steps of M_i in $\overline{W}_i$.

Remark: By lemma 1, there is a processor of $\overline{W}_i$ which simulates P_i correctly relative to M. This is the main representant of P_i. But in $\overline{W}_i$ and in other $\overline{W}_j$'s, too, there are processors which simulate P_i but make mistakes during the simulation. These are its potential representants.

Part 2: For each $i \in [1,n]$ transport the information about the last h(f(n)) steps P_i has executed from its main representant to its potential representants.

Remark: This can be done because $W_{g(n)}$ is a g(n)-distributor.

Part 3: Each potential representant of some P_i uses the information got in part 2 for computing the right configuration of P_i relative to M.

Obviously we have simulated h(n) steps of M. Let now $p \in \mathbb{N}$, $p>1$ be fixed. We may choose $f(n) \approx n^{1/p}$, $h(n) \approx \alpha \cdot \log(n)$ for some suitable $\alpha>0$ and $g(n) = \lfloor n^{1+\frac{1}{p-1}} \rfloor$.

Let T(n) be the time necessary to simulate h(n) steps of a PC with n processors by $W_{g(n)}$.

Then the above algorithm shows

$T(n) \leq a_0$ for some $a_0>0$, if $n<c$. If $n>c$, then

$$T(n) \leq \frac{h(n)}{h(f(n))} \; [T(f(n)) + 0\,(\log(g(n)) + h(n))]$$

$$\approx p \cdot T(n^{1/p}) + 0(\log(n)).$$

Thus $T(n) = 0(\log(n) \log\log(n))$ which quarantees a time loss of $0(\log\log(n))$.

We can improve this result in the following way. At the top of the above recursion we choose $f(n) \approx n^{1/\log\log(n)}$ instead of $n^{1/p}$. For the resulting subproblems of size $n^{1/\log\log(n)}$ we apply the above algorithm.

Thus we obtain for the size of M_0: $g(n) \approx n \cdot g(n^{1/\log\log(n)}) = n \cdot (n^{1/\log\log(n)})^{1+1/(p-1)}$ $\leq n^{1+\beta/\log\log(n)}$ for some $\beta>0$. Thus we may choose $g(n) = \lfloor n^{1+\beta/\log\log(n)} \rfloor$.

As we may choose $h(n) = 0(\log(n))$ we obtain:

$$T(n) = 0\left(\log(n) \cdot \frac{\log\log(n)}{\log(n)}\right) \cdot \left(T(n^{1/\log\log(n)}) + 0(\log(n))\right)$$

$$= 0(\log\log(n)) \cdot \left(\log(n^{1/\log\log(n)}) \cdot \log\log(n^{1/\log\log(n)}) + 0(\log(n))\right)$$

$$= 0(\log\log(n) \cdot \log(n)).$$

Theorem 2: Let $g(n) = \lfloor n^{1+\beta/\log\log(n)} \rfloor$ for some suitable $\beta>0$.

Then $W_{g(n)}$ is n-universal with time loss $\log\log(n)$.

Chapter 2: The Time - Processor Trade-Off

Let M_0 be n-universal and M a PC with n processors [1,n], the processors of M_0 let be [1,m]. The degree of the graph G_0 of M_0 let be d, thatone of the graph G of M let be c.In the sequel we shall identify the graph of a PC to the PC itself.

A simulation of T steps of M by M_0 is a sequence $(B_{1,t},\ldots,B_{n,t},W_t)_{t \leq T}$ with the properties:

For every $t \leq T$, $B_{1,t},\ldots,B_{n,t}$ are pairwise disjoint subsets of the vertex set [1,m] of M_0. $B_{i,t}$ is the set of representants of the vertex i of M at time t. W_t is a set of pathes in M_0. It contains for every representant x of some i at time t a path from x to one representant of each neighbour of i in M at time t-1. If k_t is the length of a longest path of W_t, then k_t is called the t-time loss and $\frac{1}{T}\sum_{i=1}^{T} k_t$ the time loss of the simulation. If $h:=\max\{\sum_{i=1}^{n} \#B_{i,t},\ t\leq T\}$, then we say that the simulation uses h representants.

A simulation with time loss at most k using at most h representants is called a (h,k)-simulation.

Obviously, the simulations from chapter 1 are (g(n),0(log log(n)) - simulations. It seems to be very unlikely that reasonable simulations can be constructed which are not of this type. Therefore we call a n-universal PC which only uses (h,k)-simulations n-universal of the general type with time loss k using h representants. For such PC's we prove:

Theorem 3: Let M_0 be a n-universal PC of the general type with m processors and time loss k, using h representants, then $h \cdot k = \Omega(n \log(n)/\log\log(n))$ or $m = n^{\Omega(n \log(n)/h)}$.

As $h \leq m$, we obtain the following time-processor trade-off:

Theorem 4: Let M_0 be a n-universal PC of the general type with m processors and time loss k, then $m \cdot k = \Omega(n \log(n))/\log\log(n))$.

Now we prove theorem 3.

The idea of this proof is as follows:

To each (h,k)-simulation of a graph with n vertices by M_0, we attach a fragment, i.e. an object which still specifies the graph being simulated. For technical reasons we only consider graphs which contain a balanced, binary tree. The set of these graphs let be called E_n, Now the number Y of fragments of (h,k)-simulations of graphs from E_n is an upper bound for the number of graphs from E_n which can be simulated by M_0 with time loss k using h representants.

(Note that this bound is smaller then the number of (h,k)-simulations, because different such simulations may have the same fragment.)

On the other hand we bound $\#E_n$ from below. As every graph from E_n must be simulated by M_0 with a (h,k)-simulation, $y \geq \#E_n$, which will prove the theorem.

We first state the bound for $\#E_n$. A proof can be found in [2].

Lemma 2: $\#E_n \geq n^{\frac{c-3}{2}n} \cdot 2^{-an}$ for some a>0.

Before defining and counting the fragments, we state some estimations from [2] which we will need in the sequel.

Lemma 3: a) For all $k,n \in N$, $1 \leq k \leq n$, $\binom{n}{k} \leq n^k$.

b) $\#\{(a_1,\ldots,a_n) \in (N \setminus \{0\})^n \mid \sum_{i=1}^{n} a_i \leq h\} \leq 2^h$

c) Let $(a_1,\ldots,a_n),(b_1,\ldots,b_n) \in (N \setminus \{0\})^n$.

Let $p \in N$ such that $p \cdot a_i \geq b_i$ for every $i \in [1,n]$,

and $\sum_{i=1}^{n} a_i \leq h$, $\sum_{i=1}^{n} b_i \leq h$. Then $\prod_{i=1}^{n} \binom{p \cdot a_i}{b_i} \leq e^{2h} \cdot p^h$.

Now we define the fragments. Let D be a balanced, binary tree with vertices $[1,n]$. D has depth $\lfloor \log(n) \rfloor$.
Now let $A \in N$ be fixed, $A \leq n$. A will be specified later.
Let $r \in N$ and $V_1,\ldots,V_r$ be r subsets of $[1,n]$ of cardinality A, which cover $[1,n]$, such that for every $i \in [1,r]$, the subgraph of D induced by V_i is a balanced, binary tree of depth $\lfloor \log(A) \rfloor$. Obviously, $V_1,\ldots,V_r$ can be chosen such that $r \leq \frac{2n}{A}$ and every $i \in [1,n]$ is contained in at most two of the V_i's.
We assume that $T \geq 2\lfloor \log(A) \rfloor + 1$. Let $(B_{1,t},\ldots,B_{n,t},W_t)_{t \leq T}$ be a (h,k)-simulation for some graph from E_n. For $t \in [1,T]$ let k_t be the t-time loss of the simulation.
We count the number of graphs for which there is a (h,k)-simulation as follows:
For some t_0 we count the number of possible choices of $B_1,\ldots,B_n = B_1^{t_0},\ldots,B_n^{t_0}$ in a strategy. Afterwards we estimate the number of possible choices of sets S of edges of graphs which can be simulated by a strategy with the above representants at time t_0 and (t_0+1)-time loss k_{t_0+1}. Unfortunately, this method, i.e. the choice of $(B_1,\ldots,B_n,S)$ as fragments, is to weak for our purpose, because there are too many choices for $B_1,\ldots,B_n$. Therefore we first fix the representants $B'_1,\ldots,B'_r$ of r suitably chosen vertices of G - one from each V_i - at time $t_0-2\lfloor \log(A) \rfloor$. There number is not too large if t_0 is chosen reasonably. As all considered graphs contain a balanced binary tree, after having fixed $B'_1 \ldots B'_r$ the number of choices of $B_1,\ldots,B_n$ decreases considerably.
Formally a fragment is defined as follows:
Let $t_0 \in [2\lfloor \log(A) \rfloor, T-1]$ be chosed such that $\sum_{t=t_0-2\lfloor \log(A) \rfloor+1}^{t_0+1} k_t)$ is minimal relative to the choice of t_0. This sum is called R_0.
Now a fragment of $(B_{1,t},\ldots,B_{n,t},W_t)_{t \leq T}$ is specified by a tupel

$(B_1,\ldots,B_n,B'_1,\ldots,B'_r,S)$ as follows:
$(B_1,\ldots,B_n) = (B_{1,t_0},\ldots,B_{n,t_0})$.

If $j \in [1,r]$ and $i_j \in V_j$ such that $B_{i_j,t_0-2\lfloor \log(A) \rfloor}$ has a minimal cardinality relative to the choice of i_j, then $B'_j = B_{i_j,t_0-2\lfloor \log(A) \rfloor}$.

$S:=\{(x,y) \in [1,m]^2 / x \in B_{i,t_0}$ and there is an $i \in [1,n]$,

such that there are two (t_0+1)-transport pathes in W_{t_0+1} which join

x and y to the minimal element of $B_{i,t_0+1}\}$.

Let R be the number of graphs from E_n for which there is a (h,k)-simulation in M_0, and Y the number of fragments of (h,k)-simulations for graphs from E_n.

Obviously a fragment still specifies the graph being simulated. Therefore, the following holds:

Prop. 1: $R \leq Y$.

Before we bound Y, we state some easy properties of the fragment described above.

Prop. 2: a) $K_{t_0+1} \leq R_0 \leq 2k(2\lfloor \log(A) \rfloor + 1)$ b) $\sum_{i=1}^{r} \#B_i' \leq \frac{2h}{A}$.

c) For every $j \in [1,r]$ and every $i \in V_j$, $B_i \subset U_{R_0}(B_j')$. (Let G=(V,E) be a graph, $B \subset V$, $a \in N$, then $U_a(B)$ is the set of vertices from V, which can be reached by a path of length at most a from some vertex from B.)

Now we bound Y.

Prop. 3: $y \leq m^{\frac{2h}{A}} \cdot d^{(h+2cn)(5k \log(A))} \cdot e^{4h} \cdot (\frac{h}{n})^n$.

Proof: First we bound the number Y_1 of all tupels $(B_1,\ldots,B_n,B_1',\ldots,B_r')$, which belong to a fragment of a(h,k)-simulation of a graph from E_n.

Claim 1: $Y_1 \leq m^{\frac{2h}{A}} \cdot e^{4h} \cdot d^{h(R_0+1)}$.

Proof: Let the cardinalities $h_1,\ldots,h_n$, $h_1',\ldots,h_r'$ of $B_1,\ldots,B_n$, $B_1',\ldots,B_r'$ be fixed.

- By lemma 2.b) there are at most 2^{2h} possible choices of $h_1,\ldots,h_n$, $h_1',\ldots,h_r'$.
- There are at most $\prod_{i=1}^{r} \binom{m}{h_i'}$ possible choices of $B_1',\ldots,B_r'$.
- For $j \in [1,r]$ let $V_j' \subset V_j$ chosen such that $V_1',\ldots,V_r'$ form a disjoint partition of $[1,n]$.

By prop. 2.c) it follows for every $j \in [1,r]$ and every $i \in V_j'$: There are at most

$$\binom{h_j' \cdot d^{R_0+1}}{h_i}$$ possible choices for B_i.

Therefore we obtain:

$$Y_1 \leq 2^{2h} \cdot \prod_{q=1}^{r} \binom{m}{h'_q} \prod_{j=1}^{r} \prod_{i \in V'_j} \binom{h'_j \cdot d^{R_0+1}}{h_i}$$

Applying lemma 3.a) and c) we obtain

$$Y_1 \leq 2^{2h} \cdot m^{\sum_{i=1}^{r} h'_i} \cdot d^{h(R_0+1)} \cdot e^{2h}.$$

By prop. 2.b), $\sum_{i=1}^{r} h'_i \leq \frac{2h}{A}$, which proves claim 1.

Now we bound for some fixed sets $B_1,\ldots,B_n$, $B'_1,\ldots,B'_r$ the number Y_2 of fragments of (h,k)-simulations which can be formed by these sets.

<u>Claim 2</u>: $Y_2 \leq (\frac{h}{n})^n \cdot d^{2(k_{t_0+1}+1)cn}$.

<u>Proof</u>: If $(B_1,\ldots,B_n , B'_1,\ldots,B'_r , S)$ is a fragment of a (h,k)-simulation it follows for S:

- There are at most n different first components of pairs occuring in S, one in each B_i, $i \in [1,n]$.
- At most c second components belong to each first component x.

They are contained in $U_{2(k_{t_0}+1)}(x)$.

For $i \in [1,n]$ let $h_i = \#B_i$. Then there are at most $\prod_{i=1}^{n} h_i \leq (\frac{h}{n})^n$ possible choices for the n first components of the pairs of S.

In order to fix the second components for some first component x, there are at most

$$\binom{d^{2k_{t_0+1}+1}}{c}$$ possible choices.

Therefore it follows by lemma 3.a):

$$Y_2 \leq (\frac{h}{n})^n \cdot \binom{d^{2k_{t_0+1}+1}}{c}^n$$

$$\leq (\frac{h}{n})^n \cdot d^{(2k_{t_0+1}+1)cn}.$$

As $Y \leq Y_1 \cdot Y_2$, prop. 3 is proved by claim 1 and 2 and the bounds for R_0 and k_{t_0+1} from prop. 2.a).

Now we are able to prove theorem 3.

By lemma 2, $\#E_n \geqq n^{\frac{c-3}{2}n} \cdot 2^{-an}$.

W.l.o.g. we may assume that $c \geqq 4$.

As pointed out when describing the idea of the proof, we get:

$$n^{\frac{c-3}{2}n} \cdot 2^{-an} \leq 2^{\frac{2h}{A}} \cdot e^{4h} \cdot d^{(h+2cn)(5k\log(A))} \cdot \left(\frac{h}{n}\right)^n .$$

Therefore,

$$m \geqq 2^{\frac{A}{2h}\left(\left(\frac{c-3}{2}\right) n \log(n) - a\, n - 4h \log(e)\right)} \cdot 2^{\frac{A}{2h}\left(-\log(d)(h+2cn)(5k\log(A)) - \log\left(\frac{h}{n}\right) n\right)} .$$

Let a_1, $a_2 > 0$ be chosen such that $\frac{c-3}{2} > a_2 = a_1 (4\log(e) + 5(2c+1)\log(d))$.

and let $h \cdot k \cdot \log(A) \leqq a_1 n \log(n)$.

Then $\log\left(\frac{h}{n}\right) \leqq \log\log(a_1 n)$ and it follows:

$$m \geqq 2^{\frac{A}{2h}\left(\left(\frac{c-3}{2} - a_2\right) n \cdot \log(n) - a \cdot n - n \cdot \log\log(a_1 n)\right)}$$

$$\geqq n^{\Omega\left(\frac{A\, n}{h}\right)} .$$ Now we choose $A = \lfloor \log(n) \rfloor$ and obtain theorem 3.

References:

[1] Z. Galil, W.J. Paul: A Theory of Complexity of Parallel Computation. Proc. of the 13th Annual ACM Symp. on Theory of Computing, Milkwaukee, May 1981, pp. 247-262.

[2] F.Meyer auf der Heide: Efficiency of Universal Parallel Computers. Interner Bericht des Fachbereichs Informatik der J.W. Goethe-Universität Frankfurt, 2.82.

[3] W.J. Paul: Komplexitätstheorie. Teubner Verlag, Stuttgart, 1978.

[4] A. Waksman: A Permutation Network. Journal of the ACM, 15(1) (1968) pp. 159-163.

Coroutines and Processes in Block Structured Languages.

A. Kreczmar
Institute of Informatics
University of Warsaw, PKiN
VIII floor, 00901 Warsaw, Poland

T. Müldner
School of Computer Science
Acadia University, Wolfville
Nova Scotia, BOP IXO, Canada

ABSTRACT.

This paper considers the semantics of coroutines and processes in block structured languages; in particular, the problem of existence of static and dynamic environments. It is shown that a definition of inaccessible module instances may result in an inconsistent meaning of some operations. Both an Algol-like language and a SIMULA-like language, (with pointers yet without coroutines), are proven to have well-defined semantics. The examples provided in this paper show that some coroutine and concurrent operations may, however, destroy the static environment.

1. INTRODUCTION.

The problem of the existence of the static and dynamic environments in block structured languages with coroutines and processes seems to be up-to-date, see e.g. ADA, [10]. The literature on coroutines and processes is rich and diverse see e.g. [7], [8] [9].

Should the structure of the module instances reflect an actual storage management system, it has to include an operation which deallocates inaccessible instances. The deletion of an instance, however, may perturb the normal program execution since the structure of static and dynamic connections could be destroyed. For completeness, Section 2 quotes the well-known results concerning the semantics of Algol-like languages. The following section comprises the corresponding analysis of language with pointers yet without coroutines. Section 4 introduces coroutine and semi-coroutine operations, and examines their semantics. The last section extends the analysis to the languages with concurrent processes. A conclusion is that the languages with coroutines and processes do not satisfy the basic requirement of an existence of the static environment. Therefore, a new approach to storage management and referencing mechanisms is needed.

2. BLOCK STRUCTURED LANGUAGES.

This section will introduce some basic concepts and recall the main properties of Algol-like languages (see [2,3,11]). Let Y be any syntactic entity, such as a variable or a module. We write Y **decl** M for Y is declared in the module M. For any program, the set T of all its modules with the relation **decl** forms a tree denoted **T[decl]** = <T,decl> with the main block (MB) as its root. For any binary relation R, denote by R+ (R*) the transitive (and reflexive) closure of R.

A module N is a static container (cf [2]) for the occurrence of the identifer X in a module M, N = SC(X,M), if (i) X **decl** N, (ii) M **decl*** N, (iii) there is no module N' for which M **decl*** N' **decl+** N and X **decl** N'. #

The instances of a module M will be denoted by P(M), Q(M), etc. (with indexes, if necessary), or simply by P, Q, etc. A state of the program execution is considered as a finite set of instances that exist when a snap-shot of the execution is taken. The states will be denoted by S, S', etc.
The changes of states will now be considered. According to the syntactic structure for an occurrence of the identifier X in the module M, the instance P(N) of the module N = SC(X,M) is accessed. The instance P is called the dynamic container for the occurrence of X in M, F = DC(X, M) (compare [2]). For any instance P (except of MB) another instance Q, called the syntactic father of P, will be uniquely defined (see def. 2). The relation between P and Q will be denoted by P => Q. The main property of => is
(2.1) if P(M) => Q(N) then M **decl** N. #
The relation P => Q will sometimes be denoted by P.SL = Q, because P's **S**tatic **L**ink points to Q.

Definition 1.

The sequence $P_k,\ldots,P_1$ is the static chain of the instance P_k, if P_{i+1} => Pi for i = k-1,..,1; and P_1 is the instance of the main block. #

The existence of the static chain of the currently executed instance will be proved later (see 2.5). From (2.1) and the above definition, it follows:
(2.2) If $P_k(M_k)$, $P_{k-1}(M_{k-1}),\ldots,P_1(M_1)$ is a static chain of the instance P_1 then $M_k,\ldots,M_1$ forms a path from M_k to the root MB, in the tree **T[decl]**. #
(2.3) If $P_k(M_k)$, $P_{k-1}(M_{k-1}),\ldots, P_1(M_1)$ is the static chain of the instance P_k then for any occurrence of an identifier Y, such that the static container $SC(Y,M_k)$ exists, there is a unique j, $1 \leq j \leq k$, for which $M_j = SC(Y,M_k)$. #
For any state S of a program execution we define a structure **S[syn]** = <S, =>>. This structure reflects the syntactic structure of the program. When a control enters a module, say M, a new instance P(M) is generated. Therefore the structure **S[mem]** with the operation **insert**(P) is introduced. The control structure of the program will be described by means of another structure **S[dyn]** = <S,->> where the relation -> determines a dynamic father. If P -> Q we shall also write P.DL = Q because P' S **D**ynamic **L**ink points to Q. An active instance at state S is the instance which is being executed at S. In all sections, except the last, we consider sequential languages for which at most one instance is active at a given state. Below, the relations =>, and -> are defined, and moreover, the transitions between states are determined:

Definition 2.

Consider a state S at which an instruction **call** F is executed in the active

instance P(N). Suppose that the static container M = SC(F,N) and the static chain of M exist. Then, by (2.2), a unique instance R(M) of the module M belongs to this static chain. The generation of a new instance Q(F) results in the following actions: (i) **insert**(Q) for **S[mem];** (ii) add an edge Q => R for **S[syn];** (iii) add an edge Q **->** P for **S[dyn];** (iv) the instance Q becomes active. The termination of the instance Q with the dynamic father P (Q->P) results in the following actions:
(i) delete the edge Q **->** P for **S[dyn];**
(ii) the instance Q becomes active. #

The following propositions describe the properties of the structures **S[syn]**, **S[dyn]**. The proofs are straightforward and are therefore omitted.

(2.4) If P **=>** Q then non Q ->* P. #

(2.5) The structure **S[syn]** is a tree; the static chain of the active instance P forms a path from P to the root (so this chain always exists). #

(2.6) The structure **S[dyn]** consists of a chain, (called operational chain) with the active instance as its leaf, and a number of isolated nodes. #

Clearly, any real memory management system cannot afford allocating more and more memory fields without any garbage collection. Therefore, the structure **S[mem]** will have an additional operation **delete**(P) which deallocates the instance P. This operation, however, may cause the structures **S[syn]** and **S[dyn]** to no longer be graphs.

If

[P] ⟶ [Q]

then after **delete**(Q) we could obtain

[P] ⟶ ?

We shall call such an edge a pseudo-edge, and a structure with nodes and pseudo-edges, a pseudo-graph.

The termination effect (def. 2) is redefined by adding the action.

(iii) **delete**(Q) for **S[mem].** #

We shall investigate the following questions:

(2.7) When an instance becomes inaccessible, and what does it really mean?

(2.8) When the inaccessible instances should be deallocated?

(2.9) What are the consequences of the deallocation for the semantics of the language?

For an Algol-like language, an instance Q, is said to be accessible from the instance P at a state S iff P ->* R =>* Q (for some instance R.) The instance Q is said to be inaccessible in a state S, iff Q is not accessible from the active instance.

The following proposition answers the question 2.7:

(2.10) A terminated instance is inaccessible at any state.

The proof goes by induction. Let a state S' satisfy (2.10), and state S be obtained from S' as a result of a termination of the instance P. Then P is inaccessible from the dynamic father Q of P, because this contradicts (2.4).

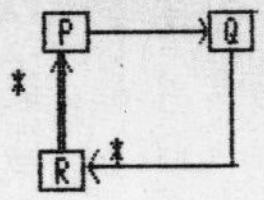

If P' ≠ P is a terminated instance accessible from Q (which is active at S): P -> Q ->* R =>* P' then P' would be accessible from P at S', which contradicts the inductive assumption. #

The proofs of the following propositions are simple enough to be left to the reader:

(2.11) The structure **S[syn]** is a tree, the active instance being its leaf. #

(2.12) The structure **S[dyn]** consists of an operational chain the active instance being its leaf. #

(2.13) The syntactic environment of the active instance is always defined, i.e. the static chain of the active instance P(M) exists and contains all the dynamic containers for all occurrences of identifiers in M. #

In accordance with the above follows the well known property of standard implementation of block structured languages follows:

(2.14) A block structured language is "stack implementable", i.e. **insert** and **delete** operations of **S[mem]** are performed in the LIFO scheduling strategy. #

In the following sections we shall investigate the semantical properties of the languages which extend an Algol-like language with the following properties:

- storage management, the terminated instances are accessible;
- control structure, the instance can be re-entered;
- parallelism, more than one active instance may exist at a time.

3. POINTER LANGUAGES.

The main feature of a language with pointers is that a terminated instance can be accessed via the pointer, (i.e. reference variables) the value of which is the address of the instance. Using SIMULA notation (certify [6]) for a reference variable X of a module type M, the instruction

X: = **new** M results in a generation of memory field for the instance P(M), an execution of M's instruction (if any), and eventually, assigning the address of P(M) to X. The relation between X and P(M) will be denoted by X ->> P(M). Similarly, Q ->> P means that the instance P is pointed to by an attribute of the instance Q. The static container for dotted identifier is defined as follows: Consider the occurrence of X.W in a module N. The module N' = SC(X,N) contains the declaration of, e.g. **var** X:M. Therefore, the module N" = SC(M,N') contains the declaration of M. If M has the attribute W, then M = SC(X.W,N), otherwise the program is syntactically incorrect. Note that (2.2) from Section 2 still holds, while (2.3) is no longer true. Consider the following:

Example 1.

```
unit N: class;
  ...
  unit M: class;
    var W: integer;
  end M;
  ...
  unit N1: class;
    var X: M;
    unit N2: class;
      ...
      ... X.W ....
      ....
    end N2;
    ...
    X:= new M;
    ...
    end N2;
    ...
    X: = new M;
    ...
  end N1;
  ...
end N;
```

Then we have P(N2) =>+ P(N1) =>+ P(N) and P(M) =>+ P(N) where X points to P(M), hence P(SC(X.W,N2)) does not belong to the static chain of P(N2). #

A generation and a termination of an addressable instance are described as follows:

Definition 3.

The description of a generation is similar to that of Def. 2. However, if a new instance Q(N) is indirectly generated from the active instance P(M), via X.N, then the syntactic father of Q is the object pointed to by X. Now let us consider a termination. Let P be the dynamic father of the instance Q, i.e., Q-> P. Then the following actions will be performed: (i) **delete** Q -> P for **S[dyn]** (i.e. Q.DL becomes none): (ii) the instance P becomes active; (iii)if Q is an addressable instance generated by means of X:=**new** M instruction, then X points to Q. #

From this definition the analogon of (2.4) follows immediately:

(3.1) If P => Q, then **non** Q ->* P. #

Note that a structure **S[syn]** does not have to be a tree any longer: Suppose that the generation X:= **new** M takes place within the body of a procedure F, M is declared in F1 and F is called from R:

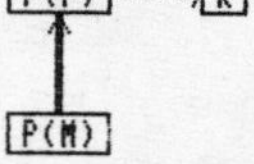

After the termination of F, R becomes active, P(F) is deleted, but P(M) remains alive and without a syntactic father:

This situation will not harm the execution of a program provided P(M) will be inaccessible. The latter notion has to be redefined in a language with pointers:

Definition 4.

An instance Q is accessible from an instance P at a state S iff

P -> * R=>* R' ->>* Q for some instances R, R'. #

(3.2) If Q is non-addressabble, and

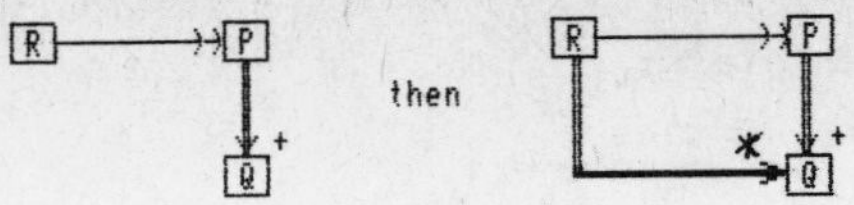

Proof. P(M) =>+ Q(M') so M is nested in M'. Moreover, R(N) ->> P(M) , so N contains the declaration of variable X of type M. Therefore, a static chain of R contains an instance Q'(M'). Our purpose is to show that Q = Q'. Suppose the contrary is true. Two different instances of the same module may communicate only via non-local variables, or via parameters. The first case is excluded, i.e. the reference to P cannot be transmitted in a remote expression via Q to Q.SL because M' is a non-addressable module (i.e. procedure /block instance). The second case is excluded because M is nested in M' and a parameter of M' has to be of a type which is visible from M'. #

(3.3) If Q is non-addressable and

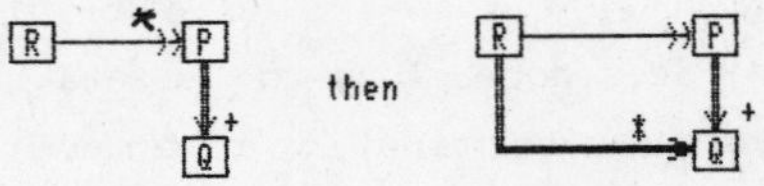

#.

A terminated non-addressable instance may be a root of static sub-tree. A structure **S[syn]** is a pseudo-tree with pseudo-edges. By virtue of (3.3), if Q is a non-addressable instance and there is a reference chain between an instance P and a node of Q's subtree **STQ** then P belongs to **STQ**:

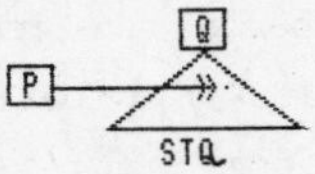

The analogons of (2.5) and (2.6) are the following:

(3.4) The structure **S[syn]** consists of a single tree **S[T]** and a number of pseudo-trees. Any instance P accessible from the active instance belongs to **S[T]**.

(3.5) The structure **S[dyn]** consists of a chain and a number of isolated vertices, the active instance is the leaf of the chain.

Proof. These propositions will be proved by simultaneous induction. If S' consists solely of the instance of MB, then the proof is trivial. Let S' be a state with the active instance Q(M). Consider a generation of an instance P(N). Put S = S' u (P). If P is directly generated by means of a **new** N instruction then N is visible from M; so the syntactic father R(N') of P(N) belongs to the static chain of Q(M):

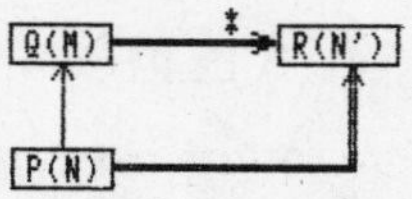

From the inductive assumption R(N') belongs to **S'[T]**, so R(N) belongs to **S[T]**. Therefore, **S[T]** consists of **S'[T]** augmented by the leaf P(N). Any instance accessible from P at state S is accessible at the state S', either from Q or from R, therefore from the inductive assumption, (3.4) holds. If P is indirectly generated by means of **X.new** N instruction then

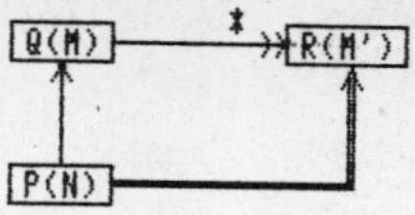

By the inductive assumption R belongs to **S'[T]** and so to **S[T]**. Therefore (3.4) holds. Now the termination of Q will be considered. Put S=S'- (Q). The only non-trivial case is that of non-addressable Q. Clearly **S'[T] = S[T] - STQ,** so we shall prove that

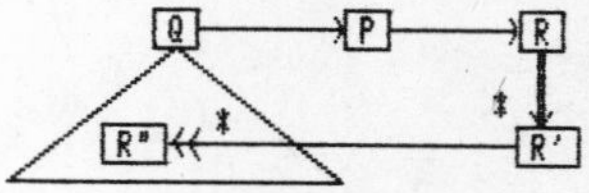

is not possible. Note that R ≠ R" = Q cannot hold because Q is non-addressable. Hence R =>* Q and from (3.3) R' =>* Q:

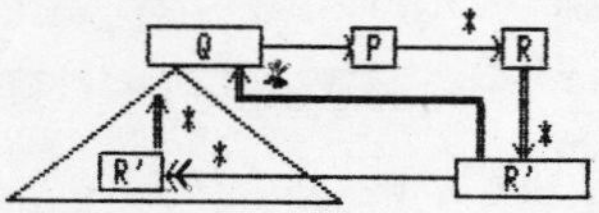

Therefore Q ->* R and R =>* Q which contradicts (3.1). #

The following analagon to (2.10) holds:

(3.6) Any accessible instance belongs to the tree **S[T]**. Hence, the syntactic and dynamic environment of the active instance is always defined as follows: the static chain of the active instance exists, and moreover, the dynamic containers (for all the occurrences of identifiers in Q) belong to the tree **S[T]**. #

Let us return now to the questions (2.7)-(2.9). A language with pointers is not "stack implementable" and we encounter one of the most difficult implementation problems. There are two well-known memory management techniques, (see [3]): - **retention** technique, which retains an instance as long as this instance is accessible (this requires expensive garbage collection to search inaccessible instances); - **deletion** technique, which deletes non-addressable instances immediately after termination. The latter technique may be fully exploited by virtue of (3.4); together with a non-addressable instance, the entire subtree of this instance may be deallocated. The reader may refer to [1], and [2] for more detailed discussion of the subject and application to the implementation of universal programming language LOGLAN.

4. COROUTINE LANGUAGES.

The term "coroutines" is used for the module instances able to cooperate in a sequential fashion. This means that the execution of a coroutine instance can be suspended, and at the same time the operations of another coroutine instance are resumed. The coroutine instance may create a number of module instances that are

dynamically contained within it (e.g. some
instances of procedures and blocks). These module instances form a coroutine
chain, say Y:

$$\boxed{\text{active instance}} \longrightarrow .. \longrightarrow \boxed{\text{coroutine head}} \longrightarrow (\text{NONE})$$

chain Y

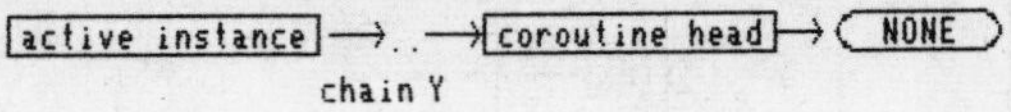

The control transfer from a coroutine chain to another one is a result of a
certain coroutine operation, say **attach**. The suspended coroutine
chain, say Z, will be pictured as follows:

$$\boxed{\text{active instance}} \longrightarrow .. \longrightarrow \boxed{\text{coroutine head}}$$

chain Z

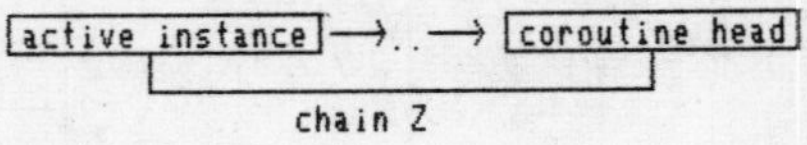

One can define the result of **attach** in the following way:

$$\boxed{\text{active instance}} \longrightarrow .. \longrightarrow \boxed{\cdot} \longrightarrow .. \longrightarrow \boxed{\cdot} \longrightarrow .. \longrightarrow (\text{NONE})$$

chain Z   chain Y

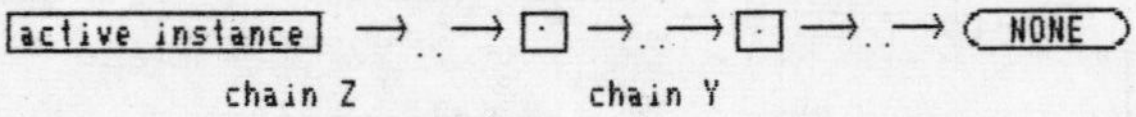

One can also define this result as follows:

$$\boxed{\text{active instance}} \longrightarrow .. \longrightarrow \boxed{\text{coroutine head}}$$

chain Y

$$\boxed{\text{active instance}} \longrightarrow \longrightarrow \boxed{\text{coroutine head}} \longrightarrow (\text{NONE})$$

chain Z

In this section we shall consider the second possibility, because we regard
processes to be considered the special cases of coroutines.

A coroutine is generated by **new** instruction. The generation is completed when
return instruction is performed; if Q(C) is a coroutine instance with a dynamic
father R:

$$\boxed{Q} \longrightarrow \boxed{R}$$

then **return** will suspend Q and resume R:

          $\boxed{\text{active R}}$

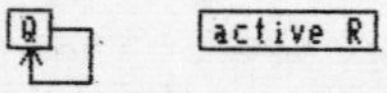

The main program MB is considered to be a coroutine instance pointed to by a
system variable **main**. The user is alowed to use this variable only in the
instruction **attach(main)**. A chain is active if control executes its active
instance, otherwise it is suspended. Directly from the definitions follows:
(4.1) A coroutine chain contains neither generated nor terminated coroutine
instances except of the head of a chain. #
The analogon to (3.1) has the following form:
(4.2) If P => Q and Q does not belong to the dynamic chain leading to the head of
a suspended coroutine chain then **non** Q - >* P. #
Lemma (3.2) is still valid while another auxiliary lemma is necessary to prove the
analagons of (3.4), (3.5):
(4.3) If a suspended coroutine head R is accessible at a state S, then any
instance of its chain is in S[T].
Proof. The only non-trivial case is that of a termination of a non-addressable
instance Q. Consider the coroutine chain of R and the instance Q with the dynamic
father P:

$$\boxed{Rk} \longrightarrow .. \longrightarrow \boxed{Ri} \longrightarrow \boxed{Ri-1} \longrightarrow .. \longrightarrow \boxed{R1} \longrightarrow \boxed{R}$$

Proof goes by induction on k. Suppose that R_{i-1} belongs to **S[T]**. If R_i = Q then R_i does not belong to the chain of R after the termination of Q, so (4.3) holds. Suppose that R_i =>+ Q. The instance R_i cannot be created in R_{i-1} directly, because R_{i-1} =>* R_i.SL implies R_{i-1} belongs to **STQ**. Therefore R_i is created in R_{i-1} indirectly by means of X.**new** M, so R_{i-1} =>* R'->>* R_i. SL. The instance Q is non-addressable, so Q ≠ R_i.SL; and from (3.3)

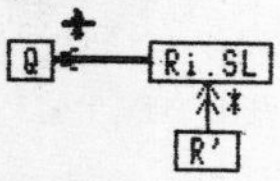

implies

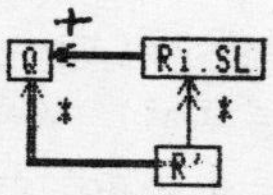

Now R_{i-1} =>* R' =>* Q implies that R_{i-1} belongs to **STQ** which contradicts the inductive assumption. #

The analogons of (3.4), (3.5) have the following form:

(4.4) The structure **S[syn]** consists of a tree **S[T]** and a number of pseudo-trees. The active instance and any accessible instance belongs to **S[T]**. #

(4.5) The structure **S[syn]** consists of a single operating chain, a number of suspended coroutine chains, and a number of isolated vertices. The active instance is a leaf of the operating chain. #

The following example illustrates (4.3).

Example 2.

Consider the following the program:

```
begin
unit B: procedure;
   var X: C;
   unit C: coroutine;
      begin
         return;
         call A;
         ...
      end C;
   begin
      X: = new C:
      attach(X);
   end B;
   unit A: procedure;
      begin
         attach(main)
      end A;
begin
   call B;
   ...
end
```

Just after the execution of **attach(main)** the state of computation looks as follows:

Thus the head Q(C) belongs to the subtree with the root Q(B), while the instance Q(A) does not. After the termination of Q(B), the head Q(C) will be inaccessible. #

Note that in virtue of the above propositions, the proposition (3.6) still holds. For some applications semi-coroutines are necessary. There is an additional operation **detach** on semi-coroutine which returns control to the callee, i.e. the coroutine head which recently resumed this semi-coroutine. Unfortunately, such a semi-coroutine operation may destroy a syntactic environment: if one adds **detach** after the instruction "**call** B" in the example 2, then after the termination of Q(B) we have:

Hence, Q(A) is active, Q(C) is accessible from Q(A), but Q(C) does not belong to **S[T]**. This example shows that (4.4) does not fully hold. The structure **S[syn]** consists of a tree **S[T]** and a number of pseudo-trees but accessible instances need not belong to **S[T]**. So some kind of run-time checking is indispensable. Note that the dynamic structure is not harmed by the operation detach.

5. PARALLEL LANGUAGES.

We consider a coroutine as a particular kind of a process; for a program with processes more than one instance may be active at a time. There is an important difference, however, between coroutines, and processes which are performed by a single multiplexed processor. In the former case the switch of the control from one coroutine chain into another one is programmable, and so it cannot happen behind the scenes. In the latter case, it is the scheduler which switches the control, so a user has no control of this, and has to consider all the active processes as the operating ones.

The operations on processes are simply extensions of those on coroutines; **stop** suspends a process; **resume**(X) resumes the process pointed to by X. It is easy to see that the basic theorems describing with syntactic and dynamic structure slightly generalize (4.3) and (4.4):

(5.1) The structure **S[syn]** consists of a tree **S[T]** with main program being its root, and a number of pseudo-trees. #

(5.2) The structure **S[dyn]** consists of a number of operating chains, and a number of suspended process chains, suspended coroutine chains, and isolated vertices. The active instances are the leafs of the operating chains. #

For parallel languages a syntactic environment may be destroyed, and so appropriate memory management systems have to be developed. A **retention** technique delays a process termination if that could destroy a syntactic environment of another process. A **deletion** technique deletes inaccessible instances, but a process may explicitly wait for the termination of his sons.

It is worthwhile to notice that one can consider a programmable deallocation technique: an instruction, say **kill**(X) deallocates a memory field pointed to by X, (in PASCAL: **dispose**, in ADA: **free**). The point is that such an operation can be "secure", i.e. the access to memory instances killed as a side-effect of these instructions results in run-time error. Because of the lack of space, further issues of memory management systems and of processes synchronization will be considered in a forthcoming paper.

BIBLIOGRAPHY

[1] Bartol, W. M., Kreczmar, A., Lao, M., Litwiniuk, A., Müldner, T., Oktaba, H., Salwicki, A., Szczepanska-Wasersztrum, D., Report on the Programming Language Loglan 79. Internal Report, University of Warsaw.

[2] Bartol, W. M., Kreczmar, A., Litwiniuk, A., Oktaba, H., Semantics and Implementation of Prefixing at many Levels. IInf UW Report NR 94 Institute of Informatics, University of Warsaw.

[3] Berry, D. M., Block Structure: Retention vs. Deletion. Proc. Third Symposium on Theory of Computation, 1971, The MIT Press, 1979.

[4] Bobrow, D. G., Wegbreit, B., A Model and Stack Implementation of Multiple Environments. BBN Report 2334, 1972.

[5] Brinch-Hansen, P., Operating System Principles. Prentice Hall, 1973.

[6] Dahl, O. J., Myhrhaug, B., Nygaard, K., Common Base Language. NCC S-22, October, 1970.

[7] Dahl, O. J., Wang, A., Coroutine Sequencing in a Block Structured Environment. BIT 1971, pp. 425-49.

[8] Lindstrom, G., Soffa, M. L. Referencing and Retention in Block Structured Coroutines. ACM TOPLAS Vol. 3, N 3, July 1981.

[9] Naur, P., (Ed.), Revised Report on the Algorithmic Language ALGOL 60. CACM 6, 1963, pp. 1-17.

[10] Organick, E. I., Computer System Organization. The B5700/6700 Series. Academic Press 1973, New York.

[11] Reference Manual for the ADA Programming Language, United States Depart. of Defense, July 1980.

[12] Wegner, P., Programming Languages - Concepts and Research Directions. In: Research Directions in Software Technology, edited by P. Wegner.

[13] Wirth, N., The Programming Language Pascal. Acta Informatica 1971, 1, pp. 35-63.

A GENERAL SCHEME FOR SOME DETERMINISTICALLY PARSABLE GRAMMARS AND THEIR STRONG EQUIVALENTS
(Extended Abstract)

Anton Nijholt
Twente University of Technology
Dept. of Computer Science
PO Box 217, 7500 AE Enschede
The Netherlands

Jan Pittl
Research Inst. Math. Machines
Loretanske Nam. 3
11855 Prague 1
Czechoslovakia

1. INTRODUCTION

In the past years there have been many attempts to fill in the gap between the classes of LL(k) and LR(k) grammars with new classes of deterministically parsable grammars. Almost always the introduction of a new class was accompanied by a parsing method and/or a grammatical transformation fitting the following scheme. If parsers were at the centre of the investigation the new method used to be designed to possess certain advantages with respect to already existing ones. As far as transformations were concerned the intention was to produce methods of transforming grammars into "more easily" parsable ones.

The problem of finding classes of context-free grammars which can be transformed to LL(k) grammars has received much attention. Parsing strategies and associated classes of grammars generating LL(k) languages have been extensively studied (among others cf. e.g. [6,14,18]). An equally interesting class of grammars is the class of strict deterministic grammars [8,9], a subclass of the LR(0) grammars with elegant theoretical properties. Generalizations of this concept have been introduced by Friede[3] and Pittl[15]. The purpose of this paper is to show how the above mentioned classes of grammars can be dealt with within a general framework originated by Nijholt[12]. Roughly speaking, we study the phenomena corresponding e.g. to the relationship between strong LL(k) and LL(k) grammars. A general scheme using adjectives "strong" and "weak" is shown to be applicable for the description of the grammar families under consideration.

PRELIMINARIES

In the remainder of this section we review several concepts of formal language theory. The reader is referred to Aho and Ullman[1] or Harrison[7] for further details.

A <u>context-free grammar</u> (abbreviated a CFG) is denoted by $G = (N,T,P,S)$. Define $V = N \cup T$. Troughout the paper we assume all the grammars under consideration to be reduced.

Let $\alpha \in V^*$. The <u>length</u> of the word α is denoted by $|\alpha|$; the symbol Λ is reserved for the <u>empty string.</u> For any nonnegative integer k the expression $k : \alpha$ denotes α if $|\alpha| < k$, otherwise the prefix of α of length k. Furthermore we define

$$T^{*k} = \{u \in T^* \mid |u| \leq k\}.$$

The following operations relate to derivations in G. For any $\alpha \in V^*$ and $A \in N$ we define

$$FIRST_k(\alpha) = \{u \in T^{*k} \mid \alpha \overset{*}{\Longrightarrow} w \text{ and } k : w = u \text{ for some } w \in T^*\}$$

$$FOLLOW_k(A) = \{u \in T^{*k} \mid S \overset{*}{\Longrightarrow} \beta A \gamma \text{ and } u \in FIRST_k(\gamma) \text{ for some } \beta, \gamma \in V^*\}$$

The $FIRST_k$ operator can be extended to handle subsets X of V^*:

$$FIRST_k(X) = \{u \in T^{*k} \mid u \in FIRST_k(\alpha) \text{ for some } \alpha \in X\}$$

Finally, we recall the definitions of four wellknown classes of grammars. The first two concepts we present describe grammars introduced by Rosenkrantz and Stearns[17].

<u>DEFINITION 1.1.</u> Let $G = (N,T,P,S)$ be a CFG, $k \geq 0$. The grammar G is called an <u>LL(k) grammar</u> iff for all $A \in N$, $w \in T^*$ and $\alpha, \beta, \gamma \in V^*$, if

$$S \overset{*}{\underset{L}{\Longrightarrow}} wA\alpha \underset{L}{\Longrightarrow} w\beta\alpha$$

$$S \overset{*}{\underset{L}{\Longrightarrow}} wA\alpha \underset{L}{\Longrightarrow} w\gamma\alpha$$

$$FIRST_k(\beta\alpha) \cap FIRST_k(\gamma\alpha) \neq \emptyset$$

then $\beta = \gamma$.

<u>DEFINITION 1.2.</u> Let $G = (N,T,P,S)$ be a CFG, $k \geq 0$. G is called a <u>strong LL(k) grammar</u> iff for any $A \in N$ and $\beta, \gamma \in V^*$, if $A \to \beta$ and $A \to \gamma$ are in P then $FIRST_k(\beta FOLLOW_k(A)) \cap FIRST_k(\gamma FOLLOW_k(A)) \neq \emptyset$ implies $\beta = \gamma$.

Among various (and different) definitions of LR(k) grammars we have chosen the one due to Geller and Harrison[5].

<u>DEFINITION 1.3.</u> Let $G = (N,T,P,S)$ be a CFG, $k \geq 0$. The grammar G is said to be <u>LR(k)</u> iff $S \overset{+}{\Longrightarrow} S$ impossible and for all $A, A' \in N$; $\alpha, \alpha', \beta, \beta', \gamma \in V^*$ and $w, w', x \in T^*$, if

$$S \overset{*}{\underset{R}{\Longrightarrow}} \alpha A w \underset{R}{\Longrightarrow} \alpha\beta w = \gamma w$$

$$S \overset{*}{\underset{R}{\Longrightarrow}} \alpha' A' x \underset{R}{\Longrightarrow} \alpha'\beta' x = \gamma w'$$

and $k : w = k : w'$ then $(A \to \beta, |\alpha\beta|) = (A' \to \beta', |\alpha'\beta'|)$.

Before we can give the definition of the fourth class to be dealt with we need a few preliminaries. Let Q be a set. A <u>weak partition</u> of Q is a set π of nonempty subsets of Q such that for each $q \in Q$ there is some $B \in \pi$ such that $q \in B$. The elements of π are called blocks of π. For p, $q \in Q$ we write $p \equiv q \pmod{\pi}$ iff $p \in B$ and $q \in B$ for some block B of π. A weak partition π of Q is called a <u>partition</u> of Q iff its blocks are pairwise disjoint. The following grammar family was introduced by Harrison and Havel[8].

<u>DEFINITION 1.4.</u> Let G = (N,T,P,S) be a CFG, let π be a partition of $V = N \cup T$. Such a partition is called <u>strict</u> iff T forms a block of π and for all A, $A' \in N$ and α, β, $\beta' \in V^*$, if $A \to \alpha\beta$, $A' \to \alpha\beta'$ are in P and $A \equiv A' \pmod{\pi}$ then either

(i) both $\beta, \beta' \neq \Lambda$ and ${}^{(1)}\beta \equiv {}^{(1)}\beta' \pmod{\pi}$, or

(ii) $\beta = \beta' = \Lambda$ and $A = A'$.

<u>DEFINITION 1.5.</u> A CFG G = (N,T,P,S) is called <u>strict deterministic</u> iff there exists a strict partition π of V.

2. GRAMMARS TRANSFORMABLE TO LL(k) GRAMMARS

In this section we shortly review some definitions of classes of grammars which have the property that they can be transformed to LL(k) grammars. We do not go into proofs or historical details. These can be found in Nijholt[12] and in Soisalon-Soininen and Ukkonen[18].

In order to intuitively characterize the different classes of grammars to be defined we give an intuitive idea of their parsing strategies. In Figure 1 we have displayed the following situation. There exist terminal strings w, x, y and z, a nonterminal A and symbols X_1, $X_2, \ldots, X_p$ in V, such that $A \to X_1 \ldots X_p$ is a production and there exist derivations

$$S \overset{*}{\Longrightarrow} wAz, \quad X_1 \overset{*}{\Longrightarrow} x, \text{ and } \quad X_2 \ldots X_p \overset{*}{\Longrightarrow} y.$$

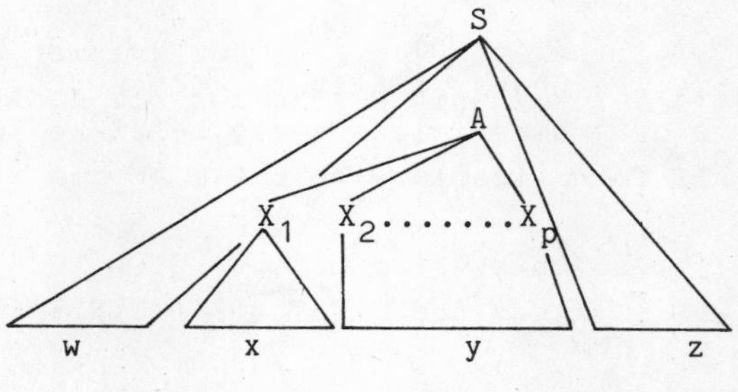

Figure 1. Parsing strategies.

In the following table we have collected six parsing strategies which are illustrated with the help of Figure 1. The following abbreviations are used:

LL : reading from the left using left parses [17]
PLC: predictive left corner grammars [12]
LP : left part grammars [12,14]
LC : left corner grammars [18]
PLR: predictive LR-grammars [18]
LR : reading from the left using right parses [5]

GRAMMAR	READ	RECOGNITION of A	READ	RECOGNITION of $A \to X_1 \ldots X_p$
LL	w	k : xyz	w	k : xyz
PLC	w	k : xyz	wx	k : yz
LP	w	k : xyz	wxy	k : z
LC	wx	k : yz	wx	k : yz
PLR	wx	k : yz	wxy	k : z
LR	wxy	k : z	wxy	k : z

Table I. Parsing strategies.

With the help of Figure 1 the table should be read as follows. Consider the terminal string wxyz. The production $A \to X_1X_2 \ldots X_p$ depicted in this parse tree of wxyz can be recognized with certainty after scanning

(i) w and k : xyz if the grammar is LL(k)
(ii) wx and k : yz if the grammar is PLC(k) or LC(k)
(iii) wxy and k : z if the grammar is LP(k), PLR(k) or LR(k)

However, if the grammar is PLC(k) or LP(k), then the lefthand side A of the production $A \to X_1X_2 \ldots X_p$ is already recognized after scanning w and k : xyz. If the grammar is PLR(k), then A is recognized after scanning wx and k : yz.

It is necessary to formalize the above intuitive ideas in order that the specific properties of grammar classes may be picked up. It is instructive to consider this formalization for LL(k) grammars.

LEMMA 2.1. Let $G = (N,T,P,S)$ be an LL(k) grammar, $k \geq 0$, $w \in T^*$, β, $\gamma \in V^*$ and $n \geq 0$. If $S \overset{n}{\underset{L}{\Rightarrow}} w\beta$, $S \overset{n}{\underset{L}{\Rightarrow}} w\gamma$ and $FIRST_k(\beta) \cap FIRST_k(\gamma) \neq \emptyset$ then $\beta = \gamma$.

PROOF. Cf. [1], Lemma 8.1. □

Here we will not pay attention to a formal definition of PLC(k) grammars (cf.[12]) but instead we immediately define LP(k) grammars. In [14] these grammars were originally called Ch(k) grammars. We give here a slight restatement of the original definition.

DEFINITION 2.1. Let G = (N,T,P,S) be a CFG, $k \geq 0$. G is said to be an LP(k) grammar iff for any $A \in N$; $\alpha, \beta, \beta', \gamma, \gamma' \in V^*$ and $w \in T^*$, if

$$S \overset{*}{\underset{L}{\Rightarrow}} wA\gamma \underset{L}{\Rightarrow} w\alpha\beta\gamma \quad \text{and} \quad S \overset{*}{\underset{L}{\Rightarrow}} wA\gamma \underset{L}{\Rightarrow} w\alpha\beta'\gamma'$$

and $FIRST_k(\beta\gamma) \cap FIRST_k(\beta'\gamma') \neq \emptyset$ then ${}^{(1)}\beta = {}^{(1)}\beta'$.

The "strong" variant of this class (strong LP(k) grammars) is defined analogously to the LL(k) case by demanding that ${}^{(1)}\beta = {}^{(1)}\beta'$ for any two productions of the form $A \to \alpha\beta$ and $A \to \alpha\beta'$ such that

$$FIRST_k(\beta FOLLOW_k(A)) \cap FIRST_k(\beta' FOLLOW_k(A)) \neq \emptyset.$$

We refer the reader to [12,14] for more detailed treatments on the class of LP(k) grammars. For the purposes of comparison we only give a result related to Lemma 2.1.

LEMMA 2.2. Let G = (N,T,P,S) be an LP(k) grammar, $k \geq 0$, $w \in T^*$, $\beta, \gamma \in V^*$ and $n \geq 0$. If $S \overset{n}{\underset{L}{\Rightarrow}} w\beta$, $S \overset{n}{\underset{L}{\Rightarrow}} w\gamma$ and $FIRST_k(\beta) \cap FIRST_k(\gamma) \neq \emptyset$ then ${}^{(1)}\beta = {}^{(1)}\gamma$.

PROOF. Cf. [12], Lemmas 12.3 and 12.4. □

A probably better known class of grammars generating LL(k) languages is represented by LC(k) grammars (cf. [1]). We consider here the characterization of this class given by Soisalon-Soininen and Ukkonen[18] in terms of rightmost derivations. Recall that a production $A \to \beta$ is said to satisfy the LR(k) condition iff the body of Definition 1.3 is satisfied for it. The underlining in the following two definitions denotes that the underlined substrings are not rewritten in the rightmost derivation.

DEFINITION 2.2. A CFG G = (N,T,P,S) is said to be an LC(k) grammar if $S \overset{+}{\underset{R}{\Rightarrow}} S$ is not possible, each Λ-production satisfies the LR(k) condition and if for each $w, w', y, y' \in T^*$; $\alpha, \alpha', \alpha'', \beta, \gamma \in V^*$; $X \in V$; $A, A' \in N$ and production $A \to X\beta$ in P, the conditions

(i) $S \overset{*}{\underset{R}{\Rightarrow}} \alpha A w \underset{R}{\Rightarrow} \alpha X \beta w \overset{*}{\underset{R}{\Rightarrow}} \alpha X y w$

(ii) $S \overset{*}{\underset{R}{\Rightarrow}} \alpha' A' w' \underset{R}{\Rightarrow} \alpha' \alpha'' X \gamma w' \overset{*}{\underset{R}{\Rightarrow}} \alpha' \alpha'' X y' w'$

(iii) $\alpha' \alpha'' = \alpha$ and $k : yw = k : y'w'$,
always imply that $\alpha A = \alpha' A'$ and $\beta = \gamma$.

We have included the condition that $S \overset{*}{\underset{R}{\Rightarrow}} S$ is not possible for an LC(k) grammar. Otherwise the following ambiguous grammar with productions $S \rightarrow S \mid a$ is to be called LC(0) (cf.[5] where similar problems are treated for LR(k) definitions). Finally the following class of grammars has been shown [18] to generate LL(k) languages.

DEFINITION 2.3. A CFG $G = (N,T,P,S)$ is said to be a PLR(k) grammar if G is LR(k) and if for each $w, w', y, y' \in T^*$; $\alpha, \alpha', \alpha'', \beta, \gamma \in V^*$; $X \in V$; $A, A' \in N$ and production $A \rightarrow X\beta$ in P, the conditions

(i) $S \overset{*}{\underset{R}{\Rightarrow}} \alpha A w \underset{R}{\Rightarrow} \alpha X \beta w \overset{*}{\underset{R}{\Rightarrow}} \alpha X y w$

(ii) $S \overset{*}{\underset{R}{\Rightarrow}} \alpha' A' w' \underset{R}{\Rightarrow} \alpha' \alpha'' X \gamma w' \overset{*}{\underset{R}{\Rightarrow}} \alpha' \alpha'' X y' w'$

(iii) $\alpha' \alpha'' = \alpha$ and $k : yw = k : y'w'$
always imply that $\alpha A = \alpha' A'$.

In Figure 2 we present the relationships between the classes of grammars which have been mentioned in this section. All arrows denote proper inclusions.

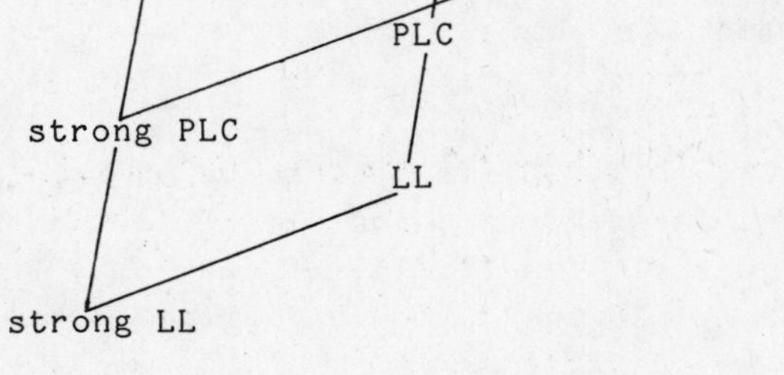

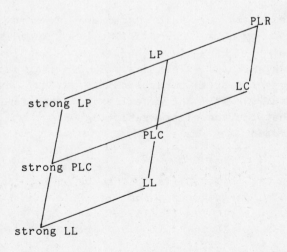

Figure 2. First inclusion diagram.

This paper is not meant to bring a discussion on the transformations converting grammars into LL(k) ones. However, for the sake of completeness, Hammer's "k-transformable" grammars [6] should be mentioned to provide such a transformation.

3. STRICT DETERMINISTIC GRAMMARS WITH LOOKAHEAD

Harrison and Havel[8] mentioned the possibility of generalizing their results by a suitable incorporation of lookahead. One of the approaches leading to the goal has appeared in Friede[4]. For notational purposes we prefer to call these grammars strong SD(k) instead of the original denotation having sounded as partitioned LL(k) grammars.

DEFINITION 3.1. Let $G = (N,T,P,S)$ be a CFG, $k \geq 0$. G is said to be a strong SD(k) grammar iff there exists a partition π of V such that T forms a block of π and for all $A, A' \in N$, $\alpha, \beta, \beta' \in V^*$, if $A \to \alpha\beta$, $A' \to \alpha\beta'$ are in P, $A \equiv A' \pmod{\pi}$ and

$$\mathrm{FIRST}_k(\beta\mathrm{FOLLOW}_k(A)) \cap \mathrm{FIRST}_k(\beta'\mathrm{FOLLOW}_k(A')) \neq \emptyset$$

then either

(i) both $\beta, \beta' \neq \Lambda$ and ${}^{(1)}\beta \equiv {}^{(1)}\beta' \pmod{\pi}$, or

(ii) $\beta = \beta' = \Lambda$ and $A = A'$.

To justify our terminology we refer the reader to compare the above definition with the one describing strong LP(k) grammars (Section 2).

THEOREM 3.1. Let $G = (N,T,P,S)$ be a strong LP(k) grammar, $k \geq 0$. Then G is a strong SD(k) grammar.

PROOF. It follows immediately from the definitions that the partition $\pi = \{\{A\} \mid A \in N\} \cup \{T\}$ satisfies the desired properties. □

This inclusion is proper since LP(k) grammars generate merely LL(k) languages whereas strong SD(k) ones were shown to generate all deterministic context-free languages (cf.[3]). A more intriguing generalization of strict deterministic grammars has been given by Pittl[15]. This latter generalization was obtained as a characterization of an existing class of grammars, namely, the LLP(k) grammars (cf. Lomet[10]).

DEFINITION 3.2. Let $G = (N,T,P,S)$ be a CFG, $k \geq 0$. We define

$$M_k(G) = \{(A,u) \mid A \in N \text{ and } u \in \mathrm{FOLLOW}_k(A)\}.$$

Let π be a weak partition of $M_k(G)$. Such a weak partition is called admissible iff for any (A,u), $(A',u') \in M_k(G)$, $\alpha, \beta, \beta' \in V^*$, if $A \to \alpha\beta$, $A' \to \alpha\beta'$ are in P, $(A,u) \equiv (A',u') \pmod{\pi}$ and

$FIRST_k(\beta u) \cap FIRST_k(\beta' u') \neq \emptyset$ then either

(i) both β, β' are in TV^*, or

(ii) $\beta = C\gamma$, $\beta' = C'\gamma'$ for some $C, C' \in N$, $\gamma, \gamma' \in V^*$ and $(C,z) \equiv (C,z') \pmod{\pi}$ for all $z \in FIRST_k(\gamma u)$ and $z' \in FIRST_k(\gamma' u')$, or

(iii) $\beta = \beta' = \Lambda$ and $A = A'$.

In [15] it is shown that LLP(k) grammars are exactly those possessing an admissible weak partition. For this reason in [12] they were renamed as weak SD(k) grammars.

DEFINITION 3.3. Let $G = (N,T,P,S)$ be a CFG, $k \geq 0$. G is called a weak SD(k) grammar iff there exists an admissible weak partition of $M_k(G)$.

Again, we wish to relate the new concept to previously defined ones. An admissible weak partition with disjoint blocks will be called an admissible partition.

LEMMA 3.1. Let $G = (N,T,P,S)$ be a CFG, $k \geq 0$. The grammar G is strong SD(k) iff there exists an admissible partition π of $M_k(G)$ such that for any block B of π and $(A,u) \in M_k(G)$, $(A,u) \in B$ implies $(A,v) \in B$ for all $v \in FOLLOW_k(A)$.

PROOF. Let π be an admissible partition of $M_k(G)$ which satisfies the above condition. Define $\pi' = \{\{A \mid (A,u) \in B\} \mid B \in \pi\} \cup \{T\}$. Then π' is a partition of V possessing the desired properties. On the other hand let π' be a partition of V mentioned in Definition 3.1. Then the partition $\pi = \{\{(A,u) \mid A \in B \text{ and } u \in FOLLOW_k(A)\} \mid B \in \pi' - \{T\}\}$ yields clearly the result. □

THEOREM 3.2. Let $G = (N,T,P,S)$ be a strong SD(k) grammar, $k \geq 0$. Then G is weak SD(k).

PROOF. An immediate consequence of Lemma 3.1. □

It can be shown that the above inclusion is proper. Weak SD(k) grammars can be characterized in an interesting way by means of leftmost derivations.

THEOREM 3.3. Let $G = (N,T,P,S)$ be a CFG, $k \geq 0$. Then G is a weak SD(k) grammar iff for any $n \geq 0$, $A, A' \in N$, $\alpha, \beta, \beta', \gamma, \gamma' \in V^*$ and $w \in T^*$, if

$$S \overset{n}{\underset{L}{\Longrightarrow}} wA\gamma \underset{L}{\Longrightarrow} w\alpha\beta\gamma$$

$$S \overset{n}{\underset{L}{\Longrightarrow}} wA'\gamma' \underset{L}{\Longrightarrow} w\alpha\beta'\gamma'$$

$$\mathrm{FIRST}_k(\beta\gamma) \cap \mathrm{FIRST}_k(\beta'\gamma') \neq \emptyset$$

then either (i) both β, β' are in TV^*, or
(ii) both β, β' are in NV^*, or
(iii) $\beta = \beta' = \Lambda$ and $A = A'$.

PROOF. Cf. [15], Theorem 3.2.(c). □

This characterization allows us to compare the classes of LP(k) and weak SD(k) grammars.

THEOREM 3.4. Let $G = (N,T,P,S)$ be an LP(k) grammar, $k \geq 0$. Then G is a weak SD(k) grammar.

PROOF. Use Lemma 2.2. and Theorem 3.3. □

As mentioned in [9], a lot of erroneous results has appeared in the literature connected with the conversion of rightmost derivations to leftmost ones. These technical difficulties can be overcome using the approach presented in Pittl[15]. The crucial result of that paper we recall is that proving any weak SD(k) grammar to be LR(k). We next improve it by showing these grammars to be included in an interesting subclass of LR(k) grammars introduced by Ukkonen[19,20].

DEFINITION 3.4. Let $G = (N,T,P,S)$ be a CFG, $k \geq 0$. G is called to be a weak PLR(k) grammar iff it is LR(k) and for all $A, A' \in N$, $\alpha, \alpha', \alpha'', \beta, \beta' \in V^*$, $w, w' \in T^*$ and $X \in V$, if

$$S \overset{*}{\underset{R}{\Rightarrow}} \alpha A w \underset{R}{\Rightarrow} \alpha X \beta w \quad \text{and} \quad S \overset{*}{\underset{R}{\Rightarrow}} \alpha' A' w' \underset{R}{\Rightarrow} \alpha'\alpha'' X \beta' w' = \alpha X \beta' w'$$

and $\mathrm{FIRST}_k(\beta w) \cap \mathrm{FIRST}_k(\beta' w') \neq \emptyset$
then $\alpha = \alpha'$ (i.e. $\alpha'' = \Lambda$).

Clearly, any PLR(k) grammar is weak PLR(k). The inclusion is proper due to the different classes of languages generated.

THEOREM 3.5. Let $G = (N,T,P,S)$ be a weak SD(k) grammar, $k \geq 0$. Then G is weak PLR(k).

PROOF. A slight modification of the proof of Theorem 5.2.[15] which proves G to be LR(k) can be shown to yield the required argument. □

The inclusion mentioned in the theorem is proper since there are left recursive PLR(k) grammars. By [15] no such grammar can be weak SD(k). Figure 3 summarizes the results concerning relationships between the families of grammars. An arrow means a proper inclusion.

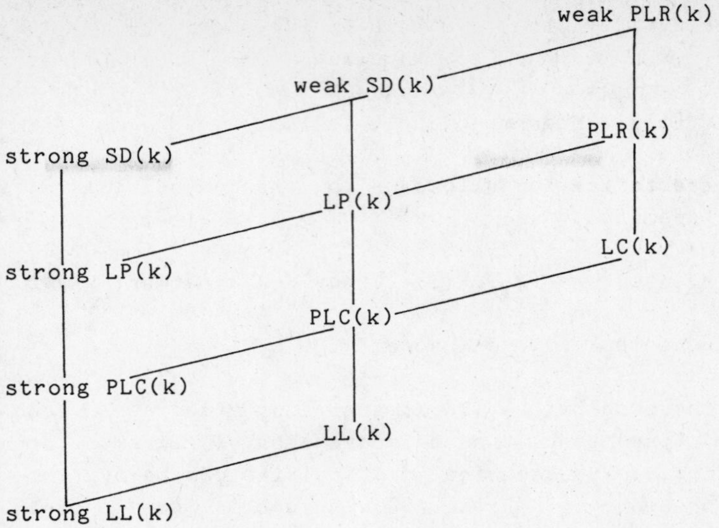

Figure 3. Second inclusion diagram.

4. TRANSFORMATIONS TO "STRONG" GRAMMARS

Most of the grammatical concepts treated in this paper originated from the attempts to facilitate parser construction for deterministic languages. From this point of view "strong" versions of grammars appeared very attractive. Indeed, the utilization of $FOLLOW_k$ sets instead of local follow sets for each sentential form yields considerable improvements in parser size. As typical examples strong LL(k) grammars and simple LR(k) grammars [2] deserve to be mentioned. This fact has lead to the investigation of transformations converting grammars into their "strong" counterparts (cf. [2,17]). We next show all these classes of grammars to possess a certain "common denominator". We present a general method providing "strong" grammars for all the types of grammar families known to the authors.

<u>TRANSFORMATION.</u> Input: A CFG $G = (N,T,P,S)$, $k \geq 0$. Output: A CFG $\tau(G) = (N',T,P',S')$. Method: Let $Y \subseteq M_k(G)$, $\alpha \in V^*$. Then we define

$$SUCC(Y,\alpha) = \{(B,v) \mid (A,u) \in Y,\ A \to \alpha B\beta \in P,\ v \in FIRST_k(\beta u) \text{ for some } B \in N \text{ and } \beta \in V^*\}$$

Let $l_m(G) = \max\{|\alpha| \mid A \to \alpha \text{ is in } P\}$. Next a set π_c of subsets of $M_k(G)$ is to be created in three phases.

Step 1. Initially let $\pi_c = \emptyset$. Then place the set $\{(S,\Lambda)\}$ into π_c as an unmarked element.

Step 2. If a set $Y \in \pi_c$ is unmarked then for all $\alpha \in V^*$ such that $|\alpha| \leq l_m(G)$ compute the set SUCC(Y,α). If this set is nonempty then place it into π_c unmarked. Then mark Y.

Step 3. Repeat Step 2. until all sets in π_c are marked.

Clearly this algorithm is guaranteed to halt since $M_k(G)$ is a finite set. Now the grammar $\tau(G) = (N',T,P',S')$ is constructed as follows. Define $S' = (\{(S,\Lambda)\},S)$ and

$$N' = \{(Y,A) \mid Y \in \pi_c \text{ and } (A,u) \in Y \text{ for some } u \in T^{*k}\}$$

The set P' contains only the productions described below. For any production $A \to X_1 \ldots X_n$ in P, where $A \in N$, $n \geq 0$, $X_i \in V$, $1 \leq i \leq n$, P' involves all the productions $B \to Z_1 \ldots Z_n$ such that $B = (Y,A)$, $Y \in \pi_c$, $(A,u) \in Y$ for some $u \in T^{*k}$ and $Z_i = X_i$ if $X_i \in T$, $Z_i = (\mathrm{SUCC}(Y,X_1 \ldots X_{i-1}),X_i)$ if $X_i \in N$, $1 \leq i \leq n$.

This transformation represents a generalization of a similar one used in Pittl[15], Theorem 4.2. To facilitate the investigation of its properties we introduce a homomorphism $\phi : V'^* \to V^*$ by defining $\phi(a) = a$ for all $a \in T$ and $\phi((Y,A)) = A$ for all $(Y,A) \in N'$. Induction arguments on the length of the derivations prove the following two assertions.

LEMMA 4.1. Let $G = (N,T,P,S)$ be a CFG, $k \geq 0$, $Z \in V'$, $\gamma \in V'^*$ and $Z \overset{*}{\Longrightarrow}_{\tau(G)} \gamma$. Then $\phi(Z) \overset{*}{\Longrightarrow}_G \phi(\gamma)$.

LEMMA 4.2. Let $G = (N,T,P,S)$ be a CFG, $k \geq 0$, $X \in V$, $\alpha \in V^*$ and $X \overset{*}{\Longrightarrow}_G \alpha$. Then there are $X' \in V'$ and $\alpha \in V'^*$ such that $\phi(X') = X$, $\phi(\alpha') = \alpha$ and $X' \overset{*}{\Longrightarrow}_{\tau(G)} \alpha'$.

We conclude that $L(G) = L(\tau(G))$. It is easy to see that the pairs of derivations corresponding to each other are structurally equivalent with respect to the homomorphism ϕ. One can easily recuperate any parse of a word w in L(G) from a parse of w according to $\tau(G)$. Similar results appear in Moura[11]. A comparison of his results with ours has not yet been done. The next lemmas are almost direct consequences of the definitions.

LEMMA 4.3. Let $G = (N,T,P,S)$ be a CFG, $k \geq 0$, $(Y,A) \in N'$. Then $\mathrm{FOLLOW}_k^{\tau(G)}((Y,A)) = \{u \in T^{*k} \mid (A,u) \in Y\}$.

LEMMA 4.4. Let $G = (N,T,P,S)$ be a CFG, $k \geq 0$, $n \geq 0$, $(Y,A) \in N'$, $\alpha, \beta \in V'^*$ and $(B,v) \in Y$. If $S' \overset{n}{\Longrightarrow}_{\tau(G)} \alpha(Y,A)\beta$ then there is $\gamma \in V'^*$

such that $S' \overset{n}{\Rightarrow}_{\tau(G)} \alpha(Y,B)\gamma$ and $v \in FIRST_k^{\tau(G)}(\gamma)$.

It remains to verify that τ produces the desired output.

THEOREM 4.1. Let $G = (N,T,P,S)$ be a CFG, $k \geq 0$. If G is an LL(k) (PLC(k), LP(k)) grammar then $\tau(G)$ is a strong LL(k) (strong PLC(k), strong LP(k)) grammar respectively.

THEOREM 4.2. Let $G = (N,T,P,S)$ be a CFG, $k \geq 0$. If G is a weak SD(k) grammar then $\tau(G)$ is a strong SD(k) grammar.

PROOF (hint). The partition π of V' ensuring $\tau(G)$ to be strong SD(k) is constructed as follows. Let $Y \in \pi_c$. Define

$$B_Y = \{(Y,A) \mid (A,u) \in Y \text{ for some } u \in T^{*k}\}$$

and

$$\pi = \{B_Y \mid Y \in \pi_c\} \cup \{T\}. \square$$

THEOREM 4.3. Let $G = (N,T,P,S)$ be a CFG, $k \geq 0$. If G is an LR(k) grammar then $\tau(G)$ is a simple LR(k) grammar.

Due to its generality, our transformation is far from being optimal for many classes of grammars.

ACKNOWLEDGEMENTS. Part of these results first appeared in an internal report of McMaster University (Report No. 80-CS-25) in 1980. Independently, Friede[4] has obtained similar results.

REFERENCES

1. A.V. Aho and J.D. Ullman. The Theory of Parsing, Translation, and Compiling. Vols. 1 and 2, Prentice Hall, N.J., 1972 and 1973.

2. F.L. DeRemer. Simple LR(k) grammars. Comm. ACM 14 (1971), 453-460.

3. D. Friede. Partitioned LL(k) grammars. In: Automata, Languages and Programming. H.A. Maurer (ed.), Lect. Notes in Comp. Sci. 71, Springer, Berlin, 1979, 245-255.

4. D. Friede. Partitioned context-free grammars. TUM-I8115, December 1981, Institut fuer Informatik, Technische Universitaet Muenchen.

5. M.M. Geller and M.A. Harrison. On LR(k) grammars and languages. Theoret. Comput. Sci. 4 (1977), 245-276.

6. M. Hammer. A new grammatical transformation into deterministic top-down form. MAC TR-119, Mass. Inst. of Technology, 1974.

7. M.A. Harrison. Introduction to Formal Language Theory. Addison-Wesley, Reading, Mass., 1978.

8. M.A. Harrison and I.M. Havel. Strict deterministic grammars. J. Comput. System Sci. 7 (1973), 237-277.

9. M.A. Harrison and I.M. Havel. On the parsing of deterministic languages. J. Assoc. Comput. Mach. 21 (1974), 525-548.

10. D.B. Lomet. The construction of efficient deterministic language processors. Ph.D. Thesis, Univ. of Pennsylvania, 1969.

11. A. Moura. Syntactic equivalence of grammar classes. Ph.D. Thesis, Univ. of California at Berkeley, September 1980.

12. A. Nijholt. Context-Free Grammars: Covers, Normal Forms, and Parsing. Lect. Notes in Comp. Sci. 93, Springer, Berlin, 1980.

13. A. Nijholt. Parsing strategies: A concise survey. In: Mathematical Foundations of Computer Science. J. Gruska and M. Chytil (eds.), Lect. Notes in Comp. Sci. 118, Springer, Berlin, 1981.

14. A. Nijholt and E. Soisalon-Soininen. Ch(k) grammars - A characterization of LL(k) languages. In: Mathematical Foundations of Computer Science. J. Becvar (ed.), Lect. Notes in Comp. Sci. 74, Springer, Berlin, 1979, 390-397.

15. J. Pittl. On LLP(k) grammars and languages. Theoret. Comput. Sci. 16 (1981), 149-175.

16. J. Pittl. On LLP(k) parsers. J. Comput. System Sci. 24 (1982), 36-68.

17. D.J. Rosenkrantz and R.E. Stearns. Properties of deterministic top-down grammars. Information and Control 17 (1970), 226-256.

18. E. Soisalon-Soininen and E. Ukkonen. A method for transforming grammars into LL(k) form. Acta Informatica 12 (1979), 339-369.

19. E. Ukkonen. Transformations to produce certain covering grammars. In: Mathematical Foundations of Computer Science. J. Winkowski (ed.), Lect. Notes in Comput. Sci. 64, Springer, Berlin, 1978, 516-525.

20. E. Ukkonen. A modification of the LR(k) method for constructing compact bottom-up parsers. In: Automata, Languages and Programming. H.A. Maurer (ed.), Lect. Notes in Comput. Sci. 71, Springer, Berlin, 1979, 646-658.

A DECIDABILITY RESULT ABOUT SUFFICIENT-COMPLETENESS OF AXIOMATICALLY SPECIFIED ABSTRACT DATA TYPES

Tobias Nipkow , Gerhard Weikum

Institut für Praktische Informatik
Technische Hochschule Darmstadt
D-6100 Darmstadt

Abstract

The problem of deciding whether an axiomatic specification of an abstract data type is sufficiently-complete is known to be in general unsolvable. Regarding axioms as directed rewrite rules instead of symmetric equations a specification defines a reduction relation on terms. It is proved that in the subclass of left-linear axiomatic specifications the property of sufficient-completeness is decidable, if the corresponding reduction relation is normalizing and confluent. The presented algorithm can also be used to determine a set of constructors for a specified data type.

1. Introduction

In the last few years the theory of abstract data types has become an interesting and promising subject of research. Today there is a common agreement that data types are not simply sets of objects but also comprise the executable operations on these objects. From a mathematical point of view, data types are therefore algebraic structures. This paradigm has had a great impact on modern computer science.

Abstract data types should be specified abstractly without referring to concrete storage representations. The axiomatic method ([ADJ 78], [GH 78]) especially fits this purpose. It describes the semantics of the operations of a data type by characterizing properties as equational laws. An example of such a specification is the following FIFO queue.

Example 1.1

```
type QUEUE is
  sorts QUEUE,NAT
  operations
    Zero  : Ø -> NAT
    Succ  : NAT -> NAT
    Newq  : Ø -> QUEUE
    Append: QUEUE × NAT -> QUEUE
    Front : QUEUE -> NAT
    Length: QUEUE -> NAT
    Remove: QUEUE -> QUEUE
```

axioms

```
Front(Newq) = Zero 1
Front(Append(Newq,i)) = i
Front(Append(Append(q,i),j)) = Front(Append(q,i))
Length(Append(q,i)) = Succ(Length(q))
Remove(Newq) = Newq
Remove(Append(Newq,i)) = Newq
Remove(Append(Append(q,i),j)) = Append(Remove(Append(q,i)),j)
```

One striking point of this specification is that it is obviously, in a yet imprecise sense, incomplete, because the effect of the operation "Length" applied on the empty queue "Newq" cannot be derived from the axioms. Theoretically, this means that new values such as "Length(Newq)" are introduced into the primitive type NAT thus violating the principle of modularity (cf. [BD 81]). The specification becomes complete and indeed correct, if the equation

Length(Newq) = Zero

is added. Of course, there are situations in which it is much more difficult to decide whether a specification is complete or not.

Guttag has precisely defined this kind of completeness and has established the name "sufficient-completeness" for it (cf. [GH 78]). He has shown that this important property of axiomatic specifications is in general undecidable. We, on the other hand, prove in our paper that sufficient-completeness is decidable for a large subclass of axiomatic specifications. However, we avoid similarly strong restrictions as the sufficient conditions given in [GH 78]. Our result is principally based on interpreting equations asymmetrically as term-rewrite rules.

2. Background

In this section we summarize the most important theoretical results about axiomatic specifications and their interpretation as term-rewrite systems.

Definition 2.1

Let S be a set of sorts, i.e. names of data types resp. their carriers. A signature Σ over S is a set of functions resp. function symbols, each of which is assigned an arity and a range type by maps Dom: $\Sigma \rightarrow S^*$ and Typ: $\Sigma \rightarrow S$.

The set of all well-formed terms of a signature Σ is called Σ_*, and we

1 We are not interested in the specification of errors or "exceptions" as you might call them.

use $(\Sigma \cup V)_*$ for the set of all Σ-terms with variables from a denumerable S-sorted set V. Σ_* is the so-called Σ-word algebra, i.e. it is freely generated by the operations of Σ. If one looks upon V as a set of constants, then $(\Sigma \cup V)_*$ can also be regarded as a word algebra. When there is no ambiguity about the signature, we shall write T for $(\Sigma \cup V)_*$.

In the following, the map "Typ" will be extended to T.

Definition 2.2

A relation $R \subseteq T \times T$ is called type-preserving, iff for all $(l,r) \in R$: $Typ(l) = Typ(r)$.

Definition 2.3

Let Σ be a signature and V a denumerable set of variables, both over a set S of sorts. A (ground) substitution is a type-preserving function $\sigma: V \to \Sigma_*$. The uniquely determined homomorphic extension of σ to $(\Sigma \cup V)_*$ will also be named σ.

Definition 2.4

Let $t \in (\Sigma \cup V)_*$ be a term of a signature Σ with variables. $t' \in \Sigma_*$ is called an instance of t, iff there is a substitution σ such that $t' = \sigma(t)$.

Two terms $t_1, t_2 \in (\Sigma \cup V)_*$ are unifiable, iff there exists a term $t' \in \Sigma_*$ which is an instance of t_1 and also an instance of t_2.

We now precisely define what an axiomatic specification as that of example 1.1 is.

Definition 2.5

An equational or axiomatic specification of the data type T is a triple (S,Σ,E), where:

- S is a finite set of sorts with $T \in S$.
- Σ is a finite signature over S.
- $E \subseteq (\Sigma \cup V)_* \times (\Sigma \cup V)_*$ is a finite set of type-preserving equations with variables from a denumerable S-sorted set V.

The above definition characterizes one sort T as the so-called "type of interest" (cf. [GH 78]), whereas the other sorts are assumed to be somehow predefined. We shall call the sorts of S-{T} primitive types. Those types usually have in turn operations themselves. Assuming that the signature Σ of a given axiomatic specification always also includes all the relevant operations on primitive types, the "primitive" functions form the subset $P_T := \{f \in \Sigma \mid Dom(f) \in (S-\{T\})^* \wedge Typ(f) \in (S-\{T\})\}$ of Σ. The expressions that can be constructed of P_T are called primitive terms. For the set of all primitive terms of a data type T we shall write $(P_T)_*$ or P_* for short. Furthermore, a term $t \in (\Sigma \cup V)_*$ that contains variables is called "primitive", iff it is an element of $(P \cup V')_*$, where $V' := \{x \in V \mid Typ(x) \neq T\}$. In example 1.1 the signature P consists of the operations "Zero" and "Succ".

Occasionally it might be useful or even necessary to restrict the syntactic form of axiomatic specifications.

Definition 2.6

A term $t \in (\Sigma \cup V)_*$ is called linear, iff every variable occurs at most once in t. We say that an axiomatic specification (S,Σ,E) resp. its set E of axioms is left-linear, iff for all $(l,r) \in E$: l is linear.

Left-linear specifications will play an important role in chapter 3. We now turn to the algebraic semantics of axiomatic specifications.

Definition 2.7

An axiomatic specification (S,Σ,E) defines the following relation

$\xrightarrow[E]{} \subseteq \Sigma_* \times \Sigma_*$:

$t_1 \xrightarrow[E]{} t_2 :\Leftrightarrow$ There exist an axiom $(l,r) \in E$ and a substitution σ such that t_1 contains $\sigma(l)$ as a (not necessarily proper) subterm, and t_2 is the same as t_1 but with a single occurence of $\sigma(l)$ replaced by $\sigma(r)$.

$\xrightarrow[E]{}$ is called reduction relation of (S,Σ,E).

A more formalized definition is included e.g. in [NW 82]. An essential point of 2.7 is the orientation of the equations E which are normally interpreted symmetrically. We intentionally distinguish left side and right side and thus actually get directed rewrite rules instead of equations. For this reason axioms are often also called rule schemes. In the following, we shall use $\xrightarrow[E]{+}$ for the transitive closure of $\xrightarrow[E]{}$, $\xrightarrow[E]{*}$ for the transitive-reflexive closure and $\xleftrightarrow[E]{*}$ or $=_E$ for the transitive-reflexive-symmetric closure. $t_1 =_E t_2$ (where $t_1, t_2 \in \Sigma_*$) means that one can deduce the "equality" of t_1 and t_2 from the axioms E with the usual logical rules of inference. Therefore $=_E$ is called the equational theory of the axiomatically specified type $T = (S,\Sigma,E)$ (cf. [Ka 80]).

As can easily be seen, $=_E$ is the smallest congruence relation on Σ_* that includes all instances of the axioms E, i.e. the set $\{(\sigma(l),\sigma(r)) \mid (l,r) \in E \wedge \sigma \text{ is a substitution}\}$. The quotient algebra $\Sigma_*/=_E$ is called the initial algebra of (S,Σ,E). Each model of a specification (S,Σ,E), i.e. every finitely generated S-sorted Σ-algebra in which the axioms E are valid, is a homomorphic image of $\Sigma_*/=_E$. For that reason the initial algebra often is regarded as the semantics of an axiomatic specification (cf. [ADJ 78]).

It is well-known that the equational theory of a specification (S,Σ,E) is in general undecidable. This does of course not affect the underlying mathematics but is, however, an annoying aspect for computer scientists. The search for a subclass of axiomatic specifications in which the "equality" is decidable has led to the asymmetric interpretation of equations and consequently to further studies of the reduction relation $\xrightarrow[E]{}$. We therefore next consider universal properties of relations which will afterwards be applied to $\xrightarrow[E]{}$.

Definition 2.8

Let $R \subseteq M \times M$ be a (binary) relation on a set M. An element $x \in M$ is in normal form or irreducible w.r.t. R, iff there is no $y \in M$ such that xRy. Otherwise x is called "reducible". We say that $z \in M$ is a normal form of x (w.r.t. R), iff xRz and z is in normal form.

The set of all normal forms of an element $x \in M$ w.r.t. a relation $R \subseteq M \times M$ is denoted by $\mathcal{N}_R(x)$. As usual, R^* stands in the following for the transitive-reflexive closure of R.

Definition 2.9

A relation $R \subseteq M \times M$ is normalizing, iff $\forall x \in M$: $\mathcal{N}_R(x) \neq \emptyset$. R is called Noetherian, iff there exists no infinite chain $x_1 R x_2 R \ldots$ w.r.t. R. R is called confluent, iff $\forall x,y,z \in M$: $(xR^*y \wedge xR^*z \Rightarrow \exists w \in M: yR^*w \wedge zR^*w)$.

Each Noetherian relation is normalizing, but the inversion is in general not true. If a relation $R \subseteq M \times M$ is normalizing and confluent, then there exists exactly one normal form for every $x \in M$.

We can now state a relationship between the reduction relation $\xrightarrow[E]{}$ of an axiomatic specification (S,Σ,E) and the equational theory $=_E$, i.e. between the directed and the symmetric interpretation of axioms. Reductions are under certain conditions as expressive as equations. This is the essence of the following Church-Rosser property.

Theorem 2.1 (cf. [CF 58])

Let (S,Σ,E) be an axiomatic specification of which the reduction relation $\xrightarrow[E]{}$ is confluent. For all $t_1, t_2 \in \Sigma_*$ the following equivalence holds: $t_1 =_E t_2 \iff \exists t \in \Sigma_*: t_1 \xrightarrow[E]{*} t \wedge t_2 \xrightarrow[E]{*} t$.

Theorem 2.1 is the basis of an operational semantics of axiomatically specified data types (cf. [Wa 77]) that coincides, under certain conditions, with the (initial) algebraic semantics. Our interest in regarding axioms as term-rewriting systems primarily stems from the following important proposition.

Theorem 2.2

Let (S,Σ,E) be an axiomatic specification of which the reduction relation $\xrightarrow[E]{}$ is normalizing and confluent. Then $=_E$ is decidable.

Similar versions of this fundamental theorem appear in many papers such as e.g. [KB 70]. Throughout the whole rest of this paper we shall look upon an axiomatic specification as a finite description of the corresponding reduction relation.

3. The Main Result and its Proof

Before giving our main result and embarking on the task of proving it we have to make the notion of sufficient-completeness more precise.

Definition 3.1

Let $T = (S,\Sigma,E)$ be an axiomatically specified data type. T is sufficiently-complete, iff for every term $t\in\Sigma_*$ of primitive sort there exists a primitive term t' such that the "equality" of t and t' is derivable from the axioms, i.e. iff

$\forall t\in\Sigma_*: Typ(t)\neq T \Rightarrow \exists t'\in P_*: t =_E t'$

where P_* denotes the set of all primitive terms.

The original definition in [GH 78] did not explicitly state in which deductive system the "equality" of t and t' is to be derived, but Kapur ([Ka 80]) confirms that it should be the equational theory $=_E$.

Clearly the two major problems in deciding whether a specification is sufficiently-complete are the unrestricted universal quantifier and the undecidability of $=_E$. To motivate our efforts in removing these problems we will now state our main theorem and develop its proof subsequently step by step. However, we will omit all proofs of lemmas, because they are mostly technical and tedious. They are contained in the full version of this paper which is part of [NW 82].

Theorem 3.1

Let $\xrightarrow[E]{}$ be the reduction relation belonging to the axiomatically specified type $T = (S,\Sigma,E)$. If E is left-linear, $\xrightarrow[E]{}$ is confluent and normalizing, and no left-hand side of E is primitive, then the sufficient-completeness of T is decidable.

The first step will be the replacement of $=_E$ by a more convenient relation.

Lemma 3.1

If $\xrightarrow[E]{}$ is a confluent and normalizing reduction relation belonging to a specification T = (S,Σ,E) where no left-hand side of E is primitive, then T is sufficiently-complete, iff

$\forall t \in (\Sigma_* - P_*): Typ(t) \neq T \Rightarrow \exists t' \in \Sigma_*: t \xrightarrow[E]{} t'$

Thus the preconditions "confluent", "normalizing" and "non-primitive" are accounted for. Similar results which do not need the confluence of $\xrightarrow[E]{}$ and therefore merely provide sufficient criteria are given in [Mu 80] and [BD 81]. Lemma 3.1 enables us to reduce the problem of finding an equivalent primitive term for a given term t to testing t for reducibility, which is obviously recursive.

The next step consists of removing the universal quantifier, as we still have to check infinitely many terms. Our approach is as follows: We partition the set of all terms into finitely many subsets such that the elements in one subset are either all reducible (w.r.t. $\xrightarrow[E]{}$) or all in normal form. This leads to a further reduction of the test for sufficient-completeness: Instead of testing infinitely many terms for reducibility we can confine ourselves to representatives of the finitely many classes of the above partition.

The construction of this partition is based upon the following observation: In testing a term t for reducibility, i.e. matching it against the left-hand sides of the set E of rule schemes, we merely consider the subterms of t which are not larger than a given height m, the maximum height of all left-hand sides. Thus the reducibility of a term is characterized by the finite set of its subterms up to a maximum height. The partition mentioned above places all terms with the same set of subterms into the same class. However, it must be stressed that these arguments apply only to left-linear axioms: Matching the (non-linear) term f(x,x) against a term t requires not only f to occur inside t but also both subterms of f to be identical. Thus the relevant depth of subterms can not be fixed in advance. This accounts for the precondition of left-linearity. We will now formalize these ideas.

Definition 3.2

height: $\mathcal{T} \rightarrow \mathbb{N}$ computes the height of a term.

$height(x) := 1$ for all $x \in V$

$height(f(t_1,\ldots,t_k)) := 1+\max\{height(t_i) \mid 1 \le i \le k := |Dom(f)|\}$

For $n \in \mathbb{N}$ the following sets are defined:

$\mathcal{T}_n := \{t \in \mathcal{T} \mid height(t) \le n\}$

$\Sigma_n := \{t \in \Sigma_* \mid height(t) \le n\}$

T_n and Σ_n are the sets of all terms up to height n with and without variables respectively.

top_n , sub_n : $T \rightarrow 2^{T_n}$

$top_n(t) := \{l \in T \mid height(l) \leq n \wedge l$ is linear $\wedge$ l is unifiable with t$\}$

$sub_n(t) := \{l \in T \mid height(l) \leq n \wedge l$ is linear $\wedge$
l is unifiable with a subterm of t$\}$

$\sim_n \subseteq T \times T$

$t_1 \sim_n t_2 \;:\!\Leftrightarrow\; top_n(t_1) = top_n(t_2) \wedge sub_n(t_1) = sub_n(t_2)$

Two terms are equivalent modulo $\sim_n$, iff they do not differ up to depth n and the sets of their subterms are the same.

In the sequel we will state some important properties of these sets and relate them to the main idea as discussed above.

Lemma 3.2

For all $n \in N$: $\sim_n$ is decidable.

Lemma 3.3

Let $\xrightarrow[E]{}$ be the reduction relation generated by a left-linear axiomatic specification (S,Σ,E), and let $m := \max\{height(l) \mid (l,r) \in E\}$.
For $n \in N$ $\sim_n$ is an equivalence relation, and for $n \geq m$, $t,t' \in \Sigma_*$:
$t \sim_n t'$ implies
1) Typ(t) = Typ(t')
2) t is primitive (i.e. $\in P_*$) iff t' is primitive (if $m \geq 2$)
3) t is reducible w.r.t. $\xrightarrow[E]{}$ iff t' is reducible w.r.t. $\xrightarrow[E]{}$

Thus $\sim_m$ is the relation we have been looking for. Since $\sim_m$ is an equivalence the quotient set $\Sigma_*/\sim_m$ exists, and the $\sim_m$-classes have the required properties:
Testing all non-primitive terms of primitive sort for reducibility is achieved by testing one term out of each non-primitive $\sim_m$-class not of type T, i.e. each class that contains only non-primitive terms of a primitive type.

Lemma 3.4

For all $n \in N$: $\Sigma_*/\sim_n$ is finite.

So we know in addition that only finitely many $\sim_m$-classes exist and thus that the test is recursive provided that at least one representative for each non-primitive $\sim_m$-class is available. This is the last problem to solve, generating members of each equivalence class. This will be done in the following fashion: Instead of explicitly constructing them we enumerate $\Sigma_*/\sim_m$ by the successive generation of the Σ_i (for i=1,2,...) until $\Sigma_i/\sim_m = \Sigma_{i+1}/\sim_m$. In this case $\Sigma_i/\sim_m = \Sigma_*/\sim_m$ holds.

We mentioned above that $\sim_n$ is an equivalence relation on Σ_* for $n \in N$. More than that, even the following property holds.

Lemma 3.5

For $n \in N$: $\sim_n$ is a congruence on Σ_*.

This property of $\sim_n$ is in turn crucial for the proof of the next lemma.

Lemma 3.6

Let $k, n \in N$ such that $\Sigma_k/\sim_n = \Sigma_{k+1}/\sim_n$. Then $\Sigma_j/\sim_n = \Sigma_k/\sim_n$ holds for all $j > k$.

With the help of these assorted lemmas we now can prove our main result.

Proof of Theorem 3.1

From the previous discussions we know that it suffices to test one member out of each of the finitely many non-primitive $\sim_m$-classes where m is the maximum height of all left-hand sides of E. Since $\Sigma_i \subseteq \Sigma_{i+1} \subseteq \Sigma_*$ for all $i \in N$ the inequations $\Sigma_i/\sim_m \subseteq \Sigma_{i+1}/\sim_m \subseteq \Sigma_*/\sim_m$ hold, and as $\Sigma_*/\sim_m$ is finite there must be a $k \in N$ such that $\Sigma_k/\sim_m = \Sigma_{k+1}/\sim_m$. Because of lemma 3.2 this k can be determined effectively. By virtue of lemma 3.6 $\Sigma_j/\sim_m = \Sigma_k/\sim_m$ holds for all $j > k$, and because the Σ_i enumerate Σ_* we get $\Sigma_k/\sim_m = \Sigma_*/\sim_m$. Thus Σ_k contains at least one representative for each $\sim_m$-class of Σ_* and T is sufficiently-complete, iff all non-primitive terms in Σ_k which are not of type T are reducible. Since Σ_k is computable and finite and reducibility is decidable, sufficient-completeness is recursive for T. □

It should be noted that this theorem is only applicable to a class of data types with certain properties, confluent and normalizing reduction relation, which are in their turn undecidable (cf. [HO 80]). Sufficient conditions for both properties, however, have been extensively studied in the literature.

The proof of theorem 3.1 directly yields a decision procedure for sufficient-completeness of data types satisfying the preconditions of 3.1. However, this algorithm is extremely inefficient as the complexity increases at least exponentially with m. This is because the growth of the size of the Σ_i is exponential in i. Nevertheless we will present the algorithm as a program in a PASCAL-like language:

Algorithm 3.1

```
function SuffCompl ( (S,Σ,E): axiomatic specification): boolean;
  (* Assert: (S,Σ,E) satisfies the conditions of theorem 3.1 *)
  var i,m: integer;
  begin
    SuffCompl := true;
    m := max{2,max{height(l)|(l,r)∈R}};
    i := 1;
    while Σ_i/~_m ≠ Σ_{i+1}/~_m do i := i+1;
    for all t∈Σ_i while SuffCompl do
        if Typ(t)≠T and t∈(Σ_*-P_*) and "t is in normal form"
        then SuffCompl := false
  end (* SuffCompl *);
```

4. Conclusion

There are several directions to which one might extend the results of our paper. First of all, a considerably more efficient algorithm for deciding sufficient-completeness should be developped in order to get a practically usable tool for checking axiomatic specifications.

Another desirable extension would, of course, be to weaken the restrictions we imposed on specifications in theorem 3.1. We conjecture that also without left-linearity sufficient-completeness remains decidable. Our proof would, however, have to be changed radically, because most of the presented lemmas do not hold for non-linear specifications.

As far as the confluence and normalization of reduction relations are concerned, we have a strong feeling that these two properties are essential prerequisites for the decidability of sufficient-completeness in any class of specifications, whereas our motivation for demanding left-linearity is of technical nature. Permutative axioms like commutativity of an operation are thus excluded, because the corresponding reduction relation is not normalizing. It seems that another kind of reducibility is needed to handle such cases. We have in mind some sort of "reduction modulo equivalence" (cf. [Hu 80]), i.e. an approach that operates partly on classes of terms instead of single terms.

At last we want to point out a connection between the problem of deciding sufficient-completeness and the task of determining a set of constructors for an axiomatically specified data type T = (S,Σ,E).

In this context, "constructors" means a subset $C_T \subseteq \Sigma$ with Typ(f)=T for all $f \in C_T$ such that $\forall t \in \Sigma_*$: Typ(t)=T => $\exists t' \in (C_T \cup P_T)_*$: $t =_E t'$ (cf. [GH 78]). It is a trivial exercise to transfer our solution for deciding sufficient-completeness to the problem of finding a set of constructors.

References

[ADJ 78] J.A. Goguen, J.W. Thatcher, E.G. Wagner, J.B. Wright; An Initial Algebra Approach to the Specification, Correctness and Implementation of Abstract Data Types; in: R.T. Yeh (ed.); Current Trends in Programming Methodology Vol. IV; Prentice-Hall, Englewood Cliffs 1978

[BD 81] M. Bergman, P. Deransart; Abstract Data Types and Rewriting Systems: Application to the Programming of Algebraic Abstract Data Types in PROLOG; in: Proc. 6th CAAP Genova 1981; LNCS 112 Springer-Verlag, Berlin-Heidelberg-New York 1981

[CF 58] H.B. Curry, R. Feys; Combinatory Logic Vol. I; North-Holland, Amsterdam 1958

[GH 78] J.V. Guttag, J.J. Horning; The Algebraic Specification of Abstract Data Types; Acta Informatica Vol.10 No.1, pp. 27-52,1978

[HO 80] G. Huet, D. Oppen; Equations and Rewrite Rules: A Survey; Technical Report, SRI International, 1980; also in: R. Book (ed.); Formal Languages: Perspectives and Open Problems; Academic Press, New York 1980

[Hu 80] G. Huet; Confluent Reductions: Abstract Properties and Applications to Term Rewriting Systems; Journal of the ACM Vol.27 No.4, pp. 797-821, 1980

[Ka 80] D. Kapur; Towards a Theory for Abstract Data Types; Ph.D. Thesis, MIT Cambridge (Mass.), 1980

[KB 70] D.E. Knuth, P.B. Bendix; Simple Word Problems in Universal Algebras; in: J. Leech (ed.); Computational Problems in Universal Algebras; Pergamon Press, Oxford 1970

[Mu 80] D.R. Musser; On Proving Inductive Properties of Abstract Data Types; in: Proc. 7th ACM Symposium on Principles of Programming Languages 1980

[NW 82] T. Nipkow, G. Weikum; Operationale Semantik axiomatisch spezifizierter Abstrakter Datentypen; Diplomarbeit Fachbereich Informatik, Technische Hochschule Darmstadt, 1982

[Wa 77] M. Wand; Algebraic Theories and Tree Rewriting Systems; Technical Report No. 66 Computer Science Department, Indiana University, Bloomington 1977

TWO REMARKS ON THE POWER OF COUNTING

Christos H. Papadimitriou and Stathis K. Zachos
Laboratory of Computer Science, M.I.T.
Cambridge, USA

August 1982

ABSTRACT

The relationship between the polynomial hierarchy and Valiant's class #P is at present unknown. We show that some low portions of the polynomial hierarchy, namely deterministic polynomial algorithms using an NP oracle at most a logarithmic number of times, can be simulated by one #P computation. We also show that the class of problems solvable by polynomial-time nondeterministic Turing machines which accept whenever there is an odd number of accepting computations is idempotent, that is, closed under usage of oracles from the same class.

KEYWORDS: Counting problems, oracle computation, polynomial hierarchy, parity problems, machine simulation.

1. INTRODUCTION

Counting Turing machines, and the class #P of counting problems that can be solved by such machines in polynomial time, were first introduced and studied by Valiant [Va1]. The relationship of #P with other complexity classes has since been an intriguing open question. It is well known that NP is contained in #P (we use the term #P originally meant for a class of functions, to denote the class of languages which are accepted in polynomial deterministic time with one invocation of a #P computation). Furthermore, Simon [Si] showed some close relationships between #P and the probabilistic class PP [Gi]. On the other hand, it was suspected that #P lies above the whole polynomial hierarchy [St], but no proof of this is known to date. Angluin [An] showed that #P appropriately relativized, is more powerful than Σ_2^P.

We were interested in showing that, in the unrelativized case, the class $\Delta_2^P = P^{NP}$ is contained in #P. What we were able to show is that a portion of Δ_2^P, namely the class $P^{NP[\log]}$ of problems solvable by polynomial-time algorithms using a logarithmic number of calls to an NP oracle, is indeed contained in #P. This class contains, for example, the problem of testing whether a given undirected graph has a unique optimum clique [Pa] (it is not known, however, whether this problem is complete for $P^{PN[\log]}$). It also contains the class D^P [PY] of languages that are the intersection of a language in NP and one in coNP. Furthermore, there is a whole hierarchy of classes of languages definable as NP predicates combined by Boolean connectives. The ith level of this hierarchy consists of all languages that can be expressed as the union of i languages in D^P. The limit of this hierarchy turns out to be identical to the class of languages recognized by polynomial algorithms using a bounded number of calls to an NP oracle, and thus is also a subset of #P, by our result.

The technique used in the proof of this theorem employs a simple way of encoding a computation with oracle branchings into the number of accepting computations of a single nondeterministic computation, which can then be computed by a counting Turning machine, and then decoded. This technique seems to be useful in simulations by counting machines. Using a variant of this technique, we show an interesting property of the class ⊕P of problems that can be solved by Turing machines which accept if the number of accepting computations is odd. A typical (complete) problem in ⊕P is the set of all graphs that have an odd number of Hamilton circuits. ⊕P can be considered as a more moderate version of the counting idea. The relationship between ⊕P and NP is not known, although it is suspected that NP is weaker [Va2]. What we show is that $\oplus P^{\oplus P} = \oplus P$, and thus ⊕P appears to behave differently from NP. This fact had been proved independently by Valiant [Va2].

2. DEFINITIONS

For basic Turing machine definitions see [GJ, LP]. All computation paths of a nondeterministic Turing machine on a particular input (or the computations from any given configuration) form a tree. We do not insist that all leaves of this tree have the same depth (this can be achieved by a variety of padding techniques). We shall need to define certain notation for manipulating nondeterministic computation trees. If $C_1,...,C_k$ are configurations of a Turing machine (equivalently, the computation trees starting from these configurations), then CHOOSE($C_1,...,C_k$) denotes the computation tree consisting of a new root, which has nondeterministic branches to all these computations. Also, APPEND(C_1,C_2) denotes the computation tree consisting of the computation tree of C_1 with a copy of C_2 hanging from each accepting leaf of C_1. Finally, $DUPL_n$ denotes a computation tree which has exactly n accepting leaves.

If M is a nondeterministic Turing machine, we let COUNT(M,x) denote the number of accepting computations of M on input x. Thus, NP can be defined as the class of languages L for which there is a nondeterministic Turing machine M such that L = {x | COUNT(M,x)>0}. #P is the class of languages that can be recognized by a deterministic polynomial-time algorithm which uses only once an oracle computing COUNT. $P^{NP[log]}$, a subclass of $\Delta_2^P = P^{NP}$, is the set of problems solvable by deterministic polynomial-time algorithms which use an oracle in NP a number of times which is at most proportional to the logarithm of the length of the input of the algorithm. Finally, $\oplus$P is the class of all languages L, for which there exists a nondeterministic Turing machine M such that L = {x | COUNT(M,x) mod 2 = 1}.

3. THE MAIN THEOREM

In this Section we prove the following:

THEOREM 1: $P^{NP[log]} \subseteq$ #P.

PROOF: Suppose that L is a language recognized by a deterministic Turing machine M with an oracle in NP, so that at most p(|x|) steps, and at most log(|x|) oracle steps are used in the computation on input x. Assume without loss of generality that the oracle queries are of the form (M',x'), asking whether a nondeterministic Turing machine M' accepts an input x' in time p(|x|). We also assume that

M always asks exactly $\lfloor \log|x| \rfloor$ queries. We shall design a deterministic polynomial algorithm which decides L by using one computation of COUNT.

The idea is the following: By multiplying the number of leaves in different subtrees of the computation tree of M by exorbitantly large numbers, we can unambiguously encode the outcomes of all the oracle calls along all possible computation paths of M. (Notice that M, although deterministic, has a polynomial number of computation paths, due to the oracle steps.)

The algorithm first constructs, based on M and x, a nondeterministic Turing machine N, as follows. N is programmed basically like M, except in the query configurations. If the query (M',x') is the ith query asked by M, and M goes to configuration C_1 if the answer is "yes", and C_o if "no", then N executes the nondeterministic program shown below:

$$\text{CHOOSE}(\text{ID}_o(M',x'),\text{APPEND}(\text{DUPL}_{k(i)},C_1),\text{APPEND}(\text{DUPL}_{k(i)^2},C_o)),$$

where $\text{ID}_o(M',x')$ denotes the initial configuration of the machine M' on input x', and the k(i)'s are integers to be defined later. In words, N nondeterministically chooses among three possibilities: either to simulate M' on x' and stop; or to assume the answer is "yes" and amplify the subsequent computation by a factor of k(i); or finally to assume the answer is "no", in which case the answer is amplified by $k(i)^2$ (see the figure below for a pictorial presentation of the construction using computation trees).

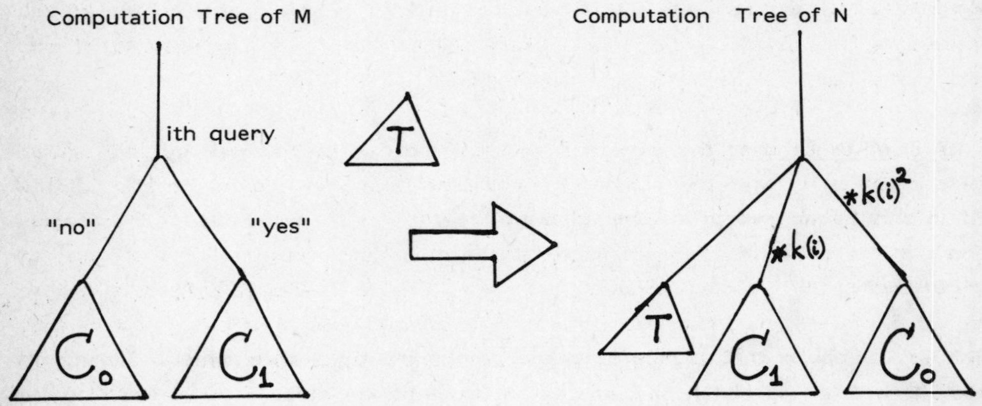

ith query: Does T have an Accepting Leaf ?

The full algorithm is the following:

```
ALGORITHM A;
 BEGIN
   construct N as described above;
   n ← COUNT(N,x);
   i ← 1;
   WHILE n > 1 DO
   BEGIN
     IF n MOD k(i) = 0 THEN n ← n DIV k(i)^2
          ELSE n ← (n MOD k(i)^2) DIV k(i);
     i ← i + 1
   END;
   IF n = 1 THEN accept ELSE reject
 END.
```

The k(i)'s are defined by the following equations:

$$k(\lfloor \log|x| \rfloor) = 2^{p(|x|)}$$
$$k(i) = k(i+1)^4$$

Thus, k(i) increases rapidly as i decreases (or, equivalently, as we proceed from later to earlier queries). The maximum value of k(i) is k(1), which is $2^{p(|x|)|x|^2/4}$. Notice that this number is of length polynomial in |x|, and therefore our construction produces a nondeterministic Turing machine N which still obeys a polynomial bound on the depth of all computations. It is this growth of the k(i)'s, a necessary ingredient for our arguments, which limits the applicability of our proof to the case of logarithmically many queries.

We shall argue that the algorithm above accepts x iff M does. We shall show, by induction on i, that the number n in the beginning of the ith iteration of the main loop of the algorithm A denotes the number of accepting leaves of the computation subtree of N, which corresponds to the computation subtree of M starting at the ith query. This certainly holds for i = 1. Assume now that it holds after the first i-1 iterations. Suppose that the ith query has answer "no". This means that there is no accepting path of M' on the queried x'. Since such paths are the only paths in the subtree of N which are not multiplied by a multiple of k(i), and since the number of such paths cannot exceed k(i)-1, this is equivalent to saying that the value of n before the ith iteration (by induction hypothesis the total number of such paths) is divisible exactly by k(i). Thus the THEN branch of the test is taken, and the new value of n is n DIV $k(i)^2$, which is exactly the number of accepting computations in the subtree of N corresponding to C_o. This is because the growth of the k(i)'s is such that the total number of leaves in the subtree of N corresponding to C_o (or for that matter to C_1) is less than k(i). Similarly, if the answer to the ith query is "yes", then the ELSE branch is taken, and n becomes the number of accepting leaves in a subtree of N that corresponds to C_1. The induction is complete.

Therefore, after the last execution of the loop, the value of n is the number of accepting computations of M after the last oracle step. This number is of course 1 or 0, depending on whether x is accepted by M or not. QED.

Notice that we can prove the same way a stronger result, namely that P can simulate a logarithmic number of queries from PP. PP is defined as the class of languages L for which there is a nondeterministic Turing machine M such that all computations of M on input x have length exactly p(|x|) for some polynomial p(.), and $L = \{x \mid COUNT(M,x) > 2^{p(|x|)-1}\}$. PP is known to contain NP [Gi].

4. PARITY COUNTING

A variant of the proof technique of the previous section can be used to show the following result:

THEOREM 2: $\oplus P^{\oplus P} = \oplus P$.

PROOF: Let L be a language recognized by a parity machine M which uses as an oracle another parity machine M'. We shall design a parity machine N which accepts L with no oracles. N is programmed exactly like M, except in the oracle steps. Suppose that M is at an oracle step with query (M',x'), and let C_1 be the configuration corresponding to a "yes" answer, and C_o to "no". At this query step, N does the following:

$$\text{CHOOSE}(\text{APPEND}(\text{ID}_o(M',x'),C_1),\text{APPEND}(\text{CHOOSE}(\text{ID}_o(M',x'),\underline{\text{accept}}),C_o)).$$

In words, the number of accepting leaves of C_1 is multiplied by the number of accepting leaves of M' on x', whereas the number of accepting leaves of C_o is multiplied by that of M' on x' plus one.

We now claim that N accepts x iff M does. To see this, notice that each leaf of the computation of M corresponds to a number of leaves in the computation of N which is the product of as many numbers as there are oracle steps in the computation leading to the leaf. If the path leading to the leaf corresponds to the correct answer to the query, then the multiplicant is odd, otherwise it is even. So, the leaf contributes an odd number to the total count (and thus it is taken into account as an accepting computation) iff it corresponds to correct answers to all the queries asked along the path. It follows that the total number of leaves of N is odd iff the total number of leaves of M, corresponding to correct sequences of oracle answers - that is, the leaves of M that are finally counted - is odd. QED.

REFERENCES

[An] D. Angluin "On counting problems and the polynominal-time hierarchy", Theoretical Computer Science 12 (1980), pp. 161-173

[GJ] M.R. Garey, D.S. Johnson Computers and Intractability: A Guide to the Theory of NP-completeness, Freeman, 1979.

[Gi] J. Gill "Computational complexity of probabilistic Turing machines", SIAM J. Computing 6 (1977), pp. 675-695.

[LP] H.R. Lewis, C.H. Papadimitriou Elements of the Theory of Computation, Prentice-Hall, 1981.

[Pa] C.H. Papadimitriou "The complexity of unique solutions", Proc. 13th FOCS Conference, 1982, to appear.

[PY] C.H. Papadimitriou, M. Yannakakis "The complexity of facets (and some facets of complexity", Proc. 14th STOC, pp. 255-260, 1982. Also to appear in JCSS.

[Si] J. Simon "On the difference between one and many" Proc. 4th Intern. Colloquium on Automata, Languages and Programming, pp. 480-491, 1977.

[St] L.J. Stockmeyer "The polynamial-time hierarchy", Theoretical Computer Science, 3 (1977), pp. 1-22.

[Va1] L.G. Valiant "The complexity of computing the permanent", Theoretical Computer Science, 8 (1979), pp. 181-201.

[Va2] L.G. Valiant, private communication, August 1982.

SOME OPERATIONS AND TRANSDUCTIONS THAT PRESERVE RATIONALITY

by J.-E. PIN and J. SAKAROVITCH
Université Paris VI et CNRS
Laboratoire d'Informatique Théorique
4, PLACE Jussieu 75230 PARIS Cedex 05

1. Introduction

When a language theorist encounters a new operation on languages, his first impulse is to know whether this operation preserves rational languages. If the answer appears to be positive, he proceeds immediately to the construction of a more or less complicated automaton to solve the problem. However there are many operations on languages, many language theorists (see the references) and many different constructions to study these many operations. The aim of this paper is to show that almost all of these constructions are a particular case of a general and simple approach. It is fair to say immediately that a few operations are overlooked, such as the star operation, complementation and reversal. However the scope of our method is quite broad, broader indeed than one would expect, and goes from "classical" operations such as union, intersection, concatenation, quotient, shuffle, inverse and direct morphisms, etc..., to less classical ones such as infiltration, Dyck reduction, longest common prefix, Straubing's counting, etc. It includes also questions that are not expressed directly as operations on languages, as, for example, Reutenauer's theorem on TOL-systems. The interest of the method is not only to give a unified framework for all these results. Statements of the form "such an operation preserves rational languages" can readily be refined into "such an operation preserves star-free languages" or even more generaly "such an operation preserves such a variety of rational languages".

The key idea of our construction is to consider an operation

$\varphi : A_1^* \times \dots \times A_n^* \to A^*$ as the inverse of a transduction

$\tau : A^* \to A_1^* \times \dots \times A_n^*$ (when it is possible). Then, given monoids $M_1, \dots, M_n$ recognizing the languages $L_1, \dots, L_n$ of $A_1^*, \dots, A_n^*$, respectively, we are able to construct a monoid M recognizing $(L_1, \dots, L_n)\varphi$ as soon as the transduction τ admits a matrix representation. At this point the term "matrix representation" is intentionally imprecise. The following definition gives a first approach to the notion. Let μ be a morphism from A^* into the monoid of $k \times k$ matrices (for some k), whose entries are subsets of $A_1^* \times \dots \times A_n^*$. Roughly speaking the transduction τ is then asked to be such that, for every u in A^*, $u\tau$ is a fixed linear expression of the entries of $u\mu$. Thus, for instance, the Kleene-Schützenberger theorem says that every rational transduction admits a matrix representation with *rational* subsets as entries. However one can replace "linear expression" by "polynomial expression" and even by "series" in the previous definition. In any case the construction of a monoid M that recognizes $(L_1,\ldots,L_n)\varphi$ *only depends on the morphism* μ and on $M_1,\ldots,M_n$. Therefore if φ is an operation, we proceed as follows : we first check whether φ can be expressed as the inverse of a transduction τ . This applies in most cases (except for star and complementation). Now the construction of M reduces to finding a matrix representation for τ. This is possible in most cases (except for reversal) and in general τ even admits a "linear" matrix representation. However the following example, which is an extension of a classical exercise in language theory, shows that non-linear matrix representations might be required : given a language L of A^*, divide the words of L into $(2n+1)$ equal segments (if possible) for any *prime* number $2n+1$: $\zeta(L)$ is the set of all medial segments one can obtain this way. Then if L is rational, $\zeta(L)$ is rational.

2.- Matrix representations of transductions

We refer the reader to [3] for undefined terms of this article.

Let M be a monoid (with unit 1). We denote by $P(M)$ the *power set* of M : $P(M)$ is a semiring with union as addition and the usual product of subsets as multiplication. The set of *rational subsets* of M, denoted Rat M is the smallest subsemiring of $P(M)$ containing the finite sets and closed under the star operation. As usual we denote by $P(M)^{n\times n}$ the set of matrices of size n with entries in $P(M)$.

A subset P of M is *recognized by a morphism* $\eta : M \to N$ if $P = P\eta\eta^{-1}$, that is, if there exists a subset Q of N such that $P = Q\eta^{-1}$. In this case we also say that N *recognizes* P. Note that if N is a submonoid of N', then N' also recognizes P.

P is a *recognizable* if it is recognized by a *finite* monoid.

Kleene's theorem states that a language is recognizable iff it is rational.

Let M and N be two monoids. A *transduction* $\tau : M \to N$ is a mapping from M into $P(N)$. One extends τ to a mapping $P(M) \to P(N)$ by setting $P\tau = \bigcup_{m\in P} m\tau$. The *inverse transduction* $\tau^{-1} : N \to M$ is defined by $Q\tau^{-1} = \{m \in M \mid m\tau \cap Q \neq \emptyset\}$. The transduction is rational if the set

$\{(m, n) \in M \times N \mid n \in m\tau\}$ is a rational subset of $M \times N$.

Let A be an alphabet and let M be a monoid.

Definition 2.1 A transduction $\tau : A^* \to M$ admits a *linear matrix representation* (λ,μ,ν) if there exist $n > o$, a morphism $\mu : A^* \to \mathcal{P}(M)^{n\times n}$, a row vector $\lambda \in \mathcal{P}(M)^{1\times n}$, a column vector $\nu \in \mathcal{P}(M)^{n\times 1}$ such that for all $f \in A^*$, $f\tau = \lambda.f\mu.\nu$.

The theorem of Kleene- Schützenberger (cf. [3]) states that a transduction $\tau : A^* \to M$ is rational iff it admits a linear matrix representation with entries in Rat M.

Every monoid morphism $M \to N$ can be extended to a morphism $\mathcal{P}(M) \to \mathcal{P}(N)$ and, for each $n > o$, to a morphism $\mathcal{P}(M)^{n\times n} \to \mathcal{P}(N)^{n\times n}$.

The following elementary result is efficient for most of the applications we have in view.

Theorem 2.1 Let $\tau : A^* \to M$ be a transduction that admits a linear matrix representation (λ, μ, ν) and let P be a subset of M recognized by a morphism $\eta : M \to N$. Then the language $P\tau^{-1}$ is recognized by the monoid of matrices $A^*\mu\eta$.

Proof Let $Q = P\eta$ and let R be the subset of $A^*\mu\eta$ defined by

$R = \{m \in \mathcal{P}(N)^{n\times n} \mid \lambda\eta.m.\nu\eta \cap Q \neq \emptyset\}$.

Then by a routine calculation :

$$\begin{aligned} R(\mu\eta)^{-1} &= \{f \in A^* \mid f\mu\eta \in R\} = \{f \in A^* \mid \lambda\eta.f\mu\eta.\nu\eta \cap Q \neq \emptyset\} \\ &= \{f \in A^* \mid f\tau\eta \cap Q \neq \emptyset\} = \{f \in A^* \mid f\tau \cap Q\eta^{-1} \neq \emptyset\} \\ &= \{f \in A^* \mid f\tau \cap P \neq \emptyset\} = P\tau^{-1} \end{aligned}$$

Corollary 2.2 Let $\tau : A^* \to M$ be a transduction that admits a linear matrix representation. If P is a recognizable subset of M, $P\tau^{-1}$ is a recognizable - hence rational - language of A^*.

The extension of theorem 2.1 requires some preliminaries.

Let M be a monoid and let Ξ be an alphabet. We denote by $M * \Xi^*$ * the free product (or coproduct) of the monoids M and Ξ^*. The monoid $M * \Xi^*$ can be identified with the set of words of the form $m_o\zeta_1 m_1 \ldots \zeta_n m_n$ (where $m_o, \ldots m_n \in M$ and $\zeta_1, \ldots, \zeta_n \in \Xi$) equipped with the product

$(m_o\zeta_1\ldots\zeta_n m_n)(m'_o\zeta'_1 m'_1\ldots\zeta'_{n'} m'_{n'}) = m_o\zeta_1 m_1\ldots\zeta_n(m_n m'_o)\zeta'_1 m'_1\ldots\zeta'_{n'} m'_{n'}$.

Let $\Theta : \Xi^* \to \mathcal{P}(M)$ be a morphism, that is, a substitution from Ξ^* to M. We denote by $[\Theta] : \mathcal{P}(M * \Xi^*) \to \mathcal{P}(M)$ the semiring morphism defined by

(a) $u[\Theta] = m_o(\zeta_1\Theta)m_1\ldots(\zeta_n\Theta)m_n$ for $u = m_o\zeta_1\ldots\zeta_n m_n \in M * \Xi^*$

(b) $x[\Theta] = \bigcup_{u\in X} u[\Theta]$ for $X \in \mathcal{P}(M * \Xi^*)$

Of course we identify in this definition the element m and the set $\{m\}$.

Let $\eta : M \to N$. We also denote by η the induced morphisms $M * \Xi^* \to N * \Xi^*$ and $\mathcal{P}(M) \to \mathcal{P}(N)$. A formal verification suffices to prove the following lemma :

Lemma 2.3 Let $\eta : M \to N$ and $\Theta : \Xi^* \to \mathcal{P}(M)$ be two monoid morphisms. The following diagram is commutative :

$$\begin{array}{ccc} \mathcal{P}(M * \Xi^*) & \xrightarrow{[\Theta]} & \mathcal{P}(M) \\ \eta \downarrow & & \downarrow \eta \\ \mathcal{P}(N * \Xi^*) & \xrightarrow{[\Theta\eta]} & \mathcal{P}(N) \end{array}$$

For any positive integer n let $\Xi_n = \{\zeta_{11}, \zeta_{12}, \ldots, \zeta_{nn}\}$ be an alphabet with n^2 letters. Any matrix $m \in \mathcal{P}(M)^{n\times n}$ defines a morphism $m : {}_n^* \to \mathcal{P}(M)^{n\times n}$ by $\zeta_{ij} m = m_{ij}$. We can now generalize definition 2.1.

Definition 2.2 A transduction $\tau : A^* \to M$ admits a *matrix representation* (s, μ) if there exist $n > o$, a morphism $\mu : A^* \to \mathcal{P}(M)^{n\times n}$ and an element $s \in \mathcal{P}(M * \Xi_n^*)$ such that for all $f \in A^*$, $f\tau = s[f\mu]$.

Then theorem 2.1 can be generalized as follows

Theorem 2.4 Let $\tau : A^* \to M$ be a transduction that admits a matrix representation (s,μ) and let P be a subset of M recognized by a morphism $\eta : M \to N$. Then the language $P\tau^{-1}$ is recognized by the monoid of matrices $A^*\mu\eta$.

The proof mimics the proof of theorem 2.1 Let $Q = P\eta$ and let R be the subset of $A^*\mu\eta$ defined by

$$R = \{m \in \mathcal{P}(N)^{n\times n} \mid s\eta\,[m] \cap Q \neq \emptyset\}$$

Thus $R(\mu\eta)^{-1} = \{f \in A^* \mid s\eta\,[f\mu\eta] \cap Q \neq \emptyset\}$, hence by lemma 2.3 :

$$\begin{aligned} R(\mu\eta)^{-1} &= \{f \in A^* \mid (s[f\mu])\eta \cap Q \neq \emptyset\} = \{f \in A^* \mid s[f\mu] \cap Q\eta^{-1} \neq \emptyset\} \\ &= \{f \in A^* \mid f\tau \cap P \neq \emptyset\} = P\tau^{-1}. \end{aligned}$$

□

3.- Operations on languages

Let $L_1, \ldots, L_n$ be languages of $A_1^*, \ldots, A_n^*$ respectively and let $\eta_i : A_i^* \to M_i$ be a morphism recognizing L_i, for $1 \leq i \leq n$. Then clearly

$$\eta = \prod_{1\leq i\leq n} \eta_i : \prod_{1\leq i\leq n} A_i^* \to \prod_{1\leq i\leq n} M_i$$ recognizes the subset $L_1 \times \ldots \times L_n$ of $A_1^* \times \ldots \times A_n^*$.

Then theorem 2.1 (or theorem 2.4) gives the construction of a monoid recognizing $(L_1, \ldots, L_n)\varphi$ provided that φ satisfies the following conditions :

(1) φ is the inverse of a transduction $\tau : A^* \to A_1^* \times \ldots \times A_n^*$

(2) τ admits a linear matrix representation (resp. a matrix representation)

As we claimed in the introduction these two conditions hold for a lot of a classical operations.

3.1 Inverse morphisms and inverse substitutions

In this example conditions (1) and (2) are trivially satisfied. For example let $\sigma : A^* \to B^*$ be a substitution. Then by definition σ induces a morphism $A^* \to \mathcal{P}(B^*)$ and $u\sigma = 1.u\sigma.1$ for all $u \in A^*$. Thus $(1, \sigma, 1)$ is a linear matrix representation of σ. With the notations of theorem 2.1, $A^*\sigma\eta$ is a submonoid of $\mathcal{P}(M)$. Therefore we have obtained the following result proved in [13] for rational languages.

Proposition 3.1 Let $\sigma : A^* \to B^*$ be a substitution. If $L \subset B^*$ is recognized by M, then $L\sigma^{-1}$ is recognized by $\mathcal{P}(M)$. In particular if L is rational, $L\sigma^{-1}$ is rational.

In the same way, we get easily

Proposition 3.2 Let $\varphi : A^* \to B^*$ be a morphism. Each monoid that recognizes $L \subset B^*$ also recognizes $L\varphi^{-1}$.

3.2 Intersection and union

We note that $L_1 \cap L_2 = (L_1 \times L_2)\tau^{-1}$ where $\tau : A^* \to A^* \times A^*$ is defined by $u\tau = (u \times u) = (1 \times 1)\ (u \times u)\ (1 \times 1)$. Thus $(1 \times 1, \tau, 1 \times 1)$ is a linear matrix representation of τ. With the notations of theorem 2.1, $A^*\mu\eta$ is a submonoid of $M_1 \times M_2$. Thus

Proposition 3.3 (see [6]). Let L_1, L_2 be languages of A^* recognized by M_1, M_2 respectively. Then $L_1 \cap L_2$ is recognized by $M_1 \times M_2$.

The case of the union is a little more involved. Indeed $L_1 \cup L_2 = (L_1 \times L_2)\tau^{-1}$ where $u\tau = (u \times A^*) \cup (A^* \times u)$ for all $u \in A^*$. Thus $((1,1), \mu, (1,1)^t)$ where

$$u\mu = \begin{pmatrix} u \times A^* & 0 \\ 0 & A^* \times u \end{pmatrix}$$

is a linear matrix representation of τ. Now an instant of reflection shows that $A^*\mu\eta$ is isomorphic to a submonoid of $M_1 \times M_2$. Therefore

Proposition 3.4 (see [6]) Let L_1, L_2 be languages of A^* recognized by M_1, M_2 respectively. Then $L_1 \cup L_2$ is recognized by $M_1 \times M_2$.

3.3. Left and right quotients (or derivatives)

Let P and L be languages of A^*. Then the left quotient of L by P is the set $P^{-1}L = \{f \in A^* \mid Pf \cap L \neq \emptyset\}$. LP^{-1} is defined dually. Now if P is fixed, $P^{-1}L = L\tau^{-1}$ where $u\tau = Pu$ for all $u \in A^*$. Clearly $(P, \zeta, 1)$ - where ζ denotes the identity of A^* - is a linear matrix representation of τ. Thus

Proposition 3.5 (see [3]) Let L be a language of A^* recognized by a monoid M. Then M recognizes $P^{-1}L$ and LP^{-1} for all languages P of A^*.

Corollary 3.6 [7] If L is rational, $P^{-1}L$ and LP^{-1} are rational for all languages P.

3.4 Concatenation product

It is easy to see that $L_1 \ldots L_n = (L_1 \times \ldots \times L_n)\tau^{-1}$ where $\tau : A^* \to A^* \times \ldots \times A^*$ is the transduction defined by

$$f\tau = \{(f_1, \ldots, f_n) \in A^* \times \ldots \times A^* \mid f_1 \ldots f_n = f\}$$

Moreover τ admits the linear matrix representation (λ, μ, ν) where $\lambda = ((1,\ldots,1), 0, \ldots, 0)$ $\nu = (0, \ldots 0, (1,\ldots,1))^t$ and $\mu : A^* \longrightarrow \mathcal{P}(A^* \times \ldots \times A^*)^{n\times n}$ is defined, for all $u \in A^*$, by

$$(u\mu)_{ij} = 0 \text{ if } i > j$$

$$(u\mu)_{ij} = \{u_1, \ldots, u_n) \in A^* \times \ldots \times A^* \mid u_1 = \ldots = u_{i-1} = u_{j+1} = \ldots = u_n = 1 \text{ and } u_i u_{i+1} \ldots u_j = u\} \text{ if } i \leq j$$

In particular τ is a rational transduction. By theorem 2.1, $L_1 \ldots L_n$ is recognized by the monoid $A^*\mu\eta$. Now $A^*\mu\eta$ is a submonoid of the monoid of all square matrices of size n with entries in the finite subsets of $M_1 \times \ldots \times M_n$ such that :

(a) P is upper triangular, that is $P_{ij} = 0$ for $i > j$

(b) The ith entry of the diagonal is an element of M_i. More precisely $P_{ii} = \{(1, \ldots, 1, m_i, 1, \ldots, 1)\}$ for some $m_i \in M_i$

(c) If $(m_1, \ldots, m_n) \in P_{ij}$, then $m_k = 1$ for $k < i$ and $k > j$.

This last monoid is called by Straubing [19] the Schützenberger product of $M_1, \ldots, M_n$ and is denoted by $\Diamond_n(M_1, \ldots, M_n)$. For $n = 2$ it can be identified with the original definition of Schützenberger (see [6]). Note that in general

$$\Diamond_2(M_1, \Diamond_2(M_2, M_3)) \neq \Diamond_3(M_1, M_2, M_3) \neq \Diamond_2(\Diamond_2(M_1, M_2), M_3).$$

Therefore, we have

Proposition 3.7 Let $L_1, \ldots, L_n$ be languages recognized by $M_1, \ldots, M_n$ respectively. Then $L_1 \ldots L_n$ is recognized by $\Diamond_n(M_1, \ldots, M_n)$

A slight modification of the previous construction leads to the following result (see [12] for applications)

Proposition 3.8 If $a_1, \ldots, a_{n-1}$ are letters of A, then $L_1 a_1 L_2 \ldots a_{n-1} L_n$ is recognized by $\Diamond_n(M_1, \ldots, M_n)$

3.5 Shuffle, infiltration product

Given a word $h = a_1 \ldots a_n \in A^*$ (the a_i's are letters) and a subset $I = \{i_1, \ldots, i_r\}$ of $\{1, \ldots, n\}$ (where $i_1 < \ldots < i_r$) we denote by h_I the word $a_{i_1} \ldots a_{i_r}$. With this notation the ***shuffle*** of two words f and g is defined by

$f \circ g = \{h \in A^* \mid \quad I, J \quad I \cup J = \{1, \ldots, |h|\},\ I \cap J = \emptyset,\ h_I = f \text{ and } h_J = g\}$

and the *infiltration product* [4] is defined by

$f \uparrow g = \{h \in A^* \mid \ I, J \quad I \cup J = \{1, \ldots, |h|\},\ h_I = f \text{ and } h_J = g\}$

Shuffle and infiltration product are extended as usual to languages by setting

$$L_1 \circ L_2 = \bigcup_{f_1 \in L_1, f_2 \in L_2} f_1 \circ f_2 \qquad L_1 \uparrow L_2 = \bigcup_{f_1 \in L_1, f_2 \in L_2} f_1 \uparrow f_2$$

Now $L_1 \circ L_2 = (L_1 \times L_2)\tau^{-1}$ where $\tau : A^* \to A^* \times A^*$ is defined by $f\tau = \{(f_1, f_2) \in A^* \times A^* \mid f \in f_1 \circ f_2\}$. Since τ induces a morphism $A^* \to P(A^* \times A^*)$, τ admits the linear matrix representation $(1, \tau, 1)$. Thus one gets easily

Proposition 3.9 [11] Let L_1 and L_2 be languages of A^* recognized by M_1 and M_2 respectively. Then $L_1 \circ L_2$ is recognized by $\mathrm{Fin}(M_1 \times M_2)$, the monoid of finite subsets of $M_1 \times M_2$.

In the same way $L_1 \uparrow L_2 = (L_1 \times L_2)\tau^{-1}$ where $f\tau = \{(f_1, f_2) \in A^* \times A^* \mid f \in f_1 \uparrow f_2\}$ and by the same argument as above we obtain

Proposition 3.10 Let L_1 and L_2 be languages of A^* recognized by M_1 and M_2 respectively. Then $L_1 \uparrow L_2$ is recognized by $\mathrm{Fin}(M_1 \times M_2)$.

3.6 Morphisms

Let $\varphi : A^* \to B^*$ be a morphism. Then $\varphi^{-1} = \tau : B^* \to A^*$ is a rational transduction. It follows that φ satisfies the conditions (1) and (2) and theorem 2.1 can be applied. However the explicit construction of a linear matrix representation requires some machinery. We first define the *petal monoid* of X^* when X is a finite language of B^* [9]. Let $Q = \{(1,1)\} \cup \{(u;v) \in B^+ \times B^+ \mid uv \in X\}$. One associates to each letter $a \in B$ a relation as follows (for the sake of simplicity we use arrows instead of formal definitions) :

$(1,1) \overset{a}{\circlearrowleft}$ if $a \in X$

$(1,1) \xrightarrow{a} (a,v)$ for all $v \in B^+$ such that $av \in X$

$(ua,v) \xrightarrow{a} (u,av)$ for all $u, v \in B^+$ such that $uav \in X$

$(u,a) \xrightarrow{a} (1,1)$ for all $u \in B^+$ such that $ua \in X$

The relations defined by a, $a \in B$, generate a monoid of relations that recognizes X^*. This is precisely the petal monoid of X^*, denoted by Pet X^*. In the sequel we shall represent in the usual way relations on Q by boolean matrices of size $Q \times Q$.

Next we introduce the following

Definition 3.1 Let N be a monoid of relations on a set Q and let S be a semiring. The *substitution product* of S by N (denoted $S \circ N$) is the set of all matrices of size $Q \times Q$ obtained by substituting elements of S for the non-zero entries of matrices of N.

Let us come back to our morphism $\varphi : A^* \to B^*$. Set $X = A\varphi \cap B^+$, $I^* = 1\varphi^{-1}$ and, for all $x \in X$, $C(x) = \{a \in A \mid a\varphi = x\}$. Then one can prove - we omit the details - that φ^{-1} admits the linear matrix representation (λ, μ, ν) where $\mu : B^* \to (\text{Rat } A^*)^{Q\times Q}$ is defined, for all $a \in B$, by

$(a\mu)_{p,q} = 1$ if $q \neq (1,1)$ and 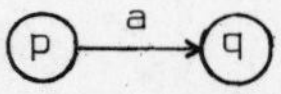

$= I^*C(ua)$ if $p = (u,a)$ $q = (1,1)$ and 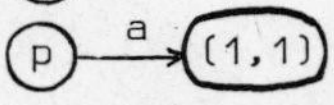

$= I^*C(a)$ if $p = q = (1,1)$ and 

$= 0$ in all other cases

$\lambda_p = 1$ if $p = (1,1)$ $\qquad$ $\nu_p = I^*$ if $p = (1,1)$

$= 0$ if not $\qquad$ $= 0$ if not

Now if L is recognized by $\eta : A^* \to M$, theorem 2.1 states that $L\varphi$ is recognized by $B^*\mu\eta$. But a straightforward verification shows that $A^*\mu\eta$ is a submonoid of Rat $M \circ$ Pet X^*. Thus

Proposition 3.11 Let $\varphi : A^* \to B^*$ be a morphism and let $X = A\varphi \cap B^+$. If $L \subset A^*$ is recognized by a monoid M, then $L\varphi$ is recognized by the substitution product Rat $M \circ$ Pet X^*.

In the case where X is a code the substitution product turns out to be a wreath product (in the sense of [15]).Therefore

Proposition 3.12 Let $\varphi : A^* \to B^*$ be a morphism such that $X = A\varphi \cap B^+$ is a code. If $L \subset A^*$ is recognized by a monoid M, then $L\varphi$ is recognized by the wreath product Rat $M \circ$ Pet X^*.

If φ is injective one can be more precise

Proposition 3.13 Let $\varphi : A^* \to B^*$ be an injective morphism and let $X = A\varphi$. If a language $L \subset A^*$ is recognized by a monoid M, then $L\varphi$ is recognized by the wreath product $M \circ$ Pet X^*.

Finally if φ is litteral (= length preserving, strictly alphabetic) we could prove the following result, obtained in [18] and [13] for rational languages.

Proposition 3.14 Let $\varphi : A^* \to B^*$ be a litteral morphism. If $L \subset A^*$ is recognized by a monoid M, then $L\varphi$ is recognized by Fin M.

3.7 Miscellaneous

We just mention here a list of operations for which theorem 2.1 applies :

- The longer common prefix of two words : see [5]
- The nabla operation, a cousin of the shuffle : see [1]
- Straubing's counting : see [20]
- Inverse of rational functions : see [17]

etc.

4.- Other applications

4.1 A result on TOL-systems

We call TOL a set $G = (A, \{\sigma_1,\dots,\sigma_n\})$ where A is an alphabet and $\sigma_1,\dots,\sigma_n$ are substitutions of A^* into A^*. Let $B = \{1,\dots,n\}$. To each word $u = i_1\dots i_r$ of B^* one associates the substitution $\sigma_u = \sigma_{i_1}\dots\sigma_{i_r}$ (the substitution associated to the empty word is the identity). The following proposition is a slight extension of a result of [14].

Proposition 4.1 Let G be a TOL-system and let K, L be two rational languages of A^*. Then $G(K,L) = \{u \in B^* \mid K\sigma_u \cap L \neq \emptyset\}$ is rational.

Indeed $G(K,L) = K\tau^{-1}$ where $\tau : B^* \to A^*$ is the transduction defined by $u\tau = L\sigma_u^{-1}$ for all $u \in B^*$. The remainder of the proof consists of verifying that τ admits a linear matrix representation. Then one applies corollary 2.2.

4.2 Reduction of the free group

Let A be an alphabet, $\bar{A}$ a copy of A and set $\tilde{A} = A \cup \bar{A}$. As is well-known the free group $F(A)$ over A is the quotient of $\tilde{A}^*$ by the congruence generated by the relations $a\bar{a} = 1$ and $\bar{a}a = 1$. We denote by D^* the set of all words congruent to 1. A word is *reduced* if it contains no occurrence of factors of the form $a\bar{a}$ or $\bar{a}a$. One can prove that every word u of A^* is congruent to a unique reduced word $u\delta$. This defines a function $\delta : \tilde{A}^* \to \tilde{A}^*$ called the *Dyck reduction*. The classical result of Benois (see [2]) can be restated as follows :

Proposition 4.2 Let R be a rational subset of $\tilde{A}^*$. Then $R\delta$ is rational.

Indeed let $\tau : \tilde{A}^* \to \tilde{A}^*$ be the transduction defined by $(a_1\dots a_n)\tau = D^*a_1D^*\dots a_nD^*$ (where $a_1,\dots,a_n$ are letters). Then one can prove - this is the difficult part of the proof - that $\tau^{-1} = \delta$. Now it is not difficult to find a linear matrix representation for τ and the result follows from corollary 2.2 □

Of course a similar result holds for the congruence generated by $a\bar{a} = 1$ $(a \in A)$ or other variants - see [16] -

4.3. Applications of the theorem 2.4

We first return to the example of the introduction. Let L be a language and let n be a positive integer. Set (cf. [8] for instance)

$$\frac{1}{2n+1} L = \{u \in A^* \mid \exists\ x,\ y \in A^* \quad |x| = |y| = n\,|u| \text{ and } xuy \in L\} \text{ and}$$

$$\zeta(L) = \bigcup_{(2n+1)\text{ prime}} \frac{1}{2n+1} L.$$ We shall prove the following result

Proposition 4.3 If L is recognized by a monoid M, then $\frac{1}{2n+1} L$ (for every $n > o$) and $\zeta(L)$ are recognized by $M \times C$ where C is a one-generator submonoid of $\mathcal{P}(M)$.

Corollary 4.4 If L is rational, $\frac{1}{2n+1} L$ (for every $n > o$) and $\zeta(L)$ are rational.

Proof Define for all $n > o$, $\tau_n : A^* \to A^*$ by $u\tau_n = A^{n|u|}\,uA^{n|u|}$ and let $\tau : A^* \to A^*$ be defined by $u\tau = \bigcup_{(2n+1)\text{ prime}} u\tau_n$. Then $L\tau_n^{-1} = \frac{1}{2n+1} L$ and $L\tau^{-1} = \zeta(L)$. Moreover τ_n admits the (non-linear) matrix representation (s_n, μ) where $u\mu = \begin{pmatrix} A^{|u|} & o \\ oo & u \end{pmatrix}$ for all $u \in A^*$ and $s_n = \zeta_{11}^{n}\zeta_{22}\zeta_{11}^{n}$. In the same way τ admits the matrix representation (s,μ) where $s = \sum_{(2n+1)\text{ prime}} s_n$. Now if L is recognized by $\eta : A^* \to M$, theorem 2.4 shows that $\frac{1}{2n+1} L$ and $\zeta(L)$ are recognized by $A^*\mu\eta$. But $A^*\mu\eta$ is isomorphic to a submonoid of $M \times C$ where C is the submonoid of $\mathcal{P}(M)$ generated by $A\eta$. □

Here is another example. Define $\sqrt{L} = \{u \in A^* \mid u^2 \in L\}$. Then $\sqrt{L} = L\tau^{-1}$ where $u\tau = u^2$ for all $u \in A^*$. Clearly τ admits the matrix representation (s,μ) where $u\mu = u$ and $s = \zeta^2$. Therefore

Proposition 4.5 If a language L is recognized by a monoid M, then M also recognizes $\sqrt{L}$. In particular if L is rational (resp. star-free), so is $\sqrt{L}$

Finally the reader who likes more complicated examples may try to prove that if $L \subset \{a,b\}^*$ is rational and if $\tau : A^* \to A^*$ is any rational transduction then

$$L' = \bigcup_{n \text{ square-free}} \{u \in A^* \mid D^* u^{\lfloor\sqrt{n}\rfloor} a^n (u\tau)^{n!}\, b \cap L \neq \emptyset\}$$ is rational.

<u>References</u>

[1] J. Beauquier On the structure of context-free languages. To appear in <u>International Journal of Computer Mathematics</u>.

[2] M. Benois Parties rationnelles du groupe libre. <u>C.R. Acad. Sci. Paris</u> sér. A 269, 1969, 1188-1190.

[3] J. Berstel Transductions and Context-Free Languages. Teubner 1979

[4] K.T. Chen, R.H. Fox and R.C. Lyndon. Free differential calculus, IV <u>Ann. of Math.</u> 68, 1958, 81-95.

[5] Ch. Choffrut A closure property of deterministic context-free languages. <u>Information Processing Letters</u> 12, 1981, 13-16.

[6] S. Eilenberg Automata, Languages and Machines. Academic Press Vol. B 1976

[7] S. Ginsburg and E.H. Spanier Quotients of context-free languages, <u>J. Assoc. Computing Machinery</u> 10, 1963, 487-492.

[8] J.E. Hopcroft, J.D. Ullman. Introduction to automata theory, languages and computation, Addison Wesley, 1979.

[9] E. Le Rest and M. Le Rest Sur le calcul du monoīde syntaxique d'un sous-monoīde finiment engendré. <u>Semigroup Forum</u> Vol 21,1980 73-185.

[10] M. Lothaire Combinatorics on words, Addison Wesley, to appear.

[11] J.-F. Perrot Variétés de langages et opérations. <u>Theoretical Computer Science</u> 7, 1978, 197-210.

[12] J.-E. Pin Hiérarchies de concaténation. Submitted.

[13] Ch. Reutenauer Sur les variétés de langages et de monoīdes, 4thGI Conference - <u>Lecture Notes in Computer Science</u> 67, Springer, 1979, 260-265.

[14] Ch. Reutenauer Sur les séries associées à certains systèmes de Lindenmayer. Theoretical Computer Science 9, 1979, 363-375

[15] J. Sakarovitch Sur la définition du produit en couronne, in <u>Colloque Codages et transductions</u> (Pirillo ed.), Florence, 1981, 285-300.

[16] J. Sakarovitch Syntaxe des langages de Chomsky, Thèse Sci. Paris, 1979

[17] M.P. Schützenberger Sur les relations rationnelles entre monoīdes libres, <u>Theoretical Computer Science</u> 3, 1976, 243-259.

[18] H. Straubing Recognizable sets and power sets of finite semigroups Semigroup Forum 18, 1979, 331-340.

[19] H. Straubing A generalization of the Schützenberger product of finite monoids. Theoretical Computer Science 13, 1981, 137-150.

[20] H. Straubing Families of recognizable sets corresponding to certain varieties of finite monoids. J. Pure and Applied Algebra, 15, 1979, 305-318.

On Algebras of Computation Sequences and Proofs of Equivalence of Operational and Denotational Semantics

Axel Poigné
Informatik II
Universität Dortmund
Postfach 50 05 00
D-4600 Dortmund 50

0. Introduction

The equivalence of operational and denotational semantics for non-deterministic schemes has been shown by Arnold and Nivat using greatest fixpoints and metrical spaces [4],[5]. In [21] we state the same result for the case of formal computations but we use least fixpoints and continuous algebras.

When we tried to extend the result to effective computations (in the sense of [4]) we found this to be impossible for arbitrary continuous algebras [22]. The reason is that our proofs use a special power domain construction which cannot be extended to arbitrary continuous algebras. In general power domain constructions identify too many subsets of a given continuous algebra which implies that an equivalence result seems to be possible only up to factorization properties of power domains in the general case. This 'negative' result is the impulse to analyze the proof techniques.

The general proceeding in scheme semantics seems to be the following:
Operational semantics is defined via some computational strategy. To any 'successful' computation sequence a meaning is given as an element of a 'domain of interpretation'. Denotational semantics is defined as a fixpoint of a function over the domain of interpretation, the function being derived from the given scheme. Equivalence of operational and denotational semantics then is established by proving first that denotational semantics corresponds to a computation strategy and second that successful computations under this strategy have the same meanings as computations under the original strategy. The proof thus depends on a cooperation of syntactic simulation of computational strategies and information hiding by the interpretation.
The aim of our paper is to seperate the syntactical and the algebraic parts of the proof. We introduce algebras of computation sequences which consist of classes of computations being mutually simulatable. The algebra of computation sequences seems to be the 'most syntactical' domain of interpretation in which operational and denotational semantics coincide. Moreover it is 'universal' in the sense that (at least for ordered algebras) proofs of equivalence of semantics are more or less straightforward consequence (obtained by purely algebraic properties) of the respective proof in an algebra of computation sequences. This shall be demonstrated for non-deterministic schemes. The intention of our paper is to gain some insight in the proof mechanism and its limitations and not so much to obtain new equivalence results.

To avoid a heavy algebraic framework we shall only consider systems of non-deterministic equations [20] which are rather simple schemes. But as in [21] the results lift to the level of program schemes if we consider algebraic theories instead of algebras. The paper consists of four parts: In the first algebras of computation sequences are introduced, the second and third gives operational and denotational semantics of non-deterministic schemes, in the fourth equivalence of the semantics is shown.

We employ the language of categories to structure our proofs. In fact - except for a few arguments on structures - we only use the notions of products, coproducts and adjoints [15], [16] to avoid lengthy definitions of uniquely induced homomorphisms.

Our work is in close relation to [4], [5], [7], [12], [19]. Due to restriction of space we restrict our attention to basic arguments and omit proofs. Also we are not able to discuss relationship to existing literature thoroughly. In [23] we shall give a full version of our paper which considers the case of deterministic schemes as well.

1. Algebras of Computation Sequences

We assume that the reader is familiar with the notions of Ω-algebras, (ω-) complete posets, (ω-) continuous functions [1], [2]. As notation we use Ω for operator domains, $a: \Omega \to \mathbb{N}_o$ for arity functions, $T_\Omega(X)$ for the canonical free term algebra over a set X. For $n \in \mathbb{N}_o$ let $\underline{n}:=\{0,\ldots,n-1\}$.

Rewritings over an algebra $A=(A,(\omega_A|\omega \in \Omega))$ will be used to model computations: A relation $\to \subseteq A\times A$ is called *rewrite relation* if it is *compatible* [13], i.e. $a_i \to a_i'$ implies $\omega_A(a_o,\ldots,a_i,\ldots,a_{a(\omega)-1}) \to \omega_A(a_o,\ldots,a_i',\ldots,a_{a(\omega)-1})$ for $a_o,\ldots,a_{a(\omega)-1}, a_i' \in A$. A *computation sequence* then is a sequence $c=(c_n|n \in \mathbb{N}_o)$ with $c_n \in A$ and with $c_n \to c_{n+1}$ or $c_n = c_{n+1}$ for all $n \in \mathbb{N}_o$.

Computation sequences naturally carry as well an algebra as an preorder structure: Let Comp' be the set of computation sequences. Then a Ω-algebra structure is given by

$$\omega_C: \text{Comp}'^{a(\omega)} \to \text{Comp}' , (c_o,\ldots,c_{a(\omega)-1}) \to (\omega c_{o,n}\ldots c_{a(\omega)-1,n}|n \in \mathbb{N}_o)$$

for $\omega \in \Omega$. A preorder is defined by

$$c \sqsubseteq c' \quad \text{iff} \quad \forall m \in \mathbb{N}_o \exists n \in \mathbb{N}_o : c_m \overset{*}{\to} c_n$$

($\overset{*}{\to}$ transitive and reflexive closure).

If we factorize by antisymmetry we obtain a Ω-algebra Comp($\to$) which we shall call *algebra of computation sequences* (w.r.t $\to$). Intuitively a congruence class [c] consists of all computation sequences where elementary computation steps are permuted.

In this paper we are interested in computations of non-deterministic recursive schemes: Let $\Omega_+ := \Omega + \{\underline{or}\}$ where Ω is an operator domain and $\underline{or}$ is an additional binary non-deterministic operator. A *system of non-deterministic equations* or *non-deterministic scheme* is a function

$$S: X \to T_{\Omega+}(X) .$$

Let $A = (A, (\omega_A | \omega \in \Omega))$ be a Ω-algebra. An *effective computation* of a scheme S in A then either replaces a variable by the right hand side of the respective equation or evaluates in the algebra - if possible - or makes a non-deterministic choice. Formally for $t, t' \in T_{\Omega+}(X+A)$

$t \rightarrow_{S,A} t'$ iff (i) $t = x$ and $t' = S(x)$

or (ii) $t = \omega a_o \ldots a_{a(\omega)-1}$ with $a_i \in A$ for $i \in \underline{a(\omega)}$ and $t' = \omega_A(a_o, \ldots, a_{a(\omega)-1})$

or (iii) $t = t_o \; \underline{or} \; t_1$ and ($t' = t_o$ or $t' = t_1$) .

We use $\rightarrow^c_{S,A}$ to denote the least compatible relation containing $\rightarrow_{S,A}$.

1.1 *Example*: Let {a,b} be a set. Then $(\{a,b\}^*, conc, \lambda, a, b)$ with concatenation, empty word and nullary operators a,b is a algebra of type $(\cdot, e, O, 1)$. The non-deterministic scheme (using infix notation)

$$S(x) := (O \cdot 1) \cdot x \; \underline{or} \; e$$

allows computations

$x \rightarrow (O\cdot 1)\cdot x \; \underline{or} \; e \rightarrow (O\cdot 1)\cdot x \rightarrow (a\cdot 1)\cdot x \rightarrow (a\cdot b)\cdot x \rightarrow ab\cdot x \rightarrow ab\cdot((O\cdot 1)\cdot x \; \underline{or} \; e\,) \rightarrow ab\cdot e \rightarrow ab\cdot\lambda \rightarrow ab$

$x \rightarrow (O\cdot 1)\cdot x \; \underline{or} \; e \rightarrow (O\cdot 1)\cdot x \rightarrow (O\cdot 1)\cdot((O\cdot 1)\cdot x \; \underline{or} \; e \rightarrow (O\cdot 1)\cdot e$

and infinite computations

$x \rightarrow^* ab\cdot x \rightarrow^* ab\cdot(ab\cdot x) \rightarrow^* ab\cdot(ab\cdot(ab\cdot x)) \rightarrow^* \ldots$

$x \rightarrow^* ab\cdot x \; \underline{or} \; e \; \rightarrow^* ab\cdot(ab\cdot x \; \underline{or} \; e) \; \underline{or} \; e \rightarrow^* \ldots$

□

Our approach basically depends on the fact that algebras of computation sequences may be understood as free structures:

A Ω-algebra is called (ω-) *complete* if the carrier is a complete poset and if the structure maps are continuous. With continuous homomorphisms this defines a category $\underline{\Omega\text{-alg -}\omega\text{-pos}}$. Let $\underline{\Omega\text{-R-alg}}$ be the category with objects being Ω-algebras A plus binary relations $R \subseteq A\times A$. Morphisms are homomorphisms $f: A \rightarrow A'$ preserving the relations, i.e. $\{(f(a), f(a')) \mid (a,a') \in R\} \subseteq R'$.

1.2 *Proposition*: (i) The forgetful functor $\underline{\Omega\text{-alg-}\omega\text{-pos}} \rightarrow \underline{\Omega\text{-R-alg}}$ has a left adjoint.

(ii) COMP:= Comp($\rightarrow^c_{S,A}$) is a free complete Ω+-algebra over the term algebra $T_{\Omega+}(X+A)$ with relation $\rightarrow_{S,A}$.

(The canonical embedding $\eta: T_{\Omega+}(X+A) \rightarrow$ COMP maps terms to equivalence classes of constant computations. For convenience we shall identify terms and the equivalence classes of constant computations)

□

Our arguments are similar to those to be found in [13] except that we point out the freeness of the structure.

2. Operational Semantics of Non-deterministic Schemes

Similar to [4], [5] we shall consider only those computation sequences to yield a result in which no possible computation - in our case substitution, non-deterministic choice or evaluation in the algebra - is infinitely often delayed. Such computation sequences we call full.

We formalize the intuitive idea in two steps:

Coproducts $T_\Omega(X)+A$ (of Ω-algebras) model evaluation of terms $t \in T_\Omega(X+A)$ as far as possible. Explicitly a coproduct $T_\Omega(X)+A$ is given by: Let Y be the smallest subset of $T_\Omega(X+A)$ such that (i) $X,A \subseteq Y$ and (ii) $\omega t_o \ldots t_{a(\omega)-1} \in Y$ if $\omega \in \Omega$, $t_o,\ldots,t_{a(\omega)-1} \in Y$ and not $\forall i \in \underline{a(\omega)}: t_i \in A$. Operations are defined by

$$\omega_Y: Y^{a(\omega)} \to Y\ ,\quad (t_o,\ldots,t_{a(\omega)-1}) \to \begin{cases} \omega_A(t_o,\ldots,t_{a(\omega)-1}) & \text{if } t_i \in A \text{ for all } i \in \underline{a(\omega)} \\ \omega t_o \ldots t_{a(\omega)-1} & \text{else} \end{cases} .$$

There is a unique homomorphic extension NF: $T_\Omega(X+A) \to T_\Omega(X)+A$ of the embedding of X and A to $T_\Omega(X)+A$ which maps each term to its *normal form* NF(t) which means that t is evaluated in the algebra A as far as possible.

For the non-deterministic operator <u>or</u> we have to choice alternatives. We observe that operators are bilinear (linear in each component) with respect to the <u>or</u>

$$\omega t_o \ldots (t_i \ \underline{\text{or}}\ t_i') \ldots t_{a(\omega)-1} = \omega t_o \ldots t_i \ldots t_{a(\omega)-1} \ \underline{\text{or}}\ \omega t_o \ldots t_i' \ldots t_{a(\omega)-1} .$$

Due to this observation we proposed in [21] the following

2.1 <u>*Definition*</u>: A (*non-deterministic*) *OI-Ω-algebra* consists of a semilattice (A,+) (+ is associative, commutative, idempotent) and a Ω-indexed family of mappings $\omega_A: A^{a(\omega)} \to A$ which are linear in each component (semilattice homomorphisms). With Ω-homorphisms being as well linear this defines a category <u>OI-Ω-alg</u>. □

As a straightforward calculation we obtain

2.2 <u>*Propositon*</u>: (compare [14]) A left adjoint P_f: <u>Ω-alg</u> $\to$ <u>OI-Ω-alg</u> to the obvious forgetful functor is given by

$$P_f(A) := \{S \subseteq A \mid S \text{ finite, non empty}\}$$
$$S + S' := S \cup S'$$
$$\omega_{P_f(A)}(S_o,\ldots,S_{a(\omega)-1}) := \{\omega_A(a_o,\ldots,a_{a(\omega)-1}) \mid a_i \in S_i\} .$$ □

$P_f(T_\Omega(X)+A)$ may be understood as a Ω+-algebra. The embedding of X and A to $P_f(T_\Omega(X)+A)$ uniquely induces a homomorphism NNF: $T_{\Omega+}(X+A) \to P_f(T_\Omega(X)+A)$ which maps a term t to the set NNF(t) of normal forms of all terms obtained as alternatives from t by evaluating the non-deterministic operator. It is convenient to understand NNF(t) as a subset of $T_\Omega(X+A)$.

Example: (1.2 continued) $NNF((0 \text{ or } 1)\cdot(x \text{ or } y)) = \{a.x, a\cdot y, b.x, b\cdot y\}$

$NNF((0 \text{ or } x)\cdot(1 \text{ or } y)) = \{ab, a\cdot y, x.b, x\cdot y\}$.

□

2.3 *Definition*: (i) Let $S^{\#}: T_{\Omega+}(X+A) \to T_{\Omega+}(X+A)$ be the unique homomorphism which maps $x \in X$ to $S(x)$ and which is the identity on A. A computation sequence $c \in COMP$ is called *full* if for all $t \in T_{\Omega+}(X+A)$ $t \leq c$ implies that $t' \leq c$ for some $t' \in NNF(S^{\#}(t))$.

(ii) For $t \in T_{\Omega+}(X+A)$ let $RES(t) := \{c \in COMP \mid c \text{ full and } t \leq c\}$.

□

In example 1.2 the first and third computation sequence is full while the second and third is not full.

2.4 *Remark*: Full computations are not necessarily maximal elements in COMP. If we take the scheme

$$x \to sy \text{ or } ss'x \ , \quad y \to s's\,y$$

the congruence classes of the sequences

$x \to sy \text{ or } ss'x \to ss'x \to ss'(sy \text{ or } ss'x) \to ss'ss'x \to \ldots$

$x \to sy \text{ or } ss'x \to sy \to ss'sy \to ss'ss'sy \to \ldots$

are full but the first sequence is not maximal.

□

The following observation is important

2.5 *Definition*: A term $t \in T_{\Omega+}(X+A)$ is said to be in *Greibach form* if $t = \omega t_o \ldots t_{a(\omega)-1}$ or $t = t_o \text{ or } t_1$ and t_o and t_1 are in Greibach form. A non-deterministic scheme $S: X \to T_{\Omega+}(X)$ is *Greibach* if $S(x)$ is in Greibach form for all $x \in X$ ([4],[5],[3]).

□

2.6 *Proposition*: If a non-deterministic scheme is Greibach then c full and $c \leq c'$ implies that c' is full for $c, c' \in COMP$.

□

Remark: For schemes being Greibach computation sequences are full iff they are successful in the sense of [19].

We shall now state a simulation result which says that for any non-deterministic computation sequence there is one in 'normal form' where all possible non-deterministic and algebraic computations take place before a substitution is executed.

Let

$$R^n_{S,A} := \{(x,t') \mid t' \in NNF(S(x))\} \subseteq T_\Omega(X)+A \times T_\Omega(X)+A$$

and $COMP_n$ be the free complete Ω-algebra over $(T_\Omega(X)+A,\ R^n_{S,A})$. An explicit representation is given as congruence classes of computation sequences with elementary computations

$$t \to^n_{S,A} t' \quad \text{iff} \quad \text{(i) } t = x \text{ and } t' \in NNF(t) \quad \text{or}$$

$$\text{(ii) } t = \omega t_o \ldots t_i \ldots t_{a(\omega)-1} \text{ and there exists a } t_i' \text{ such that } t_i \to^n_{S,A} t_i' \text{ and } t' = NF(\omega t_o \ldots t_i' \ldots t_{a(\omega)-1}).$$

For computation sequences in $COMP_n$ fullness is defined in analogy to 2.3.

2.7 *Proposition*: Let $RES_n(t) = \{c \mid c \in COMP_n \text{ full and } t' \leq c \text{ for some } t' \in NNF(t)\}$ for $t \in T_\Omega(X+A)$. Then $RES(t) = \{E(c) \mid c \in RES_n(t)\}$ with $E: COMP_n \to COMP$ induced by the embedding $T_\Omega(X)+A \to T_\Omega(X+A) \to COMP$.

□

Now the standard way to interpret recursive schemes is to use *continuous Ω-algebras* (i.e. complete Ω-algebras such that the carrier has a least element $\bot$ and homomorphisms preserve the least element but structure maps not). A continuous Ω-algebra can be extended to a continuous Ω+-algebra A by adding an operation $\bot: A \times A \to A,\ (x,y) \mapsto \bot$. Let $I: COMP \to A_\bot$ be the unique continuous Ω+-homomorphism such that **for** $x \in X$ the respective constant sequences are mapped to $\bot$ and which is the identity on A.

2.8 *Definition*: For a continuous Ω-algebra A let $RES_A(t) := \{I(c) \mid c \in RES(t)\}$. This is called *operational semantics* of a scheme S in A at $t \in T_{\Omega+}(X+A)$. □

For the initial continuous algebra CT_Ω of infinite trees [2] an infinite tree is attached to each full computation (compare [5]).

3. Denotational Semantics of Non-deterministic Schemes

To allow fixpoint semantics we add order structure to OI-Ω-algebras. Ω/E-algebras can be defined relative a category with products [16]. Hence we may introduce

3.1 *Definition*: Let <u>sl-ω-pos</u> and <u>OI-Ω-alg-ω-pos</u> be the categories of semilattices resp. OI-Ω-algebras in the category of complete posets. Explicitly all carriers are complete posets and all structure maps and homomorphisms are continuous. We shall speak of *complete semilattices* and *complete OI-Ω-algebras*. □

It should be noted that the definition is different to that given in [21] where the order structure derived from the semilattices ('$x \leq y$ iff $x+y = y$') and the poset structure are identified.

3.2 *Proposition*: Let P_c: <u>ω-pos</u> $\to$ <u>sl-ω-pos</u> be the left adjoint 'power domain construction' [24]. Then a left adjoint P'_c: <u>Ω-alg-ω-pos</u> $\to$ <u>OI-Ω-alg-ω-pos</u> is given by

$$P'_c(A,(\omega_A \mid \omega \in \Omega)) := (P_c(A),(P_c(\omega_A) \mid \omega \in \Omega)).$$ □

The proof is strictly categorical (compare [14]). It should be remarked that continuous Ω-algebras are mapped to complete OI-Ω-algebras with a least element (what might be called continuous OI-Ω-algebras).

Next we observe that given a scheme $S: X \to T_{\Omega+}(X)$ and a complete Ω-algebra A the function

$$S_A: P_c(A)^X \to P_c(A)^X, \quad f \mapsto f^\# \cdot S$$

is continuous (w.r.t. pointwise ordering) where $f^\#: T_{\Omega+}(X) \to P_f(A)$ is the unique homomorphic extension of f ($P_c(A)$ is a Ω+-algebra). As a variant of Tarski's fixpoint theorem we obtain that $FIX(S_A,f) = \bigsqcup_n S_A^n(f)$ is the least fixpoint greater than $f \in P_c(A)^X$ if $f \leq S_A(f)$ ($\bigsqcup$ -least upper bound).

To define denotational semantics on the level of computation sequences we use the domain $COMP_n$ of non-deterministic computation sequences in 'normal form'. This is necessary to ensure evaluation under the given algebra.

3.3 *Definition:* Let $e: X \to COMP_n \to P_c(COMP_n)$ be the canonical embedding. As $e \leq S_{COMP_n}(e)$ $VAL = FIX(S_{COMP_n}, e)$ is well defined. VAL is called *denotational semantics of* S.
For a continuous algebra A let $\bot: X \to P_c(A)$ map all $x \in X$ to the least element.
Trivially $VAL_A = FIX(S_A, \bot)$ is the least fixpoint of S_A. VAL_A is called *denotational semantics of* S *in* A. □

To connect the denotational semantics we observe that there is a unique continuous homomorphic extension $I_n: COMP_n \to A$ of the mapping $\bot: X \to A$, $x \to \bot$. Due to a standard argument on fixpoints we conclude from the continuity of $P_c(I_n)$

3.4 *Proposition:* $P_c(I_n)(VAL) = VAL_A$. □

4. Equivalences of the Semantics

When operational and denotational semantics are compared the strongest possible result seems to be that $VAL_A(x)$ can be characterized as a subset of the algebra A and that $RES_A(x) = VAL_A(x)$ for all $x \in X$ on the level of sets.

We assume the definitions of finite elements in a poset and of algebraic posets to be known [24] (in our context algebraic posets do not need to have a least element). It is obvious that algebras of computation sequences are algebraic. Now the development of our results depend on a variant of Plotkin's power domain construction (as in [24]).

4.1 *Definition:* Let X be an algebraic poset, $B \subseteq X$ the set of finite elements in X.

(i) A subset $Y \subseteq X$ is called *finitely generated* if there exists a sequence $(Y_n | n \in \mathbb{N}_o)$ of finite, non empty subsets of B with $Y_n \sqsubseteq Y_{n+1}$ for all $n \in \mathbb{N}_o$ such that
$Y = \{ \sqcup c | \; c: \mathbb{N}_o \to X \;\; \omega\text{-chain s.t. } \forall n \in \mathbb{N}_o: c(n) \in Y_n \}$ where
$Y \sqsubseteq Y'$ iff $\forall y \in Y \exists y' \in Y': y \leq y'$ and $\forall y' \in Y' \exists y \in Y: y \leq y'$ (*Egli-Milner*).

(ii) For subsets $Y, Y' \subseteq X$ a preorder is defined by $Y \precsim Y'$ iff for all $A \subseteq B$ being finite, non-empty $A \sqsubseteq Y$ implies $A \sqsubseteq Y'$. Let $\sim$ be the least congruence over $\precsim$. □

4.2 *Proposition:* $P_c(X) = (\{[Y]_\sim | \; Y \text{ finitely generated}\}, \precsim)$ is a free complete semi-lattice over an algebraic poset X. □

After the preliminaries we shall sketch the arguments to be used in the proof of equivalence of semantics.

4.3 *Definition:* (*Parallel substitution*) For $t, t' \in T_\Omega(X)+A$ let $t \Rightarrow_{S,A} t'$ if $t' = h(t)$ with $h: T_\Omega(X)+A \to T_\Omega(X)+A$ is a homomorphism such that $x \in X$ are mapped to some $h(x) \in NNF(S(x))$ and is the identity on A.

4.4 Lemma: (i) For $t, t' \in T_\Omega(X)+A$ $t \Rightarrow_{S,A} t'$ implies $t \xrightarrow{n^*}_{S,A} t'$.

(ii) Let $(c_n | n \in \mathbb{N}_o)$ be a sequence with $c_n \Rightarrow_{S,A} c_{n+1}$ for all $n \in \mathbb{N}_o$. Then $[(c_n | n \in \mathbb{N}_o)]$ is full (By (i) the sequence may be understood as computation sequence).

(iii) For $n \in \mathbb{N}_o$ let $Y_n(t) := \{t' \mid t \Rightarrow^n_{S,A} t'\}$. Then $Y_n : X \to COMP_n$, $x \to Y_n(x)$ generates VAL, i.e. $VAL(x) \sim \{[(c_n | n \in \mathbb{N}_o)] \mid c_o = x, c_n \Rightarrow_{S,A} c_{n+1}\}$. □

The lemma basically states that denotational semantics corresponds to parallel substitution strategy which is not too surprising.

4.5 *Lemma:* Let $c \in COMP_n$ be full. Then there exists a sequence $(c_n | n \in \mathbb{N}_o)$ with $c_n \Rightarrow_{S,A} c_{n+1}$ such that $c = [(c_n | n \in \mathbb{N}_o)]$. □

As a corollary we obtain from 4.4 (ii)+(iii) and 4.5

4.6 *Proposition:* (i) $RES_n(x) = \{[(c_n | n \in \mathbb{N}_o)] \mid c_o = x, c_n \Rightarrow_{S,A} c_{n+1}\}$ for $x \in X$

(ii) $VAL(x) \sim RES_n(x)$ for $x \in X$. □

The result states that operational and denotational semantics are equivalent in the power domain algebra $P_c(COMP_n)$ which seems to be the best possible way to compare the semantics in the given framework. The result is not satisfactory:

4.7 *Remark:* If the given non-deterministic scheme allows a computation $x \to x$ for some variable $x \in X$ then $RES_n(x) \sim \{(c \in COMP_n | x \leq c\}$. □

This is a consequence of the power domain construction which hides too much information. Because of 2.4 we cannot even expect no sharper result for schemes being Greibach.

In order to compare operational and denotational semantics on the level of continuous algebras we face the problem to understand operational semantics as an element of $P_c(A)$. But for all $x \in X$ RES(x) is finitely generated in COMP. This allows to define

$$RES_{P_c(A)}(x) := P_c(I)([RES(x)]_\sim)$$

with $P_c(I) : P_c(COMP) \to P_c(A)$. $RES_{P_c(A)}$ seems to be the best approximation of RES_A up to the equivalences induced by the power domain construction. As an immediate consequence of 2.7, 3.4 and 4.6 we obtain

4.8 *Proposition:* For a non-determin-stic scheme S and a continuous algebra A operational and denotational semantics are P_c-*equivalent*, i.e. $VAL_A(x) = RES_{P_c(A)}(x)$ for all $x \in X$. □

For the initial continuous Ω-algebra we obtain a sharper result. CT_Ω is algebraic, thus the power domain construction of 4.2 applies.

4.9 *Lemma*: (i) $I_n : COMP_n \to CT_\Omega$ (compare 3.4) maps finite elements of $COMP_n$ to finite elements of CT_Ω and for schemes being Greibach full computation sequences to maximal elements of CT_Ω. Finitely generated sets in $COMP_n$ are mapped to finitely generated sets in CT_Ω.

(ii) If $Y, Y' \subseteq CT_\Omega$ are finitely generated and if all elements of Y are maximal then $Y \sqsubseteq Y'$ implies $Y = Y'$.

□

From the above we obtain

4.10 *Theorem*: If a non-deterministic scheme is Greibach $RES_{CT_\Omega}(x) = VAL_{CT_\Omega}(x)$ for $x \in X$.

□

This is an alternative proof of equivalence of semantics to that given in [20],[21].

We cannot expect that this argument holds for arbitrary Ω-algebra, but they even do not work for algebraic Ω-algebras as the following example demonstrates.

Example: Let $\Omega = \{a,s\}$ with a being a nullary and s being a unary operator. We factorize CT_Ω by the inequation $a \leq sa$ (cf. [17]). The resulting algebra CT'_Ω is algebraic. For the scheme 'S: x → a <u>or</u> ssx' which is Greibach the equivalences

$$RES_{CT_\Omega}(x) \sim \{s^{2n}a \mid n \in \mathbb{N}_o\} \cup \{s^\omega a\} \sim \{a, s^\omega a\}$$

hold. This is disappointing as the meaning of many schemes are identified which should be different, so for instance the scheme 'S: x → a <u>or</u> sx' has the same semantics. This is due to the additional ordering which is not inherited from the ordering of computation sequences.

□

It is an open question for what kind of continuous algebras a strong result as 4.10 holds. We guess that these algebras should be very similar to the algebras used for metric interpretations in [4].

5. DISCUSSION

First of all we should remark that all our arguments given so far can be extended to non-deterministic recursive program schemes if we use the formalism of algebraic theories as proposed in [21]:

In algebraic theories elementary datas are derived operators, operations are composition, units, tupling and projections. If we construct a free algebraic theory [16] over an operator domain $\Omega + \Phi$ consisting of basic operators Ω and operator variables Φ any recursive scheme as for instance

$$\phi(x) = IF(GT\emptyset(x), MULT(x, \phi(PRED(x))), 1)$$

can be rewritten using the operators and the operations of the algebraic theory,

$$\phi = IF \circ \langle GT\emptyset, MULT \circ \langle id, \phi \circ PRED\rangle, 1\rangle \quad ,$$

yielding equations which are of the same form as the equations discussed above but which live in the environment of algebraic theories. For non-determinism the notion of OI-algebras has to be extended to the level of algebraic theories [21].

Our paper was inspired by the experience gained in [20], [21], [22] that the crucial argument in proofs of equivalence of operational and denotational semantics is a syntactical one, based on simulation of computational strategies. So we looked for a domain where the equivalence argument could be reduced to its syntactical kernel. The domain of computation sequences appeared to be adequate and it turned out that equivalence proofs for non-deterministic schemes could be reduced to a single proof on the syntactical level of computation sequences.

Our approach strictly divides between those equivalences which are induced by different notions of computation and those induced by interpretations. The first kind of equivalences is intensional, being essentially equivalences of operational semantics (in this regard least fixpoint techniques turn out to be a specific operational semantics). The second kind of equivalences is extensional, depending on the kind of phenomena which should be identified according to the meaning. The distinction seems to be reasonable from a methodological point of view. The advantage of our approach is that for both levels we use the same structural or axiomatic (in this case algebraic) framework, the connections between the levels being ensured by structure preserving maps. We believe that this kind of approach should extend to more complex notions of computation. This shall be the goal of future work. The tool of computation sequences seems to be very elementary and versatile for investigations of this kind.

More specifically with respect to non-deterministic computations we learn that we can choose between several notions of equivalence, equivalence on the level of sets being the strongest, P_c-equivalence being a weaker one. The question is, what is a 'canonical' notion of equivalence and second, how to relate a notion of equivalence to classes of algebras in which the equivalence is satisfied (For the deterministic case such classes of algebras are investigated in [8], [11]). Because of the last example we doubt that P_c-equivalence is adequate in every case.

A last remark is on the Greibach condition. One of the motivations of our approach has been to get rid of the Greibach condition originally introduced in [4], [5]. But even if our approach is more elaborate than that in [20], [21] we failed to prove strong equivalence without the Greibach condition. The failure is due to the fact that given a scheme containing a rule ' $x \to x$ <u>or</u> ...' a computation may be caused by reflexiveness or by an application of the above rule. This seems to be inherent to the one-point computation strategy in the non-deterministic case.
'no computation' and 'infinite computations being constant'. Thus it may be doubted as well if strong equivalence is a canonical notion of equivalence.

ACKNOWLEDGEMENTS: I thank the referees for pointing out several errors and for valuable suggestions for improvement.

REFERENCES

[1] ADJ-group: A junction between computer science and category theory. IBM research report RC-4526, 1973

[2] ADJ-group: Some fundamentals of order algebraic semantics. MFCS'76. LNCS 45, 1976

[3] Arnold,A.,Leguy,B.: Une proprieté des forets algébriques de Greibach. I.C. 46, 1980

[4] Arnold,A.,Nivat,M.: Metric interpretations of infinite trees and semantics of non-deterministic programs. Techn. Rep., Lille 1978

[5] Arnold,A.,Nivat,M.: Formal computations of non-deterministic recursive program schemes. Math.Syst.Th. 13, 1980

[6] Berry,G., Levy,S.J.: Minimal and optimal computations of recursive programs. JACM 26, 1979

[7] Boudol,G.: Sémantique opérationelle et algébrique des programmes recursif non-deterministes. Thèse d'Etat, Paris 7, 1980

[8] Courcelle,B.: Infinite trees in normal form and recursive equations having a unique solution. Mat. Syst. Th. 13, 1979

[9] Dubuc,E.: Kan extensions in enriched category theory. LNMath. 145, 1970

[10] Ashcroft,E.A.,Hennessy,M.C.B.: The semantics of non-determinism. 3rd ICALP, 1976

[11] Guessarian,I.: Algebraic semantics. LNCS 99, 1981

[12] Hennessy,M.C.B.,Plotkin,G.: Full abstraction of a simple programming language. MFCS'79, LNCS 74, 1979

[13] Huet,G.: Confluent reductions, abstract properties and applications to term-rewriting systems. 18th FOCS, 1977

[14] Huwig,H.,Poigné,A.: Continuous and non-deterministic completions of algebras. 3rd Hungarian Comp. Conf., Budapest 1981

[15] MacLane,S. Kategorien, Berlin-Heidelberg-New-York 1972

[16] Manes,E.G.: Algebraic theories. Berlin-Heidelberg-New-York 1976

[17] Meseguer,J.: On order-complete universal algebra and enriched functorial semantics. FCT'77, LNCS 56, 1977

[18] Meseguer,J.: Order completion monads. Math. Dpt. UCLA, 1979

[19] Nivat,M.: Non-deterministic programs: an algebraic overview. Lab. Inf. Theor. et Programmation, Paris 1980

[20] Poigné,A.: Using least fixed points to characterize formal computations of non-deterministic equations. Formaliz. of Programming Concepts, LNCS 107, 1981

[21] Poigné,A.: An order semantics for non-deterministic program schemes. 11. GI-Jahrestagung, Fachberichte Informatik 50, 1981

[22] Poigné,A.: On effective computations of non-deterministic schemes. 5th Int. Symp. on Programming, LNCS 137, 1982

[23] Poigné,A.: 'Full version of the paper', to appear as Technical Report

[24] Smyth,M.B.: Power domains, JCSS 16, 1978

SUR LES MORPHISMES QUI ENGENDRENT DES MOTS INFINIS AYANT DES FACTEURS PRESCRITS

par

Patrice Séébold

UER de Mathématiques-Université Paris VII

-:-:-:-:-

RESUME: On montre que le mot de Morse est le seul mot infini sans chevau-chement sur un alphabet à deux lettres que l'on puisse obtenir par ité-ration d'un morphisme. De plus, on montre que si un mot infini, formé des mêmes facteurs que le mot de Fibonacci, est obtenu par itération d'un morphisme, ce morphisme appartient au demi-groupe engendré par deux mor-phismes particuliers.

ABSTRACT: We show that the Morse sequence is the only infinite binary sequence without overlapping factor which can be generated by an iterated morphism. We also show that if an infinite sequence, which has the same factors as the Fibonacci sequence, can be generated by an iterated mor-phism, then this morphism belongs to a semi-group generated by two special morphisms.

1. INTRODUCTION.

Récemment, de nombreux articles sont parus concernant certaines propriétés combinatoires de mots infinis, traîtant notamment de mots sans carré, sans cube, sans chevauchement et de problèmes voisins. Depuis l'article de Thue (11) qui a le premier démontré l'existence de mots in--finis sans chevauchement et sans carré, l'étude a été reprise notamment par Arson (1) et par Morse-Hedlund (8) et, plus récemment, par Berstel (2),(3),(4), Crochemore (5), Dekking (6), Karhumäki (7) et Pansiot (9), (10) entre autres. Nous présentons dans cette communication des résultats liés à ce problème.

On appelle mot de Thue ou mot de Morse le mot infini défini comme suit: soit $A=\{a,b\}$ et soit $f:A^*\longrightarrow A^*$ le morphisme défini par $f(a) = ab$, $f(b) = ba$; le mot de Morse est le mot $\underline{\underline{M}} = \lim_{n\to\infty}(f^n(a))$. Thue a montré que ce mot est sans chevauchement. On sait aussi depuis Thue (12) qu'il existe un nombre non dénombrable de mots infinis sans chevauchement. Ils ne peuvent donc pas tous être engendrés par morphisme. Ainsi on peut se poser la question de déterminer quels sont les mots infinis sans chevauchement que l'on peut engendrer par morphisme. Nous montrons le résultat à priori assez surprenant (théorème 1) que le mot de Morse est le seul mot infini sans chevauchement que l'on puisse obtenir par itération d'un morphisme sur un alphabet à deux lettres. Ce résultat complète celui de Pansiot (9) qui a montré que l'ensemble des morphismes engendrant le mot de Morse est un monoïde libre monogène.

La même question, à savoir quels sont les morphismes qui engendrent un mot infini d'une espèce donnée, peut se poser à propos de nombreux autres mots bien connus dans la littérature. Nous ne répondons que très partiellement à cette question. En effet, nous ne considérons que le mot de Fibonacci défini comme suit: soit $A = \{a,b\}$ et soit $f:A^*\longrightarrow A^*$ le mor--phisme défini par $f(a) = ab$, $f(b) = a$; le mot de Fibonacci est le mot

$\underline{\underline{F}} = \lim_{n\to\infty}(f^n(a))$. Pansiot a montré, comme dans le cas du mot de Morse, que l'ensemble des morphismes engendrant le mot de Fibonacci est un monoïde libre monogène. Nous montrons ici (théorème 2) que tout morphisme qui engendre un mot infini formé des mêmes facteurs que le mot de Fibonacci est élément d'un demi-groupe non libre engendré par deux morphismes que nous précisons.

2. NOTATIONS ET DEFINITIONS.

Soit A un alphabet. On note A* le monoïde libre engendré par A, $|u|$ la longueur d'un mot u, ε le mot vide et $A^+ = A^* - \{\varepsilon\}$.

Un <u>mot infini</u> sur A est une application $\underline{\underline{x}}: \mathbb{N} \to A$. On l'écrit: $\underline{\underline{x}} = x_0 x_1 \ldots x_n \ldots$, $x_i \in A$ et on note $x^{[k]} = x_0 x_1 \ldots x_{k-1}$ le facteur gauche de longueur k de $\underline{\underline{x}}$.

Un morphisme $f: A^* \to A^*$ est <u>prolongeable</u> en $x_0 \in A$ si $f(x_0) = x_0 v$ pour un mot $v \in A^+$. Alors chaque mot $f^n(x_0)$ est facteur gauche propre de $f^{n+1}(x_0)$ et le mot infini $\underline{\underline{a}}$ déterminé par la condition $a^{[k]} = f^n(x_0)$ pour $k = |f^n(x_0)|$, $n \geq 0$ est la <u>limite</u> de la suite $(f^n(x_0))_{n\geq 0}$. On écrit alors: $\underline{\underline{a}} = f^w(x_0)$.

On dit qu'un mot est <u>sans chevauchement</u> s'il ne contient pas de facteur de la forme xuxux avec $x \in A$ et $u \in A^*$.

On dit qu'un mot u de A^+ <u>contient une puissance n-ième</u> s'il existe $v \in A^+$ tel que v^n soit un facteur de u.

3. RESULTATS.

Soit $A = \{a,b\}$ un alphabet à deux lettres.

<u>I)Le mot de Morse.</u>

On note $h_1: A^* \to A^*$ le morphisme défini par $h_1(a) = ab$, $h_1(b) = ba$. On appelle mot de Morse, le mot $\underline{\underline{M}} = h_1^w(a)$. On sait d'après Thue (11) et

Morse-Hedlund (8) que $\underline{\underline{M}}$ est sans chevauchement.

L'étude des morphismes engendrant des mots sans chevauchement a été poursuivie notamment par Karhumäki (7) qui a montré qu'un tel morphisme est nécessairement bipréfixe. On sait aussi depuis Thue (12) qu'il existe un nombre non dénombrable de mots infinis sans chevauchement, ce qui signi-fie qu'ils ne peuvent tous être engendrés par morphisme. Nous répondons à la question de savoir lesquels le sont par le

THEOREME 1 : $\underline{\underline{M}}$ <u>est le seul mot infini sans chevauchement commençant par a que l'on puisse obtenir par itération d'un morphisme sur un alphabet à deux lettres.</u>

II)Le mot de Fibonacci.

On note $h_2 : A^* \to A^*$ le morphisme défini par $h_2(a) = ab$, $h_2(b) = a$; on appelle mot de Fibonacci, le mot $\underline{\underline{F}} = h_2^w(a)$. On sait d'après Karhumäki (7) que $\underline{\underline{F}}$ contient des cubes, mais pas de puissance quatrième. D'autre part, on montre aisément que $\underline{\underline{F}}$ ne contient pas les mots bb, aaa, babab, aabaabaa comme facteurs. On peut donc, comme pour le mot de Morse, se poser la ques-tion de savoir quels sont les morphismes qui permettent d'engendrer des mots infinis formés des mêmes facteurs que le mot de Fibonacci. C'est à cette question que nous répondons avec le théorème 2.

On note $h_3 : A^* \to A^*$ le morphisme défini par $h_3(a) = ba$, $h_3(b) = a$.

THEOREME 2: <u>L'ensemble de tous les morphismes engendrant des mots infinis formés des mêmes facteurs que le mot de Fibonacci est le monoïde non libre</u> $\{h_2, h_3\}^+$.

4. PREUVES.

La preuve du théorème 1, bien que ne faisant pas intervenir de tech-nique nouvelle, est assez longue et compliquée. Elle repose essentielle-ment sur la démonstration de quatre lemmes.

Appelons $\mathfrak{F}_1$ l'ensemble:

$\mathfrak{F}_1 = \{ f / f : A^* \to A^*$ est un morphisme prolongeable en a tel que le mot infini $f^w(a)$ soit sans chevauchement $\}$.

(Tous les morphismes considérés ici sont prolongeables. Cette restriction n'est pas essentielle, mais facilite l'exposé.)

Le théorème 1 peut alors s'énoncer comme suit: $\mathfrak{F}_1 = \{h_1\}^+$.

L'inclusion $\{h_1\}^+ \subseteq \mathfrak{F}_1$ est évidente.

Réciproquement, soit $f \in \mathfrak{F}_1$. On sait d'après Karhumäki (7) que f est bipréfixe. Soit $\underline{\underline{x}} = f^w(a)$. Les trois remarques qui suivent sont élémen--taires, mais très utiles tout au long de la démonstration.

REMARQUE 1: <u>Pour tout</u> $n \in \mathbb{N}$, <u>les images par</u> f <u>de tous les sous-mots de</u> $\underline{\underline{x}}$ <u>de longueur</u> n <u>sont des sous-mots de</u> $\underline{\underline{x}}$, <u>donc sans chevauchement.</u>

REMARQUE 2: <u>Pour tout</u> $f \in \mathfrak{F}_1$, <u>on a</u> $f(b) \neq \varepsilon$.

REMARQUE 3: <u>Pour tout</u> $f \in \mathfrak{F}_1$, <u>on a que</u> f(a) <u>ne commence pas par la même lettre que</u> f(b) <u>et que</u> f(a) <u>ne finit pas par la même lettre que</u> f(b).

Nous sommes maintenant en mesure de démontrer le théorème 1.

LEMME 1: <u>Soit</u> $f \in \mathfrak{F}_1$, <u>si</u> $|f(a)| \leqslant 4$ <u>alors</u> $f = h_1$ <u>ou</u> $f = h_1^2$.

LEMME 2: <u>Soit</u> $f \in \mathfrak{F}_1$, <u>si</u> $|f(a)| \geqslant 5$ <u>alors</u> f(a) = abbabu <u>avec</u> $u \in A^*$.

On montre aisément ces deux lemmes en faisant une étude exhaustive de tous les cas. La démonstration du lemme 3 est, elle, plus intéressante, la méthode employée étant réutilisée plusieurs fois dans ce qui suit.

LEMME 3: <u>Soit</u> $f \in \mathfrak{F}_1$, <u>si</u> f(abba) <u>est préfixe de</u> $\underline{\underline{M}}$ <u>alors il existe</u> $k \in \mathbb{N}$ <u>tel que</u> $f = h_1^k$.

D'après le lemme 1, il suffit de considérer le cas où $|f(a)| \geqslant 5$ et, d'après le lemme 2, on a alors f(a) = abbabu, $u \in A^*$. Dans ce cas, le mot infini $f^w(a)$ commencera par f(abba).

Nous allons raisonner par l'absurde et montrer que si un morphisme f de A* dans A* est tel que f(abba) soit préfixe de $\underline{\underline{M}}$, mais que, pour tout $k \in \mathbb{N}$, $f \neq h_1^k$, alors $f \notin \mathfrak{F}_1$.

Soient, donc, $f : A^* \to A^*$ un morphisme prolongeable en a, $p = |f(a)|$ et $n \in \mathbb{N}$ tel que $2^n \leqslant p < 2^{n+1}$ et supposons que f(abba) soit préfixe de $\underline{\underline{M}}$, mais que $f \neq h_1^n$.

Deux cas se présentent:

a) $|f(a)| = 2^n$, mais alors, par hypothèse, $|f(b)| \neq 2^n$.

b) $|f(a)| \neq 2^n$.

Dans les deux cas, on montre que, quelle que soit $|f(b)|$, on est en contradiction avec le fait que $f \in \mathfrak{F}_1$, ce qui montre le lemme 3.

On notera que les lemmes 1, 2 et 3 permettent de retrouver le résultat de Pansiot (9):

COROLLAIRE: <u>Soit</u> $f: A^* \to A^*$ <u>un morphisme prolongeable en</u> a <u>et tel que</u> $f^w(a) = \underline{\underline{M}}$ <u>alors il existe</u> $n \in \mathbb{N}$ <u>tel que</u> $f = h_1^n$.

Pour achever la preuve du théorème 1, il reste à montrer le lemme 4.

LEMME 4: <u>Soit</u> $f \in \mathfrak{F}_1$ <u>alors nécessairement</u> f(abba) <u>est préfixe de</u> $\underline{\underline{M}}$.

De nouveau, d'après le lemme 1, il suffit de considérer le cas $|f(a)| \geq 5$ et, d'après le lemme 2, on a alors f(a) = abbabu, $u \in A^*$. Dans ce cas, le mot infini $f^w(a)$ commencera par f(abba). Nous allons raisonner par l'ab--surde et montrer que si un morphisme f de A* dans A* est tel que f(abba) n'est pas préfixe de $\underline{\underline{M}}$, alors $f \notin \mathfrak{F}_1$.

Nous allons commencer par énoncer un résultat intermédiaire simple mais très utile.

REMARQUE 4: <u>Soit</u> $f \in \mathfrak{F}_1$ <u>tel que</u> $|f(a)| \geq 5$, <u>alors il existe</u> $u' \in A^*$ <u>et</u> $v \in A^*$ <u>tels que</u> f(a) = abbabu'aab <u>et</u> f(b) = baabvabba <u>ou bien</u> f(a) = abbabu'abba <u>et</u> f(b) = baabvbaab; <u>de plus, dans tous les cas</u>, f(a) <u>et</u> f(b) <u>sont composés uniquement de sous-mots de la forme</u> abba <u>et</u> baab.

Cette remarque s'établit très aisément en examinant tous les cas possibles.

Soient, maintenant, $f: A^* \to A^*$ un morphisme prolongeable en a tel que $|f(a)| \geq 5$, α le préfixe de $\underline{\underline{M}}$ de longueur $|f(abba)|$ et supposons que f(abba) n'est pas préfixe de $\underline{\underline{M}}$, mais que $f \in \mathfrak{F}_1$ (donc satisfait à la remarque 4.).

Posons X = abba et Y = baab. α et f(abba) commencent tous deux par X. De plus, on sait que α commence par XYYXYXXY. Puisque f(abba) n'est pas préfixe de $\underline{\underline{M}}$, il existe un plus long préfixe α_1 commun à α et f(abba). Posons $\alpha = \alpha_1\alpha'$ avec $\alpha' \in \{X,Y\}^+$ et $f(abba) = \alpha_1\alpha''$ avec $\alpha'' \in \{X,Y\}^+$. Il ne reste alors plus qu'à examiner les différentes formes possibles de α_1 et on montre que le fait que α' soit différent de α'' fait que, dans tous les cas, $f^w(a)$ contient un chevauchement ce qui achève la démonstration du lemme 4.

Ainsi par les lemmes 1, 2 et 4 on a que, pour tout $f \in \mathfrak{F}_1$, f(abba) est préfixe de $\underline{\underline{M}}$ et, par le lemme 3, qu'un tel f s'écrit h_1^k pour un $k \in \mathbb{N}$ ce qui démontre bien le théorème 1.

Pour montrer le théorème 2, on a besoin de quelques définitions sup--plémentaires.

Appelons $FC(\underline{\underline{x}})$ l'ensemble des facteurs d'un mot $\underline{\underline{x}}$ de A*. Soient $\underline{\underline{F}}_1 = (h_3^2)^w(a)$ et $\underline{\underline{F}}_2 = h_3(\underline{\underline{F}}_1)$. On sait que $FC(\underline{\underline{F}}) = FC(\underline{\underline{F}}_1) = FC(\underline{\underline{F}}_2)$. De plus, on notera $\mathcal{G}$ le demi-groupe de morphismes engendré par h_2 et h_3 (on remarque que $\mathcal{G}$ n'est pas libre car $h_2^2 \circ h_3 = h_3^2 \circ h_2$), et on appellera $\mathfrak{F}_2$ l'ensemble: $\mathfrak{F}_2 = \{f/f:A^* \rightarrow A^* \text{ morphisme avec } FC(f^w(a)) = FC(\underline{\underline{F}})\}$.

Le théorème 2 peut alors s'énoncer comme suit: $\mathfrak{F}_2 = \mathcal{G}$.

La démonstration est composée de deux lemmes. Appelons, pour tout $n \in \mathbb{N}$, F_n le n-ième nombre de Fibonacci.

LEMME 5: <u>Soit</u> $f \in \mathfrak{F}_2$, <u>s'il existe</u> $n \in \mathbb{N}$ <u>tel que</u> $|f(a)| = F_n$ <u>alors</u> $f \in \mathcal{G}$.

Il est bien connu que, pour tout $m \in \mathbb{N}$, $\underline{\underline{F}}$ contient (m+1) facteurs de longueur m. Appelons <u>facteur spécial</u> un facteur u de $\underline{\underline{F}}$ tel que ua et ub soient tous deux facteurs de $\underline{\underline{F}}$. On sait que, pour tout $n \in \mathbb{N}$, $\underline{\underline{F}}$ contient un et un seul facteur spécial de longueur n (cf. Berstel (4)). Pour finir, appelons <u>équivalents</u> deux morphismes g et g' tels que g(a) = g'(a).

Soit u le facteur spécial de $\underline{\underline{F}}$ de longueur $F_n - 1$; ua et ub sont tous deux facteurs de $\underline{\underline{F}}$ de longueur F_n. On montre aisément qu'un de ces deux facteurs ne peut pas s'écrire f(a) pour un $f \in \mathfrak{F}_2$.

Donc $\mathfrak{F}_2$ contient au plus F_n classes de morphismes f tels que $|f(a)| = F_n$.

Nous allons maintenant montrer par récurrence que, pour tout $n \in \mathbb{N}$,

$\mathcal{G}$ contient exactement F_n classes de morphismes h tels que $|h(a)| = F_n$.

On vérifie aisément que la relation est vraie pour tout $n \leqslant 3$.

Supposons que, pour tout $n \geqslant 4$, $\mathcal{G}$ contient exactement F_n classes de morphismes h tels que $|h(a)| = F_n$ et montrons qu'alors il en est de même au rang n+1.

Il est facile de constater que $\mathcal{G}$ contient au plus $2F_n$ classes de morphismes g tels que $|g(a)| = F_{n+1}$. Or, en utilisant la relation $h_2^2 \circ h_3 = h_3^2 \circ h_2$, on montre que F_{n-2} de ces morphismes sont égaux. Donc $\mathcal{G}$ contient au plus $2F_n - F_{n-2} = F_{n+1}$ classes de morphismes g tels que $|g(a)| = F_{n+1}$.

Il reste à montrer que ces classes sont toutes deux à deux différen--tes.

Soient g_1 et g_2 deux classes de morphismes de $\mathcal{G}$ tels que $|g_1(a)| = |g_2(a)| = F_n$ et supposons $g_1(a) \neq g_2(a)$. On montre par une étude exhaustive de tous les cas que si$(h_2 \circ g_1)(a) = (h_3 \circ g_2)(a)$, alors il existe g" une classe de morphismes de $\mathcal{G}$ tels que $|g''(a)| = F_{n-2}$ et $g_1 = h_2 \circ h_3 \circ g''$, $g_2 = h_3 \circ h_2 \circ g''$.

Ainsi $\mathcal{G}$ contient exactement F_{n+1} classes de morphismes g tels que $|g(a)| = F_{n+1}$. On a alors que, pour tout $n \in \mathbb{N}$, $\mathcal{G}$ contient exactement F_n classes de morphismes h tels que $|h(a)| = F_n$ et, puisque $\mathcal{F}_2$ contient au plus F_n classes de morphismes f tels que $|f(a)| = F_n$, on a le lemme 5.

Il reste à examiner le cas où $|f(a)| \neq F_n$.

LEMME 6: <u>Soit</u> $f: A^* \longrightarrow A^*$ <u>un morphisme tel que, pour tout</u> $n \in \mathbb{N}$, $|f(a)| \neq F_n$, <u>alors</u> $f \notin \mathcal{F}_2$.

On remarque aisément qu'il suffit d'examiner le cas où f est tel que $|f(a)| \geqslant 6$. Soit $p = |f(a)|$, il existe $n \in \mathbb{N}$ tel que $F_n < p < F_{n+1}$. On sait, d'après le lemme 5, qu'il existe $g \in \mathcal{G}$ et $t \in A^+$ avec $|g(a)| = F_{n+1}$, $|t| = 5$ et tels que $f^{\omega}(a)$ commence par $g(t)$.

Posons, par exemple (les autres cas se traiteraient de manière absolu--ment similaire), $f(a) = abaabu$ avec $u \in A^+$ et $t = abaab$.

De plus posons $X = g(a)$, $Y = g(b)$, $\alpha = f(a)$ et $\beta = f(b)$. $f^{\omega}(a)$ com--mence à la fois par XYXXY et $\alpha\beta\alpha\alpha\beta$ et, comme $F_n < p < F_{n+1}$, on a $|Y| < |\alpha| < |X|$, donc il existe $X' \in A^+$ tel que $X = \alpha X'$ et $|X'| < |\alpha|$.

Pour finir, puisque si $f^w(a)$ contient XXX ou YY, $f \notin \mathcal{F}_2$, nous suppo--serons que $f^w(a)$ ne contient ni XXX, ni YY.

En appliquant une méthode similaire à celle employée dans la démons--tration du lemme 3, on montre que, dans tous les cas, $f \notin \mathcal{F}_2$.

Ainsi, par les lemmes 5 et 6, on a que $\mathcal{F}_2 \subseteq \mathcal{G}$ et comme, de façon évidente, on a $\mathcal{G} \subseteq \mathcal{F}_2$, le théorème 2 est démontré.

Pour finir, notons que puisque, pour tout $n \in \mathbb{N}$, $\mathcal{G}$ contient F_n classes de morphismes g tels que $|g(a)| = F_n$, on a que, pour tout $n \in \mathbb{N}$, il existe au moins F_n mots infinis formés des mêmes facteurs que $\underline{\underline{F}}$ et deux à deux différents. D'où le corollaire suivant du théorème 2 qui marque bien la différence entre le mot de Morse et le mot de Fibonacci:

COROLLAIRE: Il existe une infinité de mots formés des mêmes facteurs que le mot de Fibonacci et deux à deux différents.

5. DISCUSSION.

Nous venons de montrer que le mot de Morse est le seul mot infini sans chevauchement commençant par a que l'on puisse obtenir par itération d'un morphisme sur un alphabet à deux lettres. Il apparaît que la seule façon de construire d'autres mots infinis sans chevauchement sur un alphabet à deux lettres consiste à rajouter des lettres à gauche du mot de Morse. Il ne semble pas possible, avec les techniques actuelles, de construire de tels mots (sauf dans le cas d'un mot infini bilatère).

On peut également se poser la question de savoir s'il existe un mot infini ayant même ensemble de facteurs que le mot de Fibonacci et qui ne puisse pas être obtenu par itération d'un morphisme. Ceci paraît à pre--mière vue impossible puisque, pour tout $n \in \mathbb{N}$, tout préfixe de longueur F_n d'un mot formé des mêmes facteurs que le mot de Fibonacci est l'image de a par un morphisme de $\mathcal{G}$, sauf si ce préfixe est l'un des deux facteurs issus du facteur spécial de longueur F_n - 1. Mais, dans ce cas, il suffit de considérer les préfixes de longueur F_{n+1} qui commencent par ce mot.

Remerciement: Je remercie le professeur Jean Berstel pour des discussions très fructueuses au cours de la rédaction du présent travail.

6. REFERENCES.

(1) S. ARSON: Démonstration de l'existence de suites asymétriques infinies. Mat. Sb. 44 (1937), p.769-777.

(2) J. BERSTEL: Sur les mots sans carré définis par un morphisme. Springer Lecture Notes in Computer Science 71 (1979) p.16-25.

(3) J. BERSTEL: Mots sans carré et morphismes itérés. Rapport n°78-42, Institut de Programmation, Paris, 1978.

(4) J. BERSTEL: Mots de Fibonacci. LITP - Séminaire d'Informatique Théorique 1980-81. p.57-78.

(5) M. CROCHEMORE: An optimal algorithm for computing repetitions of a word Inf. Process. Letters 12 (1981), p.244-250.

(6) F. M. DEKKING: On repetitions of blocks in binary sequences. J. Combinatorial Theory (A) 20, p.292-299. (1976).

(7) J. KARHUMÄKI: On cubic-free w-words generated by binary morphisms. 1981. (à paraître).

(8) M. MORSE - G. HEDLUND: Unending chess, symbolic dynamics and a problem in semi-groups. Duke Math. J. 11 (1944) p.1-7.

(9) J. J. PANSIOT: The Morse sequence and iterated morphisms. Inf. Process. Letters 12 (1981), p.68-70.

(10) J. J. PANSIOT: Morphismes itérés et mot de Fibonacci. 1981. (à paraître).

(11) A. THUE: Über unendliche Zeichenreihen. Norske Vid. Selsk. Skr. I. Mat. Nat. Kl., Christiania (1906) n°7, p.1-22.

(12) A. THUE: Über die gegenseitige Lage gleicher Teile gewisser Zeichen-reihen. Vidensk. I. Mat. Nat. Kl., (1912) n°1, p.1-67.

-:-:-:-:-

Adresse postale:

Patrice Séébold

17 Rue des Déportés

80440 - BOVES

FRANCE

THE EQUIVALENCE PROBLEM FOR N.T.S. LANGUAGES IS DECIDABLE

by

Géraud SENIZERGUES

Université de Rennes I

et

L.I.T.P.

1.-INTRODUCTION

N.T.S. grammars were introduced by L. BOASSON (3). A context-free grammar is N.T.S. iff, using the rules "backwards" does not change the set of sentential forms (N.T.S. stands for Non Terminal Separation property). The languages generated by such grammars (they are called N.T.S. languages) are congruential and deterministic (3, 4, 7).

The main result is that this class of grammars has a dedidable equivalence problem. We notice that the class of N.T.S. languages is not contained in the union of the classes of languages already known to have a decidable equivalence problem (11, 13, 14). Nevertheless, our work uses the result of Valiant (13, 1) saying that the equivalence problem is solvable for finite-turn deterministic push down automata.

We show that the problem "G is N.T.S. ?" (for every c.f. grammar G) is decidable.

The inclusion problem is unsolvable for N.T.S. grammars (showing that this class of grammars is wide). The proof of this result uses the notion of a basic and perfect system of relations (2, 5, 9, 10).

2.- PRELIMINARIES

System of relations - congruence :

- A system of relations S on X^* is a subset of $X^* \times X^*$
- We note $f \underset{S}{\longleftrightarrow} g$ iff $\exists (u,v) \in S$, $\exists f1, f2, g1, g2 \in X^*$,

  ($f=f1\ u\ f2$, $g=g1\ v\ g2$) or ($f=f1\ v\ f2$, $g=g1\ u\ g2$)
- $\overset{*}{\underset{S}{\longleftrightarrow}}$ is the reflexive and transitive closure of $\underset{S}{\longleftrightarrow}$. It is the smallest congruence in X^* containing the set S. We call $\overset{*}{\underset{S}{\longleftrightarrow}}$ the congruence generated by S.

. Given a language $L \subset X^*$, we note $\equiv L$ its syntactic congruence : it is the greatest congruence R (for inclusion) such that, for every $f, g \in X^*$, ($f \in L$ and $f R g$) implies $g \in L$. (see 6, vol. B, p. 185).

N.T.S. grammars :

. A context-free grammar $G = (X, V, P, A)$ consists of four finite sets. X is the terminal alphabet, V an alphabet of variables, $P \subset V\times(X \cup V)^*$ and $A \subset V$ is the set of axioms of G.

. As usual, we note $\overset{*}{\underset{G}{\rightarrow}}$ the derivation. It is the smallest relation R in $(XUV)^*$ such that : R is reflexive, transitive, compatible with the product and $P \subset R$.

. We note $\overset{*}{\underset{G}{\longleftrightarrow}}$ the congruence in $(XUV)^*$ generated by P.

. For every $B \subset V$ we set :

$L(G,B) = \{f \in X^* \mid \exists v \in B,\ v \overset{*}{\underset{G}{\rightarrow}} f\}$; $\hat{L}(G,B) = \{f \in (XUV)^* \mid \exists v \in B,\ v \overset{*}{\underset{G}{\rightarrow}} f\}$
$LR(G,B) = \{f \in X^* \mid \exists v \in B,\ v \overset{*}{\underset{G}{\longleftrightarrow}} f\}$; $LR(G,B) = \{f \in (XUV)^* \mid \exists v \in B,\ v \overset{*}{\underset{G}{\longleftrightarrow}} f\}$

$L(G) = L(G,A)$; $\hat{L}(G) = \hat{L}(G,A)$

. Let us define $\pi_1(P) = \{m \in (XUV)^+ \mid \exists\ v \in V,\ (v,m) \in P\}$

We define the set of the G-irreductible words by :
$Irr(G) = (XUV)^* - (XUV)^*\ \pi_1(P)\ (XUV)^*$

Definition (3) : We call $G = (X, V, P, A)$ a N.T.S. grammar iff for every v in V, $\hat{L}(G,\{v\}) = \widehat{LR}(G,\{v\})$

. $L \subset X^*$ is called a N.T.S. language iff $L = L(G)$ for some N.T.S. grammar G.
. A grammar G is called ε-free iff $P \cap (V \times \{\varepsilon\}) = \emptyset$
Every N.T.S. grammar is equivalent to an N.T.S., ε-free grammar. In the following we deal only with ε-free, context-free grammars.

3.- EQUIVALENCE OF N.T.S. GRAMMARS

Proposition 1 : Let S_1, S_2 be systems of relations on X^* and f_i $(i \in [1,n])$, g_j $(j \in [1,m])$ words in X^*.

Let us define : $L_1 = \bigcup_{i=1}^{n} [f_i]_{\overset{*}{\underset{S_1}{\longleftrightarrow}}}$, $L_2 = \bigcup_{j=1}^{m} [g_j]_{\overset{*}{\underset{S_2}{\longleftrightarrow}}}$

If L_1 and L_2 are decidable (*) and if both syntactic congruences $\equiv L_1$, $\equiv L_2$ have decidable word-problem, then the equality of L_1 and L_2 is decidable.

(*) Recall a language L is decidable iff one can decide whether a word $f in X^*$ belongs to L or not.

Every N.T.S. languages is a finite union of classes for a finitely generated congruence (3, 4, 7) and every N.T.S. language is decidable. So, the equivalence problem for N.T.S. grammars is reduced to the word-problem for the syntactic congruence of a N.T.S. language.

Let us fix a N.T.S. grammar $G = \langle X, V, P, A \rangle$ (we suppose G is ε-free).

<u>Remark</u> : For every $(f,g) \in X^* \times X^*$, $f \equiv_{L(G)} g \iff f \equiv_{\hat{L}(G)} g$

(because G is N.T.S.)

<u>Definition</u> : For every m in $(X \cup V)^+$ we set

$L_m = \{\alpha \# \beta \mid \alpha m \beta \in \hat{L}(G) \text{ and } \alpha, \beta \in Irr(G)\}$

The dieze (noted #) is a distinguished letter.

One easily checks that $f \equiv_{\hat{L}} g \iff L_f = L_g$

<u>Proposition 2</u> : For every m in $(X \cup V)^+$, $L_m = L(A_o)$ for some one-turn d.p.d.a. A_o.

We exhibit a one-turn d.p.d.a. A such that :

(1) $L_m \subset L(A)$

(2) $L(A) \subset \{\alpha \# \beta \mid \alpha, \beta \in (X \cup V)^* \text{ and } \alpha m \beta \in \hat{L}(G)\}$

Setting $R = Irr(G) \# Irr(G)$, from inclusions (1) and (2) we conclude that $L_m = L(A) \cap R$. The intersection of a one-turn deterministic language with a rational set is a one-turn-deterministic language too. From this fact, the existence of A_o follows.

<u>Sketch of the proof</u> : The automaton has a tape, rightwards infinite, leftwards finite, in which are impressed letters (of the alphabet $X \cup V \cup \bar{X} \cup \bar{V}$) which it can read and transform ($\bar{X}$ and $\bar{V}$ are barred alphabets respectively in bijection with X and with V). It has a window of length $2(k-1)+\ell$, where k is the maximum length of the right members of rules and ℓ the length of m. This window is divided in three compartments : the left compartment (of length k-1), the middle compartment (of length ℓ) and the right compartment (of length k-1).

For example, if $G = \sigma \to \sigma\, b + x\, S$ and $A = \{\sigma\}$

$S \to S\, b + a\, b$ $m = aa$

A can be drawn as follows :

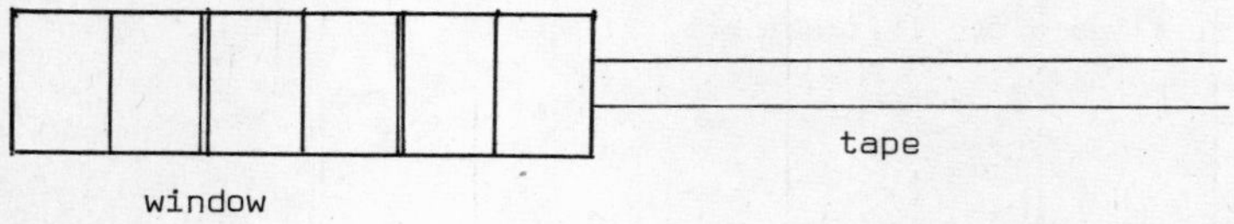

At the beginning, a word is written on the tape, which is on the right side of the window :

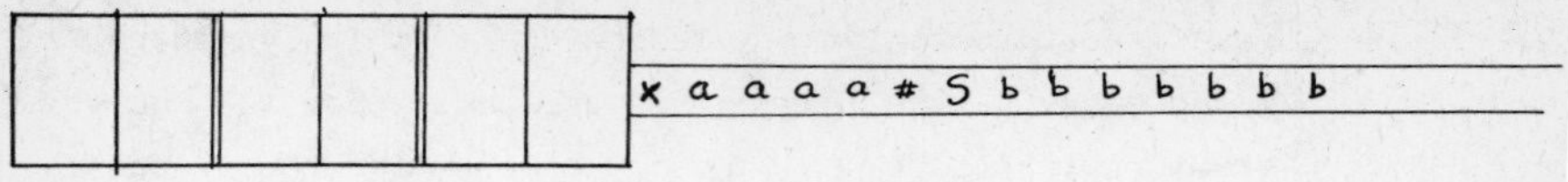

1 The automaton makes the tape run through the left compartment, as long as it does not read a #

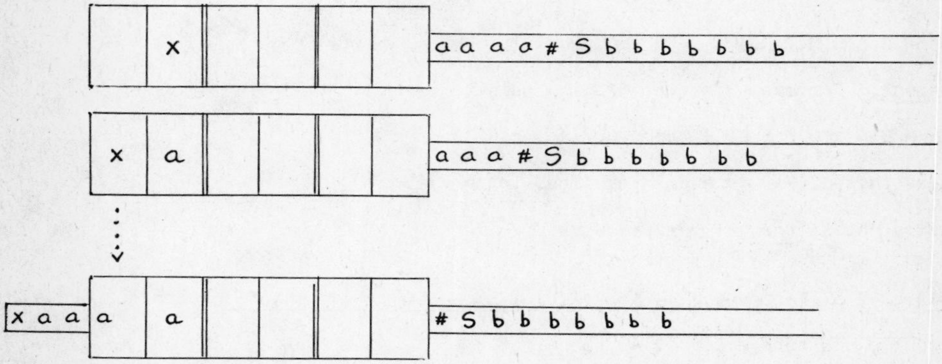

2 The first time it reads the letter #, the automaton replaces the mark # by the word $\bar{m}$ (image of m on the barred alphabet $\bar{X}$) and makes the k-1 letters following # come into the right compartment.

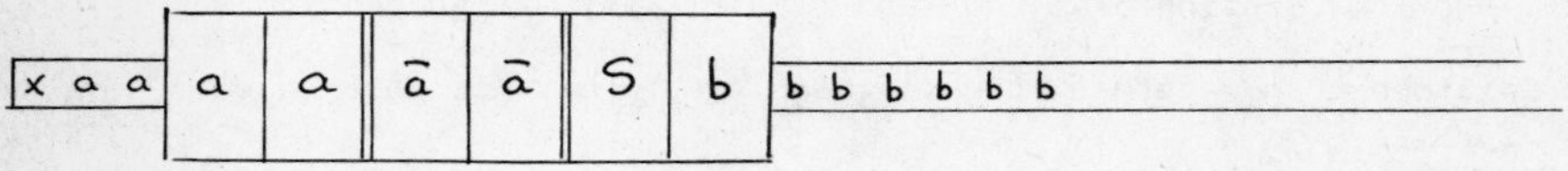

3 Then whenever the word contained in the window contains an occurence of a word f such that :

(1) there exists $v \in V$ such that $v \underset{G}{\to} f$

(2) this occurence of f is contained neither in the left compartment, nor in the right compartment.

The automaton replaces this occurence of f by the letter $\bar{v}$ (corresponding to v in the alphabet $\bar{V}$) and puts $\bar{v}$ in the middle compartment. We say that A "performs a reduction".

Then A fills again the left compartment and the right one.

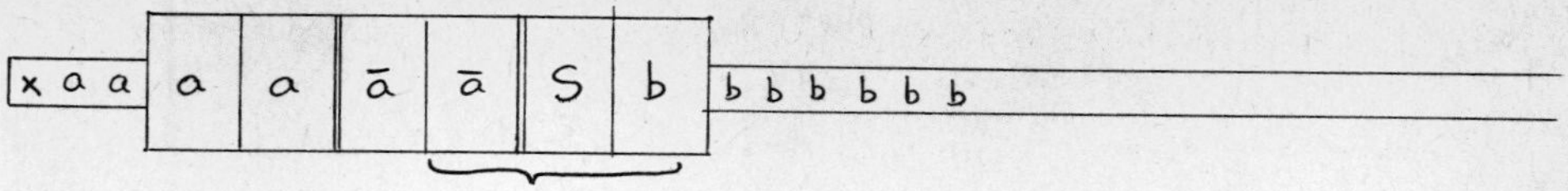

aSb $\underset{G}{\leftarrow}$ S, so A moves to the situation

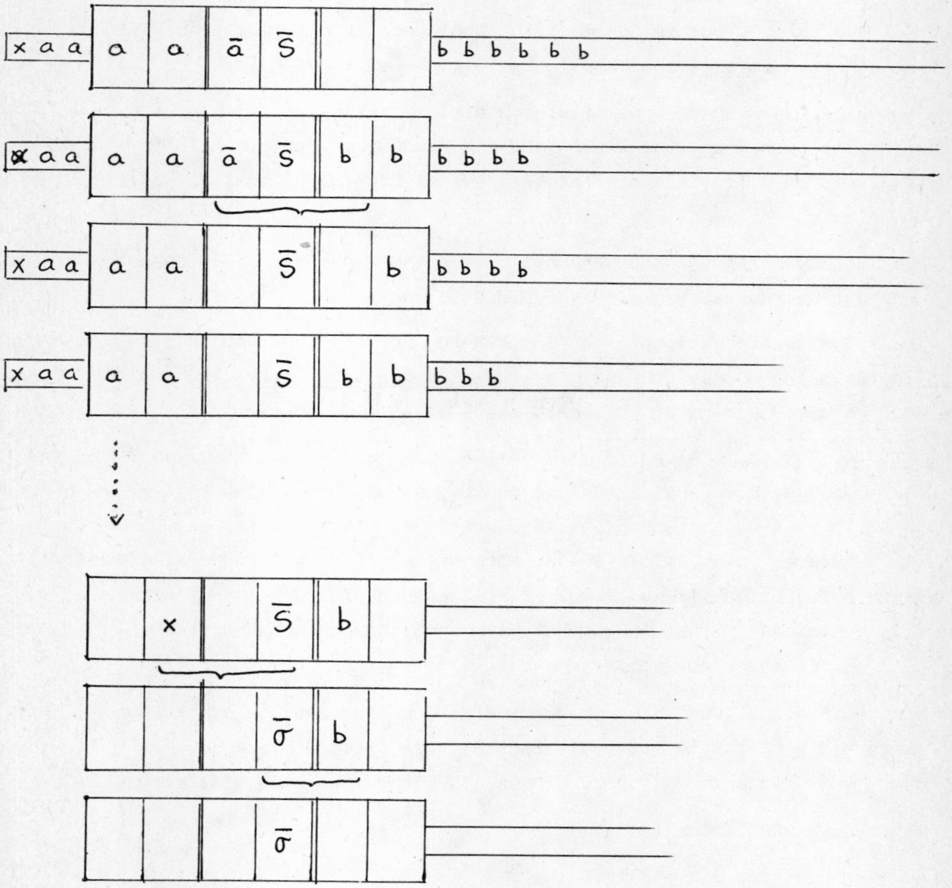

Remark : in order to build a deterministic automaton, for each triple of words $(f, \bar{g}, h) \in (XUV)^* \times (\bar{X}\bar{U}\bar{V})^* \times (XUV)^*$ such that $|f| \leq k-1$, $|\bar{g}| \leq \ell$, $|h| \leq k-1$, if there are several possible reductions, we choose (arbitrarily) one of them.

4 If no reduction of this type is possible :

- . either there is only one letter remaining on the tape (this letter is necessarily in the middle compartment)
- - if this letter is an axiom (that means a letter $\bar{v} \in \bar{V}$ such that $v \in A$) then A accepts the input-word.

- if this letter is not an axiom, then A refuses the input-word.

. or there are at least two letters remaining on the tape, then the automaton refuses the input-word.

5 - If, after performing a reduction, it reads a #, then it stops in this position.

6 - If the case 2 never occurs (that means that the input-word does not contain any letter #), then, after it has made the whole word run through the left compartment, the automaton refuses the word.

Such a machine can be simulated by a d.p.d.a : the left side of the tape is simulated by the push-down, the window and the reductions performed in this window can be simulated by a finite set of states, the right side of the tape is simulated by the input tape.

The pushdown-height increases until the automaton reads a #, then the pushdown-height decreases. Hence this d.p.d.a is one-turn.

The only transformations of an input word $\alpha\#\beta$ performed by this machine consist in replacing # by $\bar{m}$ and then reducing the word in the grammar G. So, if the word obtained at end is $\bar{\sigma}$ ($\sigma \in A$), then $\alpha\, m\, \beta \overset{*}{\underset{G}{\leftarrow}} \sigma$ so $\alpha\, m\, \beta \in \hat{L}(G)$. This gives inclusion (2).

Let $\alpha\#\beta$ ($\alpha, \beta \in (XUV)^*$) belong to L_m. After reading the letter #, the automaton is in a situation where the word written on the tape is $\alpha\, \bar{m}\, \beta$. We know that $\alpha\, m\, \beta$ reduces in an axiom $\sigma \in A$. Moreover, α, β are irreducible, hence, every possible reduction $f \underset{G}{\leftarrow} v$ involves at least one letter of $\bar{m}$. This shows that f is contained in the window, but f cannot be contained either in the left compartment, or in the right compartment.

Once this reduction has been made, the word on the tape is of the type $\alpha'\bar{g}\, \beta'$ with $|\alpha'\bar{g}\, \beta'| < |\alpha\, \bar{m}\, \beta|$, α' and β' are irreducible and $\alpha\, m\, \beta \underset{G}{\longleftrightarrow} \alpha' g\, \beta'$ so that $\alpha' g\, \beta' \in \hat{L}(G,\sigma)$. Thus the automaton will reduce $\alpha\bar{m}\beta$ in $\bar{\sigma}$ (this gives inclusion (1)).

From proposition 3-2 and from the

<u>Theorem 1 ([13])</u> : The equivalence of finite-turn d.p.d.a. is decidable, we conclude that the word-problem is decidable for the syntactic congruence of a N.T.S. language.

By proposition 3-1,

<u>Theorem 2</u> : The equivalence problem is decidable for N.T.S. grammars.

4.- DECIDABILITY OF THE N.T.S. PROPERTY

We show here that one can decide whether a given (ε-free) c.f. grammar $G = \langle X,V,P,A\rangle$ is N.T.S. or not. We start with a

Remark : G is N.T.S. iff, $\forall v \in V$, $\forall (w,m) \in P$, $w \equiv m \mod. \equiv\hat{L}(G,v)$

Hence we have to study the congruence $\bigcap_{v\in V} \equiv\hat{L}(G,v)$

Definition 1 : Let $f \in (X\cup V)^{+}$. Let T be a derivation tree and $\mu(T)$ its product. We define the set of the essential contexts of f in T (noted $EC(T,f)$) by :

$(\alpha,\beta) \in EC(T,f)$ iff $\mu(T) = \alpha f \beta$ and after marking this occurence of f in $\mu(T)$ the following conditions are realized :

(i) the youngest common ancestor of all marked leaves is the root
(ii) if a sub-tree has no marked leaf, then its depth is 0.

Example : $G = \langle\{a,b\}, \{S\}, P, \{S\}\rangle$
$P = [S \to a\,S\,S + b]$

$T_1 =$

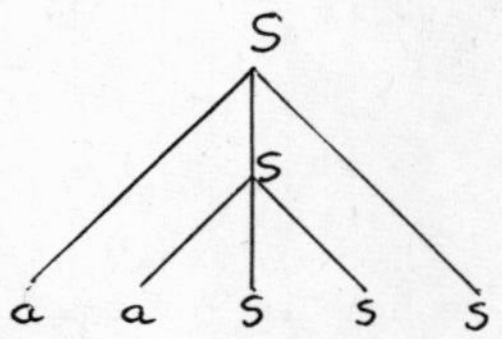

Let us take $f = SS$

If we take $\alpha = aa$ and $\beta = S$, condition (i) is not realized
If we take $\alpha = aa\,S$ and $\beta = \varepsilon$, both conditions are realized.

So, $EC(T_1, SS) = \{(aaS, \varepsilon)\}$

Let us notice that a set $EC(T,f)$ can be empty.

Definition 2 : $EC(v,f)$ is the union of all sets $EC(T,f)$ for all derivation-trees T with a root labeled v.

Proposition 1 : For every v in V and for every f in $(X\cup V)^{*}$, there exists an integer n and $2n$ rational sets $K_1,\ldots,K_i,\ldots,K_n$; $H_1,\ldots,H_i,\ldots,H_n$ such that : $EC(v,f) = \bigcup_{i=1}^{n} K_i \times H_i$.

Proposition 2 : Let f,g be words in $(X\cup V)^{+}$

$f(\bigcap_{v\in V} \equiv\hat{L}(G,v))g \iff$ (i) $\forall v\in V$, $\forall(\alpha,\beta) \in EC(v,f)$, $\alpha g\beta \in \hat{L}(G,v)$
(ii) $\forall v\in V$, $\forall(\alpha,\beta) \in EC(v,g)$, $\alpha f\beta \in \hat{L}(G,v)$

Proposition 4-1 and 4-2 together, show that the problem "$f(\bigcap_{v \in V} \equiv \hat{L}(G,v))g$?" reduces to the inclusion of a finite number of rational sets in the languages $\hat{L}(G,v)$. In the special case where we want to know if $f(\bigcap_{v \in V} \equiv \hat{L}(G,v))g$ for all $(f,g) \in P$, we can replace $\hat{L}(G,v)$ by the deterministic language $L(A_v)$ in proposition 4-2 (where A_v is a d.p.d.a performing a leftright ascending syntactic analysis in the grammar G and accepting the words which this analysis reduces in v). More precisely

Proposition 3 : G is N.T.S. iff

$\forall (w,m) \in P, \forall v \in V, \forall (\alpha,\beta) \in EC(v,m), \alpha w \beta \in L(A_v)$

As the inclusion of a finite number of rational sets in a deterministic context-free language is decidable, we obtain the

Corollary : One can decide whether a c.f. grammar is N.T.S. or not.

Remark : The problem to know if the language generated by a c.f. grammar is N.T.S. or not is unsolvable. The proof given by Hopcroft and Korenjac of the analogous statement for simple deterministic languages ([8]), still works for N.T.S. languages.

5.- UNSOLVABILITY OF THE INCLUSION PROBLEM

In this part we show that the inclusion problem for the class of N.T.S. grammars is unsolvable.

1 - Notations, definitions, preliminary results

- For every $f,g \in X^*$, we note $f \leq g$ iff $\exists\ v \in X^*$, $fv = g$
- We note $f < g$ iff $f \leq g$ and $f \neq g$
- We denote by $\tilde{f}$ the reverse image of f.
- Let $S \subset X^* \times X^*$ be a finite system of relations. We shall deal here with systems such that, $\forall (u,v) \in S$, $|u| > |v|$.

Write $f \underset{S}{\rightarrow} g$ provided $f \underset{S}{\longleftrightarrow} g$ and $|f| > |g|$. We note $\overset{*}{\underset{S}{\rightarrow}}$ the reflexive and transitive closure of $\underset{S}{\rightarrow}$.

The system S is said to be perfect iff : for all f,g, if $f \overset{*}{\underset{S}{\longleftrightarrow}} g$ then there exists a h such that $f \overset{*}{\underset{S}{\rightarrow}} h$ and $g \overset{*}{\underset{S}{\rightarrow}} h$.

We say that a word f verifies the condition (C) iff for every $(u,v) \in S$ and for every $w_0, w_1, w_2 \in X^*$:

$f = w_1 w_2 \quad u = w_0 w_1 \Rightarrow w_1 = \varepsilon$ or $w_2 = \varepsilon$

$f = w_1 w_2 \quad u = w_2 w_0 \Rightarrow w_1 = \varepsilon$ or $w_2 = \varepsilon$

$f = w_1 \, u \, w_2 \quad \Rightarrow w_1 = w_2 = \varepsilon$

The system S is basic ([2]) if, for every $(u,v) \in S$, v verifies condition (C).

Proposition 1 ([3],[12]) : if S is a finite, perfect and basic system of relations, for every finite set of words $f_1,\dots,f_i,\dots,f_n$ verifying condition (C), $\bigcup_{i=1}^{n} [f_i]_{\overset{*}{\underset{S}{\longleftrightarrow}}}$ is a N.T.S. language.

2 - Post correspondance problem and N.T.S. languages

Let φ, Ψ be non erasing homomorphisms $X^* \to Y^*$ (where X,Y are disjoint finite alphabets).

Let a,b,c be letters which do not belong to $X \cup Y$.

We define : $L_1 = \{a\, f\, b\, \widetilde{\varphi(f)}c \mid f \in X^*\}$

$L_2 = a\, X^*\, b\, Y^*\, c - \{a\, f\, b\, \widetilde{\psi(f)}\, c \mid f \in X^+\}$

The Post correspondance problem specified by φ, Ψ has a solution iff $\exists f \in X^+,\ \varphi(f) = \psi(f)$, which is equivalent to : $L_1 \not\subset L_2$

In order to show that L_1, L_2 are N.T.S. languages we define systems of relations :

$$S_1 = \{(xb\widetilde{\varphi(x)},\ b)\}_{x \in X}$$

For every $x \in X$, we define $M(x) = \{m \in X^* \mid m \nleq \widetilde{\psi(x)}$ and for every $m' \in X^*$, $m' < m \Rightarrow m' < \widetilde{\psi(x)}\}$

S_2 is composed of the following pairs of strings :

(1) $(x\, b\, \widetilde{\psi(x)},\ b)$ for all $x \in X$

(2) $(x_1 x_2 b p_2 c,\ x_2 b p_2 c)$ for all $x_1, x_2 \in X$, $p_2 < \widetilde{\psi(x_2)}$

(3) $(a b y_1\, y_2,\ a b y_1)$ for all $y_1, y_2 \in Y$

(4) $(x\, x_1 b m_1,\ x_1 b m_1)$ for all $x, x_1 \in X$, $m_1 \in M(x_1)$

(5) $(x_1\, b m_1 y,\ x_1\, b m_1)$ for all $x_1 \in X$, $m_1 \in M(x_1)$, $y \in Y$

Lemma 1 : S_1 and S_2 are perfect and basic.

Lemma 2 : $L_1 = [a\, b\, c]_{\overset{*}{\underset{S_1}{\longleftrightarrow}}}$

Lemma 3 : $L_2 = \left(\bigcup_{y \in Y} [abyc]_{\overset{*}{\underset{S_2}{\longleftrightarrow}}}\right) \cup \left(\bigcup_{\substack{x \in X \\ p < \psi(x)}} [axbpc]_{\overset{*}{\underset{S_2}{\longleftrightarrow}}}\right) \cup \left(\bigcup_{\substack{x \in X \\ m \in M(x)}} [axbmc]_{\overset{*}{\underset{S_2}{\longleftrightarrow}}}\right)$

As the words abyc, axbpc, axbmc (respectively abc) verify condition (C) withrespect to S_2 (resp. to S_1), using proposition 5-1 we conclude

Proposition 2 : The languages L_1, L_2 are N.T.S. .

As the P.C.P. for non-erasing homomorphisms is unsolvable we conclude

Theorem : The problem of inclusion for N.T.S. languages is unsolvable.

REFERENCES

[1] C.BEERI, An improvment of Valiant's decision procedure for equivalence of deterministic finite-turn pushdown machines, Theoretical Computer Science 3 (1976), p. 305-320.

[2] J. BERSTEL, Congruences plus que parfaites et langages algébriques, Séminaire d'Informatique Théorique L.I.T.P. (1975-1977) p. 123-147.

[3] L. BOASSON, Dérivations et réductions dans les grammaires algébriques

[4] L. BOASSON, G. SENIZERGUES, N.T.S. Languages are congruential and deterministic, to appear .

[5] R. BOOK, Confluent and other types of Thue systems, J.A.C.M. Vol. 29, N° 1, January 1982, pp. 171-182 .

[6] S. EILENBERG, Automata, Languages and Machines, Ac. Press (1976)

[7] C. FROUGNY, Thèse de 3ème Cycle, Une famille de langages algébriques congruenciels, Les langages à non-terminaux séparés, Paris 1980.

[8] J.E. HOPCROFT, A.J. KORENJAC, Simple deterministic languages, I.E.E.E, 7 th Symp. on switching and automate theory, p. 36-46 (1966).

[9] M. NIVAT, M. BENOIT, Congruences parfaites et quasi-parfaites, Séminaire Dubreil, 25ème année, 1971-72.

[10] M. NIVAT, Y. COCHET, Une généralisation des ensembles de Dyck, Israel J. of Maths 9 (1971), p. 389-395.

[11] M. OYAMAGUCHI, Y. INAGAKI, N. HONDA, The equivalence problem for real-time strict deterministic languages, Information and Control 45 (1980), p. 90-115.

[12] G. SENIZERGUES, Thèse de 3ème cycle, Décidabilité de l'équivalence des grammaires N.T.S, Paris 1981.

[13] L.G. VALIANT, The equivalence problem for deterministic finite-turn pushdown automata, Information and Control 25, (1974), p. 123-133.

[14] L.G. VALIANT, M.S. PATERSON, Deterministic one-counter automata, J. Computer System Science 10, p. 340-350.

Mailing Address :

Pr. G. Sénizergues
L.I.T.P.
Université Paris 7
2, Place Jussieu
75005 PARIS F.

Weakest expressible preconditions: A new tool for proving completeness results about Hoare calculi

Kurt Sieber
Universität des Saarlandes
6600 Saarbrücken
West Germany

1. Introduction

In order to establish and prove completeness results about Hoare calculi, the concepts of expressiveness and relative completeness were introduced in [Cook]. Here they are only applied to the classical Hoare calculus for while programs and can be described as follows.

The assertions and programs of a Hoare logic are always built upon a first order predicate language L and interpreted w.r.t. an interpretation I of L. L is called I-expressive, if for every while program and every formula the weakest precondition is again expressible by a formula of L. Cook's result states that whenever L is I-expressive, then the Hoare calculus is complete for L and I, i.e. all I-valid Hoare formulas can be derived from I-valid first order predicate formulas. This is called relative completeness of the Hoare calculus.

But - as was already pointed out in [BT] - Cook's result is not completely satisfying because of the following reasons. Completeness of the calculus for L and I is a first order property, i. e. it only depends on the first order theory of I and not on I itself (cf. Theorem 1). On the other hand expressiveness is not such a first order concept, as can be illustrated with the aid of Peano arithmetic. While the standard model of Peano arithmetic is expressive, all nonstandard models are not (cf. section 4).

As an immediate consequence expressiveness turns out to be a sufficient but not a necessary condition for completeness. This makes Cook's result somewhat unnatural because first it is far from being a converse of the usual soundness theorem and second it is not as strong as possible.

In this paper an alternative for the concept of expressiveness is suggested. Instead of the expressibility of the weakest precondition, only the existence of a weakest one among all expressible preconditions is required. This is now a first order concept which is indeed weaker than expressiveness, but still sufficient to imply completeness of the Hoare calculus. As a consequence the new completeness result is more natural and more general than Cook's original version.

2. Preliminaries on predicate logic and Hoare logic

A *first order predicate language* L is built upon the infinite set V of *variables*, a set F of *function symbols*, a set P of *predicate symbols* and the set of *logical symbols*, which is assumed to contain in particular the boolean constants true, false and the equality symbol. The set of *terms*, (first order predicate) *formulas* and *expressions* (i.e. quantifier free formulas), which are constructed from these symbols in the usual way, are denoted by T(L), L and Exp(L) respectively. WH(L) stands for the set of all *while programs*, in which the terms are taken from T(L) and the boolean expressions from Exp(L), and HF(L) for the set of all *Hoare formulas* {p}S{q} with $p,q \in L$ and $S \in WH(L)$.

An *interpretation* I of L consists of a nonempty set D and a function I_0, which assigns functions and predicates on D to the symbols of F and P. A *state* (for L and I) is a function $\sigma: V \to D$. The set of all states is denoted by Σ. Every term $t \in T(L)$ is interpreted as a function $I(t):\Sigma \to D$ and every formula $p \in L$ as a predicate $I(p):\Sigma \to \{true,false\}$ as usual. The semantics of a program $S \in WH(L)$ is a partial function $M_I(S)$ from states to states, which is here considered as a relation $M_I(S) \subseteq \Sigma \times \Sigma$. Based on this semantics every Hoare formula $h \in HF(L)$ is also assigned a predicate $I(h):\Sigma \to \{true,false\}$ according to the following definition:

$I(\{p\}S\{q\})(\sigma) = true$
$\Leftrightarrow$ If $I(p)(\sigma) = true$ and $(\sigma,\sigma') \in M_I(S)$, then $I(q)(\sigma') = true$

Let now w be a formula of L or HF(L) and W a subset of L. w is called *valid in* I (or: I-valid, notation: $\models_I w$), if $I(w)(\sigma) = true$ for every $\sigma \in \Sigma$; in particular I-validity of a Hoare formula expresses partial correctness. I is called a *model* of W, if every $w \in W$ is I-valid. w is called a *valid consequence* of W (notation, $W \models w$), if it is valid in all models of W.

A subset Th of L is called a *theory*, if
- Th is consistent, i.e. Th has at least one model;
- Th is closed under $\models$, i.e. Th $\models$ p and p$\in$Th are equivalent for every p$\in$L.

For every interpretation I the set Th(I) of all I-valid formulas of L is a theory.

3. Reducing Hoare formulas to first order predicate formulas

Let p,q$\in$L be formulas and S$\in$WH(L) a while program. If $\models_I \{p\}S\{q\}$ holds, then p is called a *precondition* of S and q in I, and q is called a *postcondition* of p and S in I. p is called the *weakest precondition* (wp) of S and q in I if:
I(p)(σ) = true
$\Leftrightarrow$ I(q)(σ') = true for all $\sigma'\in\Sigma$ such that $(\sigma,\sigma')\in M_I(S)$, and q is called the *strongest postcondition* (sp) of p and S in I if:
I(q)(σ') = true
$\Leftrightarrow$ there exists a $\sigma\in\Sigma$ such that I(p)(σ) = true and $(\sigma,\sigma')\in M_I(S)$.

Of course "the" weakest precondition is only uniquely determined up to equivalence in I. Hence it would be more precise to define it as a predicate and to say that the formula p "expresses" this predicate. As in this paper formulas play the central part and not predicates, such a distinction is not made, but the problem should be kept in mind. The same argument applies to the strongest postcondition.

If weakest precondition or strongest postcondition exist, they can be used to "reduce" a Hoare formula to a first order predicate formula, because they possess the following properties: If p is the wp of S and q in I, then $\models_I \{r\}S\{q\}$ and $\models_I r\supset p$ are equivalent for every formula r$\in$L; and if q is the sp of p and S in I, then $\models_I \{p\}S\{r\}$ and $\models_I q\supset r$ are equivalent for every r$\in$L.

But it is well known that weakest preconditions or strongest postconditions do not always exist, e.g. if L is the language of Presburger arithmetic or the language in [Wand]. Hence in general it can only be expected that I-validity of a Hoare formula is equivalent to I-validity of possibly infinitely many first order predicate formulas, and this can

be seen as follows:
Every while program S can be translated into an equivalent flowchart program. Let now Path(S) denote the set of all paths through this flowchart program, and define the semantics $M_I(\pi)$ of a path π to be the set of all $(\sigma,\sigma')\in M_I(S)$, such that the computation for σ takes the path π and yields the result σ'. Of course then $M_I(S) = \bigcup_{\pi\in Path(S)} M_I(\pi)$ holds.

If now {p}S{q} is a Hoare formula then for every path $\pi\in Path(S)$, the wp of π and q and the sp of p and π can be constructed independently of the interpretation I. (Such a construction is part of Floyd's inductive assertions method and is described e.g. in [Man].) Let now WP(S,q) and SP(p,S) be the sets of all these weakest preconditions and strongest postconditions respectively. Then, as an immediate consequence of the "semantical equation" mentioned above, one gets:

$$\models_I \{p\}S\{q\} \quad\Leftrightarrow\quad \models_I p \supset r \text{ for all } r \in WP(S,q)$$
$$\Leftrightarrow\quad \models_I r \supset q \text{ for all } r \in SP(p,S)$$

These equivalences imply that partial correctness is a "first order concept" in the following sense:

THEOREM 1:

Let L be a first order predicate language, I an interpretation of L and $\{p\}S\{q\}\in HF(L)$ a Hoare formula. Then

$$\models_I \{p\}S\{q\} \quad\Leftrightarrow\quad Th(I) \models \{p\}S\{q\}$$

i.e. the I-validity of a Hoare formula only depends on the first order theory of I. □

4. The new concepts

Cook has introduced the concept of expressiveness in order to formulate his completeness result. For while programs it can be defined as follows: Let L be a first order predicate language and I an interpretation of L. Then L is called I-*expressive* if for every program $S\in WH(L)$ and every formula $q\in L$ there exists a formula $p\in L$ which is the wp of S and q in I. Cook originally used strongest postconditions for the definition. Indeed both definitions are equivalent. The proof is similar to that of Theorem 2.

As was already mentioned in the introduction, we want to replace expressiveness by a weaker concept. For this purpose we define for $p,q\in L$ and $S\in WH(L)$: p is the *weakest expressible precondition* (wep) of S and q in I, if $\models_I \{r\}S\{q\}$ and $\models_I r \supset p$ are equivalent for every formula $r \in L$; q is the *strongest expressible postcondition* (sep) of p and S in I, if $\models_I \{p\}S\{r\}$ and $\models_I q \supset r$ are equivalent for every $r \in L$.

Note that we have made *properties* of weakest preconditions and strongest postconditions to *definitions*. This implies immediately that, if the wp of S and q exists in L, then it is also the wep, and if the sp of p and S exists, then it is also the sep. That the converse is not true in general can be seen with the aid of a nonstandard model of arithmetic: Let L be the language of Peano arithmetic and I its standard model. It is well known, that L is I-expressive. Consider now the program S:

y:=0; <u>while</u> y ≠ x <u>do</u> y:=y+1 <u>od</u>.

As this program terminates for every input state in I, the formula <u>false</u> is the wp (and hence also the wep) of S and <u>false</u>. Let now J be a nonstandard model of Th(I). Then <u>false</u> is also the wep of S and <u>false</u> in J, because $\models_I \{r\}S\{\underline{false}\}$ and $\models_J \{r\}S\{\underline{false}\}$ are equivalent by Theorem 1. But of course <u>false</u> is not the wp of S and <u>false</u> in J, because the program does not terminate if the input value for x is infinite. Moreover, as <u>false</u> is the only candidate for wp (up to equivalence), L is not J-expressive and this means, that expressiveness is not a first order concept.

The above argumentation gives us another insight into the nature of wep's and sep's. Although both notions were defined with respect to an interpretation I, they turned out - by Theorem 1 - to depend only on the first order theory Th(I). This observation leads us to the final definition, which concerns theories instead of interpretations and which will be the basis for the completeness results of the next section.

<u>Definition:</u>

Let L be a first order predicate language, $Th \subseteq L$ a theory and p,q,S as usual. p is called the wep of S and q in Th, if $Th \models \{r\}S\{q\}$ and $Th \models r \supset p$ are equivalent for every $r \in L$; q is called the sep of p and S in Th, if $Th \models \{p\}S\{r\}$ and $Th \models q \supset r$ are equivalent for every $r \in L$. Th is called *precondition complete* if for every $S \in WH(L)$ and every $q \in L$ the wep exists in L; it is called *postcondition complete* if for every $p \in L$ and every $S \in WH(L)$ the sep exists in L.

□

Like for expressiveness both definitions turn out to be equivalent:

Theorem 2:

A theory Th is precondition complete iff it is postcondition complete.

Sketch of the proof:
It must be described how to construct sep's from wep's and vice versa. The construction is the same as for sp's and wp's and runs as follows: Let $p,q \in L$, $S \in WH(L)$, $\bar{x}$ the list of all variables occuring free in p,q and S and $\bar{y}$ a list of new variables. Then $(\exists\bar{x}.(p\wedge\neg r))\frac{\bar{x}}{\bar{y}}$ is the sep of p and S in Th, if r is the wep of S and $\neg\bar{x}=\bar{y}$ in Th; and $(\forall\bar{x}.(r\supset q))\frac{\bar{x}}{\bar{y}}$ is the wep of S and q in Th, if r is the sep of $\bar{x}=\bar{y}$ and S in Th. But the proof is more difficult here than for wp's and sp's. It can not be carried out by a simple "calculation with states" but is based on the following lemma:

Lemma:

With the same notations as above the following statements are equivalent for every interpretation I of L:

(i) $\models_I \{p\}\,S\,\{q\}$

(ii) $\models_I \{\bar{x}=\bar{y}\}\,\underline{S}\,\{p\frac{\bar{y}}{\bar{x}} \supset q\}$

(iii) $\models_I \{p\wedge\neg q\frac{\bar{y}}{\bar{x}}\}\,S\,\{\neg\bar{x}=\bar{y}\}$ □

Let r now be the wep of S and $\neg\bar{x}=\bar{y}$ and let s be the formula $(\exists\bar{x}.(p\wedge\neg r))\frac{\bar{x}}{\bar{y}}$. Then $\models (p\wedge\neg s\frac{\bar{y}}{\bar{x}})\supset r$ can be proved, hence - by the equivalence of (i) and (iii) - s is a postcondition of p and S. On the other hand Th $\models s\supset q$ can be proved for every postcondition q by using the equivalence of (i) and (iii) for q. This means that s is indeed the sep. The proof for the wep can be done similarly with the equivalence of (i) and (ii). □

Theorem 2 is not important for this paper, because here only precondition completeness is needed. But in general it is interesting, as for more complex programming languages which include procedures postcondition completeness seems to be the adequate tool.

5. The new results

The following results refer to the usual Hoare calculus for while programs consisting of the assignment axiom, the rules of composition, conditional statement and while statement and the consequence rule. "$\vdash$" denotes derivability in this calculus. The soundness theorem can then be stated in a very general form:

If W is a subset of L then $W \vdash \{p\}S\{q\}$ implies $W \models \{p\}S\{q\}$ for every $\{p\}S\{q\} \in HF(L)$; i.e. every Hoare formula which is derivable from W, is also a valid consequence of W.

Consider now Cook's completeness result:
If L is I-expressive, then $\models_I \{p\}S\{q\}$ implies $Th(I) \vdash \{p\}S\{q\}$; i.e. every Hoare formula which is I-valid can be derived from Th(I).

In contrast to the soundness theorem it is very restrictive, and - as was already discussed in the introduction - it involves a non first order concept. With our new concepts a completeness theorem without these deficiencies can be obtained:

Theorem 3:

Let L be a first order predicate language and $Th \subseteq L$ a theory which is precondition complete. Then $Th \models \{p\}S\{q\}$ implies $Th \vdash \{p\}S\{q\}$ for every $\{p\}S\{q\} \in HF(L)$; i.e. every Hoare formula which is a valid consequence of Th, is also derivable from Th.

Sketch of the proof:
The key of the proof is the following lemma, which guarantees the existence of intermediate assertions:

Lemma:

Let $p,q \in L$ and $S_1, S_2 \in WH(L)$.
If $Th \models \{p\}S_1;S_2\{q\}$ and r is the wep of S_2 and q in Th, then $Th \models \{p\}S_1\{r\}$.

Proof of the lemma:
By the results of section 3 it is sufficient to prove $Th \models s \supset r$ for every $s \in SP(p,S_1)$. As r is the wep of S_2 and q in Th, this is equivalent to $Th \models \{s\}S_2\{q\}$ which can be proved by a simple calculation with states. □

Note that the essential difference of the old and the new approach lies in the proof of this lemma. If expressiveness is assumed, r can be chosen to be the wp of S_2 and q and the lemma can be proved "directly". But if only precondition completeness is assumed, then only the wep of S_2 and q is available and this makes it necessary to apply the above trick with the strongest postconditions of all paths.

The rest of the proof of Theorem 3 now runs as usual. The wep of while e do S od is proved to be an invariant of the loop by writing the while statement in the form

if e then S; while e do S od else x:=x fi

and applying the lemma again. The existence of intermediate assertions and loop invariants together guarantees the completeness of the Hoare calculus. □

Of course the question arises now, which theories are precondition complete. We give some examples and counter examples without proofs.

a) The theory of Peano arithmetic is precondition complete, because it is the theory of an expressive language.
b) The theory of Presburger arithmetic can not be precondition complete, because it is decidable and its Hoare logic is not recursively enumerable, and this contradicts the existence of any sound and complete Hoare calculus.
c) Every theory which has only finite interpretations is precondition complete. The main argument is that - by the compactness theorem - such a theory cannot possess interpretations of arbitrary size.
d) If L contains at least one constant symbol and one unary function symbol (to stand for zero and the successor function), then the theory of pure predicate logic, i.e. the set of all valid formulas of L, is not precondition complete. The idea of the proof is that arithmetical programs can be "simulated" in such a language.

It is an interesting open question, whether precondition complete theories can be characterized in a similar way as expressive interpretations by a lemma of Lipton's theorem (cf. [CGH]). Perhaps it is also worth while to reflect upon Lipton's theorem itself again with the aid of the new concepts.

Finally the question arises if the ideas of this paper can be transferred to other Hoare calculi which are known to be complete in the sense of Cook. At a first glance this seems to be impossible, because we have made use of the translation of while programs into flowchart programs and such a translation does not exist in the case of more complex programming languages. But note that this translation was only used to "approximate" every while program by a set of paths, i.e. of loopfree programs, and such an approximation is also possible for other programming languages.

References:

[BT] Bergstra, J.A. and Tucker, J.V.: Expressiveness and the completeness of Hoare's logic, Internal Report IW 149, Mathematisch Centrum Amsterdam (1980).

[CGH] Clarke, E.M., German, S.M. and Halpern, J.Y.: On effective axiomatizations of Hoare logics, 9th ACM Symp. on Principles of Programming Languages, 309 - 321 (1982).

[Cook] Cook, S.A.: Soundness and completeness of an axiomatic system for program verification, SIAM Journal of Computing 7, 1, 70 - 90 (1978).

[Man] Manna, Z.: Mathematical theory of computation, Mc Graw-Hill 1974.

[Wand] Wand, M.: A new incompleteness result for Hoare's system, JACM 25, 168 - 175 (1978).

A Hierarchy of Sets of Infinite Trees

Wolfgang Thomas

Lehrstuhl für Informatik II, Büchel 29/31, D-5100 Aachen

Abstract. A hierarchy of sets of infinite (valued) trees is introduced which has no counterpart in the theory of sets of infinite strings ("ω-languages"). As a consequence we obtain that for sets of infinite trees an analogue of McNaughton's fundamental theorem on ω-languages does not hold.

§1. Introduction. The subject of this paper are regular sets of infinite strings and corresponding sets of infinite trees. Recall that an ω-language is regular iff it is recognized by a Büchi automaton (cf. [5]). Two different generalizations of these automata, both introduced by Rabin [6],[7], have been developed for recognizing sets of infinite trees. The results of the present paper show that the basic characterization of regular ω-languages, due to McNaughton [3], cannot be extended to the tree languages recognized by either kind of Rabin's tree automata. (For definitions of automata see § 5.)

Mc Naughton's theorem characterizes the regular ω-languages by "limits of regular word-sets": For $W \subset A^*$, where A is a finite alphabet, let

$$\lim W = \{\alpha \in A^{\omega} \mid \text{there is a strictly increasing sequence of initial segments of } \alpha \text{ which are all in } W\}.$$

Let $\mathcal{S}(A)$ be the class of all ω-languages $\Gamma \subset A^{\omega}$ which are boolean combinations of sets lim W with $W \subset A^*$ regular. The theorem of McNaughton says that an ω-language is regular iff it belongs to $\mathcal{S}(A)$. (The original formulation stated the equivalence between the nondeterministic Büchi- and the deterministic Muller-automata.) A similar theorem for "star-free" ω-languages was proved in [10]. The paper [4] by Nivat/Perrin contains an extension to sets of strings which are infinite both to right and left.

Let us consider tree languages. In the sequel a tree over A is a map $t:\mathrm{dom}(t)\to A$ where dom(t) is a subset of $\{l,r\}^*$ closed under initial segments. (The restriction to trees with binary branching is inessential for the results of this paper and adopted only for notational convenience. For the same reason we work with valued trees rather than with trees as represented by finite of infinite terms.) Let $T_{fin}(A)$ be the set of trees t over A with dom(t) finite, and $T_{inf}(A)$ the set of trees t over A with $\mathrm{dom}(t) = \{l,r\}^*$. Concerning infinite trees with domain $\subsetneq \{l,r\}^*$ see § 4.

To introduce an analogue of $\mathcal{S}(A)$ for tree languages we refer to the regular tree languages $T \subset T_{fin}(A)$ as defined in [9]. For $T \subset T_{fin}(A)$ let

$$\lim T = \{t \in T_{inf}(A) \mid \text{there is a sequence } t_o, t_1, \ldots \text{ of finite subtrees of } t \text{ (all with the same root as } t) \text{ such that } \bigcup_{i \geq o} \mathrm{dom}(t_i) = \{l,r\}^* \text{ and each } t_i \in T\}.$$

Denote by $\mathcal{T}(A)$ the class of tree languages which are boolean combinations of sets lim T with regular $T \subset T_{fin}(A)$. In § 2 we define an infinite hierarchy of classes of tree languages $T \subset T_{inf}(A)$ such that (1) $\mathcal{T}(A)$ is located at a low level of this hierarchy and (2) the union of the hierarchy is strictly included in the class of those T recognized by Rabin's tree automata. The corresponding hierarchy for ω-languages becomes stationary at the level of $\mathcal{S}(A)$ where it reaches the class of regular ω-languages.

The definition of the hierarchy requires a finer analysis of definability of tree languages. An appropriate formalism for this purpose is monadic second-order logic.

§2. Definability in monadic second-order logic

(a) $L_{w2}(A)$ and $L_2(A)$ Let $A = \{a_1, \ldots, a_k\}$. With any $t \in T_{inf}(A)$ we associate the structure $(\{l,r\}^*, +l, +r, \leq, P_1, \ldots, P_k)$ where +l,+r are the two successor functions on $\{l,r\}^*$, $\leq$ the initial segment relation on $\{l,r\}^*$, and $P_1, \ldots, P_k \subset \{l,r\}^*$ defined by: $w \in P_j$ iff $t(w) = a_j$. We denote by t also this structure coding t. We introduce (logical) languages in which such structures can be described: the weak monadic second-order language $L_{w2}(A)$, and the monadic second-order language $L_2(A)$. In both cases the formulas are the same, built up using the following symbols: function symbols +l, +r, a binary relation symbol

$\leq$, unary predicate symbols $P_1,\ldots,P_k$, connectives $\neg,\wedge,\vee,\rightarrow,\leftrightarrow$, quantifiers $\exists,\forall$, variables $x,y,z,\ldots$ (ranging over elements of $\{1,r\}^*$) and variables $X,Y,Z,\ldots$ (ranging over subsets of $\{1,r\}^*$). The interpretation of formulas differs in $L_{w2}(A)$ and $L_2(A)$; in $L_{w2}(A)$ the set variables range only over the finite subsets of $\{1,r\}^*$, in $L_2(A)$ over arbitrary subsets of $\{1,r\}^*$. Using this convention it is clear how to define the satisfaction relation "$t \models \varphi$" for $t \in T_{inf}(A)$ and a sentence φ in either of the systems $L_{w2}(A)$, $L_2(A)$. For example, taking t_o as in the figure, we have $t_o \models \forall x(P_1x \rightarrow P_2x{+}1 \wedge P_2x{+}r)$ and, in $L_2(A)$, $t_o \models \exists X\ \forall x(Xx \leftrightarrow P_1x)$, while in $L_{w2}(A)$ the tree t_o does not satisfy the latter sentence. Call $T \subset T_{inf}(A)$ <u>$L_{w2}(A)$-definable</u> (resp. <u>$L_2(A)$-definable</u>) if there is a $L_{2w}(A)$ - (resp. $L_2(A)$-) sentence φ such that for all $t \in T_{inf}(A)$ we have $t \in T$ iff $t \models \varphi$.

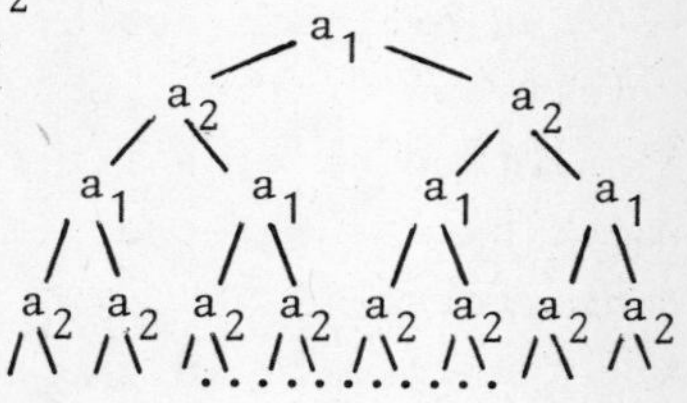

Tree t_o

Rabin showed that $T \subset T_{inf}(A)$ is $L_2(A)$-definable iff T is recognized by a tree automaton as introduced in [6]. Also he proved that $T \subset T_{inf}(A)$ is $L_{w2}(A)$-definable iff both T and $T_{inf}(A) - T$ are recognized by "special automata" [7]. Finally he showed that none of the implications "$L_{w2}(A)$- definable $\Rightarrow$ recognizable by a special automaton $\Rightarrow$ $L_2(A)$-definable" is reversible in general. The hierarchy to be set up below exhausts the class of $L_{w2}(A)$-definable tree languages.

We add a remark on the analogous notions of definability for ω-languages. In order to adapt $L_{w2}(A)$- and $L_2(A)$-definability to this case one views any $\alpha \in A^\omega$ as a structure $(\mathbb{N},+1,\leq,P_1,\ldots,P_k)$ and then proceeds in the same way as above. Büchi [1] proved that $\Gamma \subset A^\omega$ is $L_2(A)$-definable iff Γ is a regular ω-language. However, in contrast to the tree case, $L_2(A)$-definability of ω-languages coincides with $L_{w2}(A)$-definability (cf. [10]).

(b) <u>Bounded formulas. Σ_n-definability</u> We shall classify L_{w2}-sentences by the complexity of their prefix, counting only the unbounded quantifiers.

Abbreviate $x \leq y \wedge y \leq x$ by $x = y$. We call a formula φ <u>term-reduced</u> if $+1$, $+r$ occur in φ only in subformulas of the form $x{+}1 = y$, $x{+}r = y$. Any formula is equivalent to a term-reduced one (rewrite e.g. $P_1x{+}r$ as $\exists y(x{+}r = y \wedge P_1y)$). For set-variables X,Y let $X \preccurlyeq Y$ stand for $\forall z(Xz \rightarrow \exists z'(z \leq z' \wedge Yz'))$. The notations $x \preccurlyeq Y$, $X \preccurlyeq y$, $x \preccurlyeq y$ are used accordingly. Call a $L_{w2}(A)$-formula $\varphi(x_1,\ldots,x_m,X_1,\ldots,X_n)$, with free variables as indicated, bounded if φ is term-reduced and in φ only quantifiers of the form $\exists z \preccurlyeq \cdot$, $\forall z \preccurlyeq \cdot$, $\exists Z \preccurlyeq \cdot$, $\forall Z \preccurlyeq \cdot$ occur where $\cdot$ is any of the x_i or X_i.

A bounded formula $\varphi(\bar{x},\bar{X})$ speaks only about elements which are $\preccurlyeq$-bounded by $\bar{x},\bar{X}$: For example, if $\varphi(X)$ is bounded, we have for any $t,t' \in T_{inf}(A)$ and any finite $D \subset \{l,r\}^*$ that $t \models \varphi[D]$ iff $t' \models \varphi[D]$ provided t and t' agree on $\{d \mid d \preccurlyeq D\}$.

Interpreted over strings or trees, the bounded formulas characterize the regular word-sets, resp. the regular sets of finite trees. We explain the tree case: For $t \in T_{inf}(A)$ and finite $D \subset \{l,r\}^*$ denote by $t\upharpoonright D$ the finite subtree of t with domain $\{d \mid d \preccurlyeq D\}$. Then, using [2], [9], one shows: $T \subset T_{fin}(A)$ is regular iff T is defined by a bounded $L_{w2}(A)$-formula $\varphi(Y)$ in the sense that for all $t \in T_{inf}(A)$ and all finite $D \subset \{l,r\}^*$ we have $t \models \varphi[D]$ iff $t\upharpoonright D \in T$.

An $L_{w2}(A)$-formula is called a Σ_n-formula if it has the form $\exists X_1 \forall X_2 \exists X_3 \ldots \overset{\exists}{\forall} X_n \psi$ with ψ bounded. It is easy to verify that any $L_{w2}(A)$-sentence is equivalent (over $T_{inf}(A)$) to a Σ_n-sentence for suitable n. Let us denote by tree-$\Sigma_n(A)$ (resp. string-$\Sigma_n(A)$) the class of all $T \subset T_{inf}(A)$ (resp. $\Gamma \subset A^{\omega}$) which are defined by some Σ_n-sentence. For a class C (of ω-languages or tree languages) let $\mathcal{B}(C)$ be the respective boolean closure.

Lemma (a) $\mathcal{B}(\text{string-}\Sigma_2(A)) = \mathcal{S}(A)$
(b) $\mathcal{B}(\text{tree-}\Sigma_2(A)) = \mathcal{T}(A)$.

We only sketch the inclusion $\supseteq$ needed for the applications of the present paper. It suffices to consider (b). Assume $T \in \mathcal{T}(A)$, w.l.o.g. $T = \lim S$ for a regular $S \in T_{fin}(A)$. Suppose S is defined by the bounded formula $\varphi(Y)$. Then one verifies that for $t \in T_{inf}(A)$

$$t \in T \quad \text{iff } t \models \forall X \exists Y (X \preccurlyeq Y \wedge \varphi(Y)),$$

hence T is defined by the negation of a Σ_2-sentence.

While $\mathcal{B}(\text{string-}\Sigma_2(A))$ exhausts already the class of all regular ω-languages (cf. the remark on $\mathcal{S}(A)$ in § 1) and hence string-$\Sigma_n(A)$ = string-$\Sigma_{n+1}(A)$ for $n > 2$, we have for trees the following

Hierarchy Theorem. For $n \geq 0$: tree-$\Sigma_n(A) \subsetneq$ tree-$\Sigma_{n+1}(A)$.

The proof is given in § 3. Clearly by the above lemma the theorem implies that $\mathcal{T}(A)$ is strictly included in the class of all $L_{w2}(A)$-definable tree languages (= union of all tree-$\Sigma_n(A)$) and hence also in the classes of tree languages recognized by Rabin's tree automata in either version.

§3. Recursive trees and their theory

The proof of the above hierarchy theorem applies some basic recursion theory (in particular, the arithmetical hierarchy). We use recursion-theoretic notions informally (without explicitly mentioning codings), e.g. when speaking of a recursive tree or a recursive set of sentences. As usual $\emptyset^n$ is the n-th jump of $\emptyset$ (cf. [8]). For fixed $t \in T_{inf}(A)$, the set of Σ_n-sentences φ with $t \models \varphi$ is called the Σ_n-theory of t.

Lemma A. The Σ_n-theory of a recursive tree is recursive in $\emptyset^n$.

Proof. Suppose t is a recursive tree. For any $L_{w2}(A)$-formula $\varphi(X_1,\ldots,X_n)$ consider the relation $R_{t,\varphi}$ between finite subsets of $\{1,r\}^*$:

$$(D_1,\ldots,D_n) \in R_{t,\varphi} \quad \text{iff} \quad t \models \varphi[D_1,\ldots,D_n].$$

Clearly if φ is bounded, then $R_{t,\varphi}$ is recursive (via a Gödel numbering of the finite subsets of $\{1,r\}^*$). The claim follows immediately.

Lemma B. For every n there is a recursive tree t_n (over $A = \{0,1\}$) such that $\emptyset^n$ is recursive in the Σ_n-theory of t_n.

Proof. $\emptyset^n$ may be written as

$$\emptyset^n = \{k \in \mathbb{N} \mid \exists k_1 \forall k_2 \exists k_3 \ldots \overset{\exists}{\forall} k_n (k_1,\ldots,k_n,k) \in R_n\}$$

for a certain (n+1)-ary recursive relation R_n over $\mathbb{N}$. The desired tree t_n over $\{0,1\}$ is defined to have the value 1 at all $w \in \{1,r\}^*$ from a set $B_n \cup C_n$, otherwise 0. Here B_n is given by the regular expression $1^*r \cup (1^*r)^2 \cup \ldots \cup (1^*r)^n$, and

$$C_n = \{1^{k_1} r 1^{k_2} r \ldots 1^{k_n} r\, 1^{k+1} \mid (k_1,\ldots,k_n,k) \in R_n\}.$$

Obviously t_n is recursive. A picture explains the situation for n = 2, $(2,3,1) \in R_2$:

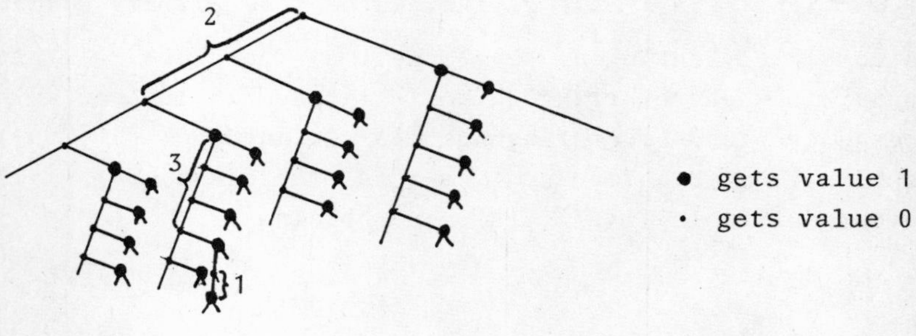

We now present for given k a Σ_n-sentence $\varphi_{n,k}$ (even a first-order one) such that $k \in \emptyset^n$ iff $t_n \models \varphi_{n,k}$, thus proving the lemma. We use the predicate letter P_1 for the elements carrying the value 1. Define

$$y \multimap x :\leftrightarrow x < y \wedge P_1 y \wedge \forall z\,(x < z \wedge z < y \rightarrow \neg P_1 z).$$

Then $\varphi_{n,k}$ says, in concise notation (λ is the empty word):

$$\exists x_1 \multimap \lambda\ \forall x_2 \multimap x_1\ \exists x_3 \multimap x_2 \ldots \overset{\exists}{\forall} x_n \multimap x_{n-1}\ P_1 x_n{+}1^{k+1}.$$

By construction of t_n we have $k \in \emptyset^n$ iff $t_n \models \varphi_{n,k}$. Clearly $\varphi_{n,k}$ may be written as a Σ_n-sentence.

Proof of Hierarchy Theorem. Trivially tree-Σ_n(A) $\subseteq$ tree-Σ_{n+1}(A). For contradiction assume tree-Σ_n(A) = tree-Σ_{n+1}(A). Then for any Σ_{n+1}-sentence φ there is a Σ_n-sentence ψ with ($t \models \varphi$ iff $t \models \psi$) for all $t \in T_{inf}(A)$. Moreover, such a ψ can be found effectively from φ: Enumerate all Σ_n-sentences (say in order $\psi_o, \psi_1, \ldots$); replace, for $i = 0,1,\ldots$, the symbols P_j by variables X_j in ψ_i and also in φ, and check whether

$$(\{1,r\}^*, +1, +r, \leq) \models \forall X_1 \ldots \forall X_k (\varphi(X_1,\ldots,X_k) \leftrightarrow \psi_i(X_1,\ldots,X_k)) ,$$

using decidability of the monadic theory of the binary tree [6]. It follows that for any fixed tree t, the Σ_{n+1}-theory of t is recursive in the Σ_n-theory of t. Applying this fact to t_{n+1}, together with Lemma B (also for t_{n+1}) and with Lemma A, we obtain that $\emptyset^{n+1}$ is recursive in $\emptyset^n$, a contradiction.

§4. Concluding Remarks

By a variation of the arguments in §2,3 one obtains also the following results:

(1) For any $n \geq o$, $\varphi_{n+1,o}$ is an example of a sentence defining a tree language $T_{n+1} \in$ (tree-Σ_{n+1})-(tree-Σ_n).

(2) Even in the deterministic version, Rabin's automata from [6] recognize tree-languages over A which are not in T(A). (For a reduction as in §3 use $\emptyset^3$ instead of an arbitrary $\emptyset^n$.)

(3) A completely analogous development of the above results is possible when referring to a first-order instead of a weak monadic second-order language. For ω-languages this is carried out in [10]. Denoting by tree-Σ_n^1(A) the class of Σ_n-first-order definable $T \subset T_{inf}(A)$, one obtains

$$\text{tree-}\Sigma_n^1(A) \subsetneq \text{tree-}\Sigma_{n+1}^1(A),$$

$$\text{tree-}\Sigma_n^1(A) \subsetneq \text{tree-}\Sigma_n(A),$$

$$\bigcup_{n\geq o} \text{tree-}\Sigma_n^1(A) \subsetneq \bigcup_{n\geq o} \text{tree-}\Sigma_n(A).$$

Note that for $L_2(A)$ the situation is different: By [1],[6] any $L_2(A)$-sentence can be reduced over $T_{inf}(A)$ to one with Σ_2-second-order prefix, over A^ω even to one with a Σ_1-second-order prefix ("Automata normal form").

(4) Concerning infinite trees with $dom(t) \subsetneq \{1,r\}^*$: The Hierarchy Theorem fails if, for instance, one considers only trees having a uniformly bounded finite number of infinite paths.

Finally we mention some problems suggested by this paper:

(1) Investigate further the structure of the (tree-$\Sigma_n(A)$)-hierarchy (e.g.,compare $\mathcal{B}(\text{tree-}\Sigma_n(A))$ with tree-$\Sigma_{n+1}(A) \cap$ tree-$\Pi_{n+1}(A)$).

(2) Characterize the hierarchy in other formalisms (automata, regular expressions,...).

(3) Decide whether membership in tree-$\Sigma_n(A)$ is decidable.

§5. Appendix: Definitions of automata

A <u>Büchi automaton</u> over A has the form $\mathcal{A} = (A,Q,q_o,\delta,F)$ where Q is a finite set of states, $q_o \in Q$ the initial state, $\delta\colon Q \times A \to 2^Q$, and $F \subset Q$. A <u>run</u> of $\mathcal{A}$ on $\alpha \in A^\omega$ is a state-sequence $s_o, s_1, \ldots$ with $s_o = q_o$, $s_{i+1} \in \delta(s_i, \alpha(i))$. $\mathcal{A}$ recognizes α if there is a run of $\mathcal{A}$ on α such that infinitely often in this run a state from F occurs.

A tree automaton in the sense of [6] (which one might call <u>Rabin automaton</u>) has the form $\mathcal{A} = (A,Q,q_o,\delta,\mathcal{F})$ where Q,q_o are as before, $\delta\colon Q \times A \to 2^{Q \times Q}$, and $\mathcal{F} \subset 2^Q$. A run of such an automaton on a tree $t \in T_{inf}(A)$ is a tree $\rho \in T_{inf}(Q)$ with $\rho(\lambda) = q_o$, $(\rho(w+1), \rho(w+r)) \in \delta(\rho(w), t(w))$ for $w \in \{1,r\}^*$. $\mathcal{A}$ accepts t if for some run of $\mathcal{A}$ on t the following holds: For each path of this run the set of states occurring infinitely often on the path belongs to $\mathcal{F}$.

A <u>special automaton</u> in the sense of [7] is defined as a Rabin automaton, with a set $F \subset Q$ replacing $\mathcal{F}$. A special automaton $\mathcal{A}$ accepts a tree t if for some run of $\mathcal{A}$ on t we have: On each path of this run a state from F occurs infinitely often.

References

[1] J.R. Büchi, On a decision method in restricted second-order arithmetic, Proc. Int. Congr. Logic, Method., Philos. Sci. 1960, Stanford Univ. Press 1962, pp. 1-11.

[2] J. Doner, Tree acceptors and some of their applications, JCSS 4 (1970), 406-451.

[3] R. McNaughton, Testing and generating infinite sequences by a finite automaton, Inf. Contr. 9 (1966), 521-530.

[4] M. Nivat, D. Perrin, Ensembles reconnaissables de mots bi-infinis, Proc. Ann. ACM Symp. on the Theory of Comp. 1982, 47-59.

[5] M.O. Rabin, Automata on infinite objects and Church's problem, Regional Conf. Ser. in Math. No. 13, Amer. Math. Soc. 1972.

[6] M.O. Rabin, Decidability of second-order theories and automata on infinite trees, Trans. Amer. Math. Soc. 141 (1969), 1-35.

[7] M.O. Rabin, Weakly definable relations and special automata, Math. Logic and Found. of Set Theory (Ed. Bar-Hillel), North-Holland, Amsterdam 1970, pp. 1-23.

[8] H. Rogers, Theory of recursive functions and effective computability, Mc Graw Hill, New York 1967.

[9] J.W. Thatcher, J.B. Wright, Generalized finite automata theory with an application to a decision problem of second-order logic, Math. Systems Theory 2 (1968), 57-81.

[10] W. Thomas, A combinatorial approach to the theory of ω-automata, Inf. Contr. 48 (1981), 261-283.

MAINTAINING ORDER IN A GENERALIZED LINKED LIST

Athanasios K. Tsakalidis

Fachbereich 1o, Universität des Saarlandes
D-66oo Saarbrücken, West Germany

Abstract: We give a representation for linked lists which allows to efficiently insert and delete objects in the list and to quickly determine the order of two list elements. The basic data structure, called an indexed BB[α]-tree, allows to do n insertions and deletions in O(n log n) steps and determine the order in constant time, assuming that the locations of the elements worked at are given. The improved algorithm does n insertions, deletions and comparisons in O(n log* n) steps.

1. Introduction:

We study the problem of performing a sequence of the following operations on a list L:

1. Insert(x,y): insert x immediately after y in the list L.
2. Delete(x): delete x from the list L.
3. Compare(x,y): return true iff x occurs before y in L.

These operations must be done on line; that is, each compare instruction must return a value before any further instructions are given.

We assume that the locations of the elements x,y are given. P. Dietz in [2] explores this problem and gives a data structure, called an indexed 2-3 tree which can perform n insertions in O(n log n) total running time and an individual comparison in O(1) time.

Keeping the comparison in O(1) time Dietz notes the following open problems:

1. A generalization of his algorithm which allows n insertions and deletions of arbitrary elements in O(n log n) total running time.
2. A modification of the algorithm which allows an individual insertion to be performed in O(log |L|) steps.

Dietz's data structure does not support insertions and deletions. In fact, a sequence of n insertions and deletions may have cost $\Theta(n^2)$.

We call a linked list generalized, if it can support efficiently insertions, deletions and comparisons.

A very simple algorithm would be to use the usual representation for linked lists. An insertion or deletion would take constant time, but comparisons could take up $O(|L|)$ time. If the list items are stored as leaves in a balanced tree scheme, the list items occuring in correct order at the leaves of the tree, insertions and deletions take $O(\log |L|)$ time. Comparisons would involve tracing back up through the tree until a common node is reached; this would also take $O(\log |L|)$ steps.

Using the weak B-tree as main structure in the last algorithm as it was defined and explored from S. Huddleston and K. Mehlhorn in [3], we can have $O(n)$ total running time for n arbitrary insertions and deletions and comparisons take $O(\log |L|)$ steps.

In this paper we give a solution for the first problem based on $BB[\alpha]$-trees, because these trees according to the results of N. Blum and K. Mehlhorn in [1] show a common behavior for both arbitrary insertions and deletions. To each item of the list we assign proper numbers which indicate the order of the items in the list: if a occurs before b in L then a's number is less than b's. Then we can do comparisons in constant time. For insertions and deletions we must renumber the respective leaves.

The main idea is that after renumbering we assign to adjacent elements such numbers that they can absorb enough operations without causing any renumbering of their adjacent elements.

Section 2 describes indexed $BB[\alpha]$-trees in detail and gives some results from [1] on these trees. In section 3 we give the algorithm and we analyse its total running time for a sequence of n arbitrary insertions and deletions. In section 4 we give some modifications to the basic data structure similar to those given in [2] for the improved algorithm. In section 5 we give an application of the algorithm to the area of CAD systems for VLSI design.

2. The main data structure

As main data structure we use a BB[α]-tree. These trees were defined by J. Nievergelt and E. Reingold [6]. The Theorems 1 and 2 and some definitions of this section are taken from [1].

Definition 1: Let T be a binary tree. If T is a single leaf, then the root-balance $\rho(T)$ is 1/2, otherwise we define $\rho(T) = |T_\ell|/|T|$, where $|T_\ell|$ is the number of leaves in the left subtree of T and $|T|$ is the number of leaves in tree T.

Definition 2: A binary tree T is said to be of bounded balance α, or in the set BB[α], for $0 \le \alpha \le 1/2$, if and only if:

1) $\alpha \le \rho(T) \le 1-\alpha$;
2) T is a single leaf or both subtrees are of bounded balance.

Theorem 1: For all $\alpha \in (1/4, 1-\sqrt{2}/2]$ there are constants $d \in [\alpha, 1-\alpha]$ and $\delta \ge 0$ (if $\alpha < 1-\sqrt{2}/2$ then $\delta > 0$) such that for T a binary tree with subtrees T_ℓ and T_r and

(1) T_ℓ and T_r in BB[α]
(2) $|T_\ell|/|T| < \alpha$ and either
   (2.1) $|T_\ell|/(|T|-1) \ge \alpha$ (i.e. an insertion into the right subtree of T occured) or
   (2.2) $(|T_\ell|+1)/(|T|+1) \ge \alpha$ (i.e. a deletion from the left subtree of T occured).
(3) ρ_2 is the root balance of T_r

we have
   (i) if $\rho_2 \le d$ then a rotation rebalances the tree,
   (ii) if $\rho_2 > d$ then a double rotation rebalances the tree.

In the next Theorem we use notations as they are given in [1] on page 316.

Theorem 2: Let $0 \le \delta \le 0.01$, $\alpha \in (1/4, 4, 1-\sqrt{2}/2]$ and let v be a node. If

(1) v causes a rebalancing operation in T_m (after the transaction was applied to T_m) and

(2) either v took part in a rebalancing operation before or v was not a node of the initial tree T_o and never took part in a rebalancing operation before and

(3) μ is the number of leaves in the subtree with root v in T_m, then at least $\lceil \delta\alpha\mu \rceil$ transactions went through v since v took part in a rebalancing operation for the last time or v was created.

For the height h(T) of T we know from [5, p. 99] that:

$$h(T) \le 1 + 1/_{\log(1/(1-\alpha))}(\log |T|-1).$$

We give some definitions on a given binary tree T.

Definition 3:

1) symord(x) denotes the number assigned to x by the symmetric traversal of T (traverse the left tree, then the root and at last the right subtree).

2) A function p: nodes $\cup$ leaves $\to \mathbb{N}_o$ labels T iff for all leaves x,y and any node v with symord(x) < symord(v) < symord(y) the following holds: $p(x) \le p(v) < p(y)$.

3) d(v) denotes the depth of a node v, where d(root(T)) = 0, T_x is the subtree with the node x as root, and w(x) the weight of x defined as $w(x) = |T_x|$. I(x) denotes the interval determined by the indices of the leaves of T_x having upper bound U_x and lower bound L_x.

Definition 4: We define c as $c = 1/\log(1/1-\alpha))$ and $e > 2(1-\alpha) + 1$. Then $h(T) \le c \log |T| + 1 - c$ and setting $\alpha \approx 1 - \sqrt{2}/2 = 0.2928$ we get $c = 2$.

Proposition 1: The function p: nodes $\cup$ leaves $\to \mathbb{N}_o$ defined as follows:

$$p(x) = \begin{cases} p(v) & \text{if x is the left son of v} \\ p(v) + \lfloor e2^{c \log |T| - d(v)} \rfloor, & \text{if x is the right son of v.} \end{cases}$$

and p(root(T)) = 0, makes T an indexed BB[α]-tree.

Proof: We explore adjacent intervalls and we show that they don't overlap. Let x,y,v,w be nodes as in figure 1.

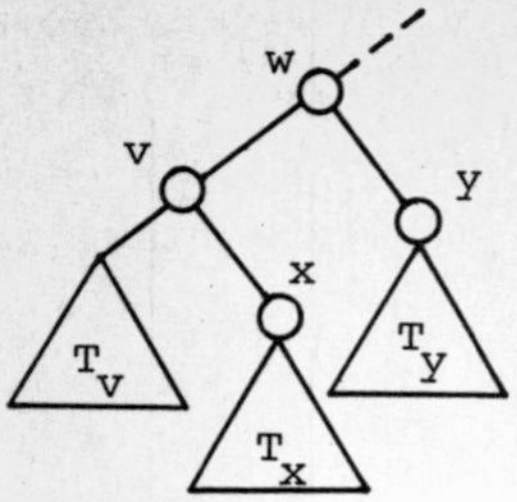

figure 1

Let $t = d(w)$, then we have

$L_y = p(w) + \lfloor e2^{c \log |T|-t} \rfloor$

Since $d(v) = t + 1$ and $p(v) = p(w)$ we have:

$p(x) = p(w) + \lfloor e2^{c \log |T|-t-1} \rfloor$

Let h_x be the height of T_x, then $h_x \leq h(T)-t-1$ and we have:

$$U_x \leq p(w) + \sum_{i=o}^{h_x} \lfloor e2^{c \log |T|-t-1-i} \rfloor \leq p(w) + \lfloor \sum_{i=1}^{h_x+1} e2^{c \log |T|-t-i} \rfloor$$

$$\leq p(w) + \lfloor e2^{c \log |T|-t}(1-2^{-h_x-1}) \rfloor < p(w) + \lfloor e2^{c \log |T|-t} \rfloor = L_y,$$

since $e2^{c \log |T|-t} \cdot 2^{-h_x-1} > 1$.

The same holds for the symmetric situation of figure 1. Hence $I(x) \cap T(y) = \emptyset$. □

3. The algorithm and its complexity

We treat both insertion and deletion in a similar way. After inserting or deleting an item we trace the path backwards to the root, we change the balance of the nodes in this path, we carry out the necessary rotations or double rotations and at last we renumber the subtree whose root is the node rotated last.

Since the labeling function $p(x)$ depends on the number of leaves, we perform an operation RENUMBER(T) which renumbers the whole tree T with respect to $|T|$.

The operation RENUMBER(T) will be executed every time the current number of leaves becomes double or half as much as the number of leaves of T after the last execution of RENUMBER(T).

Now let us give the algorithm more formally and use a fixed value n_o as an indicator for the execution of renumbering the whole tree T.

```
proc Insert(x,y) [Delete(x)]
          Let T be the current tree, v_o,v_1,...,v_k the search path from
          the leaf worked at up to the root v_k of the tree T. Let b(v_i)
          be the balance of node v_i. After inserting [deleting] x in T
          we perform the following operations:
a ← v_1; p(a) ← p(v_1);
for i = 1 to k do
    change b(v_i);
    if b(v_i) ∉ [α,1-α] then [rotate or double rotate on v_i; ]
                             [   a ← v_i; p(a) ← p(v_i)      ] fi
od;
          Let |T_s| be the number of the leaves of T by the last execu-
          tion of RENUMBER(T). We initialize |T_s| by a fixed value n_o.
if  (|T| = 2|T_s|) v (|T| = |T_s|/2) then RENUMBER(T)
                                     else renumber(a,p(a),|T_s|) fi
end;

proc RENUMBER(T)
     renumber(root(T),O,|T|)
end;

proc renumber(v,i,k)
     p(v) ← i;
          Let s_ℓ,s_r be the left and right son of v.
     renumber(s_ℓ,i,k);
     renumber(s_r,i+⌊e2^(c log k-d(v))⌋, k)
end;

proc Compare(x,y)
     return (p(x) < p(y))
end;
```

Theorem 1 guarantees the correctness of insertions and deletions. On the correctness of comparisons we show the following Proposition.

Proposition 2: Let x,y be nodes of a BB[α]-tree T which does not stay in any ancestor relationship to each other, then during the execution of n arbitrary insertions and deletions by the above algorithm $I(x) \cap I(y) = \emptyset$.

Proof: We explore the adjacent intervals from nodes x,y as they are given in figure 1.

According to Proposition 1 we have $I(x) \cap I(y) = \emptyset$ after RENUMBER(T). Let $|T| = m$ at this moment.

We explore the possibility of the subtree T_x to label its elements until the next execution of RENUMBER(T), assuming that no rotation or double rotation on x or an ancestor of x occurs during that time. Note that any such rotation or double rotation would renumber all descendants of x. In particular, this implies that d(x) has not changed and hence T_x can never include more than $(1-\alpha)^{t+2}2m$ elements.

We have

$$|I(x)| \le p(y) - p(x) = \lfloor e2^{c\log m-t} \rfloor - \lfloor e2^{c\log m-t-1} \rfloor$$

Since $e2^{c\log m-t-1}-1 < \lfloor e2^{c\log m-t} \rfloor - \lfloor e2^{c\log m-t-1} \rfloor$ it suffices to show that:

(1) $(1-\alpha)^{t+2}2m \le e\frac{m^c}{2^{t+1}} - 1$ for $0 \le t \le h(T) - 2$

For h(T) before the next execution of RENUMBER(T) we have $h(T) \le c\log(2m) + 1 - c = c\log m + 1$.

Hence it suffices to show that:

(2) $(1-\alpha)^{c\log m-i}2m \le e\frac{m^c}{2^{c\log m-i-1}} - 1$, for all integers i with

$-1 \le i \le c\log m - 2$

We rewrite (2) as

(3) $\frac{2}{(1-\alpha)^i} \le e2^{i+1}-1$, because $(1-\alpha)^{c\log m} = \frac{1}{m}$.

Since $e > 2(1-\alpha)+1$ for $1/4 < \alpha < 1 - \sqrt{2}/2$ the inequality (3) is valid for $i \ge -1$.

By deletions we have no problems. Rotations or double rotations renumber the elements in the local enviroment. □

Next we analyse the complexity of the algorithm. We tacitly assume that operations on the indices can be done in unit time. This is reasonable because each index is less than $2e|L|^c$.

Proposition 3: The algorithm performs n operations (insertions and deletions) in O(n log n) steps. The order of two elements can be determined in O(1) time.

Proof: The total running time consists of:

A: the total time needed for the balance changes and the rotations or double rotations.
B: the total time needed for the execution of renumber(a,p(a),$|T_s|$).
C: the total time needed for the execution of RENUMBER(T).

Since every balance change, rotation or double rotation needs O(1) time units, we have for n operations: A = O(n log n).

Let v be a node with weight w(v).
An execution of renumber(v,p(v),$|T_s|$) costs O(w(v)) time units. According to Theorem 2 v can cause these cost again, if Ω(w(v)) operations are going through v. Thus we charge O(1) time units for each operation going through v. Since a path consists of O(log n) nodes, we have B = O(n log n).

RENUMBER(T) causes cost O(|T|) [O(|T|/2)] after at least |T| insertions [|T|/2 deletions]. Thus we charge O(1) renumbering cost to each operation. Hence we have C = O(n).

Thus the total running time by n operations (insertions and deletions) is O(n log n).

Comparisons are executed by comparing only the indices assigned to the elements and it needs O(1) time units. □

4. Improvements to the algorithm

We use the idea of P. Dietz to improve the total running time for n arbitrary insertions and deletions. The basic data structure will be divided into two levels. Each level is indexed. The lower level trees are the leaves of the upper level tree. If each lower level tree has weight about $f(|L|)$, where f is a sublinear function, then the upper level tree about $|L|/f(|L|)$ leaves. Insert, Delete and Compare are now two step operations. If after inserting (deleting) a new lower level tree is created (deleted), then a leaf will be inserted (deleted) into the upper level tree. An operation ORGANIZE(L) will determine the roots x_i of the lower level tree with $w(x_i) \le f(|L|)$. ORGANIZE(L) will be executed every time the number of the elements in the list L doubles or halves. In the time between two executions of ORGANIZE(L) a node x_i remains a root of a lower level tree if $w(x_i) \le f(|L_s|)$, where $|L_s|$ is the size of the list at the time of the last execution of ORGANIZE(L). To compare x and y, check if they are in the same lower level tree. If so, compare directly. If not, compare their trees in the upper level tree.

Since much time is spent on renumbering deep vertices, we can save time if we use independent renumberings on the upper and lower levels (also that implies that lower level trees have to be independently renumbered). That is possible if the nodes in the lower level tree are equipped with a direct pointer to their root-leaf in the tree one level upwards. Then it can be detected in unit time whether the two nodes belong to the same lower level tree. An insertion or deletion into the lower level tree takes $O(\log f(|L|))$ time, and every $\Omega(f(|L|)\, w(v))$ such operations cause cost $O(w(v))$ by renumbering at the node v in the upper level tree.

Thus for every insertion or deletion we charge $\frac{1}{f(|L|)} \cdot \log(\frac{|L|}{f(|L|)})$ cost in the upper level tree. Hence the total running time for doing n arbitrary insertions and deletions is $O(\frac{n}{f(n)} \log\frac{n}{f(n)} + n \log f(n))$ and each comparison takes constant time.

If we choose $f(n) = O(\log n)$ then the total running time is $O(n + n \log\log n)$. We can analogously divide this data structure into k levels and we get:

Proposition 4: There is an algorithm that does n arbitrary insertions and deletions in time $O(k \cdot n + n \log^{(k)} n)$ and comparisons in time $O(k)$.

If we let k be $\log^* n$ we get:

Proposition 5: There is an algorithm that does n insertions, deletions and comparisons in time $O(n \log^* n)$.

5. Applications

In addition to the applications mentioned in [2] we give an application of the problem to the area of CAD systems for VLSI design.

Th. Lengauer und K. Mehlhorn [4] described a VLSI design system which allows chip specification on a topological level (without specifying the distances between circuit components). The circuit is laid out on a grid which can change in size dynamically. Here the elements of the ordered set are the grid lines (in the x-resp. y-direction), and the order is given implicitly by the sequence in which they appear in the plane.

Inserting new layout components may require the insertion of new grid lines. If during the design process components are taken out of the circuit such that grid lines become empty, these grid lines are deleted.

References:

1 N. Blum and K. Mehlhorn "On the average number of rebalancing operations in weight-balanced trees", Theoretical Computer Science 11 (198o), p. 3o3-32o.

2 P. Dietz "Maintaining order in a linked list", 14th ACM SIGACT Symposium on Theory of Computing (1982), p. 122-127.

3 S. Huddleston and K. Mehlhorn "A new data structure for representing sorted lists", Acta Informatica 17 (1982), p. 157-184.

4 Th. Lengauer and K. Mehlhorn "HILL-Hierarchical Layout Language, A CAD-System for VLSI-Design", Technischer Bericht A 82/1o, Universität des Saarlandes (1982).

5 K. Mehlhorn "Effiziente Algorithmen", Teubner Verlag (1977).

6 J. Nievergelt and E.M. Reingold "Binary search trees of bounded balance", SIAM Journal of Computing, Vol. 2 (1973), p. 33-43.

PERIODIC VERSUS ARBITRARY TESSELLATIONS OF THE PLANE USING POLYOMINOS OF A SINGLE TYPE*

(extended abstract)

H.A.G. Wijshoff and J. van Leeuwen

Department of Computer Science, University of Utrecht
P.O. Box 80.002, 3508 TA Utrecht, the Netherlands

Abstract. Given N parallel memory modules, we like to distribute the elements of an (infinite) array in storage such that any set of N elements arranged according to a given data template T can be accessed rapidly in parallel. Array embeddings that allow for this are called skewing schemes and have been studied in connection with vector-processing and SIMD machines. In 1975 H.D. Shapiro proved that there exists a valid skewing scheme for a template T if and only if T tessellates the plane. We settle a conjecture of Shapiro and prove that for polyominos P a valid skewing scheme exists if and only if there exists a valid periodic skewing scheme. (Periodicity implies a rapid technique to locate data elements.) The proof shows that when a polyomino P tessellates the plane without rotations or reflections, then it can tessellate the plane periodically, i.e., with the instances of P arranged in a lattice. It is also proved that there is a polynomial time algorithm to decide whether a polyomino tessellates the plane, assuming the polyominos in the tessellation should all have an equal orientation.

1. Introduction.

The problem addressed in this paper has a deep motivation from the theory of data organisation for large computers such as vector-processing and SIMD-machines (see e.g. Thurber [8]). The characterising feature of these machines is the availability of a multitude of arithmetic units and memory modules that can operate independently in parallel. Clearly the effectiveness of these machines depends to large extent on

---

* A full version of this paper is available as [10].

being able to store the data elements in the available memories such that memory conflicts are avoided whenever data are fetched.

About 1970 Budnik and Kuck [1] pointed out that nontrivial problems arise if any set of N elements from a 2-dimensional array, arranged according to some common pattern or template, must be accessed in one cycle without conflict. A data template T consists of a fixed set of N locations relative to a designated base or "handle" (0,0). An instance of T is obtained by adding a fixed displacement to all locations of T. An assignment of array elements to memories is called a skewing scheme. A skewing scheme is valid for T if it provides for the conflict-free parallel access to the data in any instance of T.

In 1975 Shapiro (see [7]) added two significant results to this theory. First of all, he proved that there exists a valid skewing scheme for T in all finite cases (square arrays) if and only if there is one for the infinite array with domain $(-\infty{:}\infty;-\infty{:}\infty)$. Secondly, he proved that there is a valid skewing scheme for T if and only if T (as a combinatorial structure) tessellates the two-dimensional plane.

WARNING. When we speak of tessellations of the plane using a template of some sort (e.g. a polyomino) we shall require throughout this paper that the templates (polyominos) in a tessellation all have equal orientation, i.e., we do not consider rotations and reflections of the objects when discussing tessellations unless explicitly stated otherwise.

General skewing schemes are not necessarily of use in practice. There is no guarantee that a skewing scheme s is finitely encoded or indeed recursive. This led Shapiro ([7], sect. IV) to consider a number of constraints to force a skewing scheme to be finitely represented in computer memory. The weakest condition is periodicity which, for the purposes of this paper, is interpreted as the condition that the instances of T that tessellate the plane have their handle in the points of a (2-dimensional) lattice. Periodicity implies a simple method to store and retrieve data elements quickly. In this paper we settle an important conjecture of Shapiro [7] and prove that for templates that have the shape of a polyomino there exists a valid skewing scheme if and only if there exists a valid periodic skewing scheme. The proof relies on the geometric interpretation of the problem. We show that when a polyomino of size N tessellates the plane, then it can tessellate the plane periodically, i.e., with its instance arranged according to an effectively computable lattice. As a corollary we show that the existence of a valid skewing scheme for a polyomino of size N can be decided in polynomial time.

The paper is organised as follows. In section 2 we give some preliminary results. In section 3 we define tessellations and derive an operational notion of periodicity for tessellations. In section 4 we derive an important condition for the existence of a periodic tessellation. In section 5 a tedious counting argument involving Euler's formula for planar graphs is given showing that whenever a tessellation with a polyomino exists, then the nodes and numbers must exist required for the condition derived in section 4. In section 6 we prove the polynomial algorithm for the existence of a tessellation with a given polyomino and offer some final comments to identify the significance of the results within the theory of geometric packing and covering.

2. Definitions and preliminary results.

Definitions 2.1 to 2.3 are from Shapiro [7].

Definition 2.1. A data template is an N-tuple $T = \{(0,0),(a_1,b_1),\dots,(a_{N-1},b_{N-1})\}$ with no two components identical and whose first element is (0,0). For consistency we let $(a_0,b_0) \equiv (0,0)$.

Definition 2.2. An instance $T(x,y)$ of a data template T is the N-tuple obtained by the componentwise addition of the displacement (x,y) to T: $T(x,y) = \{(x,y),(a_1+x,b_1+y),\dots,(a_{N-1}+x,b_{N-1}+y)\}$.

Definition 2.3. A polyomino is a data template of which the cells form a rook-wise connected set with no "holes" (when embedded in the plane).

Rook-wise connectedness means that every two cells of the template can be connected by a chain of cells within the template, with every two consecutive cells of the chain sharing a full side.

From now on we fix a polyomino P of size N and introduce some notions pertaining to its set of instances $P(x,y)$.

Definition 2.4. The relative position π of cells (x_1,y_1) and (x_2,y_2) is the "bi-directional" vector $r = \pm\overrightarrow{(x_2-x_1,y_2-y_1)}$. The relative position of $P(x_1,y_1)$ and $P(x_2,y_2)$ is the relative position of (x_1,y_1) and (x_2,y_2).

Definition 2.5. $P(x_1,y_1)$ and $P(x_2,y_2)$ overlap if there exist components (a_i,b_i) and (a_j,b_j) of P such that $(a_i+x_1,b_i+y_1) = (a_j+x_2,b_j+y_2)$.

Lemma 2.6. $P(x_1,y_1)$ and $P(x_2,y_2)$ overlap if and only if P contains two components that are in the same relative position as $P(x_1,y_1)$ and $P(x_2,y_2)$.

Proof

Clearly $P(x_1,y_1)$ and $P(x_2,y_2)$ overlap if and only if $(a_i,b_i) = (a_j,b_j) + (x_2-x_1,y_2-y_1)$ or, equivalently, $(a_j,b_j) = (a_i,b_i) + (x_1-x_2,y_1-y_2)$. □

Let $P(x_0,y_0)$ be a fixed instance of P. With every polyomino $P(x,y)$ there is a second polyomino (its "buddy") that has the same relative position to $P(x_0,y_0)$, see figure 1.

Definition 2.7. The buddy of $P(x,y)$ with respect to $P(x_0,y_0)$ is the instance $\varphi_{x_0y_0}(P(x,y)) = P(2x_0-x,2y_0-y)$.

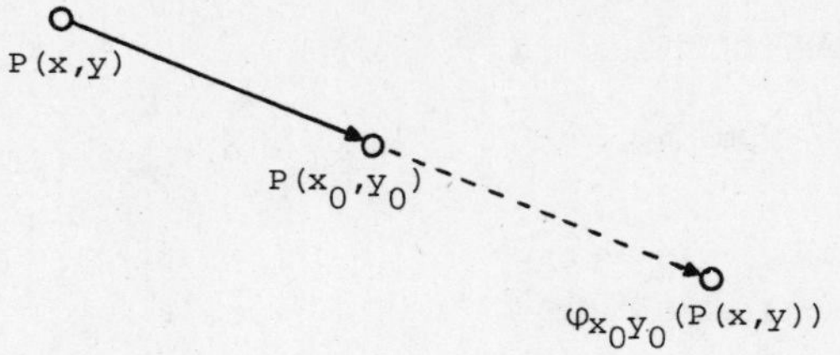

figure 1.

The mapping $\varphi_{x_0y_0}$ implicit in definition 2.7 will be important for "filling" the space surrounding $P(x_0,y_0)$.

Lemma 2.8. $\varphi_{x_0y_0}$ preserves relative positions.

By lemma 2.6 $\varphi_{x_0y_0}$ maps disjoint instances of P to disjoint images (buddies). The following result will be important.

Lemma 2.9. $\varphi_{x_0y_0}$ does not introduce overlap, i.e., if $P(x,y)$ and $P(x_0,y_0)$ are disjoint then $\varphi_{x_0y_0}(P(x,y))$ is disjoint from these two instances also.

(This lemma actually is a special case of some results of Levi [6].)

3. Tessellations.

Tessellations (or "tilings") are a familiar subject in mathematics. Definition 3.1 is from Shapiro [7] (although we have added the distinction between partial and total tessellations). It is important to note that we require the objects in a tessellation to have the same orientation. (In the literature one usually allows rotations and reflections as well.)

Definition 3.1. A partial tessellation (using P) is any collection of instances of P with the property that every cell of the plane is in at most one instance. A tessellation is said to be total if every cell of the plane is in exactly one instance of P in the collection.

If no adverb is added we assume a tessellation to be total. If there exists a total tessellation using P then we say that P "tessellates the plane".

Definition 3.2. A (total) tessellation is periodic if it is the collection of instances $P(x,y)$ with (x,y) ranging over the elements of a 2-dimensional lattice.

In the following we assume that polyominos are sets of cells on the two-dimensional grid. (Recall that polyominos have no holes.)

Definition 3.3. The boundary B of the (embedded) polyomino P is the set of grid-lines of unit length that bound the interior of P from the exterior. The size of B is denoted as $|B|$. The boundary $B(x,y)$ of $P(x,y)$ is B, shifted by $\overrightarrow{(x,y)}$.

We will number the grid-lines in B going around clockwise as $r_0, r_1, \ldots$, starting from a fixed reference element $r_0 \in B$. Shifted over $\overrightarrow{(x,y)}$ this numbering translates into a numbering $r_0(x,y), r_1(x,y), \ldots$ of $B(x,y)$. Note that numbers like $r_i(x,y)$ are merely names of grid-lines with respect to some $P(x,y)$.

Now suppose some tessellation τ is given. We say $P(x,y) \in \tau$ borders $P(x_0,y_0) \in \tau$ if $B(x,y) \cap B(x_0,y_0) \neq \emptyset$. It is clear that the boundary of $P(x_0,y_0)$ divides into consecutive segments $[r_{i_0}(x_0,y_0)..r_{i_1}(x_0,y_0)], [r_{i_2}(x_0,y_0)..r_{i_3}(x_0,y_0)], ..$ $(r_0 \leq r_{i_0} \leq r_{i_1} < r_{i_2} \leq r_{i_3} < \ldots)$ that are the borderline with instances $P(x,y)$. We assume that each segment is maximal for the particular $P(x,y)$.

Lemma 3.4. If τ is a total tessellation then each $P(x,y) \in \tau$ that borders $P(x_0,y_0) \in \tau$ generates exactly one, contiguous segment on the boundary of $P(x_0,y_0)$.

The proof shows that if two bordering polyominos would lead to two or more segments, then they would enclose a hole that can impossibly be covered by instances of P (as is required by the totality of τ). The same argument shows that even a hole enclosed by three instances P_i ($i=1..3$, with P_i bordering $P_{i(\mathrm{mod}3)+1}$) can never be covered.

Definition 3.5. A partial segmentation of $B(x_0,y_0)$ is any set of (maximal and disjoint) index segments $I_0, I_1, \ldots$ along $B(x_0,y_0)$ that are the borderline with some $P(x,y) \in \tau$. A segmentation is called total if $\bigcup_i I_i = B(x_0,y_0)$.

A segmentation of $B(x,y)$ will be denoted as $Seg(B(x,y))$. The number of segments in it will be denoted by $|Seg(B(x,y))|$. Its "length" is defined in an obvious manner.

We say that $P(x_1,y_1), \ldots, P(x_k,y_k)$ partially surround $P(x_0,y_0)$ if the polyominos (including $P(x_0,y_0)$) are all disjoint but each $P(x_i,y_i)$ $(i>0)$ borders $P(x_0,y_0)$). We say that $P(x_1,y_1) \ldots, P(x_k,y_k)$ completely surround $P(x_0,y_0)$ if, in addition, each grid-line of $B(x_0,y_0)$ is contained in some $B(x_i,y_i)$ (i>0). The size of a surrounding will be the number (k) of distinct polyominos in it. Clearly partial surroundings lead to partial segmentations and complete surroundings lead to total segmentations of $B(x_0,y_0)$. Of course lemma 3.4. applies to the elements of a complete surrounding of $P(x_0,y_0)$ just the same.

Definition 3.6. A tessellation τ is regular if the same segmentation is induced in every $B(x,y)$ with $P(x,y)\in\tau$, i.e., $Seg(P(x_1,y_1)) = Seg(P(x_2,y_2))$ for every $P(x_1,y_1)$ and $P(x_2,y_2)$ in the tessellation.

In a periodic tessellation the relative positions of the surrounding polyominos must be the same for every $P(x,y)\in\tau$. It easily follows that periodic tessellations must be regular. But the same is true of regular tessellations. Thus, "regularity" exactly characterizes periodic tessellations.

Lemma 3.7. There exists a regular tessellation using P if and only if there exist an instance $P(x_0,y_0)$ and a complete surrounding $P(x_1,y_1),\ldots,P(x_k,y_k)$ of it such that $Seg(P(x_i,y_i)) \subseteq Seg(P(x_0,y_0))$ (i>0).

4. Conditions for periodic tessellations.

Given a (partial or total) tessellation τ, let G_τ be the graph of boundaries of the instances $P(x,y)\in\tau$. The nodes of G_τ will be the (grid-)points where at least three boundaries meet. The length of an edge e will be the number of unit-length grid-lines it is composed of, denoted as $|e|$. Clearly G_τ is a planar graph with nodes of degree 3 or 4.

Definition 4.1. A three-node (four-node) is any grid-point g where three (four) non-overlapping instances of P meet. The branches of g are the three (four) edges that meet in g (taken in consecutive order).

We normally refer to the three- and four-nodes of some G_τ with τ total, but the definition applies to any local configuration of some $P(x_0,y_0)$ and a (partial or complete) surrounding. In the latter case we speak of three-nodes (four-nodes) admitted by P. An edge will simply extend to either a node or a grid-point where two boundaries part.

Lemma 4.2. Suppose P admits a three-node g with branches T_1, T_2 and T_3. Then there exists with every $P(x_0,y_0)$ a partial surrounding $P(x_1,y_1),\ldots,P(x_6,y_6)$ such that $P(x_i,y_i)$ also borders $P(x_{i+1},y_{i+1})$ for $1\leq i\leq 6$ (and $x_7\equiv y_1, x_7\equiv y_1$). The length of the partial segmentation induced is $2.|T_1|+2.|T_2|+2.|T_3|$.

Proof

Suppose P admits a three-node g as described. It means that for any $P(x_0,y_0) \approx P_0$ we can find two additional non-overlapping instances $P(x_1,y_1) \approx P_1$ and $P(x_2,y_2) \approx P_2$ that border it, with the three of them meeting in g. The typical situation is shown in figure 2. Note that each instance borders the other two along precisely two consecutive branches of g. Let $\vec{a}$, $\vec{b}$ and $\vec{c}$ be the vectors pointing from one handle to the next, starting from and returning to (x_0,y_0).

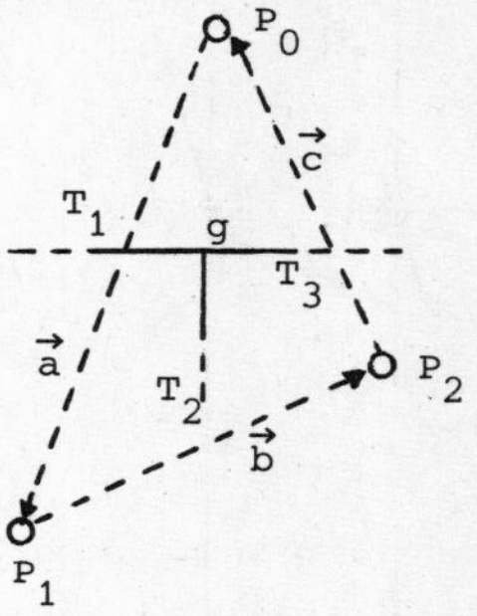

figure 2.

Consider an instance $P(x_3,y_3) \approx P_3$ located at the cell $(x_3,y_3) = (x_0,y_0)+\vec{b}(=(x_2,y_2)-\vec{a})$, see figure 3. As P_3 has the same relative position to P_0 as P_2 has to P_1, it does not overlap but does border P_0. For a similar reason it does not overlap P_2, but borders it. The connectedness and isomorphism of the polyominos are easily used to prove that P_3 cannot reach around P_0 and P_2 to intersect P_1 and thus P_3 does not overlap or even border this one. It follows that P_1, P_2 and P_3 are a correct beginning of the partial surrounding claimed in the lemma.

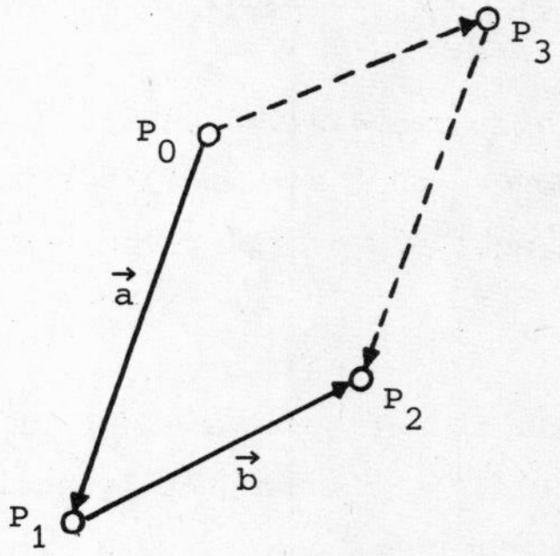

figure 3.

We use the mapping $\varphi_{x_0y_0}$ introduced in section 2 to further extend the partial surrounding. Thus let $P(x_4,y_4) = \varphi_{x_0y_0}(P(x_1,y_1)) \approx P_4$ and, going around in counter clockwise order, let $P(x_5,y_5) = \varphi_{x_0y_0}(P(x_2,y_2)) \approx P_5$ and also $P(x_6,y_6) = \varphi_{x_0y_0}(P(x_3,y_3)) \approx P_6$. The situation is indicated in figure 4. Because P_4 has the same relative position to P_3 as P_0 has to P_4, it does not overlap but borders P_3. Likewise P_6 borders P_1 but does not overlap it. Using lemma 2.8 and 2.9 it follows that P_4, P_5 and P_6 are all disjoint from P_0 as well (but they border it just like P_1, P_2 and P_3 do). We conclude that P_1 to P_6 form a partial surrounding of P_0 as claimed.

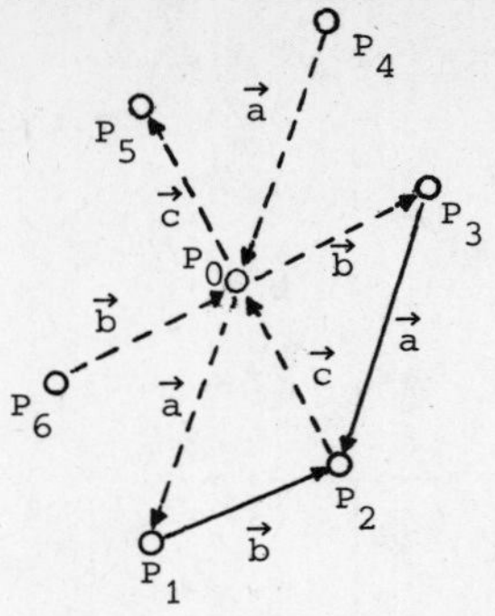

figure 4.

Finally consider the partial segmentation induced on the boundary of $P(x_0,y_0)$. The argument of lemma 3.4 proves that no other instances of P but P_1 through P_6 can border $P(x_0,y_0)$. Each P_i $(1 \leq i \leq 6)$ gives rise to exactly one segment along $B(x_0,y_0)$. This identifies the 6 segments along $B(x_0,y_0)$, with a total length equal to $|T_1|+|T_3|+|T_1|+|T_2|+|T_2|+|T_3| = 2.(|T_1|+|T_2|+|T_3|)$. □

<u>Lemma</u> 4.3. Suppose P admits a four-node g with branches T_1, T_2, T_3 and T_4. Then there exists with every $P(x_0,y_0)$ a partial surrounding $P(x_1,y_1),\dots,P(x_4,y_4)$ such that $P(x_i,y_i)$ is "near" to $P(x_{i+1},y_{i+1})$ for $1 \leq i \leq 4$ (and $x_5 \equiv x_1, y_5 \equiv y_1$). The length of the partial segmentation induced on $B(x_0,y_0)$ is equal to $2.|T_1|+2.|T_4|$.

The proof is similar to that of lemma 4.2. The notion of "near-ness" in the lemma pertains to the phenomenon that one cannot squeeze other polyominos in between that also border $P(x_0,y_0)$. By careful analysis of the proofs of lemma 4.2 and 4.3 one obtains the following fact.

<u>Corollary</u> 4.4. Let τ be a periodic tessellation using P. Then either (a) every node of G_τ is a three-node and every $P(x,y) \in \tau$ is completely surrounded by 6 other instances of P, or (b) every node of G_τ is a four-node and every $P(x,y) \in \tau$ is completely surrounded by 4 other instances of P.

<u>Corollary</u> 4.5. Let τ be an arbitrary (partial or total) tessellation of the plane using P. For all three-nodes of G_τ we have: $|T_1|+|T_2|+|T_3| \leq \frac{1}{2}|B|$ and for all four-nodes of G_τ we have: $|T_1|+|T_2|+|T_3|+|T_4| \leq |B|$, where T_1, T_2 and T_3 (and T_4) are the branches of the three-node (four-node) in question and B is the boundary of P.

Proof

Consider any three-node g of G_τ. By lemma 4.2 every $P(x_0,y_0)$ can be partially surrounded by a set of polyominos (not necessarily from τ) that induce a partial segmentation of $B(x,,y_0)$ of length $2.(|T_1|+|T_2|+|T_3|)$. Hence $|T_1|+|T_2|+|T_3|\leq\frac{1}{2}|B|$. Likewise it follows from lemma 4.3 that for every four-node g of G_τ: $|T_1|+|T_4|\leq\frac{1}{2}|B|$, and by a symmetric argument that $|T_2|+|T_3|\leq\frac{1}{2}|B|$. Hence $|T_1|+|T_2|+|T_3|+|T_4|\leq|B|$ for every four-node. □

The final result of this section is important because it establishes a local condition that is necessary and sufficient for the existence of a periodic tessellation.

Theorem 4.6. There exists a periodic tessellation of the plane using the polyomino P with boundary B if and only if

(*) P admits a three-node g with branches T_1, T_2 and T_3 such that $|T_1|+|T_2|+|T_3| = \frac{1}{2}|B|$, or

(**) P admits a four-node g with branches T_1, T_2, T_3 and T_4 such that $|T_1|+|T_2|+|T_3|+|T_4| = |B|$.

5. Obtaining periodic tessellations from arbitrary tessellations: a proof of Shapiro's conjecture.

The detailed analyses of the preceding sections will be used to prove that whenever there is a tessellation of the plane using the polyomino P, there must exist a periodic tessellation using P. Let τ be an arbitrary tessellation of the plane using P, and G_τ the corresponding graph.

Definition 5.1. The support of $g\in G_\tau$, denoted as: $Sup_\tau(g)$ or $Sup(g)$ when τ is understood, is equal to $Sup_\tau(g) = \frac{1}{2}\Sigma|e|$, with the summation extending over all (3 or 4) edges incident to g.

Lemma 5.2. In every tessellation of the plane using P there exists a three-node as in (*) or a four-node as in (**).

Proof

Let N be sufficiently large. Let G'_τ be the planar graph of nodes and edges obtained by only considering the polyominos of τ that are strictly within an N×N window. Clearly G'_τ is a connected and finite section of G_τ, with a contour C bounding the graph from its "exterior". Among the nodes along C there are many that are remnants of three-nodes or four-nodes that lost at least one branch (because it was sticking out of the window). Let K be the number of polyominos of τ strictly contained in the window and (hence) spanning G'_τ. Define factors ε (depending on τ, K and N) such that

$\varepsilon_1.K$ = the number of three-nodes along C that have degree 2 in G'_τ,

$\varepsilon'_1.K$ = the number of three-nodes along C that (still) have degree 3 in G'_τ,

$\varepsilon_2.K$ = the number of four-nodes along C that have degree 2 in G'_τ,

$\varepsilon'_2.K$ = the number of four-nodes along C that have degree 3 in G'_τ,

$\varepsilon''_2.K$ = the number of four-nodes along C that (still) have degree 4 in G'_τ.

Claim 5.2.1. For N sufficiently large each factor ε is less than $\frac{1}{2.|B|}$, where $|B|$ is the size of the boundary of P.

Proof

Note that the size of the polyomino is fixed. Thus K increases quadratically in N for $N\to\infty$. On the other hand, it is easily seen that $|C|$ increases at most linearly in N.

Now define the following values. In each case an expression is obtained either by direct reasoning or by carefully accounting the contributions to three-nodes ($\frac{1}{3}$ from each incident polyomino), four-nodes ($\frac{1}{4}$ from each incident polyomino) and/or edges ($\frac{1}{2}$ from the initial node in the clockwise ordering of B):

α_{ij} = the number of polyominos within the window (hence in G'_τ) that have i three-nodes and j four-nodes on their boundary,

α_{i*} = the number of polyominos etc. that have i three-nodes on their boundary = $= \sum_j \alpha_{ij}$,

α_{*J} = the number of polyominos etc. that have j four-nodes on their boundary = $= \sum_i \alpha_{ij}$,

t = the number of three-nodes within the window = $= \sum_i \frac{i}{3}.\alpha_{i*} + \frac{2}{3}.\varepsilon_1 K + \frac{1}{3}.\varepsilon'_1 K$,

f = the number of four-nodes within the window = $= \sum_j \frac{j}{4}.\alpha_{*j} + \frac{3}{4}.\varepsilon_2 K + \frac{2}{4}.\varepsilon'_2 K + \frac{1}{4}.\varepsilon''_2 K$,

n = the total number of nodes within the window = $= t + f$,

e = the total number of edges (branches) within the window = $= \sum_{i,j} \frac{i+j}{2}.\alpha_{ij} + \frac{1}{2}.\varepsilon_1 K + \frac{1}{2}.\varepsilon'_1 K + \frac{1}{2}.\varepsilon_2 K + \frac{1}{2}.\varepsilon'_2 K + \frac{1}{2}.\varepsilon''_2 K$,

p = the total number of parts (faces) in which the plane is divided by G'_τ = $= K + 1$.

Claim 5.2.2. $f = -\frac{1}{2}t + \frac{1}{2}\varepsilon_1 K + \varepsilon_2 K + \frac{1}{2}\varepsilon'_2 K + K - 1$.

Proof

Since G'_τ is planar we can apply Euler's polyeder formula: n+p = e+2. Hence $t+f+K+1 = e+2 \Rightarrow \sum_i \frac{i}{6}.\alpha_{i*} + \sum_j \frac{j}{4}.\alpha_{*j} = \frac{1}{6}\varepsilon_1 K - \frac{1}{6}\varepsilon'_1 K + \frac{1}{4}\varepsilon_2 K - \frac{1}{4}\varepsilon''_2 K + K - 1.$
Multiplying the latter equation by 2, the left-hand side reminds of t+2f. Straightforward manipulation shows $t+2f = \varepsilon'_2 K + \frac{1}{2}\varepsilon''_2 K = \varepsilon_1 K + 2\varepsilon_2 K + \varepsilon'_2 K + 2k - 2$, and the expression for f follows.

Suppose by way of contradiction that τ (hence G'_τ) does not contain any three-nodes satisfying (*) nor any four-nodes satisfying (**). By corollary 4.6 this means that for every three-node g: $\mathrm{Sup}(g) \leqq \frac{1}{4}|B| - \frac{1}{2}$ and for every four-node g: $\mathrm{Sup}(g) \leqq \frac{1}{2}|B| - \frac{1}{2}$.
Let L be the total edge length of G'_τ. Note that $L < \sum_{g \in G'_\tau} \mathrm{Sup}(g)$. Using the expression for f from claim 5.2.2 we can bound L as follows: $L < \sum_{\substack{g \in G'_\tau \\ g \text{ three-node}}} \mathrm{Sup}(g) + \sum_{\substack{g \in G'_\tau \\ g \text{ four-node}}} \mathrm{Sup}(g) \leqq$
$\leqq t.(\frac{1}{4}|B| - \frac{1}{2}) + f.(\frac{1}{2}|B| - \frac{1}{2}) \leqq \frac{1}{2}K.|B| + \{(\frac{1}{4}\varepsilon_1 + \frac{1}{2}\varepsilon_2 + \frac{1}{4}\varepsilon'_2).|B| - \frac{1}{2}\}K.$
As N was chosen sufficiently large, it follows from claim 5.2.1. that $\frac{1}{4}\varepsilon_1 + \frac{1}{2}\varepsilon_2 + \frac{1}{4}\varepsilon'_2 < \frac{1}{2.|B|}$. Thus our estimate on L reduces to $L < \frac{1}{2}K.|B|$.
On the other hand, if we let each of the K polyominos in G'_τ contribute one half of every bounding edge (which properly divides the length of every edge over its two bordering polyominos) then it easily follows that $L \geqq K.\frac{1}{2}|B| = \frac{1}{2}K.|B|$, a contradiction. We conclude that G'_τ (hence τ) must contain a three-node satisfying (*) or a four-node satisfying (**). □

Theorem 5.3. Let P be a polyomino. If P tessellates the plane, then there exists a periodic tessellation of the plane using P.

Proof

From lemma 5.2 and theorem 4.6. □

6. Final comments.

Our study of plane tessellations was motivated from the theory of data organisation for SIMD-machines. We argued in section 1 (see also Shapiro [7]) that only periodic tessellations are of practical interest. Thus the proof of Shapiro's conjecture has significance within this context. It is important to note that the result of theorem 5.3 is entirely effective. First of all, whenever a tessellation using a polyomino P is given in some computable manner, then the proof of lemma 5.2 shows that one can compute (by inspecting any N×N window) a three-node satisfying (*) or a four-node satisfying (**). Secondly, the results underlying theorem 4.6 show that there is an effective way to determine the two generating vectors (i.e., the basis) of the lattice of points where the polyominos P in a periodic tessellation must be placed. Clearly, given theorem 5.3 only the second observation is important, for one can always determine by trying whether P admits a three-node or a four-node with the desired property.

Theorem 6.1. Given a polyomino P, there exists an algorithm that is polynomial in the size of P to decide whether P can tessellate the plane or not.

Proof

By theorem 5.3 we only need to test the conditions for a periodic tessellation using P as expressed in theorem 4.6 Take an instance of P and test at every (grid-) point along the boundary whether 3 or 4 instances can be fitted without overlap and satisfying the length condition for the branches at the node so created. There are only polynomially many cases to consider, and each test takes at most $O(|B|^2)$ (hence: polynomial) time. □

The study of plane tessellations (tilings, pavings) with regular objects has a long history in mathematics. It has repeatedly been the subject of M. Gardner's column in the Scientific American ([2]). A systematic study of tessellations with sets of polyominos was made by Golomb [4]. In the late sixties Golomb [5] proved that the question whether an arbitrary finite set of polyominos tiles the plane (rotational symmetries etc. allowed) is equivalent to Wang's domino problem ([9]) and hence algorithmically undecidable. If the set contains only one polyomino, the decidability question is reportedly still open (Göbel [3]). Thus the results we proved in this paper, and theorem 6.1 in particular, may be viewed as a partial answer to this question for a restrictive class of tessellations (requiring polyominos to have a fixed orientation).

Severe problems arise if we attempt to generalize theorem 5.3 and e.g. relax the condition that P be a polyomino. The template T shown in figure 5 provides an example that Shapiro's conjecture does not remain valid if we do so. It is easily verified that T tessellates the plane. But it cannot tessellate the plane periodically. The existence of periodic tessellations in general, using sets of objects and allowing symmetries, is a hard problem for which only a few results have been proved. It is known (see Gardner [2d]) that there exists a set of 2 polygons which tile the plane non-periodically only. Thus there are many inspiring problems left in the study of tessellations.

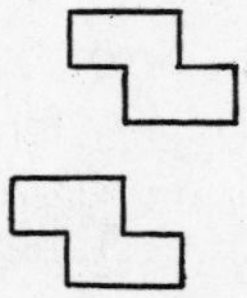

figure 5.

7. References.

[1] Budnik, P. and D.J. Kuck, The organisation and use of parallel memories, IEEE Trans. Comput. C-20 (1971) 1566-1569.

[2] Gardner, M., Mathematical games, articles in the Scientific American:
[2a] july 1975, pp. 112-117
[2b] august 1975, pp. 112-115
[2c] december 1975, pp. 116-119
[2d] january 1977, pp. 110-121

[3] Gõbel, F., Geometrical packing and covering problems, in: A. Schrijver (ed.), Packing and covering in combinatorics, Math. Centre Tracts 106, Mathematisch Centrum, Amsterdam, 1979, pp. 179-199.

[4] Golomb, S.W., Tiling with polyominos, J. Combin. Theory 1 (1966) 280-296.

[5] Golomb, S.W., Tiling with sets of polyominos, J. Combin. Theory 9 (1970) 60-71.

[6] Levi, P., Sur une generalisation du theorème de Rolle, Comp. Rend. Acad. Sci. Paris 198 (1934) 424-425.

[7] Shapiro, H.D., Theoretical limitations on the efficient use of parallel memories, IEEE Trans. Comput. C-27 (1978) 421-428.

[8] Thurber, K.J., Large scale computer architecture: parallel and associative processors, Hayden Book Comp., Rochelle Park NJ, 1976.

[9] Wang, H., Games, logic and computers, Scientific American 213 (1965) 98-106.

[10] Wijshoff, H.A.G., and J. van Leeuwen, Periodic versus arbitrary tessellations of the plane using polyominos of a single type, Techn. Rep. RUU-CS-82-11, Dept. of Computer Science, University of Utrecht, Utrecht, 1982 (submitted for publication).

INDEX OF AUTHORS